THE M68000 MICROPROCESSOR FAMILY
Fundamentals of Assembly Language Programming and Interface Design

Yu-cheng Liu
Electrical Engineering Department
The University of Texas at El Paso

 Prentice Hall, Englewood Cliffs, New Jersey 07632

Library of Congress Cataloging-in-Publication Data

Liu, Yu-cheng.
   The M68000 microprocessor family : fundamentals of assembly
language programming and interface design / Yu-cheng Liu.
    p. cm.
   Includes index.
   ISBN 0-13-566399-7
   1. Motorola 68000 series microprocessors—Programming. I. Title.
QA76.8.M6895L58 1991
004.165—dc20   90-7397
                                                          CIP

Editorial/production supervision: bookworks
Cover design: Bruce Kenselaar
Manufacturing buyers: Linda Behrens and Patrice Fraccio

© 1991 by Prentice-Hall, Inc.
A Division of Simon & Schuster
Englewood Cliffs, New Jersey 07632

The author and publisher of this book have used their best efforts in preparing
this book. These efforts include the development, research, and testing of the
theories and programs to determine their effectiveness. The author and
publisher make no warranty of any kind, expressed or implied, with regard to
these programs or the documentation contained in this book. The author and
publisher shall not be liable in any event for incidental or consequential
damages in connection with, or arising out of, the furnishing, performance, or
use of these programs.

Printed in the United States of America
10 9 8 7 6 5 4 3 2 1

ISBN   0-13-566399-7

Prentice-Hall International (UK), Limited, *London*
Prentice-Hall of Australia Pty. Limited, *Sydney*
Prentice-Hall Canada Inc., *Toronto*
Prentice-Hall Hispanoamericana, S.A., *Mexico*
Prentice-Hall of India Private Limited, *New Delhi*
Prentice-Hall of Japan, Inc., *Tokyo*
Simon & Schuster Asia Pte. Ltd., *Singapore*
Editora Prentice-Hall do Brasil, Ltda., *Rio de Janeiro*

To my family:

Anne, Janice, and Jonathan

Contents

Contents

Contents

Interfacing the FPCP to the MC68000 384
Programming the FPCP as a peripheral 386

Preface

In the past several years, microprocessors have emerged as a major field in the computer industry. For a computer engineering or computer science student, it therefore becomes increasingly important to have a fundamental knowledge about microprocessors. Although a large variety of microprocessors are in use, the Motorola M68000 microprocessor family is regarded as one of the industry's standards for 16- and 32-bit microprocessors. This book is about the M68000 microprocessor family.

Since a simple microcomputer can be implemented with just a few LSI devices, a student interested in learning microprocessors should study not only the software but also the hardware aspect of a microprocessor. This book is primarily designed as a text for a one-semester, junior-level microprocessor course that covers both programming and system design using the MC68000 microprocessor.

To make this book self-contained, Chap. 1 is included to provide an introduction to microcomputer organization and to give an overview of data formats used by the MC68000 microprocessor. The programming model of the MC68000 and its addressing modes are described in Chap. 2.

An assembly language remains as the most direct means for gaining an indepth understanding of the structure, capabilities, and limitations of a given microprocessor. Yet another important reason for learning assembly language is that many simple educational microprocessor boards can accept programs implemented only in assembly language or machine code. Chapter 3 covers the MC68000 instruction set and assembly language programming. Since the MC68000 is a popular microprocessor, various assemblers and cross-assemblers for this microprocessor are in use. In this book, we choose the syntax of Motorola assemblers. However, only minor changes need to be made in converting a sample program in this book for a specific assembler.

Chapter 4 discusses typical development tools. We select the Motorola MC68000-based single-board computer (ECB) as an example to illustrate the debugging facilities and their typical usages. The actual system made available to the student may be different. Even though the commands differ from one system to another, the concept of single-stepping, execution with breakpoints, memory and register display/modification, etc., and their usages in program development remain the same. Development tools typically found in a large multiuser development system, such as cross-assemblers, simulators, emulators, and logic analyzers, are also described in this chapter.

Chapter 5 extends the discussion of assembly language programming to multiple-module structure and examines advanced programming techniques such as recursive routines and macros. Chapter 6 covers how to implement interrupt service routines and how the MC68000 processes interrupts.

The hardware aspect of the MC68000 and microprocessor-based system design are covered in Chaps. 7 through 9. Chapter 7 discusses how the MC68000 is interfaced to the bus that provides communication between two components in the system. Chapter 8 covers commonly used I/O devices and discusses how these LSI devices are used as basic building blocks in system implementations. Various types of memory devices including static RAMs, dynamic RAMs, and read-only memories and implementations of memory modules using these memory devices are described in Chap. 9.

As VLSI technologies advance, more and more logic can be integrated into a microprocessor. This makes many of the advanced features, which were only available in minicomputers or mainframes several years ago, possible to be included in a microprocessor. For this reason, the book has an introduction to provide the reader with an overview of more advanced features of the MC68000 microprocessor family. Chapter 10 describes the enhanced features of the MC68010, MC68020, MC68030, and MC68040, including addressing mode extensions, new instructions, expanded data and address buses, and speed related improvements. Floating-point coprocessors and their interfaces to a 16-bit microprocessor (MC68000/MC68010) and 32-bit microprocessor (MC68020/MC68030) are discussed in Chap. 11. Chapter 12 introduces cache memory and virtual memory and their implementations in the M68000 family. Chapter 7 also has a section on the 32-bit VME bus, which is typically used in large systems having more than one bus master.

For an introductory course that assumes no prior knowledge of any assembly language, most of the material on advanced topics may be omitted so that the fundamental material can be covered at a slower pace.

Portions of Sections 4-4 and 9-2 of this book have been adopted from the following two books: Glenn A. Gibson/Yu-cheng Liu, *Microcomputers for Engineers and Scientists, 2/E,* ©1987, and Yu-cheng Liu/Glenn A. Gibson, *Microcomputer Systems: The 8086/8088 Family, 2/E,* ©1986, both published by Prentice Hall, Englewood Cliffs, New Jersey. The author would like to thank Prentice Hall and Dr. Glenn Gibson for the use of this material. The author would also like to thank Motorola, Inc. for supplying much of the needed information and Janice Liu for typing most of the manuscript.

Yu-cheng Liu

1

Introduction

The focus of this book is the Motorola M68000 microprocessor family. Many of the design practices and fundamental concepts can apply to other modern microprocessors as well. Before a detailed discussion of the MC68000 microprocessor is presented, it is appropriate first to provide an overview of the hardware and software organization of microcomputer systems and a description of the data formats used in processing data inside the MC68000 microprocessor.

1-1 Overview of Hardware Organization

A microprocessor-based system is composed of a microprocessor, one or more memory modules, and I/O peripheral devices, interconnected by a bus, as shown in Fig. 1-1.

A microprocessor integrates the necessary logic of a general-purpose processor into a single chip, which is able to fetch and execute instructions stored in memory. Among other logic, a microprocessor has a register set to store temporary data and addresses, a program counter (PC) to keep the location of the next instruction to be executed, an instruction register (IR) to hold the current instruction being executed, an arithmetic logic unit (ALU) to perform the operation as specified in the current instruction, and a status register (SR) to indicate condition code settings.

A typical instruction takes the microprocessor several steps to execute:

1. Fetch from memory the current instruction to be executed, whose address is in the program counter, and store it in the instruction register. Meanwhile, increment the program counter by the instruction length so that it points to the next instruction to be executed.

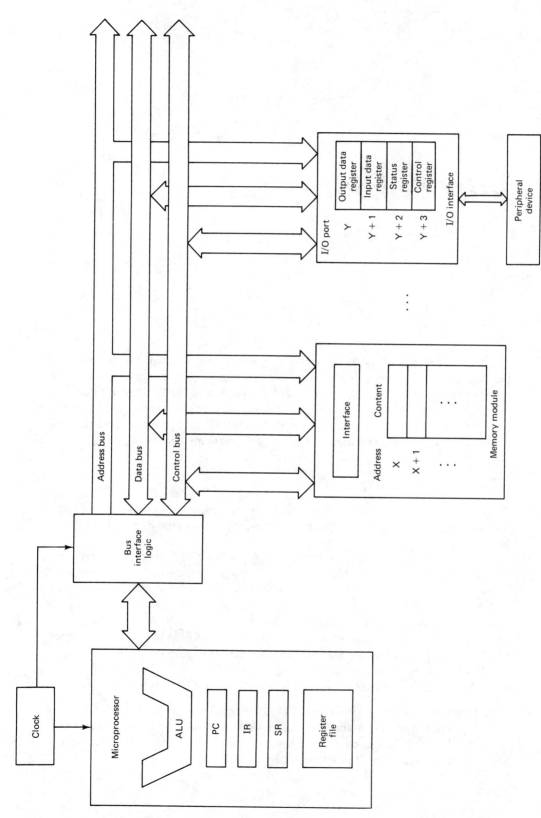

Figure 1-1 Block diagram of a microprocessor-based system.

2. Decode the operation code of the instruction in the instruction register.
3. Calculate the operand address according to the addressing mode specified in the instruction.
4. Fetch the operand from memory if a memory operand is required.
5. Perform the required operation.
6. Store the result to memory if the destination is in memory.
7. Check for pending interrupt requests. If none, the next instruction is started by returning to Step 1. Otherwise, an interrupt is processed.

Each step requires one or more clock cycles to complete, with the clock signals being generated by a clock circuit.

The processor communicates with other system components through the system bus. Normally, the processor is connected to the bus through a bus interface, which includes data transceivers, address drivers, and an interrupt management logic to resolve simultaneous interrupt requests.

System bus

The system bus is a set of conductors that can be divided into three groups, the address bus, data bus, and control bus, according to function. Each location in the memory or each programmable register in an I/O interface has a unique address assigned to it. During a data transfer, the processor sends out the address over the address bus and the data bus is used to transfer the data.

For the MC68000, an I/O register is accessed as if it were a memory location. This scheme is commonly known as *memory-mapped* I/O. Since the MC68000 uses 24 bits to specify an address, the maximum total size of memory and I/O ports is $2^{24} \approx 16$ megabytes.

The data bus of the MC68000 is 16 bits wide. This allows a 16-bit data word to be transferred in one bus cycle. In addition to a word, the MC68000 can also read/write a byte (8 bits) or a longword (32 bits) from/to a given address. However, reading or writing a longword requires two bus cycles.

The control bus is used by the processor to issue a bus command, such as read or write, and by memory or I/O devices to return an acknowledge signal. A typical control bus also provides lines for I/O devices to send interrupt requests.

Memory module

The main memory is normally organized in a modular form, with each module having its own bus interface logic. A typical system has at least a read-only memory (ROM) module and a read-write memory (RAM) module. Since ROM is nonvolatile, it normally stores a resident monitor or a bootstrap loader so that the system is ready to run whenever the power is turned on. The user's program and data are stored in RAM. The high-order bits of a memory address determine which module is to be enabled, whereas the low-order bits select the location within the enabled module.

The MC68000 may access a memory location as a byte, word, or longword.

However, to read or write a word or longword, the address must be even. As illustrated in Fig. 1-2, according to Motorola's convention, a word is stored in two consecutive locations beginning with the upper byte. This means that in reading a word from location X, the MC68000 receives two consecutive bytes from location X with the byte from X being interpreted as the upper byte and the byte from $X + 1$ as the lower byte. Similarly, a longword is stored in four consecutive locations, with the most significant byte being stored in the lowest address. Some examples to illustrate byte, word, and longword references are shown in Fig. 1-3, with all numbers given in hexadecimal form.

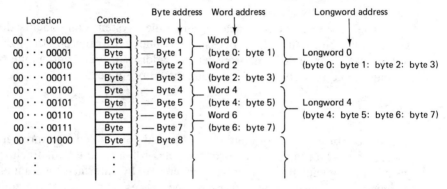

Figure 1-2 Data organization in memory.

```
                Initial Conditions

         Location   Content           Operation Performed
         (in Hex)   (in Hex)          by the MC68000                Result

            .                        1) Read location 001205      Byte received is 34.
            .                           as a byte.
            .
                                     2) Read location 001204      Word received
         001204      12                 as a word.                is 1234.
         001205      34
         001206      56               3) Read location 001204      Longword received
         001207      78                  as a longword.            is 12345678.

            .                        4) Write byte 11 into        Memory locations
            .                           location 00350C.          00350C-00350F have
            .                                                      11, BC, DE and F0.

         00350C      9A               5) Write word 1122 into      Memory locations
         00350D      BC                  location 00350C.          00350C-00350F have
         00350E      DE                                            11, 22, DE and F0.
         00350F      F0
                                     6)  Write longword           Memory locations
            .                            11223344 into            00350C-00350F have
            .                            location 00350C.         11, 22, 33 and 44.
            .
```

Figure 1-3 Examples of memory data organization.

I/O interface

Peripheral devices such as CRT terminals and printers require an interface to the system bus, which serves as a buffer. For a commonly used peripheral device, most of the required interfacing logic is provided by an LSI (large scale integration) device, called an I/O interface device. Communication between the processor and a peripheral device is accomplished via the programmable registers in the interface. These registers may include an output data register to hold the data to be transmitted to the peripheral device, an input data register to receive the data from the peripheral device, a status register to indicate if the device is ready for a data transfer or an error occurred during data transfers, and a control register to receive commands from the processor. Each register has an address assigned called an *I/O port* and is accessed as a memory location to the MC68000.

1-2 Overview of Software System

Operating system

Figure 1-4 illustrates the major components of a typical software system. An operating system is a collection of system programs, including a monitor, that is stored on a disk. When the system is turned on, the monitor becomes resident in the memory. The main functions of the monitor are to supervise the operation of the system, to manage both the hardware and software resources, and to provide an interface between the user and the system. The monitor recognizes user commands and then performs the requested tasks by loading and executing the appropriate system routines. In addition, a monitor includes file management routines and I/O drivers for system peripheral devices. They allow the user to simplify I/O programming and to create, manipulate, and delete files.

Language translators

Although a processor can execute instructions only in the binary form called *machine code*, a program can initially be written in a symbolic format. Typically a text editor is employed for creating and modifying such programs. The resulting program generated from a text editor is stored as an ASCII file called a *source module*. The source module is then translated into machine code, called an *object module*, by a language translator. An assembler and one or more compilers, such as Fortran and Pascal, are typical language translators available in a system.

Linker

In order to reduce the development time, a complex program is frequently broken down into several modules. Each module is independently developed and tested and perhaps is written in a different language. Some frequently used routines may be collected as a library file so that they can be shared by many users.

A linker combines the various object modules of a program into a single executable file called a *load module*. As an option, a linker may also produce a listing showing the loading address assigned to each object module. The load module produced by the linker is ready to be loaded into memory for execution.

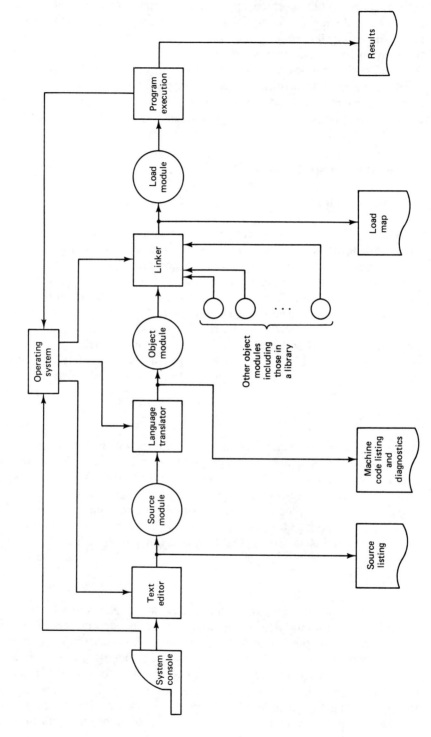

Figure 1-4 Program development and software organization.

6

1-3 Data Formats Used in the MC68000 System

A typical MC68000 instruction may operate on byte, word, or longword operands. An operand can represent either numerical or nonnumerical data. For nonnumerical data, each character is stored in 1 byte using the ASCII code. For numerical data, the MC68000 provides instructions that can directly operate on data stored in the following forms:

1. Unsigned binary
2. Signed binary
3. Packed binary coded decimal (BCD)

Unsigned binary

A nonnegative number can be represented in binary form, which uses 2 as the base. The n-bit unsigned binary equivalent $b_{n-1} \ldots b_2 b_1 b_0$ of a given number N indicates that

$$N = b_{n-1} \times 2^{n-1} + b_{n-2} \times 2^{n-2} + \cdots + b_1 \times 2^1 + b_0 \times 2^0$$

Therefore, the coefficients $b_0, b_1, \ldots, b_{n-1}$ can be obtained in that order using $n - 1$ successive divisions of N by 2. This conversion process is illustrated in the following example, assuming an 8-bit format:

	Remainder	Coefficient
2)45	1	b_0
2)22	0	b_1
2)11	1	b_2
2) 5	1	b_3
2) 2	0	b_4
2) 1	1	b_5
2) 0	0	b_6
0	0	b_7
		45 = 00101101

In order to simplify a long sequence of bits in a binary number, we can group four bits at a time, starting at the radix point, with each group being represented by a hexadecimal digit in the range of 0–9 and A–F. For example, the binary number 00101101 is represented by 2D in the hexadecimal form. Therefore, the range of an 8-bit unsigned number is 00–FF in hexadecimal or 0–255 in decimal.

Signed binary

In order to process negative numbers as well as positive numbers, negative numbers are represented in the 2's complement form. In this form, $-N$ is represented as

$$-N = 2^n - N$$

where n is the number of bits used in the representation. For example, -45 in the 8-bit 2's complement form is

$$2^8 - 00101101 = 11010011$$

which can also be obtained by complementing each bit in the binary number 00101101 and then adding 1 to the result.

In the 2's complement form, since a number is interpreted to be either positive or negative depending on its most significant bit, the number is referred to as a *signed binary number*. Using 8-bit format as an example, the following table compares the unsigned and signed interpretations of given binary numbers:

Binary representation	As unsigned number	As signed number
00000000	0	+0
00000001	1	+1
00000010	2	+2
00000011	3	+3
.	.	.
.	.	.
01111111	127	+127
10000000	128	-128
10000001	129	-127
.	.	.
.	.	.
11111111	255	-1

When a number is stored as a longword, the range of unsigned numbers is from 0 to $2^{32} - 1$, and signed numbers range from -2^{31} to $2^{31} - 1$. To extend an 8-bit signed number to a word or to a longword, 8 bits or 24 bits must be appended to the left of the number by repeating the sign bit so that the value is not changed. This operation is called *sign extension*. For example, 11011100 (DC in hexadecimal) is the 8-bit representation for decimal number -36. After being sign-extended to 32 bits, it becomes 11111111 11111111 11111111 11011100 (FFFFFFDC), which is the correct 2's complement representation for -36 in the 32-bit format.

The arithmetic operations of addition and subtraction for signed binary numbers are performed in the same way as for unsigned binary numbers. After an addition or subtraction, the result is interpreted as a signed number if signed arithmetic is intended and is interpreted as an unsigned number if unsigned arithmetic is intended. Assuming 8-bit format, the following examples illustrate signed and unsigned additions and subtractions:

Binary	As unsigned numbers	As signed numbers
00100011	35	35
+ 11001001	+ 201	+ (-55)
11101100	236	-20

Binary	As unsigned numbers	As signed numbers
01101101	109	109
+ 11001001	+ 201	+ (−55)
1 00110110	310	54

└─This carry indicates an overflow for an unsigned operation and is discarded for a signed operation.

└─Too large to be represented in 8 bits.

Binary	As unsigned numbers	As signed numbers
11011101	221	−35
− 00011010	− 26	− 26
11000011	195	−61
11011101	221	−35
− 10010000	− 144	− (−112)
01001101	77	77

As demonstrated by the preceding examples, for addition or subtraction both unsigned and signed operations can be accomplished by the same binary arithmetic instruction. But this is not true for multiplication and division, each of which requires separate instructions for unsigned and signed operations.

Fixed-point format

In addition to integers, numbers having fractional parts can be represented and operated in a binary form. A straightforward approach, referred to as *fixed-point format*, is to allocate a predefined number of bits for the integral part and for the fractional part of each number to be processed.

A fraction is converted to binary form $.a_{-1}a_{-2}a_{-3} \ldots a_{-m}$ based on the expression

$$.F = a_{-1} \times 2^{-1} + a_{-2} \times 2^{-2} + a_{-3} \times 2^{-3} + \cdots + a_{-m} \times 2^{-m}$$

Coefficients $a_{-1}, a_{-2}, a_{-3}, \ldots, a_{-m}$ can be obtained in that order by successively multiplying by 2, as follows.

0.59375	Integral Part	Coefficient
× 2		
1.1875	1	a_{-1}
× 2		
0.375	0	a_{-2}
× 2		
0.75	0	a_{-3}
× 2		
1.5	1	a_{-4}
× 2		
1.0	1	a_{-5}

$0.59375 = 0.100110 \ldots 0$

Since the position of the binary point is fixed for all numbers, a binary point is not actually stored. For example, each number can be represented by two 16-bit words, with the upper word storing the integral part, the lower word storing the fractional part, and a binary point being implied between the two words. In a fixed-point format, an arithmetic operation can be performed by processing the integral parts and the fractional parts of the two operands separately using binary arithmetic instructions.

Note that a fixed-point representation is essentially the same as an integer multiplied by a fixed-scale factor that is a power of 2. Therefore, as with integers, the range of fixed-point numbers that can be represented by a given number of bits is rather limited.

Packed BCD

In the packed BCD format, each decimal digit is encoded in 4 bits or is represented by its equivalent hexadecimal digit, with two digits being stored in 1 byte. For example, the number 3509 is stored in packed BCD as 00110101 00001001 in binary or 3509 in hexadecimal.

There is another BCD format called the unpacked BCD, in which each 4-bit encoded decimal digit is stored in 1 byte. Therefore, decimal 3509 would be stored in 4 bytes as

$$00000011 \quad 0000000101 \quad 00000000 \quad 00001001$$

The MC68000 has instructions to perform additions and subtractions directly on packed BCD numbers but not on numbers in the unpacked form. For simplicity, this book will use the term BCD to represent the packed BCD format.

A negative integer is represented in the 10's complement form in BCD, which is similar to 2's complement. For example, the 4-digit BCD equivalent of -3509 is 6491.

Floating-point formats

For scientific and engineering applications, both very large and very small numbers are frequently involved in a single calculation. A *floating-point format*, also known as a *real-number format*, can represent operands that may vary from extremely small to extremely large values and retain a constant number of significant digits during calculations. A floating-point number is divided into three fields: sign, exponent, and mantissa; i.e.,

$$X = \pm 2^{\text{exp}} \times \text{mantissa}$$

The exponent adjusts the position of the binary point in the mantissa. Decreasing the exponent by 1 moves the binary point to the right by one position. Therefore, a very small value can be represented by using a negative exponent without losing any precision. However, except for numbers whose mantissa parts fall within the range of the format, a number may not be exactly representable, thus causing a roundoff error. If leadings 0s are allowed, a given number may have more than one representation in a real-number format. But since there are a fixed number of bits in the mantissa, leading 0s increase the roundoff error. Therefore, in order to minimize roundoff errors, the leading 0s in a mantissa can be deleted by properly adjusting the exponent. A nonzero real number is said to be *normalized* when its mantissa is in the form of 1.F, where F represents a fraction.

Normally, a bias value is added to the true exponent so that the true exponent is actually the number in the exponent field minus the bias value. Using biased exponents allows two normalized real numbers of the same sign to be compared by simply comparing the bytes from left to right as if they were integers.

The MC68000 does not provide floating-point instructions. Floating-point arithmetic can be performed using a set of subroutines implemented in the MC68000 instruction set, which are normally available as a scientific library file or package. Motorola has also made available floating-point coprocessors, MC68881/MC68882, which can be used with the M68000 family to support floating-point arithmetic and other math functions efficiently. The floating-point formats supported by the Motorola are the standards proposed by the IEEE. Two floating-point standards have been proposed, the single-precision and the double-precision formats. The form, number of bytes, and approximate range for each of the two formats are shown in Fig. 1-5.

In the single-precision format, the biased exponent E and the fraction F have 8 and 23 bits, respectively, and the number is represented by the form:

$$(-1)^S \times 2^{E-127} \times 1.F$$

where S is the sign bit. Because the 1 appearing before the fraction is always present, it is implied and is not physically stored. For example, suppose that a single-precision real number is stored as follows:

$$\text{C25A8000} = \underbrace{1}_{\text{Sign}} \quad \underbrace{10000100}_{\text{Biased exponent}} \quad \underbrace{101101010 \ldots 0}_{\text{Fraction}}$$

Then the true exponent is $132 - 127 = 5$, and the floating-point number being represented is

$$-1.10110101 \times 2^5 = -110110.101$$
$$= -(2^5 + 2^4 + 2^2 + 2^1 + 2^{-1} + 2^{-3})$$
$$= -54.625$$

To illustrate the conversion of a real number to its single-precision floating-point form, consider the number 313.125. First, one should convert the integral and fractional parts to binary as follows:

$$100111001 + .001 = 100111001.001$$

After normalizing this number by moving the binary point until it is next to the first nonzero bits, it becomes:

$$1.00111001001 \times 2^8$$

From this form it is seen that

$$S = 0, \quad E = 127 + 8 = 135 = 10000111, \quad \text{and} \quad F = 00111001001$$

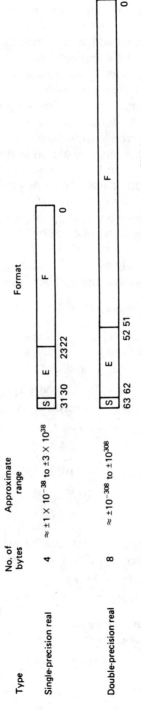

Type	No. of bytes	Approximate range	Format
Single-precision real	4	$\approx \pm 1 \times 10^{-38}$ to $\pm 3 \times 10^{38}$	S E F 31 30 23 22 0
Double-precision real	8	$\approx \pm 10^{-308}$ to $\pm 10^{308}$	S E F 63 62 52 51 0

Figure 1-5 Floating-point formats proposed by IEEE. Yu-cheng Liu/Glenn A. Gibson, *Microcomputer Systems: The 8086/8088 Family, 2/E,* © 1986. Reprinted by permission of Prentice Hall, Inc., Englewood Cliffs, New Jersey.

Thus the single-precision form of the number is:

$$\underbrace{0}_{\text{Sign}} \quad \underbrace{10000111}_{\text{Biased exponent}} \quad \underbrace{001110010010 \ldots 0}_{\text{Fraction}} = 439C9000$$

For the single-precision format, the valid range of the biased exponent is $0 < E < 255$. Consequently, the numbers that can be represented are from $\pm 2^{-126}$ to $\pm 2^{128}$, approximately $\pm 1 \times 10^{-38}$ to $\pm 3 \times 10^{38}$. A biased exponent of all 1s is reserved to represent infinity or "not-a-number." At the other extreme, a biased exponent of all 0s is used to represent $+0$ (all 0s with a $+$ sign) and -0 (all 0s with a $-$ sign).

The double-precision floating-point format has 11 exponent bits and 52 fraction bits. As with the single-precision real format, the first nonzero bit in the mantissa is implied and not stored. As a result of the larger exponent field, the range of representable nonzero numbers in the double-precision real format is extended to approximately $\pm 10^{-308}$ to $\pm 10^{308}$. The increased number of fraction bits improves the precision of the real number to 11 decimal digits from 7 as in the single-precision real format.

ASCII code

Nonnumerical data are commonly stored using the ASCII code, which stands for the American Standard Code for Information Interchange. Data are represented by a string of ASCII characters, with each character being stored in 1 byte. The ASCII code is a 7-bit alphanumeric code; hence it includes 128 characters. As can be seen from Fig. 1-6, the ASCII code includes digits 0–9 and letters A–Z, both upper- and lowercase. In addition, the code also provides special symbols such as arithmetic operators and typical control characters used in input/output. For example, sending a carriage return character (0D) to a printer would cause its printing head to move to the left margin. When the ASCII code is used for inputting or outputting data, an optional parity bit can be attached to each ASCII character as the most significant bit, making the total number of bits per character equal to eight. Parity bits enable the system to detect errors during data transfers.

For a peripheral device employing the ASCII code, numbers are transferred between the device and the computer as sequences of ASCII-coded digits. For example, the number 4125 would be sent as 34, 31, 32, and 35. After the computer receives ASCII-coded numbers, they must be converted to binary or BCD if arithmetic operations are to be performed. Conversely, before a number in binary or BCD can be output, it first needs to be converted to the corresponding ASCII-coded digits.

1-4 Motorola's Microprocessor Evolution

Advances in the very large scale integration (VLSI) technology have made it possible to fabricate a powerful central processing unit (CPU) into a single-chip microprocessor. Because so much electronic circuitry is available in a small microprocessor, it is capable of performing complex tasks at a high speed. The

ASCII Char.	Hex. Code	Control Character	ASCII Char.	Hex. Code	Control Character	ASCII Char.	Hex. Code	Control Character
NUL	00	Null	+	2B		V	56	
SOH	01	Start heading	,	2C		W	57	
STX	02	Start text	–	2D		X	58	
ETX	03	End text	.	2E		Y	59	
EOT	04	End transmission	/	2F		Z	5A	
ENQ	05	Inquiry	0	30		[	5B	
ACK	06	Acknowledgment	1	31		\	5C	
BEL	07	Bell	2	32		]	5D	
BS	08	Backspace	3	33		^	5E	
HT	09	Horizontal tab	4	34		_	5F	
LF	0A	Line feed	5	35		`	60	
VT	0B	Vertical tab	6	36		a	61	
FF	0C	Form feed	7	37		b	62	
CR	0D	Carriage return	8	38		c	63	
SO	0E	Shift out	9	39		d	64	
SI	0F	Shift in	:	3A		e	65	
DLE	10	Data link escape	;	3B		f	66	
DC1	11	Device control 1	<	3C		g	67	
DC2	12	Device control 2	=	3D		h	68	
DC3	13	Device control 3	>	3E		i	69	
DC4	14	Device control 4	?	3F		j	6A	
NAK	15	Neg. acknowledge	@	40		k	6B	
SYN	16	Synchronous/Idle	A	41		l	6C	
ETB	17	End trans. block	B	42		m	6D	
CAN	18	Cancel data	C	43		n	6E	
EM	19	End of medium	D	44		o	6F	
SUB	1A	Start special seq.	E	45		p	70	
ESC	1B	Escape	F	46		q	71	
FS	1C	File separator	G	47		r	72	
GS	1D	Group separator	H	48		s	73	
RS	1E	Record separator	I	49		t	74	
US	1F	Unit separator	J	4A		u	75	
SP	20	Space	K	4B		v	76	
!	21		L	4C		w	77	
"	22		M	4D		x	78	
#	23		N	4E		y	79	
$	24		O	4F		z	7A	
%	25		P	50		{	7B	
&	26		Q	51		|	7C	
'	27		R	52		}	7D	
(	28		S	53		~	7E	
)	29		T	54		DEL	7F	Delete-rubout
*	2A		U	55				

Figure 1-6 ASCII code. Glenn A. Gibson/Yu-cheng Liu, *Microcomputers for Engineers and Scientists, 2/E*, © 1987. Reprinted by permission of Prentice Hall, Inc., Englewood Cliffs, New Jersey.

processing power and complexity of microprocessors have been increasing dramatically, and this trend is continuing. Figure 1-7 illustrates the rapid growth of Motorola's microprocessor family. As can be seen from the figure, the growth started from the MC6800, originally introduced in 1974, to the MC68000 and its derivatives with a performance improvement of more than 10 times.

The MC6800 is an 8-bit microprocessor in which both data bus and accumulators are 8 bits wide. Its instructions can operate only on byte operands. In addition to expanded instruction set and addressing modes, its successor, the MC6809, can perform 16-bit arithmetic operations using a single instruction. However, the data bus of the MC6809 remains 8 bits wide. The MC68000 increases the width of data registers to 32 bits and also expands the data bus to 16 bits. This architectural improvement substantially increases the speed, especially for 32-bit data operations. Meanwhile, the maximum memory capacity has been increased to 16 megabytes from the 64 kilobytes of both MC6800 and MC6809.

In addition to the general-purpose microprocessors, there is another growth path from MC6800 to MC6802 and MC6801. The processors along this path are called single-chip microcomputers, or microcontrollers. A typical microcomputer chip, such as the MC6801, has a CPU, a certain amount of ROM and RAM, a programmable timer, a serial I/O interface, and a parallel I/O interface. By integrating these commonly used peripheral and interfacing devices into a single IC package, a microcomputer chip can reduce the chip count and simplify the design for microprocessor-based control-type applications.

The M68000 family consists of several microprocessors, all of which use the same basic instruction set and machine code formats. Therefore, each microprocessor maintains upward user code compatibility within the family. The major members of this microprocessor family and their key features are summarized below.

MC68000: The basic model of the M68000 microprocessor family.

MC68008: An 8-bit version of the MC68000. Since it employs an 8-bit data

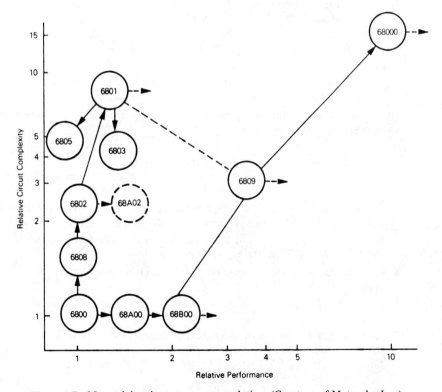

Figure 1-7 Motorola's microprocessors evolution. (Courtesy of Motorola, Inc.)

bus, the MC68008 can be used in a hardware system that was built for an MC6809 with minimal modifications.

MC68010: An enhanced version of the MC68000. The MC68010 has additional instructions and architectural improvements to support virtual memory when used in conjunction with a memory management unit.

MC68020: The 32-bit member in the family. Both the data and address buses are 32 bits in width. The MC68020 also has an on-chip instruction cache memory, and instructions to provide coprocessor interface.

MC68030: An enhanced version of the MC68020. The MC68030 has a virtual memory management logic and a data cache in addition to the instruction cache.

MC68040: The third generation 32-bit member in the family. The MC68040 includes separated memory management units for data and instruction, expanded on-chip caches, and a floating-point arithmetic unit.

EXERCISES

1. Convert the following decimal numbers to 16-bit binary numbers (give your answers in hexadecimal):
   (a) 81 (b) −21 (c) 1230 (d) −1501 (e) 15000

2. Convert the following unsigned hexadecimal numbers to decimal numbers.
   (a) 003A (b) 00F2 (c) F0F0 (d) 8001

3. Convert the following signed hexadecimal numbers to decimal numbers.
   (a) 003A (b) 00F2 (c) F0F0 (d) 8001

4. Find the 2's complement of the following signed hexadecimal numbers (give your answers in hexadecimal):
   (a) 003A (b) 00F2 (c) F0F0 (d) 8001

5. Given the signed hexadecimal numbers $A = 003A$ $B = 00F2$ $C = F0F0$ $D = 8001$ interpret the signed result of each of the following operations:
   (a) $A - B$ (b) $A + B$ (c) $A - C$ (d) $B + D$

6. Compare the ranges of n-bit unsigned binary, n-bit signed binary, n-bit unsigned BCD, and n-bit signed BCD formats for $n = 16, 24,$ and 32. Give your answers in decimal.

7. Find the 10's complement in BCD for each of the following decimal numbers.
   (a) 3456 (b) 7025 (c) 0015 (d) 9999

8. Give the smallest nonzero positive single-precision real number (give your answer in hexadecimal).

9. Give the largest positive single-precision real number (give your answer in hexadecimal).

10. Assume that the following hexadecimal numbers represent single-precision floating-point numbers:
    (a) C1A4C000 (b) CCEB7652 (c) BE180000 (d) 4640E680
    Determine their decimal equivalents.

11. Convert the following decimal numbers to single-precision real numbers (give your answers in hexadecimal):

(a) -11.375 (b) $-3,590,144$ (c) 0.625 (d) -54.625

12. Does 0.1 have an exact representation in a floating-point format? Justify your answer.

13. Express the following character strings in their ASCII equivalents (give your answers in hexadecimal):

(a) The MC68000 microprocessor (b) -12.205 (c) $(A + B) * C = A * C + B * C$

2

MC68000 Architecture

2-1 Register Set

The MC68000 is an internal 32-bit processor, meaning that each register has 32 bits and the processor can perform arithmetic and logic operations on 32-bit operands. Figure 2-1 is a block diagram showing all the registers in the MC68000 that are directly accessible to the user.

The register set is divided into two groups, the data registers and the address registers. There are eight data registers, denoted by D0–D7. Each can be used as a source or destination operand in a typical instruction. A data register may be accessed as a byte, a word, or a longword. For a byte operation, only the least significant byte, i.e., bits 7–0, is used as an operand. The remaining 24 bits are not affected by the byte operation. Similarly, for a word operation, only the least significant half of the register can be used.

The address registers are primarily for generating memory operand addresses. Therefore, their accesses are more restrictive when compared to the data registers. An address register cannot be referenced as a byte operand. When specified as a source, an address register can be accessed as a word (its lower 16 bits) or longword operand. But, when used as a destination in a word operation, the operand word is sign-extended to a longword before being stored into the destination address register. This means that the entire register will be affected regardless of whether the operation size is word or longword. In addition, address registers are allowed to be a valid destination operand only in those special instructions designed for address operations, such as move address (MOVEA), add address (ADDA), subtract address (SUBA), and compare address (CMPA).

As shown in Fig. 2-1, there are nine address registers, two of which also serve as the system stack pointers. The two stack pointers are the supervisor

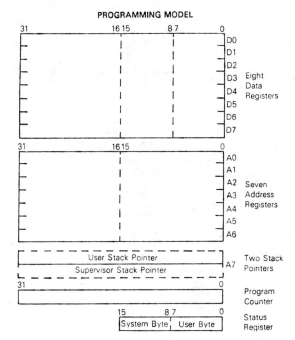

PROGRAMMING MODEL

Eight Data Registers

Seven Address Registers

Two Stack Pointers

Program Counter

Status Register

Figure 2-1 The MC68000 register set. (Courtesy of Motorola, Inc.)

stack pointer (SSP) and the user stack pointer (USP). In a subroutine call or some other instructions, the active system stack pointer (SP) is automatically used for saving and restoring the return address and other information. The active system stack pointer is the SSP in the supervisor mode and the USP in the user mode. The address registers are referenced by A0–A7, with A7 (or SP) representing either the SSP or the USP, depending on the supervisor bit in the status register.

As any other microprocessor, the MC68000 has a program counter and a status register. The program counter (PC) always points to the next instruction to be executed. Unlike a general purpose register, it cannot be explicitly specified as an operand in any instruction except as an index register. During a branch-type instruction, the destination is loaded into the PC. For any other instruction, its contents are incremented by the instruction length as the instruction is executed. Although the program counter and address registers are 32 bits long, only the lower 24 bits are used for addressing the memory. This limits the programming space to 16 megabytes.

2-2 Status Register

The status register has 16 bits and is divided into the system byte and user byte, as shown in Fig. 2-2. The user byte contains five condition flags. The remaining 3 bits in the user byte are not used and remain zero. The condition flags contain information on the result of the last processor operation. Their settings can be

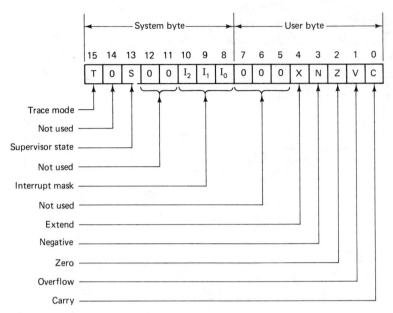

Figure 2-2 Status register.

tested by conditional branch instructions. The five condition flags are summarized next.

The carry (C) flag is set to 1 if a carry is generated out of the most significant bit of the result. Otherwise, it will be cleared. Assume that A and B represent the two operands involved in the operation and R represents the result. Then, in addition A + B, the generation of the C flag can be described by the Boolean expression:

$$C = A_{m-1} \cdot B_{m-1} + \overline{R_{m-1}} \cdot A_{m-1} + \overline{R_{m-1}} \cdot B_{m-1}$$

where A_{m-1} is the most significant bit (MSB) of operand A, B_{m-1} is the MSB of B, and R_{m-1} is the MSB of R. For example, 43210000 + A1230000 will cause the carry flag to be cleared. On the other hand, 43210000 + D1230000 will set the flag to 1. However, in subtraction A − B, setting the C flag to 1 indicates a borrow by the most significant bit in the result. In this case, the C flag is generated by

$$\overline{A_{m-1}} \cdot B_{m-1} + R_{m-1} \cdot \overline{A_{m-1}} + R_{m-1} \cdot B_{m-1}$$

The overflow (V) flag is set when the result exceeds the maximum number that can be represented in the 2's complement notation for the destination operand size. An overflow occurs when the addition of two positive numbers produces a negative result or when the subtraction of a positive number from a negative number produces a positive result. For example, 70000000 + 40000000 and D0000000 − 70000000 both cause an overflow. On the other hand, D0000000 + 70000000 and D0000000 − B0000000 both clear the overflow flag. The overflow flag is meaningful in signed arithmetic operations. For an unsigned operation, the carry flag should be used to test for a possible overflow. In general, the V flag is set if there is a carry/borrow from the MSB but no carry/borrow into the MSB or there is a carry/borrow into the MSB but no carry/borrow from the MSB.

The zero (Z) flag indicates whether the result is zero or not. It is set to 1 if the result is zero and is cleared if the result is nonzero.

The negative (N) flag is set to 1 when the result is negative and to 0 when the result is positive. In other words, the N flag is set equal to the most significant bit of the result.

The extend (X) flag is set in the same way as the carry flag. Unlike the C flag, the extend flag is not affected by data movement, logic, and comparison operations. This flag is designed to facilitate programming of multiple-precision arithmetics. In a double-precision instruction, the X flag is always used as in implied operand.

The upper byte of the status register can be modified only by privileged instructions executed in the supervisor mode. Bits 11, 12, and 14 are not used and are filled with zeros. The remaining bits serve special processor control functions.

The interrupt mask bits (I_2 I_1 I_0) allow the processor to ignore low-priority interrupt requests. When an interrupt request is received, its priority, which is from 1 to 7 with 7 being the highest, is compared with the mask level set by I_2 I_1 I_0. If the interrupt priority is not greater than the mask level, the request is ignored. This allows the processor to recognize interrupt requests with higher priorities while ignoring requests with lower priorities. Because request level 7 cannot be masked, the processor will ignore all interrupt requests except the one with priority 7 whenever I_2 I_1 I_0 is set to 111.

The trace (T) bit is used to enable the single-stepping facility. When the T bit is 1, a trace exception occurs upon completion of the current instruction execution. This bit is especially useful in program debugging because it allows the user to trace a program instruction by instruction.

The supervisor (S) bit specifies the processor's privilege level. If this bit is 1, the processor is in the supervisor state; otherwise, it is in the user state. The supervisor state, in which all instructions can be executed, is typically reserved for the operating system. In the user state, an attempt to execute a privileged instruction will cause a trap. This prevents a user program from changing vital processor control functions and therefore provides a protection for the system software in a multiprogramming environment. Those instructions that have access to the entire status register typically are privileged.

After a reset, the processor is initially in the supervisor state. Change from the supervisor state to the user state can be accomplished by clearing the S bit. Since the S bit is not accessible in the user state, a transition back to the supervisor state can be accomplished only through exception processing such as traps.

2-3 Machine Instruction Format

An MC68000 machine instruction may consist of one to five words, with the first word being called the *operation word*. The operation word includes an operation code, or *op code*, which defines the operation to be performed. If the operand is not implied, the operation word will have an addressing mode field that specifies how the operand address—i.e., the effective address—is calculated. Additional indicators such as operation size and second operand may also be included for some instructions. For those addressing modes that require additional information—i.e., immediate data, an index register, or a displacement—the operation word is followed by one or more extension words, which are considered as part of the instruction. The general format of a machine instruction is shown in Fig. 2-3.

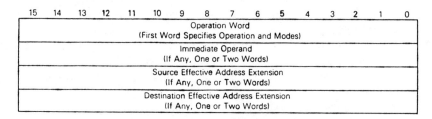

15	14	13	12	11	10	9	8	7	6	5	4	3	2	1	0
Operation Word (First Word Specifies Operation and Modes)															
Immediate Operand (If Any, One or Two Words)															
Source Effective Address Extension (If Any, One or Two Words)															
Destination Effective Address Extension (If Any, One or Two Words)															

Figure 2-3 General instruction format. (Courtesy of Motorola, Inc.)

The format of an operation word varies from one instruction group to the next. Figure 2-4 shows the general operation word for the group of single-operand instructions and immediate instructions. Typical instructions in this group are clear (CLR), negate (NEG), compare immediate (CMPI), and add immediate (ADDI). The size field whose encoding is given in Fig. 2-5 specifies the operand length. In the assembler notation, the operand length is indicated by an instruction postfix, which is .B for byte, .W for word, or .L for longword.

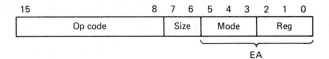

Figure 2-4 Operation word format of single-operand or immediate instructions.

Size Field	Operation Size	Assembler Syntax	Example
00	Byte	OPR.B	CLR.B (Clear a byte)
01	Word	OPR.W	CLR.W (Clear a word)
10	Longword	OPR.L	CLR.L (Clear a longword)

Figure 2-5 Encoding of the size field.

The effective address (EA) field is divided into two 3-bit subfields. The mode bits define the addressing mode, whereas the register bits indicate which register is to be used in forming the effective address. Figure 2-6 summarizes the 12 valid addressing modes and their encodings. Each is discussed in the next section.

There are many instructions that require two operands—for example, add, subtract, and move instructions. The operand to store the result is called the *destination* and the other operand is called the *source*. In order to reduce the

Mode	Register	Addressing Mode	Basic Assembler Syntax
000	Data register number	Data register direct	Dn
001	Address register number	Address register direct	An
010	Address register number	Address register indirect (ARI)	(An)
011	Address register number	ARI with postincrement	(An)+
100	Address register number	ARI with predecrement	-(An)
101	Address register number	ARI with displacement	d(An)
110	Address register number	ARI with index	d(An,Ri.X)
111	000	Absolute short	$XXXX
111	001	Absolute long	$XXXXXXXX
111	010	Program counter with displacement	d(PC)
111	011	Program counter with index	d(PC,Ri.X)
111	100	Immediate	#XXXX

Note: The index size indicator .X may be .W (word) or .L (longword).

Figure 2-6 The mode and register fields.

instruction size, for a typical double-operand instruction, only one operand is specified by the EA field, and the other operand is restricted to be a data register. Only a few instructions are capable of performing memory-to-memory operations. In such cases the addressing mode is implied by the instructions. The only exception is the move (MOVE) instruction, which allows both operands to be specified by EA addressing modes. The operation word format for double-operand instructions is given in Fig. 2-7.

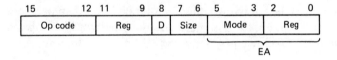

D = 0   (Dn) OP (EA) → Dn
D = 1   (EA) OP (Dn) → EA

Figure 2-7 Double-operand instruction format.

A branch instruction such as the BEQ (branch if equal) and BLT (branch if less than) does not have an EA field. Instead, the machine code has a condition field that specifies the condition to be tested and a displacement field to store the branch distance in bytes using the 2's complement form. Figure 2-8 shows the branch instruction format. The branch location is the sum of the displacement

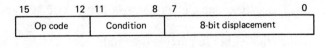

Figure 2-8 Machine code format of conditional branch instructions.

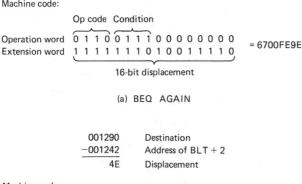

```
        0010A0      Destination
       −001202      Address of BEQ + 2
        −0162       Displacement
```

Machine code:

```
                    Op code  Condition
                   ⏞        ⏞
Operation word   0 1 1 0 0 1 1 1 0 0 0 0 0 0 0 0     = 6700FE9E
Extension word   1 1 1 1 1 1 1 0 1 0 0 1 1 1 1 0
                 ⏟_____⏟
                        16-bit displacement
```

(a) BEQ AGAIN

```
        001290      Destination
       −001242      Address of BLT + 2
           4E       Displacement
```

Machine code:

```
                Op code  Condition  8-bit displacement
               ⏞        ⏞         ⏞
Operation word  0 1 1 0 1 1 0 1 0 1 0 0 1 1 1 0     = 6D4E
```

(b) BLT.S EXIT

Figure 2-9 Examples of machine code for conditional branch instructions.

and the content of PC, which is the address of the branch instruction plus 2. If the branch distance is not within the range of − 128 to 127 bytes, an extension word is required to provide a 16-bit displacement.

Since the 1-word branch is shorter and faster than the 2-word branch, it is advantageous to use the 1-word branch whenever possible. For a backward branch, the assembler is able to determine whether an 8-bit or 16-bit displacement should be used. For a forward branch, the assembler assumes a 2-word instruction unless the branch instruction is followed by a postfix .S (short), which forces a 1-word instruction.

Figure 2-9 illustrates how to determine the displacement in a conditional branch instruction. In these examples, it is assumed that the addresses assigned to instructions

```
        BEQ        AGAIN
```

and

```
        BLT.S      EXIT
```

and labels AGAIN and EXIT are hexadecimal 001200, 001240, 0010A0, and 001290, respectively.

There are some instructions that either require no operands (such as RESET) or the operands are implied, such as RTS (return from subroutine) and TRAPV (trap on overflow). In these instructions, the entire operation word is used as the op code. The machine code formats of all MC68000 instructions are given in Appendix A.

2-4 Addressing Modes

The MC68000 supports 12 addressing modes for accessing operands, each of which is discussed shortly. For a memory operand, the address is calculated in the 32-bit 2's complement form. However, only the lower 24 bits of the result are actually used for the operand address. It is important to point out that in accessing a memory operand as a word or longword, its effective address must be evaluated to an even address. Otherwise, error will occur when that instruction is executed.

Data register direct

In the data register direct mode, the operand address is the data register specified in the instruction. The content of that data register is treated as the operand required for the operation. The action of this addressing mode is graphically described in Fig. 2-10, along with an illustrative example. The sample instruction

    CLR.W   D3

clears the lower word in data register D3 and leaves the upper word unchanged.

Register direct addressing is the fastest and most compact addressing mode because no memory reference operation is required for accessing the operand.

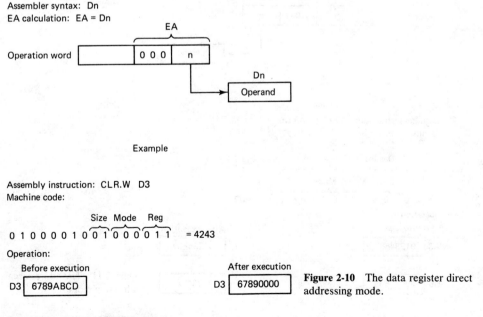

Figure 2-10 The data register direct addressing mode.

Address register direct

In the address register direct mode, the content of the specified address register is the operand required for the operation. The action of this addressing mode is graphically described in Fig. 2-11, along with an illustrative example. In this example, the instruction

        MOVE.L   A3,D5

copies the longword in address register A3 to data register D5.

Unlike the data register direct, a byte operation cannot be performed using the address register direct addressing mode. Furthermore, this addressing mode may not be used for specifying a destination operand except in few address-related instructions.

Address register indirect

In the address register indirect mode, the specified address register contains the memory address of an operand. This addressing mode is graphically described in Fig. 2-12, along with an illustrative example. In this example, the instruction

        CLR.L   (A3)

clears the longword beginning at memory location 001234, which is the address stored in address register A3.

Assembler syntax: An
EA calculation: EA = An

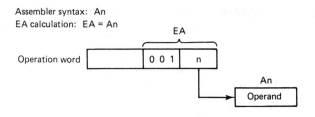

Example
Assembly instruction: MOVE.L   A3,D5
Machine code:

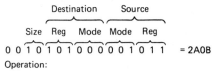

Operation:

Figure 2-11 The address register direct addressing mode.

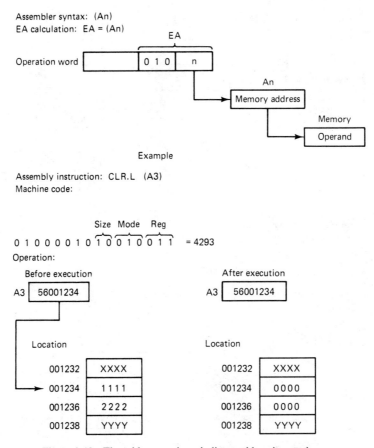

Assembler syntax: (An)
EA calculation: EA = (An)

EA

Operation word | | 0 1 0 | n |

An
Memory address

Memory
Operand

Example

Assembly instruction: CLR.L (A3)
Machine code:

Size Mode Reg
0 1 0 0 0 0 1 0 1 0 0 1 0 0 1 1 = 4293

Operation:

Before execution

A3 | 56001234 |

After execution

A3 | 56001234 |

Location

001232	XXXX
001234	1111
001236	2222
001238	YYYY

Location

001232	XXXX
001234	0000
001236	0000
001238	YYYY

Figure 2-12 The address register indirect addressing mode.

With the address register indirect mode, the same instruction can be repeated to operate on several different operands by changing the content of the address register each time.

Address register indirect with postincrement

In the address register indirect with postincrement mode, the content of the specified address register is used as the memory address of an operand. After the operation, the content of the address register is incremented by 1, 2, or 4, depending on whether it is a byte, word, or longword operation. Therefore, after the instruction execution, the same address register points to the next operand in sequence. This addressing mode is graphically described in Fig. 2-13, along with an illustrative example. In the example, the instruction

        CLR.B   (A3)+

clears the byte at location 012344 taken from register A3 and then increments the

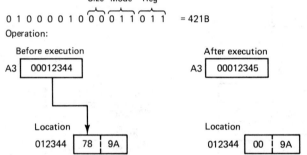

Assembler syntax: (An)+

EA calculation: EA = (An); An + 1, 2 or 4 → An

Operation word

Example

Assembly instruction CLR.B (A3)+
Machine code:

```
        Size  Mode  Reg
0 1 0 0 0 0 1 0 0 0 0 1 1 0 1 1   = 421B
Operation:
```

Before execution

A3 00012344

After execution

A3 00012345

Location

012344 78 ¦ 9A

Location

012344 00 ¦ 9A

Figure 2-13 The address register indirect with postincrement addressing mode.

content of A3 by 1, pointing to the next byte in sequence. Should the same instruction be executed again, the next byte, which is 9A, would be cleared and the content of register A3 would become 00012346.

The postincrement register indirect mode is especially useful for processing a one-dimensional array from low address to high address. This addressing mode is also used to implement the operation of retrieving data from the stack. Because the system stack pointer is used in interrupt processing and as an implied operand in some instructions, its content must remain on a word boundary. To ensure this, if A7 is used as the address register in the postincrement addressing mode, register A7 will be incremented by 2 for a byte or word operation and by 4 for a longword operation.

Address register indirect with predecrement

In the address register indirect with predecrement mode, the selected address register is first decremented by 1, 2, or 4, depending on whether the operation size is byte, word, or longword. Then, its content is used as a memory operand address. If the address register used is A7, it will be decremented by 2 instead of 1 for byte operations. The action of the predecrement addressing mode is graphically described in Fig. 2-14, along with an illustrative example. In this example, address register A3 initially has 00003458. During the execution of

    CLR.B   −(A3)

register A3 is first decremented by 1, and the resulting address is then used as the memory location to clear the data byte.

This addressing mode is typically used to process a linear array, starting from its last element toward its first element, and to push data onto a stack.

Address register indirect with displacement

In the address register indirect with displacement mode, the effective address is the sum of the content of the selected address register and a sign-extended displacement. An extension word is required to specify the 16-bit displacement. This

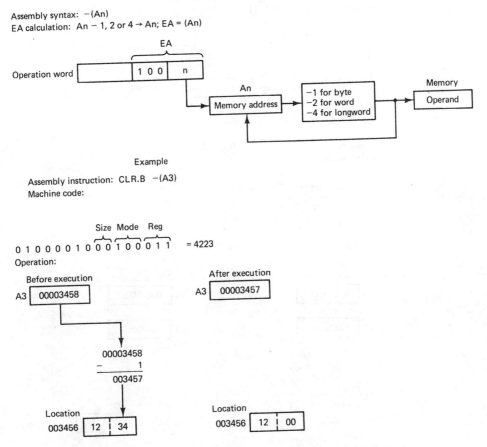

Figure 2-14 The address register indirect with predecrement addressing mode.

Sec. 2-4 Addressing Modes

addressing mode is graphically described in Fig. 2-15, along with an illustrative example. In the sample instruction

MOVE.B   18(A5),D3

the source address is the sum of decimal 18 plus the content of register A5, which is hexadecimal 002000. The instruction copies the data byte from the source address to the least significant byte in register D3.

The address register indirect with displacement mode is useful in accessing elements in an array. With the address register pointing to the beginning of the array, the displacement can be used as an offset to select the element in the array for processing.

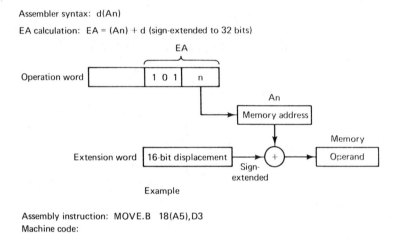

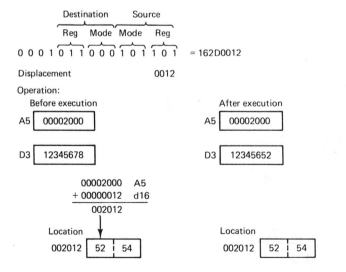

Figure 2-15 The address register indirect with displacement addressing mode.

Address register indirect with index

In the address register indirect with index mode, the effective address is the sum of the content of the selected address register, an index, and a displacement. The index whose size is word or longword can be taken from either a data or an address register. The displacement is always a byte and is sign-extended to 32 bits before the addition.

An extension word, whose format is given in Fig. 2-16, is required to specify the index register and displacement. The D/A bit indicates whether the index register is a data register (0) or an address register (1). The index register number is designated by bits 14–12, and the index size is specified by the W/L bit, 0 for 16 bits and 1 for 32 bits.

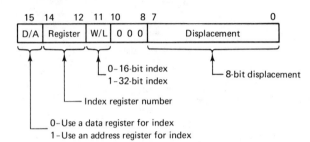

Figure 2-16 Extension word format for the address register indirect with index addressing mode.

The action of the index addressing mode is graphically described in Fig. 2-17, along with an illustrative example. In the sample instruction

        MOVE.W   − 2(A3,D5.W),$3600(A6)

the source address is specified in the index addressing mode, which is the sum of − 2, the content of A3, and the lower word of D5. The destination address is specified in the address register indirect with displacement mode. The dollar sign in the displacement $3600 indicates that the number is given in the hexadecimal form.

The address register indirect with index mode is very flexible, in that two address components can be varied at execution time. It is frequently used in processing two-dimensional arrays such as matrices and tables. For example, suppose that a two-dimensional array is stored in memory column by column. If the address register points to the beginning of the array and the displacement is set to the relative position of the ith element in a column, then by changing the index, each element in the ith row can easily be accessed.

Absolute short

In the absolute short addressing mode, the effective address is specified by the displacement in the extension word. The 16-bit displacement is sign-extended before it is used. Therefore, the addressable memory range is 000000–007FFF

Assembler syntax: d(An,Ri.X) (X = W for 16-bit index or L for 32-bit index)
EA calculation: EA = (An) + (Ri.X) (sign-extended if X = W)
                   + d (sign-extended)

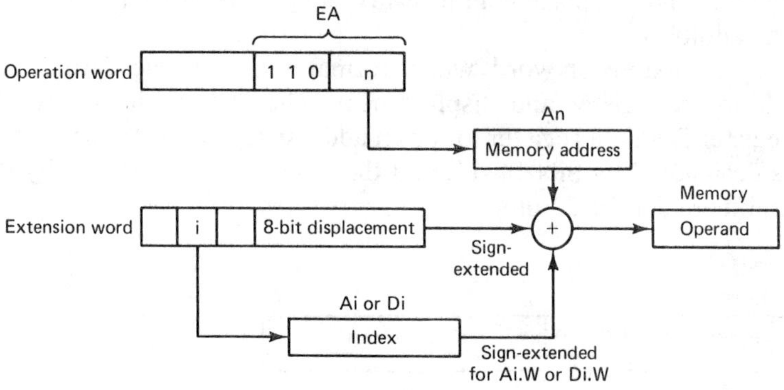

EA

Operation word | | 1 1 0 | n |

An
Memory address

Memory

Extension word | | i | 8-bit displacement | → (+) → Operand

Sign-
extended

Ai or Di
Index

Sign-extended
for Ai.W or Di.W

Example

Assembly instruction: MOVE.W −2(A3,D5.W),$3600(A6)
Machine code:

Destination   Source
Reg Mode   Mode Reg
0 0 1 1 1 1 0 1 0 1 1 1 0 0 1 1

D/A Reg W/L   Displacement
0 1 0 1 0 0 0 0 1 1 1 1 1 1 1 0   = 3D7350FE3600

Displacement   3600

Operation:

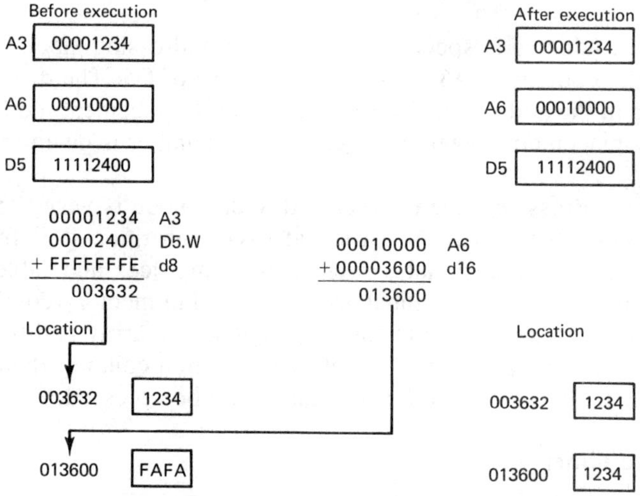

Before execution   After execution

A3 | 00001234 | A3 | 00001234 |

A6 | 00010000 | A6 | 00010000 |

D5 | 11112400 | D5 | 11112400 |

  00001234 A3   00010000 A6
  00002400 D5.W   + 00003600 d16
+ FFFFFFFE d8   013600
  003632

Location   Location

003632 | 1234 | 003632 | 1234 |

013600 | FAFA | 013600 | 1234 |

Figure 2-17 The address register indirect with index addressing mode.

and FF8000–FFFFFF. No register is involved in this addressing mode. The action of the absolute short addressing mode is graphically described in Fig. 2-18, along with an illustrative example. The sample instruction

CLR.W $3000

clears the memory word located at hexadecimal location 003000. This addressing mode is typically used to access simple memory operands.

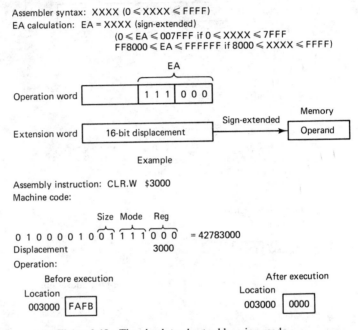

Figure 2-18   The absolute short addressing mode.

Absolute long

The absolute long addressing mode is the same as the absolute short addressing mode except that the full 24-bit effective address is stored in the second and third words of the instruction. This allows an instruction to access any memory location directly. The action of the absolute long addressing mode is graphically described in Fig. 2-19, along with an illustrative example.

Program counter relative with displacement

The program counter relative with displacement mode is similar to the address register with displacement addressing mode in that the effective address is the sum of a sign-extended displacement and a base address. In this mode, the base address is the current content of the program counter, which points to the extension word. The displacement in this case represents the distance in bytes be-

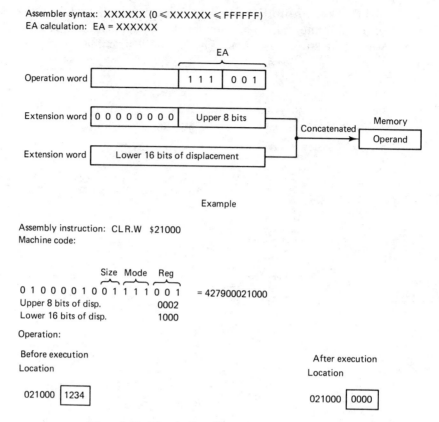

Assembler syntax: XXXXXX (0 ≤ XXXXXX ≤ FFFFFF)
EA calculation: EA = XXXXXX

Example

Assembly instruction: CLR.W $21000
Machine code:

```
                Size  Mode  Reg
0 1 0 0 0 0 1 0 0 1 1 1 1 0 0 1   = 427900021000
Upper 8 bits of disp.        0002
Lower 16 bits of disp.       1000
```

Operation:

Before execution
Location

021000 | 1234 |

After execution
Location

021000 | 0000 |

Figure 2-19 The absolute long addressing mode.

tween the instruction and the referenced operand, which is independent of where the program is stored in memory. Therefore, by using the PC relative with displacement addressing mode, an instruction can become position-independent. The action of this addressing mode is graphically described in Fig. 2-20 along with an illustrative example. In this example, it is assumed that the instruction

        MOVE.W $1200(PC),D3

is stored beginning at location 122000. Therefore, during its execution PC points to 00122002. This address is added by $1200 to form the source operand address.

The PC relative with displacement addressing mode is not allowed for specifying destination operands.

Program counter relative with index

The program counter relative with index mode is the same as the register indirect with index addressing mode except that the current content of the program counter is used as the base address. An extension word is required that has the same format as the one given in Fig. 2-16. When calculating the effective address, the content of PC is the address of the extension word. The action of this addressing mode is graphically described in Fig. 2-21, along with an illustrative example. As with the PC relative with displacement mode, the major advantage of having this mode is to support position-independent programming. A destination effective address may not be given in the PC relative with index addressing mode.

Assembler syntax: d(PC)
EA calculation: EA = (PC) + d (sign-extended)

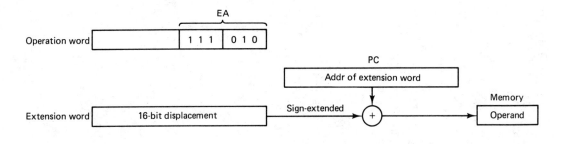

Example

Assembly instruction: MOVE.W $1200(PC),D3
Machine code:

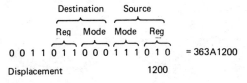

Operation:

Assume that the instruction starts at 122000

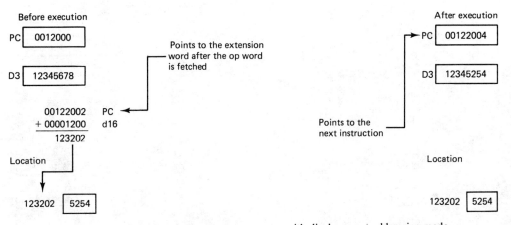

Figure 2-20 The program counter with displacement addressing mode.

Assembler syntax: d(PC,Ri.W) (X = W for 16-bit index or L for 32-bit index)
EA calculation: EA = (PC) + (Ri.X) (sign-extended)
+ d (sign-extended)

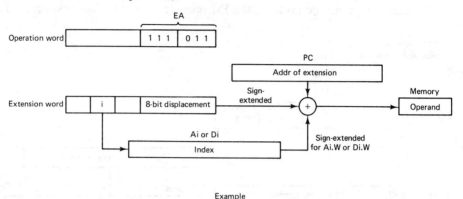

Example

Assembly instruction: MOVE.L −20(PC,A2.L),D1
Machine code:

```
          Destination   Source
          Reg   Mode   Mode   Reg
0 0 1 0 0 0 1 0 0 0 1 1 1 0 1 1
D/A Reg W/L        Displacement        = 223BA8EC
1 0 1 0 1 0 0 0 1 1 1 0 1 1 0 0
```

Operation:

Assume that the instruction starts at 010200

Figure 2-21 The program counter with index addressing mode.

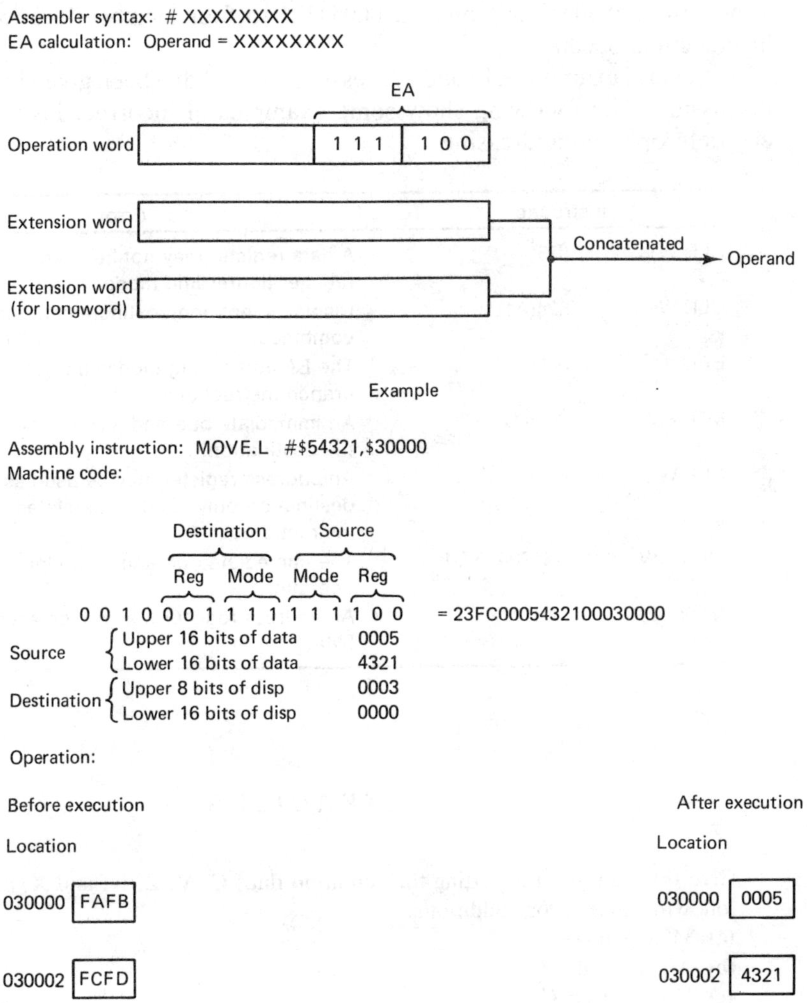

Assembler syntax: # XXXXXXXX
EA calculation: Operand = XXXXXXXX

EA

Operation word | 1 1 1 | 1 0 0

Extension word

Extension word
(for longword)

Concatenated ——→ Operand

Example

Assembly instruction: MOVE.L #$54321,$30000
Machine code:

```
              Destination    Source
            ┌─────────┐  ┌────────┐
            Reg  Mode  Mode  Reg
            ┌──┐┌───┐┌───┐┌──┐
 0 0 1 0 0 0 1 1 1 1 1 1 1 0 0    = 23FC0005432100030000
Source    { Upper 16 bits of data    0005
          { Lower 16 bits of data    4321
Destination { Upper 8 bits of disp   0003
            { Lower 16 bits of disp  0000
```

Operation:

Before execution

Location

030000 | FAFB

030002 | FCFD

After execution

Location

030000 | 0005

030002 | 4321

Figure 2-22 The immediate addressing mode.

Immediate

In the immediate mode, the operand itself is stored in the extension word as part of the instruction. If the immediate operand is a longword, two extension words are required. The immediate addressing mode provides a convenient way for referencing constants that are occasionally used in a program. Obviously, immediate operands may serve only as source operands. The action of the immediate addressing mode is graphically described in Fig. 2-22, along with an illustrative example. The sample instruction

    MOVE.L   #$54321,$30000

moves the hexadecimal constant 00054321 to four memory locations starting at hexadecimal 30000.

Several examples of valid addressing modes have been given in the preceding discussion. The following show some examples of incorrect instructions due to errors in operand addressing.

Instruction		Error
CLR.W	(D3)	A data register may not be used in the indirect register addressing mode.
CLR.W	$24(A1)+	Displacement and postincrement may not be combined.
BEQ	(A1)	The EA addressing modes do not apply to branch instructions.
MOVE.W	D1,#12	An immediate operand may not be used for the destination.
CLR.W	A1	An address register may be used as the destination only in address-related instructions.
MOVE.W	#$123456,D1	The immediate operand is too large for a word operation.
MOVE.B	A1,D1	An address register may not be accessed as a byte.

EXERCISES

1. Give the sum and the setting for condition flags C, V, Z, N, and X, after each of the following 16-bit word additions:
   (a) 3456 + 6543
   (b) AFFF + B123
   (c) 1234 + EDCC
   (d) 1234 + 4321
   (e) AFED + 1234

2. Give the difference and the setting for condition flags C, V, Z, N, and X, after each of the following 16-bit word subtractions.
   (a) 1234 − 1212
   (b) 1234 − 4321
   (c) 4321 − AFFF
   (d) AFE0 − B000
   (e) AFE0 − 4321

3. For each of the given arithmetic operations, indicate whether or not an overflow could occur. If yes, show an example.
   (a) Positive + positive
   (b) Positive − positive
   (c) Negative + negative
   (d) Negative − negative

4. What is a privileged instruction?

5. Assume that the interrupt mask $I_2 I_1 I_0$ in the status register is set to 101. Determine the priorities of the interrupts that can be recognized by the MC68000.

6. Determine the machine code for each of the following instructions.
   (a) CLR.W $-\$120(A2)$
   (b) CLR.L   56(A3,A6.L)
   (c) MOVE.B $-(A3),-2(A3,D1.W)$
   (d) MOVE.W $3600,3600
   (e) MOVE.L   #$54,$1234(A3)
   (f) BLT   LABEL   (Assume that the addresses assigned to the instruction and the operand are 001200 and 0011A4, respectively.)
   (g) BEQ   LABEL   (Assume that the addresses assigned to the instruction and the operand are 002400 and 003620, respectively.)

7. Indicate the error in each of the following instructions.
   (a) MOVE.B   A3,D1
   (b) CLR.W $4567
   (c) CLR.W   36(A3)+
   (d) CLR.L $-(D3)$
   (e) MOVE.W $1234(A3,D2.L),$1234
   (f) CLR.W   #$1234
   (g) CLR.W $12(A1.W,A2.W)

8. Suppose that the initial conditions are:

Registers	Locations
A1: 00001202	001200: 1111
A2: 00001204	001202: 2222
D1: 01020304	001204: 3333
D2: F0F1F2F3	001206: 4444
	001208: 5555
	00120A: 6666

Assuming that the initial conditions as given are the same for each of the following instructions, show the results in all affected registers (except PC) and locations for each instruction.
   (a) CLR.L $-(A1)$
   (b) CLR.W   D2
   (c) MOVE.B $1205,D1
   (d) MOVE.W   (A2)+,1200
   (e) MOVE.L   D1,$-(A2)$
   (f) MOVE.L   (A1)+,D2

9. Each of the following is a machine code for the CLR instruction:
   (a) 429D
   (b) 427150EE
   (c) 42B83600
   (d) 42AE2400
   Translate each instruction into symbolic form.

10. What is the difference between the following two instructions?
    MOVE.W $1234,D1   and   MOVE.W   #$1234,D1

3

Assembly Language Programming and Basic Instructions

A program can be written directly in machine instructions, but it is a tedious process to code each instruction in binary or even in hexadecimal form. Furthermore, a program written in machine code is difficult to read and modify. In most cases, assembly language instructions are in one-to-one correspondence with machine instructions. With assembly language, a programmer can use mnemonics for op codes and symbols for memory locations and operands, thus simplifying the programming. A utility program called an assembler will then translate (or assemble) the assembly language program into binary code before the program is executed.

3-1 Symbols

Figure 3-1 shows a sample program in assembly language along with the assembled machine code. In many cases, especially for a multiprogramming system, the user does not know where the program will be loaded for execution. The assembler can be directed to assemble a program into relocatable code. In this situation, the assembler assumes the beginning address of the program to be zero and assigns each instruction an address that is relative to the program origin. In Fig. 3-1, the second column shows the relative address of each instruction and the third column gives the machine code. When the program is loaded into memory for execution, the relative addresses that have been referenced as operands in the program must be converted to physical or absolute addresses.

Consider that the sample program is to be loaded into memory starting at location 002000 for execution. Now, the symbols ARRAY and SIZE correspond to actual addresses 002000 and 002030, respectively. Therefore, the immediate

```
1    000000                              SECTION  0
2    000000                      ARRAY   DS.L     12
3    000030   000C               SIZE    DC.W     12
4             0000 0002          CONST   EQU      2
5    000032   227C 0000 0000     START   MOVEA.L  #ARRAY,A1
6    000038   3238 0030                  MOVE.W   SIZE,D1
7    00003C   5341                       SUBQ.W   #1,D1
8    00003E   4282                       CLR.L    D2
9    000040   143C 0002                  MOVE.B   #CONST,D2
10   000044   22C2               LOOP    MOVE.L   D2,(A1)+
11   000046   D482                       ADD.L    D2,D2
12   000048   51C9 FFFA                  DBF      D1,LOOP
13   00004C   4E72 2000                  STOP     #$2000
14                                       END      START
```

Machine code before relocation

Figure 3-1 A sample assembly language program.

operand #ARRAY in the MOVEA.L instruction and the operand address SIZE in the MOVE.W instruction must be adjusted accordingly from the machine code given in Fig. 3-1. Among other things, a linker performs this relocation operation as follows.

Physical address = relative address + relocation factor (the physical address of the program origin)

The result is given in Fig. 3-2 along with a duplicate of the source code for comparison. The figure also shows the correct machine code if the program is to be loaded starting at location 032500 for execution. A symbol such as ARRAY and SIZE, whose associated value (not the content) is relative to the program origin,

```
002000                           ARRAY   DS.L     12
002030   000C                    SIZE    DC.W     12
         0000 0002               CONST   EQU      2
002032   227C 0000 2000          START   MOVEA.L  #ARRAY,A1
002038   3239 0000 2030                  MOVE.W   SIZE,D1
00203E   5341                            SUBQ.W   #1,D1
002040   4282                            CLR.L    D2
002042   143C 0002                       MOVE.B   #CONST,D2
002046   22C2                    LOOP    MOVE.L   D2,(A1)+
002048   D482                            ADD.L    D2,D2
00204A   51C9 FFFA                       DBF      D1,LOOP
00204E   4E72 2000                       STOP     #$2000
                                         END      START
```

(a) Machine code after being relocated to 002000.

```
032500                           ARRAY   DS.L     12
032530   000C                    SIZE    DC.W     12
         0000 0002               CONST   EQU      2
032532   227C 0003 2500          START   MOVEA.L  #ARRAY,A1
032538   3239 0003 2530                  MOVE.W   SIZE,D1
03253E   5341                            SUBQ.W   #1,D1
032540   4282                            CLR.L    D2
032542   143C 0002                       MOVE.B   #CONST,D2
032546   22C2                    LOOP    MOVE.L   D2,(A1)+
032548   D482                            ADD.L    D2,D2
03254A   51C9 FFFA                       DBF      D1,LOOP
03254E   4E72 2000                       STOP     #$2000
                                         END      START
```

(b) Machine code after being relocated to 032500.

Figure 3-2 Program relocation.

is called *relocatable*. On the other hand, the operand #CONST represents a fixed value 2, which is not dependent on the location of the program. Such a symbol, whose value will not change when the program is relocated, is called *absolute*. The reader should not confuse the absolute addressing mode discussed in Chap. 2 with an absolute address or absolute symbol. For this reason, perhaps a more appropriate name for absolute addressing mode is direct memory addressing mode.

For a simple system, a user may have control over where to load a program for execution. In this case the assembler can be directed to assemble the program with its first instruction starting at a given address. The resulting machine code is called absolute code; it will execute properly if and only if it is loaded into memory starting at the same address as specified. Therefore, an absolute code is inflexible as far as memory allocation is concerned but requires no relocation.

3-2 Assembly Language Statement Format

An assembly language statement has the following general format:

Label   Operator   Operand,Operand   Comment

The label field is optional. When present, it is a user-defined symbol representing the address associated with the instruction. This address can then be referenced symbolically by other instructions in the program. Since a label identifies a particular statement, the same symbol may not appear in more than one label field. A label, which may have up to eight alphanumeric characters, must begin in column 1 with a letter and be terminated by a space. The comment field is also optional. If present, it begins with a space which separates the operand and comment fields. If column 1 of a statement line is an asterisk *, the entire line is treated as a comment. Comments will be ignored by the assembler and will not affect program execution. However, they will be shown in the assembly listing, making the program more readable.

The operator field may contain a mnemonic code for an MC68000 instruction, an assembler directive also known as a *pseudoinstruction*, or a macro call. For those instructions that can handle more than one operand size, a postfix is required to specify the operation size. If a postfix is not given in the operator field, the assembler assumes the size option to be word. The possible operation size postfixes are as follows.

Symbol	Meaning	Example	
.B	Byte	CLR.B	DC.B
.W	Word	MOVE.W	DS.W
.L	Longword	MOVE.L	DS.L

For a branch instruction, a postfix .S is optional to indicate a one-word instruction.

The operand field depends on the operator and may have more than one operand. Two operands are separated by a comma, with the source followed by the destination. For example, in the instruction

```
ADD.W       D2,XYZ
```

D2 is the source operand, and XYZ is the destination operand where the sum is to be stored.

In general, an operand that represents an address or immediate data may include an expression consisting of integers and defined labels combined by the following operators:

+	Addition
−	Subtraction
*	Multiplication
/	Division
−	Negation
( )	Parentheses

An expression may also include the current location counter, which is the address assigned to the first word of the current instruction. The current location counter is denoted by an asterisk (*), which is treated as a relocatable symbol. For example, the instruction

```
BEQ       *−24
```

will branch 24 bytes backward from the instruction if the Z flag is 1.

An integer can be specified in different forms as indicated by the base designators as follows:

Format	Meaning	Example
$N	N in hexadecimal	$34, −$5AFF0000
N (no designator)	N in decimal	12, −3600
@2	N in octal	@177777, −@32
%N	N in Binary	%110, −%10101010
'string'	ASCII character string	'AB' (same as $4142)

If a number does not have a base designator, it is treated as a decimal number.

The basic rule for a valid expression is that it must be either relocatable or absolute. Otherwise, its value cannot be adjusted at link time. Based on the definitions of relocatable and absolute terms, as given in Sec. 3-1, it can be seen that the allowable operations for combining terms are the following.

Operation	Result
Relocatable expression − relocatable expression	Absolute
Relocatable expression ± absolute expression	Relocatable
Absolute expression + relocatable expression	Relocatable
Absolute expression ± absolute expression	Absolute
Absolute expression */ absolute expression	Absolute

Note that a relocatable term subtracted by another relocatable term becomes an absolute expression. This is so because the difference between the two terms remains contant when the program is relocated. Assume that X, Y, and Z are relocatable symbols defined in the program. Some examples of valid and invalid expressions are shown next.

X + 6 − Z	Relocatable
X + (Y − Z)	Relocatable
(X − Y)*2 − 6	Absolute
* − 10	Relocatable
$FF00 − 12 + X	Relocatable
− 1234	Absolute
1000 − X	Invalid
X*2	Invalid
X + Y + 6	Invalid

Addressing Mode	Assembler Format	Example	
Data register direct	Dn	CLR.W MOVE.B	D3 D2,$1000
Address register direct	An, SP (same as A7)	CLR.L MOVEA.W	A2 #$1000,SP
Address register indirect	(An)	CLR.B MOVE.W	(A3) #-$24,(A4)
ARI with postincrement	(An)+	CLR.W MOVE.L	(A2)+ (SP)+,D0
ARI with predecrement	-(An)	CLR.B MOVE.L	-(A1) D0,-(SP)
ARI with displacement	Expression(An)	CLR.W JMP	OFFSET+2(A1) NEXT(A2)
ARI with index	Expression(An,Ri.X)	CLR.B MOVE.W	-$12(A1,A2.L) 0(A1,D2.W)
Absolute short	Expression	CLR.W JMP	$6FFF $2000
Absolute long	Expression	JMP MOVE.W	DONE ARY+4,$12500
PC with displacement	Expression(PC)	MOVE.W MOVE.W	ARY+4(PC),D2 $240(PC),D2
PC with index	Expression(PC,Ri.X)	MOVE.W MOVE.M	AA(PC,D2.W),D3 12(PC,D2.W),D3
Immediate	#Expression	MOVE.L MOVE.W	#LAB-$12,D2 #'12',D2
Relative (branch only)	Expression	BLT BEQ.S	*-24 LAB+12

Figure 3-3 General forms for specifying an operand.

An operand may have one of several general forms depending on its addressing mode, as shown in Fig. 3-3. Also included in the figure are some coding examples. The expression portion of an operand will be assembled into a displacement or immediate data in the given instruction. Since the displacement size varies from one addressing mode to the next, an expression must evaluate to a number within the valid range of the displacement for a given addressing mode. For example, the displacement size is 16 bits in the ARI with displacement addressing mode. Therefore, in the

        CLR.W   OFFSET + 2(A1)

instruction, the operand will be incorrect if the value associated with OFFSET is higher than or equal to $FFFE.

For a given instruction, not all addressing modes are available. Exactly which addressing modes can be used varies from instruction to instruction. In order to simplify the description of those addressing modes available in each instruction, which will be discussed later, the addressing modes are classified into eight categories, as listed in Fig. 3-4. The four basic categories are:

Data: Consists of the addressing modes that may be used as a data operand. Since the content of an address register is considered an address, the address register direct mode is not included in this category.

Memory: Consists of the addressing modes that specify a memory operand. Obviously, the data and address register direct modes do not belong to this category.

Control: Consists of the addressing modes that refer to a memory address without an associated size. For example, a jump and subroutine call are unsized instructions and therefore use the control addressing modes. Note

Addressing Mode	Data	Memory	Control	Alterable	Data Alterable	Memory Alterable	Control Alterable	All
Data register direct	X			X	X			X
Address register direct				X				X
Address register indirect	X	X	X	X	X	X	X	X
ARI with postincrement	X	X		X	X	X		X
ARI with predecrement	X	X		X	X	X		X
ARI with displacement	X	X	X	X	X	X	X	X
ARI with index	X	X	X	X	X	X	X	X
Absolute short	X	X	X	X	X	X	X	X
Absolute long	X	X	X	X	X	X	X	X
PC with displacement	X	X	X					X
PC with index	X	X	X					X
Immediate	X	X						X

Figure 3-4 Categories of EA addressing modes.

that the register indirect with postincrement/predecrement modes are not included in this category. The reason is that both modes need to update a pointer by 1, 2, or 4, depending on the operation size associated with the instruction.

Alterable: Consists of the addressing modes that refer to an operand that is writable (or alterable). By this definition, a destination operand can be specified only by using an alterable addressing mode. Note that the MC68000 is designed in such a way that the program counter relative with displacement/index addressing modes are not allowed for specifying a destination operand. This restriction is intended to discourage a user from writing a self-modifying code in which a program may change its instructions during execution.

The destination operand addressing of some instructions is further limited to the data, memory, or control category. Those addressing modes in both data and alterable categories are represented by the data alterable category. The memory alterable and control alterable categories are defined in a similar way.

In the later discussion of individual instructions, if an instruction has an EA (effective address) field, we will specify its allowable addressing modes using the categories just defined. The following are some examples:

CLR	EA	EA: Data alterable addressing modes
MOVE	EA,EA	Source EA: All addressing modes
		Destination EA: Data alterable addressing modes
MOVE	EA,CCR	EA: Data addressing modes
SUB	EA,Dn	EA: All addressing modes
SUB	Dn,EA	EA: Memory alterable addressing modes
SUBQ	#Data,EA	EA: Alterable addressing modes
JMP	EA	EA: Control addressing modes

The control alterable addressing modes are used only in the MOVEM instruction for specifying its destination operand. No instructions use memory addressing modes alone.

Let us use an example to illustrate the EA field for a given instruction. As noted before, the EA addressing modes of a CLR instruction are limited to the data alterable category. Therefore, the following instructions are invalid:

CLR.L	A2
CLR.W	VAR(PC)
CLR.W	VAR(PC,D2.W)
CLR.B	#24

On the other hand, the same addressing modes are valid for specifying a source in the subtract instruction, as shown:

SUB.L	A2,D1
SUB.W	VAR(PC),D1
SUB.W	VAR(PC,D2.W),D1
SUB.B	#24,D1

```
          Directives                                  Function

      ORG       Expression (Absolute)      Initialize the location counter
                                           and instruct the assembler to
                                           assemble the program into
                                           absolute code.

      END       Expression                 Terminate the assembly process.
                                           The operand field is optional.

Label EQU       Expression                 Assign the value evaluated from
                                           the expression to the label.

Label DC.X      Expression,Expression,...  Reserve memory locations and
                                           assign initial values to these
                                           locations.

Label DS.X      Expression (Absolute)      Reserve memory locations with
                                           no initial values being specified.
```

Notes: 1. A label is not permitted for the ORG and END directives, is
          required for the EQU directive, and is optional for the DC
          and DS directives.
       2. The postfix .X, which specifies the operand size, is .B (byte),
          .W (word), or .L (longword).

Figure 3-5 Frequently used assembler directives.

3-3 Assembler Directives

Assembler directives are similar to declarative statements in a typical high-level language in that they are not executed during program execution. Instead, they are used to instruct the assembler to reserve storage and to invoke certain control functions during the assembly process. Figure 3-5 lists those assembler directives most often used.

The ORG (origin) directive sets the program origin—i.e., the location counter—to the value evaluated from the operand expression. The statement following the ORG directive will be assigned the address as specified in the operand field. The machine code is generated with all addresses being assigned absolute values. Therefore, the program will execute properly as long as the machine code is loaded into memory starting from the same location, as specified in the ORG statement. For a simple system, this absolute programming is typical because no link is required. It is possible for a program to have more than one ORG directive in order to load a program into several separate areas. For example,

```
          ORG       $2000
START     MOVEA.L   #STACK+$600,SP
          .
          .                       ;other code
          .
          ORG       $3000
VAR1      DS.W      5
VAR2      DS.B      8
          .
          .                       ;other storage definition
          .                       ;directives
          ORG       $5000
STACK     DS.W      $300
          .
          .
          .
```

divides the program into three portions, separating code, data, and stack. The first portion starts from location $2000, where the MOVEA.L instruction is stored. The data area starts from location $3000, with VAR1 corresponding to $3000, and a stack of $300 words is reserved, with its lowest address being $5000, which is the upper limit of the stack.

A program must have one and only one END directive, which is the last statement in the program. The END directive terminates the assembly process. If an optional operand is present, it indicates the entry point of the program, which is the address of the first instruction to be executed. In case a main program and several subprograms are assembled independently and then combined into one load module, the main program should be terminated by an END directive with an operand, whereas each of the subprograms should be terminated by an END with no operand. This is because the execution of a subprogram is always initiated in a calling program. Consequently, the entry point of the entire program must reside in the main program.

The EQU (equate) directive enables the label to represent the expression in the operand field. Although it is not necessary, this directive provides some conveniences in program coding.

First, the EQU directive allows short names to replace frequently used lengthy expressions, thus reducing actual coding. Second, it allows meaningful names to represent constants or expressions, thus making a program more readable. Third, when a frequently used constant or address is replaced with a name, it is easy to change that constant or address in the program if necessary. For example, the instruction sequence

```
IOREG        EQU          $8AFE
             .
             .
             .
             MOVEA.L      #IOREG,A1
             .
             .
             .
             MOVE.B       IOREG,D2
             .
             .
             .
             MOVE.B       (A2)+,IOREG
             .
             .
             .
```

refers to the address of an I/O device register, which is $8AFE in many instructions. Should the I/O register address be changed due to a hardware reconfiguration, only the EQU statement must be modified, and then the program must reassembled in order to use the same program. Without using an EQU directive, every instruction in which the address $8AFE appears must be modified.

The DS (define storage) and DC (define constant) directives are, respectively, equivalent to the DIMENSION and DATA declaration statements in FORTRAN language. Both directives require a size postfix .X, where X is B for byte, W for word, or L for longword. An optional label represents the location of the first element of the reserved memory.

The operand expression in a DS directive must evaluate to an absolute number that specifies how many bytes, words, or longwords are to be reserved. No initial values will be assigned to the reserved memory block.

The DC directive reserves space and stores the values associated with the operands in the reserved locations. The location of the first element will be aligned to an even address if word or longword is specified.

Figure 3-6 shows several examples of storage definition directives with the indicated initial contents for the reserved spaces. As can be seen from the figure, the byte following the last element of the ARY2 block has been skipped due to the word alignment caused by the next DC.W statement.

3-4 Data Movement Group

The MC68000 has a total of 56 instructions. The basic ones will be discussed in this chapter. In describing the operations of individual instructions, we will use some special symbols and abbreviations. Their meanings are as follows:

Abbreviation	Meaning	Symbol	Meaning
An	Address register	X[n:m]	Bits n−m of X
Dn	Data register	(x)	Content of X
PC	Program counter	→	Left operand is moved to right operand
Rn	Data or address register		
SR	Status register	↔	Exchange left and right operands
CCR	Condition code register		
SSP	Supervisor stack pointer	∧	Logical AND operator
USP	User stack pointer	∨	Logical OR operator
SP	Active stack pointer, i.e., A7	⊕	Logical exclusive-OR operator
SRC	Source operand	$\overline{X}$	Complement of X
DST	Destination operand	*	Indicates that a condition flag is set or cleared according to the result
EA	Effective address		
I	Immediate data		
I8	8-bit immediate data	−	Indicates that a condition flag is not affected
I3	Immediate data with a value of 1 to 8		
		u	Indicates that a condition flag setting is undefined
D8	8-bit displacement		
D16	16-bit displacement		

The MC68000 provides nine data transfer instructions, which are summarized in Fig. 3-7. The instructions in this group are used to load data into a data register or memory location, to load an address into an address register, and to move status to or from the status register. Also included in the group are instructions to transfer data to or from multiple registers.

```
                                              Location    Contents
                ORG     $3000                   3000       3A78
                DC.W    $3A78,-17,'AB'          3002       FFEF
      ARY1      DS.W    4                       3004       4142
      ARY2      DS.B    7              (ARY1)   3006       ----
      SIZE      DC.W    ARY2-ARY1               3008       ----
      ADDR      DC.L    ARY2                    300A       ----
                                                300C       ----
                                       (ARY2)   300E       ----
                                                3010       ----
                                                3012       ----
                                                3014       ----
                                       (SIZE)   3016       0008
                                       (ADDR)   3018       0000
                                                301A       300E
```

Note: - means undefined.

Figure 3-6 Examples of the DC and DS directives.

Mnemonic	Size or Postfix	Operand Format	Allowable EA Modes	Operation	Condition Flags N Z V C X
MOVE (Move data)	.B[1], .W, .L	EA,EA	SRC: All DST: Data alterable	(SRC EA) -> DST EA	* * 0 0 -
MOVE (Move condition codes or status register)	Word	EA,CCR or SR[2] SR,EA	Data Data alterable	(EA) -> CCR or SR SR -> EA	* * * * * - - - - -
MOVE (Move user stack pointer)	Longword	USP,An[2] An,USP[2]		USP -> An An -> USP	- - - - -
MOVEA (Move address)	.W, .L	EA,An	All	(EA) -> An	- - - - -
MOVEQ (Move quick)	Longword	#I8,Dn		I8 (sign-extended) -> Dn	* * 0 0 -
MOVEM (Move multiple registers)	.W, .L	Reg List,EA EA,Reg List	Control alterable or predecrement Control or postincrement	Registers -> EA (EA) -> Registers	- - - - -
MOVEP (Move peripheral data)	.W, .L	Dx,D16(Ay) D16(Ay),Dx		Dx -> DST (SRC) -> Dx	- - - - -
EXG (Exchange registers)	Longword	Rx,Ry		Rx <-> Ry	- - - - -
SWAP (Swap register halves)	Word	Dn		Dn[31:16] <-> Dn[15:0]	* * 0 0 -
LEA (Load effective address)	Longword	EA,An	Control	EA -> An	- - - - -
PEA (Push effective address)	Longword	EA	Control	EA -> -(SP)	- - - - -

Notes: 1. Byte operation is not allowed if the source operand is
          an address register.
       2. MOVE EA,SR   MOVE USP,An   and MOVE An,USP are
          privileged instructions.

Figure 3-7 Data movement instructions.

The MOVE, MOVEA, and MOVEQ instructions

The MOVE instruction, depending on its operand formats, can transfer a byte, word, or longword from register to register, between register and memory, and from memory to memory. This instruction can also move a word to or from the status register and a longword between the user supervisor stack point and an address register. When the USP is specified as an operand or SR as the destination, the instruction becomes privileged and therefore cannot be executed in the user mode.

The MOVEA (move address) instruction provides a means of initializing an address register. Only a word or longword operand is allowed to be transferred into the specified address register. For a word operation, the source operand is sign-extended before being loaded into the address register.

The MOVEQ (move quick) is a short form of the move instruction for transferring an immediate operand to a data register. The immediate operand is limited to the range of −128 to 127. The operation size is implied to be longword. Therefore, the 8-bit immediate operand is sign-extended to 32 bits before being loaded into the destination, which must be a data register. Some assemblers can distinguish the three forms, move data, move address, and move quick, because each has a unique operand format. For such assemblers, the same instruction mnemonic MOVE can be used for MOVEA and MOVEQ as well, and the respective op code is assembled according to the operands.

To illustrate the actions of move instructions, assume that $D1 = 56789ABC$, $A1 = 01020304$, and $CCR = 00010001$ are the initial conditions before each instruction is executed. Then, each of the following instructions will have the indicated results.

MOVE	#0,CCR	No register or memory is affected, $N = 0, Z = 0, V = 0, C = 0, X = 0$
MOVE.W	A1,D1	$D1 = 56780304$, $N = 0, Z = 0, V = 0, C = 0, X = 1$
MOVEA.W	D1,A1	$A1 = FFFF9ABC$, $N = 0, Z = 0, V = 0, C = 1, X = 1$
MOVEQ	#−10,D1	$D1 = FFFFFFF6$, $N = 1, Z = 0, V = 0, C = 0, X = 1$

The MOVEM and MOVEP instructions

The MOVEM (move multiple registers) instruction transfers words or longwords between a register list and consecutive memory locations. In the case of a word transfer to the registers, each memory word is sign-extended before bing loaded into the respective register. The registers to be transferred can be specified either by listing the individual registers separated with slashes (/) or by giving the starting and ending registers. In the memory, the contents of the selected registers are always stored in such a way that D0 corresponds to the lowest address, D1 to the next, . . . , followed by A0 to A7, with A7 corresponding to the highest memory address.

The memory operand address can be specified by any control alterable addressing mode or the predecrement mode if the transfer is from registers to memory. For the other transfer direction, the effective address can be specified by

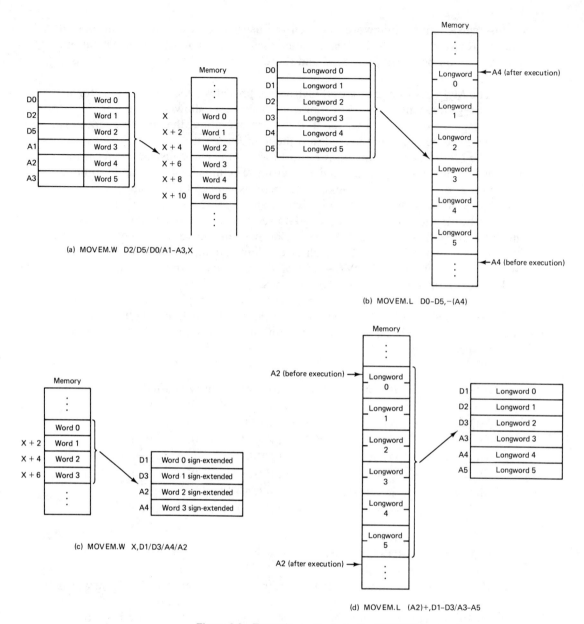

Figure 3-8 Examples to illustrate the MOVEM instruction.

any control addressing mode or the postincrement mode. Several examples are given in Fig. 3-8.

A typical application of the MOVEM instruction is to save and restore registers in a subroutine. After entering a subroutine, all registers can be saved into the system stack by

MOVEM.L   D0 – D7/A0 – A6, – (A7)

Before returning to the calling program, these registers can be restored to their original contents by

      MOVEM.L   (A7) + ,D0 − D7/A0 − A6

Note that although the instruction

      MOVEM.L   (A7),D0 − D7/A0 − A6

would also restore the saved register contents, the stack pointer A7 will not be updated to the appropriate value, which points to the original stack top.

The MOVEP (move peripheral data) instruction is designed to facilitate I/O programming. Many I/O interface ICs are 8-bit devices. In order to simplify the connection between a 16-bit data bus and an 8-bit I/O device, the device is connected either to the lower byte or to the higher byte of the data bus. When connected to the lower byte of the data bus, all internal registers of the device are accessed via consecutive odd addresses. In the other configuration, all internal registers are assigned consecutive even addresses. The MOVEP instruction can input or output data from or to two (for word operation) or four (for longword operation) consecutive I/O registers. Only the address register indirect with displacement addressing mode is allowed for specifying the I/O ports. The other operand in the instruction is always a data register. Figure 3-9 shows the results from two sample MOVEP instructions.

The EXG and SWAP instructions

The EXG (exchange) instruction interchanges the contents of two registers, whereas the SWAP instruction exchanges the lower word of the specified data register with its upper word. As implied by the instruction, the operand size for EXG is longword and for SWAP is word.

The LEA and PEA instructions

The LEA (load effective address) instruction transfers the source operand address rather than its content to the destination address register. Therefore, the instruction

      MOVEA.L   #OPER,A1

is equivalent to

      LEA   OPER,A1

The PEA instruction pushes the memory address of its source into the system stack. This instruction is typically used to pass parameter addresses to a subroutine through the stack. The source operand of both the LEA and PEA instructions must be a memory operand.

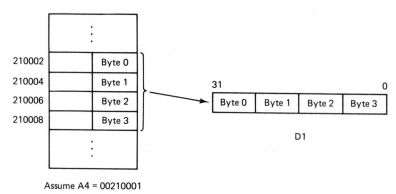

Assume A4 = 00210001

(a) MOVEP.L 2(A4),D1

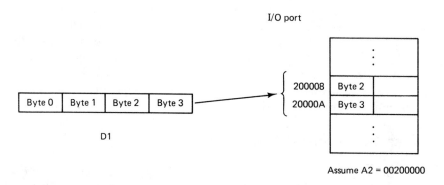

Assume A2 = 00200000

(b) MOVEP.W D1,8(A2)

Figure 3-9 Two examples of the MOVEP instruction.

In order to illustrate some of the instructions described, suppose that we wish to write a simple instruction sequence that will move four longwords from array ABC to the beginning of array XYZ. A straightforward implementation is as follows:

```
MOVE.L      ABC,XYZ
MOVE.L      ABC+4,XYZ+4
MOVE.L      ABC+8,XYZ+8
MOVE.L      ABC+12,XYZ+12
```

The same operation can be accomplished by two instructions

```
MOVEM       ABC,D0-D3
MOVEM       D0-D3,XYZ
```

Yet another approach is illustrated by the following instruction sequence:

```
MOVEA.L        #ABC,A1
MOVEA.L        #XYZ,A2
MOVE.L         (A1)+,(A2)+
MOVE.L         (A1)+,(A2)+
MOVE.L         (A1)+,(A2)+
MOVE.L         (A1)+,(A2)+
```

In this approach, using the postincrement addressing mode the same MOVE.L instruction is repeated to move the next element. Therefore, this instruction sequence can be easily modified as an iterative loop to transfer a large number of elements between the two arrays.

3-5 Compare Group

A compare instruction subtracts the left operand (source) from the right operand (destination). The operands may be bytes, words, or longwords. The result is not saved but is used to update all condition flags except the X flag. The five compare instructions are summarized in Fig. 3-10. The CMP (compare) instruction requires the destination operand to be a data register. Therefore, it would be incorrect to compare a memory operand VAR and a data register D1 with the instruction

```
CMP D1,VAR
```

The correct instruction in this case is

```
CMP VAR,D1
```

The CMPA (compare address) instruction is used when the destination operand is an address register and consequently the operation size is limited to either word or longword. The CMPI (compare immediate) instruction is for comparing an immediate operand with a destination operand, which can be specified by any data alterable addressing mode. Most assemblers can distinguish between these three

Mnemonic	Size or Postfix	Operand Format	Allowable EA Modes	Operation	Condition Flags N Z V C X
CMP (Compare)	.B[1], .W, .L	EA,Dn	All	Dn - (EA)	* * * * -
CMPA (Compare address)	.W, .L	EA,An	All	An - (EA)	* * * * -
CMPI (Compare immediate)	.B, .W, .L	#I,EA	Data alterable	(EA) - I	* * * * -
CMPM (Compare memory)	.B, .W, .L	(Ax)+,(Ay)+		ROPR - LOPR	* * * * -
TST (Test)	.B, .W, .L	EA	Data alterable	(EA) - 0	* * 0 0 -

Note: 1. Byte operation is not allowed if the source operand is an address register.

Figure 3-10   Comparison instructions.

instructions by the operands, thus allowing CMP to be used for CMPA and CMPI as well. A memory operand may be compared with another memory operand using a CMPM (compare memory) instruction, but both operands must use the postincrement addressing mode. The TST (test) instruction, having only one operand, is a special form of comparison instructions, which compares the operand with 0.

The flag setting resulting from a compare instruction can be tested by a subsequent conditional branch instruction for various relations between the compared operands. The four basic relations are equal, not equal, smaller than, and larger than, some of which may be combined for additional relations. Whether or not two operands are equal is indicated simply by the Z flag: 1 for equal and 0 for not equal.

However, to determine which operand is smaller (or larger) depends on whether the operands are interpreted as signed or unsigned numbers. For example, suppose that registers D1 and D2 have 0000001A and 0000FFF0, respectively. Then, D2.W (-16) is smaller than D1.W (26) as 16-bit signed numbers. But, when interpreted as unsigned numbers, D2.W (65520) is larger than D1.W (26). The terms *greater* and *less* are commonly used for comparing signed numbers, and *higher* and *lower* are used for comparing unsigned numbers. Therefore, the relation between the two operands above can be described as D2.W is less than D1.W, or D2.W is higher than D1.W.

Let us consider the flag settings to be tested for some relations. For example, D2.W is less than D1.W if and only if one of the two conditions is true:

1. D2.W $-$ D1.W is negative (N = 1) and no overflow occurs (V = 0).
2. D2.W $-$ D1.W is positive (N = 0) and an overflow occurs (V = 1). (This may occur when D2.W has a negative number and D1.W has a large positive number.)

Translated into a Boolean expression, the condition for "less than" becomes

$$N \oplus V = 1$$

As another example, D2.W is higher than D1.W if and only if D2.W $-$ D1.W is nonzero and no borrow occurs in the subtraction. This condition can be simply stated as

$$C + Z = 0$$

Suppose that D1 = 0000001A and D2 = 0000FFF0. Then, the instruction

```
CMP.W       D1,D2
```

will set the flags, based on the operation FFF0 $-$ 001A, as follows:

$$Z = 0, \qquad N = 1, \qquad V = 0, \qquad C = 0$$

As can be predicted, $N \oplus V = 1$ and $C + Z = 0$.

3-6 Control Transfer Group

The sequence in which the instructions of a program are executed is controlled by the program counter. As each instruction is executed, the length of the instruction is added to the PC, so that it points to the next instruction in sequence. A control transfer instruction alters this sequential execution by loading a target address into the PC. Only the relative addressing mode may be used in a branch instruction (unconditional, conditional, or iterative) to specify the destination. This limits the branch distance to $\pm 32K$ bytes. Unlike a branch, a jump instruction may use any control addressing modes. We will describe the branch instructions first; they are summarized in Fig. 3-11. The set byte conditionally instructions are also included in the figure because the same conditions that can be tested in the branch conditionally instructions apply to those instructions as well.

Mnemonic	Size or Postfix	Operand Format	Allowable EA Modes	Operation	Condition Flags N Z V C X
BRA (Branch)	.S or none	DST		DST -> PC	- - - - -
Bcc (Branch conditionally)	.S or none	DST		If cc then DST -> PC	- - - - -

DBcc (Decrement and branch conditionally)	Unsized	Dn,DST		If $\overline{cc}$ then
				Dn.W - 1 -> Dn.W
				If Dn.W $\neq$ -1 then
				DST -> PC
					- - - - -

Scc (Set conditionally)	Byte	EA	Data alterable	If cc then FF -> EA else 00 -> EA	- - - - -

Where cc designates the condition to be tested as given below.

Syntax	Test Condition	Flag Setting for Causing a Branch in Bcc or a Termination in DBcc, or FF to Be Moved to EA in Scc
BEQ, DBEQ, SEQ	Equal	Z = 1
BNE, DBNE, SNE	Not equal	Z = 0
BGT, DBGT, SGT	Greater	Z + (N $\oplus$ V) = 0
BLT, DBLT, SLT	Less	N $\oplus$ V = 1
BGE, DBGE, SGE	Greater or equal	N $\oplus$ V = 0
BLE, DBLE, SLE	Less or equal	Z + (N $\oplus$ V) = 1
BVS, DBVS, SVS	Overflow	V = 1
BVC, DBVC, SVC	No overflow	V = 0
BPL, DBPL, SPL	Plus	N = 0
BMI, DBMI, SMI	Minus	N = 1
BHI, DBHI, SHI	Higher	C + Z = 0
BLS, DBLS, SLS	Lower or same	C + Z = 1
BCS, DBCS, SCS	Carry set (Lower)	C = 1
BCC, DBCC, SCC	Carry clear (Higher or same)	C = 0
DBF, SF	False (Never)	None
DBT, ST	True (Always)	None

Figure 3-11 Branch and conditional set instructions.

The Bcc and BRA instructions

A Bcc (branch conditionally) instruction has the form

    Bcc   DST

where cc represents the condition to be tested. If the test condition is true, control is transferred to the destination indicated by DST. Otherwise, the next instruction following the conditional branch is executed. When the optional postfix .S is present, the instruction is to be assembled as a one-word instruction which requires the branch distance to be within the range of -128 to 127 bytes. As shown in Fig. 3-11, there are 14 different conditions that can be tested. The first two conditions, EQ and NE, can be used for both signed and unsigned arithmetics. The next eight conditions, GT, LT, GE, LE, VS, VC, PL, and MI, are intended for signed arithmetic. The last four conditions, HI, LS, CS, and CC, are for unsigned arithmetic. The BRA (branch) instruction is an unconditional branch instruction that always causes a branch.

To illustrate how to use conditional and unconditional branch instructions, consider the flowchart given in Fig. 3-12. Suppose that the variables A and B store 16-bit signed integers. Then, the required control flow shown in the figure can be implemented as follows:

```
              MOVE.W      AA,D0
              CMP.W       BB,D0
              BGT.S       CHECKB
              TST.W       D0
              BGE.S       INCA
              BRA.S       ZEROA
INCA          ADDQ.W      #1,AA
              BRA.S       NEXT
CHECKB        CMPI.W      #-5,BB
              BLE.S       ZEROA
              SUBQ.W      #1,AA
              BRA.S       NEXT
ZEROA         CLR.W       AA
NEXT            .
                .
                .
```

As explained before, the postfix .S is typically used in a forward branch when the branch distance is less than 128 bytes.

The DBcc instructions

A DBcc (decrement and branch conditionally) instruction performs the operation of decrement and branch until the specified termination condition is true. The

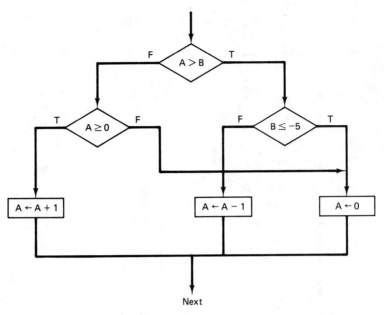

Figure 3-12 Example of logic flow.

general form of a decrement and branch conditionally instruction is

    DBcc   Dn,DST

The instruction first tests the condition specified by cc for loop termination. If the specified condition is met, no branch has taken place and execution continues with the next instruction in sequence. If the condition is *not* met, the lower word of the counter indicated by Dn is decremented by 1. If the resulting count is not equal to −1, a branch is made to the instruction whose label is indicated by DST. Otherwise, execution continues with the next instruction. It should be noted that the decrement operation in a DBcc instruction does not affect any condition flags.

As an example to illustrate the operation of DBcc instructions, consider the following instruction sequence:

    NEXT   .

               .

               .
           CMP.L   LIMIT,D3
           DBGE   D2,NEXT

Suppose that initially D2 has $00010001. Then, during the first iteration of this sequence, it would branch to NEXT and decrement D2 to $00010000 if D3 is less than memory operand LIMIT. Otherwise, the instruction following DBGE would be executed. Should this instruction sequence be repeated again, a branch would not take place because the content of D2 would become $0001FFFF, e.g., −1 in D2.W.

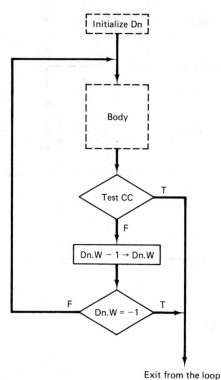

Figure 3-13 Logic flow of the DBcc instructions.

Exit from the loop

As can be seen from Fig. 3-13, this DBcc instruction group is designed to simplify the implementation of looping. It should be emphasized that only the lower word of the counter register Dn is used in a DBcc instruction, and this counter should be initialized with the value of one less than the maximum number of iterations desired.

All 14 test conditions for the Bcc instructions can be used as termination conditions for the DBcc instructions. In addition, the termination condition can be specified as always false (DBF) or always true (DBT). For the DBF instruction, looping is terminated only when Dn.W $= -1$. On the other hand, the DBT instruction will not branch regardless of the content of Dn.

The program in Fig. 3-14 illustrates how to implement a loop for a given number of iterations. The example moves the character string in array STG into

```
            ORG      $2000
STG         DC.B     'A CHARACTER STRING TO BE REVERSED'
RVDSTG      DS.B     31
SIZE        DC.W     31                    ;NO OF CHARACTERS IN STG
START       MOVEA.W  #RVDSTG,A1            ;A1 POINTS TO ONE BYTE AFTER THE
*                                          ;LAST CHARACTER IN STG
            MOVEA.W  A1,A2                 ;A2 POINTS TO THE FIRST BYTE OF RVDSTG
            MOVE.W   SIZE,D7              ;USE D7 AS LOOP COUNTER
            SUBQ.W   #1,D7                ;D7 = SIZE - 1
LOOP        MOVE.B   -(A1),(A2)+
ENDLP       DBF      D7,LOOP
            STOP     #$2000
            END      START
```

Figure 3-14 A program to store a character string in the reversed order.

```
                ORG       $2000
ARRAY           DC.W      5,-1,100,10,35,-7,11,53,-2,75
SIZE            DC.W      10
MIN             DS.W      1
MAX             DS.W      1
START           MOVEA.W   #ARRAY+2,A1
                MOVE.W    SIZE,D7           ;USE D7 AS LOOP COUNTER
                SUBQ.W    #2,D7
                MOVE.W    ARRAY,D0          ;USE D0 FOR MIN, D0 = ARRAY(1)
                MOVE.W    D0,D1             ;USE D1 FOR MAX, D1 = ARRAY(1)
LOOP            CMP.W     (A1),D0           ;D0 <= ARRAY(I+1)?
                BLE.S     NEXT
                MOVE.W    (A1),D0           ;IF D0 IS NOT SMALLER, D0 = ARRAY(I+1)
                BRA.S     AGAIN
NEXT            CMP.W     (A1),D1           ;D1 >= ARRAY(I+1)?
                BGE.S     AGAIN
                MOVE.W    (A1),D1           ;IF D1 IS NOT LARGER, D1 = ARRAY(I+1)
AGAIN           ADDA.W    #2,A1             ;A1 = A1 + 2, i.e., I = I + 1
ENDLP           DBF       D7,LOOP
                MOVE.W    D0,MIN
                MOVE.W    D1,MAX
                STOP      #$2000
                END       START
```

Figure 3-15   A program to find the maximum and the minimum values in an array.

array RVDSTG in the revised order. Since the program's addressing range does not exceed 00FFFF, 16 bits are sufficient to specify any address. Otherwise, the two MOVEA.W instructions to initialize registers A1 and A2 should be replaced with two MOVEA.L instructions. The loop counter D7 used in the DBF instruction is initialized with the string size, which is 31, minus 1. During the first 30 times when DBF instruction is executed, it branches back to LOOP because the content of D7.W is greater than −1. During the 31st time when the DBF is executed, D7.W is decremented to −1, causing the looping to be terminated. A STOP instruction is used to terminate the program execution, which causes the MC68000 to stop if in the supervisor mode. In the user mode, this instruction causes a trap and passes the control to the monitor.

Another example that combines Bcc and DBcc instructions is given in Fig. 3-15. The program searches through a given integer array and finds the minimum and the maximum values. This example assumes that the numbers to be searched are 16-bit signed integers stored beginning at address ARRAY and that SIZE has the number of elements in the integer array.

The Scc instructions

An Scc (set conditionally) instruction tests the condition specified by the cc field, as does a Bcc or DBcc instruction. Unlike the Bcc and DBcc, the test result in an Scc instruction does not cause a branch. Instead, it is used to set the destination operand either to FF (if the condition is met) or to 00 (if the condition is not met). The destinations operand, which is a byte, can be specified by any data alterable addressing mode. The same 16 conditions testable in the DBcc instructions, including the F (false) and T (true), can apply to the Scc instructions. Note that the SF instruction will set the destination to 00, whereas the ST will set the destination to FF.

The Scc instructions are handy when an indicator byte needs to be set or cleared depending on a test result. For example, the Pascal statement

```
IF    X >= Y    THEN    FLAG := TRUE
                ELSE    FLAG := FALSE;
```

Mnemonic	Size or Postfix	Operand Format	Allowable EA Modes	Operation	Condition Flags N Z V C X
JMP (Jump)	Unsized	EA	Control	EA -> PC	- - - - -
NOP (No operation)	Unsized	None		No operation	- - - - -
STOP (Stop)	Unsized	#I		I -> SR; Stop	* * * * *

Note: STOP is a privileged instruction.

Figure 3-16 Jump, no operation, and stop instructions.

can be implemented as

```
MOVE.W    XX,D1
CMP.W     YY,D1
SGE       FLAG
```

Without using an Scc instruction, an implementation would require five instructions.

Another application of the Scc instructions is to save certain tested conditions for later use in the program. Let us consider the example of evaluating the following logic expression:

$$(A > B) \quad OR \quad (B < C) \quad AND \quad (C > D)$$

This requires three comparisons, A and B, B and C, and C and D. By using Scc instructions, the result of each comparision can be saved on a 1-byte Boolean variable so that these test results can then be combined with logic instructions.

The JMP, NOP, and STOP instructions

Figure 3-16 summarizes three additional control transfer instructions. The NOP (no operation) instruction has no effect on program execution. Like the CONTINUE statement in FORTRAN, this instruction provides a location to be branched to from other places in the program.

The STOP instruction is a privileged instruction whose operand must be immediate. In the supervisor mode, this instruction loads the immediate word into the status register and then stops.

The JMP (jump) instruction causes an unconditional transfer to the target location. Unlike a BRA instruction, the JMP can address a target anywhere in memory. Furthermore, this instruction may use any control addressing mode to specify the target address.

As an example to illustrate the flexibility in determining the target address in a JMP instruction, suppose that a jump table is defined as follows:

```
          ORG    $2000
TABLE     DC.L   LABEL1
          DC.L   LABEL2
          DC.L   LABEL3
```

Then, the instructions

```
MOVEA.L     TABLE(A1),A0
JMP         (A0)
```

can jump to three different locations, depending on the content in A1: LABEL1 when A1 = 0, LABEL2 when A1 = 4, and LABEL3 when A1 = 8.

Control constructs

Quite often, the logic flow of a program is too complex for the program to be directly coded in assembly language. Two tools have commonly been used as programming aids. One is flowchart and the other is pseudocode. A pseudocode is a mixture of English and Pascal-like control constructs used to describe the logic flow of a program.

The logic flow of a typical program can be broken down as combinations of the following six basic control constructs in addition to simple sequencing:

1. IF *condition*
      THEN *action 1*;
2. IF *condition*
      THEN *action 1*
      ELSE *action 2*;
3. FOR *counter* = *initial* TO *final value*
      DO *action 1*;
4. REPEAT *action 1*
      UNTIL *condition*;
5. WHILE *condition*
      DO *action 1*;
6. CASE *selector* OF
      action 1,
      action 2,

         .

         .

         .

      action N;

For each of these control constructs, a flowchart illustrating its control sequence and an example of assembly language implementation are given in Fig. 3-17. In these examples, memory operands are assumed to be defined as words. Even though a REPEAT and a WHILE construct could be implemented using the Bcc instructions, in many cases it is desirable to include a limit on the number of iterations as a possible exit condition in order to eliminate endless looping. For such cases, the DBcc instructions are preferable over the Bcc instructions.

To implement a rather complex task, usually a flowchart or pseudocode composed of the basic control constructs is used to formulate the flow of control first. Then the flowchart or pseudocode can be translated into assembly language in a straightforward manner. The following example illustrates this idea.

Suppose that we wish to write a program to sort an array of N elements into descending order using bubble sort. Starting at the beginning of the array, this sorting scheme compares two adjacent elements each time and exchanges them if necessary. Therefore, after a complete pass through the array, the smallest element reaches the bottom of the list. This operation is repeated for the remaining $N - 1$ elements during the second pass, $N - 2$ elements the third pass, and so on.

As can be seen, the entire sorting process requires a total of $N - 1$ passes. In order to reduce the execution time, a flag can be used to detect early termination. This flag indicates whether or not at least one element exchange has occurred in a given pass. If the indication is that no exchange has occurred in the pass, the array is already in descending order and, therefore, there is no need to go through the remaining passes.

The flow of control required to implement a bubble sort with a detection for early termination can be described by the flowchart in Fig. 3-18, and by the following pseudocode:

```
FOR Count1 = N − 1 TO 1
  DO 0 → Flag;
    0 → I;
    FOR I = 0 to Count1
      DO IF A(I) < A(I + 1)
          THEN A(I) ↔ A(I + 1);
          1 → Flag
          ENDIF;
        I + 1 → I
    ENDLOOP;
    IF Flag = 0
      THEN terminate the loop;
    Count1 − 1 → Count1
ENDLOOP;
```

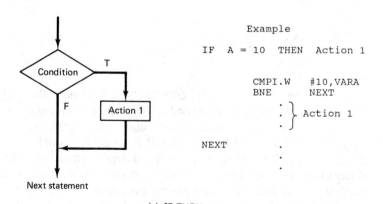

(a) IF-THEN

Figure 3-17 Implementation of basic control constructs.

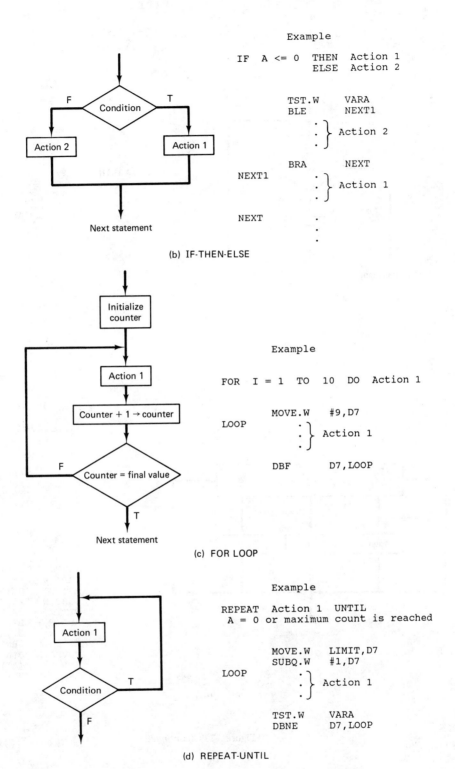

Example

```
IF  A <= 0  THEN  Action 1
            ELSE  Action 2
```

```
        TST.W    VARA
        BLE      NEXT1
         .    ⎫
         .    ⎬ Action 2
         .    ⎭
        BRA      NEXT
NEXT1    .    ⎫
         .    ⎬ Action 1
         .    ⎭
NEXT     .
         .
         .
```

(b) IF-THEN-ELSE

Example

```
FOR  I = 1  TO  10  DO  Action 1
```

```
        MOVE.W   #9,D7
LOOP     .    ⎫
         .    ⎬ Action 1
         .    ⎭
        DBF      D7,LOOP
```

(c) FOR LOOP

Example

```
REPEAT  Action 1  UNTIL
A = 0 or maximum count is reached
```

```
        MOVE.W   LIMIT,D7
        SUBQ.W   #1,D7
LOOP     .    ⎫
         .    ⎬ Action 1
         .    ⎭
        TST.W    VARA
        DBNE     D7,LOOP
```

(d) REPEAT-UNTIL

Figure 3-17 (*continued*)

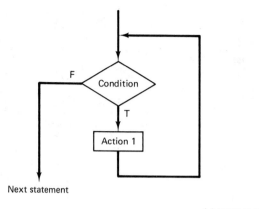

(e) WHILE-DO

```
                    Example

WHILE   A <= 10 and maximum count
    is not reached   DO   Action 1


              MOVE.W    LIMIT,D7
AGAIN         CMPI.W    #10,VARA
              DBGT      D7,LOOP
              BRA       NEXT
LOOP          .      ⎫
              .      ⎬   Action 1
              .      ⎭

              BRA       AGAIN
NEXT          .
              .
              .
```

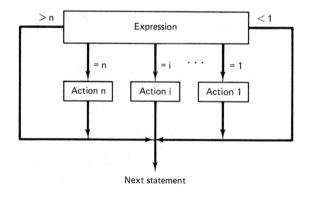

Next statement

(f) CASE

```
                    Example

CASE    I   OF
            Action 1,
            Action 2,
            Action 3,
            Action 4,
            Action 5;


BRTBL    DC.L      LABEL1    ;Action 1
         DC.L      LABEL2    ;Action 2
         DC.L      LABEL3    ;Action 3
         DC.L      LABEL4    ;Action 4
         DC.L      LABEL5    ;Action 5
            .
            .
            .

         MOVE.W    VARI,D7
         CMPI.W    #5,D7
         BGT.S     SKIP
         SUBQ.W    #1,D7
         BLT.S     SKIP
         ADD.W     D7,D7
         ADD.W     D7,D7
         MOVEA.L   #BRTBL,A0
         MOVEA.L   0(A0,D7.W),A1
         JMP       (A1)
SKIP     BRA       NEXT
```

Figure 3-17 (*continued*)

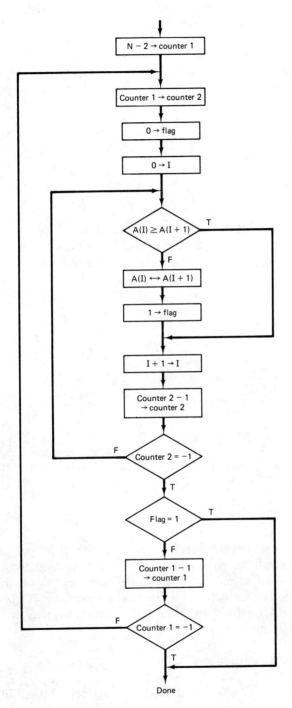

Figure 3-18 Flowchart for a bubble sort of N elements with early termination.

After translating the flowchart or pseudocode into assembly language, the resulting program is as shown in Fig. 3-19. In the program, we assume that the numbers to be sorted are 16-bit integers stored beginning at ARRAY and variable NN has the number of words in this array.

It is worth mentioning that the size of the array ARRAY can be calculated automatically by the assembler at assembly time. Suppose that in the program, the statement

         NN   DC.W   10

is replaced by

         NN   DC.W   (* – ARRAY)/2

Then the assembler can calculate the actual number of data words defined in ARRAY and use that size as the initial value for N. This allows the programmer to add or delete items from ARRAY without having to remember to change the data size in N.

```
               ORG      $2000
ARRAY          DC.W     5,-1,100,10,35,-7,11,53,-2,75
NN             DC.W     10
START          MOVE.W   NN,D7             ;USE D7 AS COUNTER1
               SUBQ.W   #2,D7
LOOP1          MOVE.W   D7,D6             ;USE D6 AS COUNTER2
               CLR.B    D5                ;USE D5 AS FLAG
               MOVEA.W  #ARRAY,A0         ;USE A0 AS POINTER AND I = 1
LOOP2          MOVE.W   (A0)+,D0          ;D0 = A(I)
               CMP.W    (A0),D0           ;A(I) >= A(I+1)?
               BGE.S    ENDLP2            ;YES, CHECK NEXT ELEMENT
               MOVE.W   (A0),-2(A0)       ;NO, A(I) <-> A(I+1)
               MOVE.W   D0,(A0)
               MOVE.B   #1,D5             ;FLAG = 1
ENDLP2         DBF      D6,LOOP2
               TST.B    D5
ENDLP1         DBEQ     D7,LOOP1
DONE           STOP     #$2000
               END      START
```

Figure 3-19 Implementation of a bubble sort.

3-7 Binary Arithmetic Group

The MC68000 instruction set provides binary arithmetic instructions for performing signed and unsigned additions, subtractions, multiplications, and divisions. In addition and subtraction instructions, operands may be bytes, words, or long-words. For a multiplication or division instruction, the operand size is word. Also included in this group are two instructions designed to simplify the implementation of multiple-precision additions and subtractions.

Addition and subtraction instructions

Figure 3-20 summarizes the MC68000 instructions for performing binary additions and subtractions. Each instruction in this group has two operands. An addition instruction adds the left operand into the right operand and stores the sum in the right operand. A subtraction instruction subtracts the left operand from the right

Mnemonic	Size or Postfix	Operand Format	Allowable EA Modes	Operation	Condition Flags N Z V C X
ADD (Add binary)	.B[1], .W, .L	EA,Dn Dn,EA	All Memory alterable	(EA) + Dn -> Dn Dn + (EA) -> EA	* * * * *
ADDA (Add address)	.W, .L	EA,An	All	(EA) + An -> An	- - - - -
ADDI (Add immediate)	.B, .W, .L	#I,EA	Data alterable	I + (EA) -> EA	* * * * *
ADDQ (Add quick)	.B, .W, .L	#I3,EA[2]	Alterable	I3 + (EA) -> EA	* * * * *
ADDX (Add with X flag)	.B, .W, .L	Dx,Dy -(Ax),-(Ay)		Dx + Dy + X -> Dy (SRC) + (DST) + X -> DST	* * * * *
SUB (Subtract binary)	.B, .W, .L	EA,Dn Dn,EA	All Memory alterable	Dn - (EA) -> Dn (EA) - Dn -> EA	* * * * *
SUBA (Subtract address)	.W, .L	EA,An	All	An - (EA) -> An	- - - - -
SUBI (Subtract immediate)	.B, .W, .L	#I,EA	Data alterable	(EA) - I -> EA	* * * * *
SUBQ (Subtract quick)	.B, .W, .L	#I3,EA[2]	Alterable	(EA) - I3 -> EA	* * * * *
SUBX (Subtract with X flag)	.B, .W, .L	Dx,Dy -(Ax),-(Ay)		Dy - Dx - X -> Dy (DST) - (SRC) - X -> DST	* * * * *

Notes: 1. Byte operation is not allowed if the source operand is an address register.
2. If An is specified, the size indicator must be .W or .L, and the condition flags will not be affected.

Figure 3-20 Binary addition and subtraction instructions.

operand and stores the difference in the right operand. The same instructions are applicable to both signed and unsigned operands.

The ADD (add binary) and SUB (subtract binary) instructions require at least one operand to be a data register. The ADDA (add address) and SUBA (subtract address) instructions are for adding and subtracting an address. Therefore their destination operands must be address registers and the operand size must be either word or longword. The ADD and SUB instructions can operate on immediate operands and store results to data registers, whereas the ADDI (add immediate) and SUBI (subtract immediate) instructions can add and subtract an immediate value to/from a memory operand as well as to/from a data register. Most assemblers can distinguish between these three pairs of instructions by the operands, allowing ADD to be used for ADDA and ADDI and SUB to be used for SUBA and SUBI.

ADDQ (add quick) and SUBQ (subtract quick) are short forms of the ADDI and SUBI instructions, respectively. The immediate operand in an ADDQ or SUBQ instruction is limited to the range of 1 to 8. The ADDX (add extended) and SUBX (subtract extended) instructions are for implementing multiple-precision additions and subtractions.

All condition flags, including the X flag, are affected by the addition and subtraction instructions. The only exception is when an address register is used as the destination. In this case, none of them is affected.

As an example involving addition and subtraction instructions, suppose that a 16-bit integer matrix [A] of M rows and N columns is stored in memory by

```
            ORG     $2000
MATA        DC.W    -3,0,5,2,11,-3,-1,9,0,-5,4,11,1,1,0,2,-3,4,-5,5,2,3,6,1
II          DC.W    3                   ;ROW SUBSCRIPT I
JJ          DC.W    2                   ;ROW SUBSCRIPT J
KK          DC.W    4                   ;ROW SUBSCRIPT K
MM          DC.W    4                   ;NO. OF ROWS
NN          DC.W    6                   ;NO. OF COLUMNS
START       MOVEA.W #MATA,A0            ;A0 = ADDRESS OF A(1,L) WITH L = 1
            MOVE.W  II,D0
            SUBQ.W  #1,D0
            ADD.W   D0,D0               ;D0 = INDEX FOR I, (II - 1)*2
            MOVE.W  JJ,D1
            SUBQ.W  #1,D1
            ADD.W   D1,D1               ;D1 = INDEX FOR J, (JJ - 1)*2
            MOVE.W  KK,D2
            SUBQ.W  #1,D2
            ADD.W   D2,D2               ;D2 = INDEX FOR K, (KK - 1)*2
            MOVE.W  NN,D7               ;D7 = NO. OF COLUMNS
            SUBQ.W  #1,D7               ;USE D7 AS COUNTER
LOOP        MOVE.W  0(A0,D2.W),D6
            ADD.W   0(A0,D0.W),D6
            SUB.W   0(A0,D1.W),D6       ;D6 = A(K,L) + A(I,L) - A(J,L)
            MOVE.W  D6,0(A0,D2.W)       ;A(K,L) = D6
            ADDA.W  MM,A0
            ADDA.W  MM,A0               ;A0 = ADDRESS OF A(1,L+1), A0 + 2*MM
ENDLP       DBF     D7,LOOP
            STOP    #$2000
            END     START
```

Figure 3-21 A program to add the *i*th row and subtract the *j*th row from the *k*th row of an $M \times N$ matrix.

columns. Let $A_{i,j}$ represent the element in the *i*th row and *j*th column. Then, the elements are stored in the sequence

$$A_{1,1}, A_{2,1}, A_{3,1}, \ldots, A_{M,1}, A_{1,2}, A_{2,2}, \ldots, A_{M,2}, \ldots, A_{M,N}$$

The program in Fig. 3-21 adds the *i*th row into and subtracts the *j*th row from the *k*th row; i.e.,

$$A_{k,l} = A_{k,l} + A_{i,l} - A_{j,l} \quad \text{for} \quad l = 1, 2, \ldots, N$$

As can be seen, the address register indirect with index addressing mode is ideal for accessing elements in a matrix. The address of element $A_{i,j}$ can be formed as the sum of beginning address of matrix [A], offset of the *j*th column, and offset of the *i*th element within the column. Therefore an element $A_{i,j}$ could be specified as MATA(A0,D0.W) where MATA is the matrix address, A0 has the column offset, and D0.W contains the row offset. However, since the displacement size in the index addressing mode is limited to 8 bits, this form cannot be applied in our example. An alternative is to address $A_{i,j}$ as 0(A0,D0.W) with A0 having the beginning address of the *j*th column.

In this example, register A0 serves as a base register pointing to the beginning of a column. Three data registers are used for storing the indices associated with subscripts *i*, *j*, and *k*. After each iteration of the loop, the column length is added to register A0 so that it points to the next column, whereas the three index registers remain unchanged.

Multiple-precision addition and subtraction

The ADD and SUB instruction can handle at most one longword at a time. For applications in which each operand requires more than 32 bits to store, double-precision addition or subtraction can be performed by using two additions or subtractions. Consider the following two 64-bit additions:

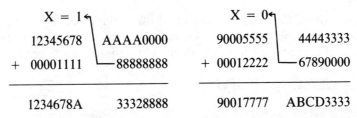

$$\begin{array}{cc} X = 1 & X = 0 \\ \begin{array}{ll} 12345678 & \text{AAAA0000} \\ +\ \ 00001111 & \text{88888888} \end{array} & \begin{array}{ll} 90005555 & \text{44443333} \\ +\ \ 00012222 & \text{67890000} \end{array} \\ \hline \begin{array}{ll} 1234678\text{A} & \text{33328888} \end{array} & \begin{array}{ll} 90017777 & \text{ABCD3333} \end{array} \end{array}$$

In both cases the correct answer is obtained by adding the lower 32 bits (using ADD) and then adding the upper 32 bits with the X flag (using ADDX). Note that the same procedure is valid for both signed and unsigned operands.

Similarly, a 64-bit subtraction can be implemented by subtracting the lower 32 bits (using SUB) and then subtracting the upper 32 bits and the X flag (using SUBX). In this case, the X flag indicates the borrow caused by the subtraction of the lower 32 bits. This procedure can be verified by the following examples:

$$\begin{array}{cc} \begin{array}{ll} 12345678 & \text{AAAA0000} \\ -\ \ 00001111 & \text{88888888} \\ X = 0 \end{array} & \begin{array}{ll} 90005555 & \text{44443333} \\ -\ \ 00012222 & \text{67890000} \\ X = 1 \end{array} \\ \hline \begin{array}{ll} 12344567 & \text{22217778} \end{array} & \begin{array}{ll} 8\text{FFF}3332 & \text{DCBB3333} \end{array} \end{array}$$

To illustrate how to program 64-bit additions and subtractions, suppose that we wish to compute

$$X = Y + Z - \$12FF$$

where X, Y, and Z are defined as 64-bit variables. Based on the Motorola convention, the upper 32 bits of each variable are stored first, followed by the lower 32 bits. An instruction sequence to accomplish this computation is as follows:

```
MOVE.L      YY,D1
MOVE.L      YY+4,D0
ADD.L       ZZ+4,D0
MOVE.L      ZZ,D2
ADDX.L      D2,D1
SUBI.L      #$12FF,D0
CLR.L       D2
SUBX.L      D2,D1
MOVE.L      D1,XX
MOVE.L      D0,XX+4
```

Two points should be made for this example. First, even though the instructions

```
MOVE.L      XX,D2
```

and

```
CLR.L       D2
```

clear the C flag, they do not affect the X flag, which stores the carry or borrow of the previous operation. Second, the immediate operand has only 32 bits, but it is still necessary to use a 64-bit subtraction. This is because the instruction

```
SUBI.L      #$12FF,D0
```

will cause a borrow if the content of D0 is lower than 12FF.

As shown in Fig. 3-20, the ADDX and SUBX instructions have two operand formats. One is data register to data register, as illustrated in the preceding example. The other operand format is from memory to memory, with each operand specified by the predecrement addressing mode. This form is particularly useful in implementing multiple-precision operations, in which case each operand consists of more than two segments.

To illustrate the memory-to-memory additions, let us simulate a 64-bit addition by using multiple-byte additions. The following instruction sequence adds Y into X with each having 64 bits:

```
        MOVEA.W     #YY + 8,A0
        MOVEA.W     #XX + 8,A1
        MOVEQ       #7,D7
        ADDI.W      #0,D7
LOOP    ADDX.B      - (A0), - (A1)
        DBF         D7,LOOP
```

In the example, unlike the other 7 bytes, the addition of the least significant byte should not include the X flag. An instruction such as

```
ADDI.W      #0,D7
```

or

```
MOVE      #0,CCR
```

guarantees that the X flag is zero when the ADDX.B instruction is executed during the first iteration.

Miscellaneous arithmetic instructions

Some miscellaneous instructions are frequently used in binary arithmetic operations. These instructions are summarized in Fig. 3-22. The EXT (sign extend) instruction converts a byte or word register operand to a word or longword by extending the sign bit of the operand. The NEG (negate) instruction forms the 2's complement of the destination operand, effectively reversing its sign. If the operand is zero, the sign is not changed. For a byte operation, if the operand is $80 ($-128$), the operand remains unchanged but the V flag is set to 1. The same is true when $8000 or $80000000 is negated as a word or as a longword, respec-

Mnemonic	Size or Postfix	Operand Format	Allowable EA Modes	Operation	Condition Flags N Z V C X
EXT (Sign extend)	.W, .L	Dn		Dn.B sign-extended -> Dn.W or Dn.W sign-extended -> Dn.L	* * 0 0 -
NEG (Negate)	.B, .W, .L	EA	Data alterable	0 - (EA) -> EA	* * * * *
NEGX (Negate with extend)	.B, .W, .L	EA	Data alterable	0 - (EA) - X -> EA	* * * * *
CLR (Clear)	.B, .W, .L	EA	Data alterable	0 -> EA	0 1 0 0 -

Figure 3-22 Miscellaneous binary arithmetic instructions.

tively. The NEGX (negate with X flag) instruction is for negating a double-precision number. The CLR (clear) instruction clears the destination operand to zero.

To illustrate some of these instructions, suppose that we wish to compute

$$X = |X - 5| + Y$$

where X is defined as a longword and Y as a word. An instruction sequence to accomplish this is given next:

```
        SUBQ.L    #5,XX
        BGE.S     PLUS
        NEG       XX
PLUS    MOVE.W    YY,D0
        EXT.L     D0
        ADD.L     D0,XX
```

Multiplication and division instructions

The binary multiplication and division instructions are summarized in Fig. 3-23. The multiplication instructions multiply two 16-bit operands and produce a 32-bit result, which is stored in the destination data register. The MULS (signed multiply) instruction treats the operands as signed numbers to yield a signed product.

Mnemonic	Size or Postfix	Operand Format	Allowable EA Modes	Operation	Condition Flags N Z V C X
MULS (Signed multiply)	Word	EA,Dn	Data	(EA) * Dn[15:0] -> Dn Product is signed	* * 0 0 -
MULU (Unsigned multiply)	Word	EA,Dn	Data	(EA) * Dn[15:0] -> Dn Product is unsigned	* * 0 0 -
DIVS (Sign divide)	Word	EA,Dn	Data	Dn / (EA) Quotient (signed) -> Dn[15:0] Remainder (same sign as dividend) -> Dn[31:16]	*[1]* * 0 -
DIVU (Unsigned divide)	Word	EA,Dn	Data	Dn / (EA) Quotient (unsigned) -> Dn[15:0] Remainder (unsigned) -> Dn[31:16]	*[1]* * 0 -

Note: 1. N, Z, and V flags are set according to the quotient.

Figure 3-23 Multiply and divide instructions.

For the MULU (unsigned multiply) instruction, the operands are interpreted as unsigned numbers.

To distinguish the MULS and MULU instructions, suppose that before each instruction is executed, the initial conditions are as follows:

	Content in hex	As unsigned decimal	As signed decimal
Location XX	0003	3	3
Location YY	B000	45056	−20480
D0[15:0]	00A0	160	160
D1[15:0]	FF00	65280	−256

Then, each of the following instructions will have the indicated result:

MULS XX,D0 D0 = 000001E0 $(3 \times 160 = 480 \text{ decimal})$

MULU XX,D0 D0 = 000001E0 $(3 \times 160 = 480 \text{ decimal})$

MULS XX,D1 D1 = FFFFFD00 $(3 \times (-256) = -768 \text{ decimal})$

MULU XX,D1 D1 = 0002FD00 $(3 \times 65280 = 195840 \text{ decimal})$

MULS YY,D1 D1 = 00500000 $(-20480 \times (-256)$

$= 5242880 \text{ decimal})$

MULU YY,D1 D1 = AF500000 $(45056 \times 65280$

$= 2941255680 \text{ decimal})$

Both the DIVS (signed divide) and DIVU (unsigned divide) instructions divide the 32-bit dividend stored in the destination data register by the 16-bit source operand being specified. The 16-bit remainder is returned in the upper half of the destination data register, and the 16-bit quotient is returned in the lower half of the register. For the DIVS instruction, the sign of the quotient is determined by the algebra rule and the remainder has the same sign as the dividend.

There are two possible errors that may occur during a division. If the divisor is zero, a divide-by-zero error occurs, which causes a trap. The other error is division overflow, which occurs when the quotient is too large to be stored in 16 bits. This overflow error will occur if the divisor is smaller than the upper 16 bits of the dividend. A division overflow sets the V flag to 1, but the destination is unaffected. During a division, the N and Z flags are also conditionally set according to the quotient not the remainder.

To illustrate the action of the two division instructions, suppose that the following are the initial register and memory contents:

Location XX: 0012   (decimal 18)

Location YY: FFAE   (decimal −82)

Location ZZ: FF00   (unsigned decimal 65280)

Register D0:   00000308   (decimal 776)

Register D1:   FFFFFE00   (decimal −512)

Assuming that these are the initial conditions before each of the following instructions, the instructions will have the indicated results.

Instruction	Result in hex	Quotient	Remainder
DIVU XX,D0	D0 = 0002002B	decimal 43	decimal 2
DIVS XX,D1	D1 = FFF8FFE4	decimal −28	decimal −8
DIVS YY,D0	D0 = 0026FFF7	decimal −9	decimal 38
DIVS YY,D1	D1 = FFEC0006	decimal 6	decimal −20
DIVU ZZ,D0	D0 = 03080000	decimal 0	decimal 776
DIVU ZZ,D1	D1 = FFFFFE00	V flag = 1 to indicate a division overflow.	

As an example involving a combination of binary arithmetic operations, suppose that we wish to compute

$$X = 5 \times Y + Z/W$$

where Y, Z, and W are 16-bit signed integers, and to store the result into a long-word X. An instruction sequence to accomplish this is given next:

```
MOVE.W    YY,D0
MULS      #5,D0
MOVE.W    ZZ,D1
EXT.L     D1
DIVS      WW,D1
EXT.L     D1
ADD.L     D1,D0
MOVE.L    D0,XX
```

As another example of binary arithmetic instructions, the program in Fig. 3-24 performs the matrix multiplication

$$[A] = [B] \times [C]$$

where [A], [B], and [C] are $M \times L$, $M \times N$, and $N \times L$ matrices, respectively. It is assumed that each element in the matrices is a 16-bit integer. Matrix [A] is computed based on the formula

$$A_{i,j} = \sum_{k=1}^{n} B_{i,k} \times C_{k,j}$$

```
              ORG        $2000
       *      MATRIX A = MATRIX B X MATRIX C
       MATA   DS.W       20
       *      MATRIX B, SIZE IS M X N
       MATB   DC.W       3,-1,-2,0,1,5,1,2,3,0,4,6
       *      MATRIX C, SIZE IS N X L
       MATC   DC.W       1,0,1,3,-1,5,2,0,1,-3,2,-2,4,2,3
       MM     DC.W       4               ;NO. OF ROWS (M) IN MATRIX B
       NN     DC.W       3               ;NO. OF COLUMNS (N) IN MATRIX B
       LL     DC.W       5               ;NO. OF COLUMNS (L) IN MATRIX C
       START  MOVE.W     #MATA,A0        ;A0 = ADDRESS OF A(1,1), USE A0 AS
       *                                 ;POINTER TO THE CURRENT ELEMENT IN A
              MOVE.W     #MATC,D3        ;D3 = ADDRESS OF C(1,1), USE D3 AS
       *                                 ;POINTER TO THE CURRENT COLUMN IN C
              MOVE.W     LL,D7           ;USE D7 AS COUNTER FOR LOOP1
              SUBQ.W     #1,D7           ;D7 = L - 1
       *      FOR EVERY COLUMN IN C DO LOOP1
       LOOP1  MOVE.W     #MATB,D2        ;D2 = ADDRESS OF B(1,1), USE D2 AS
       *                                 ;POINTER TO THE CURRENT ROW IN B
              MOVEA.W    D3,A2           ;USE A2 AS POINTER TO THE CURRENT
       *                                 ;ELEMENT IN C, INITIALIZE A2 TO C(1,J)
              MOVE.W     MM,D6           ;USE D6 AS COUNTER FOR LOOP2
              SUBQ.W     #1,D6           ;D6 = M - 1
       *      FOR EVERY ROW IN B DO LOOP2
       LOOP2  MOVEA.W    D2,A1           ;USE A1 AS POINTER TO THE CURRENT
       *                                 ;ELEMENT IN B, INITIALIZE A1 TO B(I,1)
              CLR.L      D0              ;USE D0 TO STORE PARTIAL PRODUCT
              MOVE.W     NN,D5           ;USE D5 AS COUNTER FOR LOOP3
              SUBQ.W     #1,D5           ;D5 = N - 1
       *      LOOP3 ADDS B(I,K) * C(K,J) INTO D0  FOR EVERY ELEMENT IN B'S ROW AND
       *      C'S COLUMN (i.e., K = 1 TO N)
       LOOP3  MOVE.W     (A1),D1         ;D1 = B(I,K)
              MULS       (A2)+,D1        ;D1 = B(I,K) * C(K,J), A2 POINTS TO
       *                                 ;C(K+1,J)
              ADD.L      D1,D0
              ADDA.W     MM,A1
              ADDA.W     MM,A1           ;A1 POINTS TO B(I,K+1)
       ENDLP3 DBF        D5,LOOP3        ;END OF LOOP3
              MOVE.W     D0,(A0)+        ;STORE THE RESULT INTO A(I,J), A0
       *                                 ;POINTS TO THE NEXT ELEMENT
              ADDQ.W     #2,D2           ;D2 POINTS TO B(I+1,1)
              MOVEA.W    D3,A2           ;RESET A2 TO POINT TO C(1,J)
       ENDLP2 DBF        D6,LOOP2        ;END OF LOOP2
              ADD.W      NN,D3
              ADD.W      NN,D3           ;D3 POINTS TO C(1,J+1)
       ENDLP1 DBF        D7,LOOP1        ;END OF LOOP1
              STOP       #$2000
              END        START
```

Figure 3-24 A program to multiply an $M \times N$ matrix by an $N \times L$ matrix.

As each matrix is stored column by column, the addresses of elements $A_{i,j}$, $B_{i,k}$, and $C_{k,j}$ can be calculated as

$$\text{Address of } A_{i,j} = \text{address of } A_{1,1} + 2 \times [(j - 1) \times M + (i - 1)]$$

$$\text{Address of } B_{i,k} = \text{address of } B_{1,1} + 2 \times [(k - 1) \times M + (i - 1)]$$

$$\text{Address of } C_{k,j} = \text{address of } C_{1,1} + 2 \times [(j - 1) \times N + (k - 1)]$$

In the program, the address of $A_{1,1}$ is MATA, the address of $B_{1,1}$ is MATB, and the address of $C_{1,1}$ is MATC. Furthermore, the dimensions M, L, and N are given as 16-bit integers stored in variables MM, LL, and NN, respectively.

In order to eliminate address calculation for each $A_{i,j}$, the program calculates the elements in matrix $[A]$ column by column. In this sequence, the next element to be calculated has the address following the current one. In referencing $B_{i,k}$ or $C_{k,j}$ during the nested iterations, the next element is either in the same row or in the same column of the current element. In either case, we can use the ADDA instruction to add a constant into the corresponding address register to point to the next element. The constant to be added is two if the next element is in the current column and is two times the column size if the next element is in the current row.

Double-precision multiplication and division

An unsigned 32×32 bit multiplication can be carried out by using four 16×16 bit multiplications and then adding together the partial products. Let $a2^{16} + b$ and $c2^{16} + d$ represent the two 32-bit operands to be multiplied. The following multiply operation shows how a 32×32 multiplication can be performed using 16×16 bit multiplications.

$$
\begin{array}{r}
a2^{16} + b \\
\times \quad c2^{16} + d \\
\hline
ad2^{16} + bd \\
ac2^{32} + \quad bc2^{16} \\
\hline
ac2^{32} + (ad + bc)2^{16} + bd
\end{array}
$$

Based on this illustration, a procedure to perform an unsigned 32×32 bit multiplication is outlined as follows.

1. Use the MULU instructions to form partial products bd, bc, ad, and ac, with each having 32 bits.
2. Save the lower 16 bits of bd as the least significant 16-bit segment of the final product.
3. Add ad, bc, and the upper 16 bits of bd together.
4. Save the lower 16 bits of the sum from Step 3 as the next higher 16-bit segment of the final product.
5. Add the upper 16 bits of the sum, including the possible carry from Step 3 into ac.
6. Save the sum from Step 5 as the upper 32 bits of the final product.

A signed 32×32 bit multiplication can be accomplished by first multiplying the magnitudes of the two operands and then negating the result if the two operands have different signs. A more efficient method is to perform unsigned multiplication and then make corrections to the result if either the multiplier or multiplicand is negative. Let us consider the case that X is positive and Y is negative. In the 32-bit 2's complement form, Y is equal to $2^{32} - Y^*$, where Y^* is the magnitude. The correct answer for a signed multiplication of X and Y is

$$XY \text{ (signed multiplication)} = -XY^* = 2^{64} - XY^*$$

When X and Y are multiplied as two unsigned numbers, the product becomes

$$XY \text{ (unsigned multiplication)} = X(2^{32} - Y^*) = X2^{32} - XY^*$$

Because

$$2^{64} - XY^* = X2^{32} - XY^* + 2^{32}(2^{32} - X) = X2^{32} - XY^* - X2^{32}$$

the correct signed 64-bit product can be obtained by subtracting X from the upper 32 bits of the unsigned product of X and Y. A similar argument can be made if X is negative or both X and Y are negative. Therefore, a signed 32×32 bit multiplication can be implemented as follows. First, treat both operands as unsigned numbers and perform a double-precision multiplication. Then, the result is corrected by subtracting from its upper 32 bits the multiplier if the multiplicand is negative and the multiplicand if the multiplier is negative.

Unlike multiplication, the implementation of unsigned double-precision division cannot be accomplished by using the DIVU instruction. However, the special case of dividing 64 bits by 16 bits can be implemented by using single-precision division repeatedly. This is illustrated as follows:

$$
\begin{array}{r}
q_3 2^{48} + q_2 2^{32} + q_1 2^{16} + q_0 \\
\hline
a)\overline{b2^{48} + c2^{32} + d2^{16} + e} \\
\underline{r_3 2^{48} + c2^{32}} \\
r_2 2^{32} + d2^{16} \\
\underline{\phantom{r_2 2^{32} + d2^{16}}} \\
r_1 2^{16} + e \\
\hline
r_0
\end{array}
$$

where q_3 and r_3 are the quotient and remainder resulting from b/a, q_2 and r_2 are the quotient and remainder resulting from $(r_3 2^{16} + c)/a$, etc. As can be seen, during each division the new 32-bit dividend is formed by concatenating the remainder from the previous division and the next-lower 16-bit segment of the original dividend.

A generalized unsigned double-precision division, i.e., a division of 64 bits by 32 bits, can be accomplished by using the same algorithm employed to build the hardware of an integer divider. For simplicity, let us use an 8-bit dividend and 4-bit divisor in the example to explain a basic binary division algorithm. A step-by-step division of 00111010 (58) by 1011 (11) in the binary form is as shown.

```
            0101      (Quotient)
   1011)00111010
         0000
         1110
         1011
         0111
         0000
         1110
         1011
          011      (Remainder)
```

The example suggests that a binary division can be accomplished by repeating the sequence of subtracting the divisor or 0 from the upper part of the dividend, entering the next quotient bit, and shifting the dividend. This leads to a well-known binary division algorithm called the *restoring algorithm*, which is illustrated in Fig. 3-25.

Applying the binary division algorithm just illustrated, an unsigned 64-bit by 32-bit division can be implemented by the following procedure:

1. Load the upper 32 bits and lower 32 bits of the 64-bit dividend into registers Di and Dj and the 32-bit divisor into register Dk, and set the count to 32.
2. If Di $\geq$ Dk, a division overflow is detected and the process is terminated.
3. Shift register pair Di and Dj to the left by 1 bit.
4. Compare Di and Dk. If Di $<$ Dk, clear bit 0 of Dj. Otherwise, subtract Dk from Di, and set bit 0 of Dj to 1.
5. Decrement the count by 1. If count is not zero, go to Step 3. Otherwise, the process is terminated, register Di has the remainder, and register Dj has the quotient.

A signed double-precision division is accomplished by performing an unsigned division and then determining the sign of the quotient and remainder according to the sign rule.

Conversion between binary and decimal

When numerical data are entered to the computer system via a terminal, decimal numbers are used most of the time. In many cases, each decimal digit is sent from the terminal to the computer as an ASCII code. Similarly, results to be displayed

R	Q	Action
0 0 1 1	1 0 1 0	Load the dividend 00111010 into register pair RQ.
0 1 1 1	0 1 0 0	Shift RQ to the left by 1 bit.
- 1 0 1 1		Subtract the divisor from R.
1 1 0 0 + 1 0 1 1 0 1 1 1	0 1 0 0 0 1 0 0	Because the result in R is negative, restore the old value by adding back the divisor and clear bit 0 of Q.
1 1 1 0	1 0 0 0	Shift RQ to the left by 1 bit.
- 1 0 1 1		Subtract the divisor from R.
0 0 1 1	1 0 0 1	Because the result in R is positive, set bit 0 of Q to 1.
0 1 1 1	0 0 1 0	Shift RQ to the left by 1 bit.
- 1 0 1 1		Subtract the divisor from R.
1 1 0 0 + 1 0 1 1 0 1 1 1	0 0 1 0 0 0 1 0	Because the result in R is negative, add the divisor back to R and clear bit 0 of Q.
1 1 1 0	0 1 0 0	Shift RQ to the left by 1 bit.
- 1 0 1 1		Subtract the divisor from R.
0 0 1 1	0 1 0 1	Because the result in R is positive, set bit 0 of Q to 1.
Remainder	Quotient	

Figure 3-25 The restoring unsigned binary division algorithm.

on a terminal or to be printed through a printer are normally in the decimal form. Therefore, in order to perform arithmetic operations using the binary arithmetic instructions described in this section, the input data must first be converted from decimal to binary. Because results from computations are in binary, they need to be converted back to decimal before being sent to a terminal or printer. The whole process from input to output is outlined in Figure 3-26.

Since the hexadecimal representation of a given ASCII-coded decimal digit is $30 plus the BCD digit, the conversion between the two forms is simple. Conversion between unpacked BCD and binary is based on the relationship

$$d_n d_{n-1} \cdots d_1 d_0 = ((\cdots (d_n \times 10 + d_{n-1})10 \cdots)10 + d_1)10 + d_0$$

where $d_n, d_{n-1}, \ldots, d_0$ represent the decimal digits. A conversion from unpacked BCD to binary requires successive multiplications by 10, whereas a conversion from binary to unpacked BCD requires successive divisions by 10.

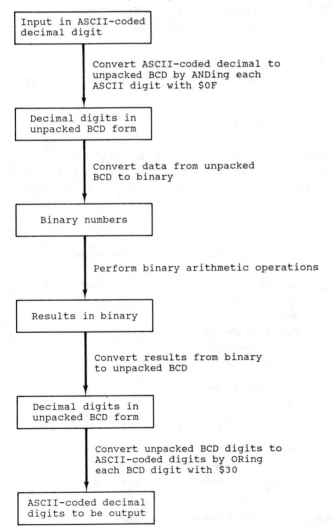

Figure 3-26 Conversion process required for performing binary operations on ASCII-coded numeric data.

```
                ORG         $2000
INPNUM          DC.B        '-16352
SIZE            DC.B        12
ERCODE          DC.B        0
BINNUM          DS.L        1
SIGN            DC.B        0
START           CLR.L       D0                      ;CLEAR D0 FOR PARTIAL SUM
                CLR.B       ERCODE                  ;CLEAR ERROR CODE
                MOVEA.W     #INPNUM,A0              ;A0 AS POINTER POINTS TO INPNUM
                CMPI.B      #'-',(A0)+              ;IF NEGATIVE
                BEQ.S       MINUS                   ;THEN SET SIGN TO 1
                CMPI.B      #'+',-1(A0)             ;IF POSITIVE
                BEQ.S       PLUS                    ;THEN SET SIGN TO 0
                SUBA.W      #1,A0                   ;UNSIGNED, DECREMENT POINTER BY 1
PLUS            MOVE.B      #0,SIGN
                BRA.S       CONVER
MINUS           MOVE.B      #1,SIGN
*
*STARTING FROM THE MOST SIGNIFICANT DIGIT CONVERT AN ASCII DIGIT TO BCD.
*IF IT IS A BLANK, EXIT FROM THE LOOP. IF IT IS AN INVALID DIGIT, SET
*ERROR CODE TO 2.
*
CONVER          CLR.L       D1                      ;CLEAR THE UNUSED BYTES
                MOVE.B      (A0)+,D1
                CMPI.B      #' ',D1                 ;IS IT A BLANK?
                BEQ.S       ENDCVT                  ;IF YES, EXIT
                CMPI.B      #'0',D1
                BLT.S       ERROR                   ;LESS THAN 0?
                CMPI.B      #'9',D1                 ;GREATER THAN 9?
                BGT.S       ERROR
                AND.B       #$0F,D1                 ;CONVERT TO BCD
*
*MULTIPLY PARTIAL SUM BY 10 AND CHECK FOR OVERFLOW
*
                ADD.L       D0,D0                   ;D0 = 2*D0
                BVS.S       OVERFL
                MOVE.L      D0,D2                   ;SAVE 2*D0
                ADD.L       D0,D0                   ;D0 = 4*D0
                BVS.S       OVERFL
                ADD.L       D0,D0                   ;D0 = 8*D0
                BVS.S       OVERFL
                ADD.L       D2,D0                   ;D0 = 10*D0
                BVS.S       OVERFL
                EXT.W       D1                      ;EXTEND THE NEXT DIGIT TO A LONGWORD
                EXT.L       D1
                ADD.L       D1,D0                   ;ADD IT INTO PARTIAL SUM
                BVS.S       OVERFL
                BRA         CONVER                  ;REPEAT FOR DIGIT D(I+1)
*
*CHECK SIGN.  IF PLUS, STORE RESULT.  OTHERWISE, TAKE 2'S COMPLEMENT.
*
ENDCVT          TST.B       SIGN
                BEQ.S       STORE                   ;IF SIGN IS MINUS,
                NEG.L       D0                      ;TAKE 2'S COMPLEMENT
STORE           MOVE.L      D0,BINNUM               ;RETURN THE BINARY EQUIVALENT
                BRA.S       DONE
ERROR           MOVE.B      #1,ERCODE               ;IF AN INVALID DIGIT IS DETECTED,
*                                                   ;SET CODE TO 1 AND BINNUM TO 0
                CLR.L       BINNUM
                BRA.S       DONE
OVERFL          MOVE.B      #2,ERCODE               ;IF AN OVERFLOW OCCURS SET CODE TO 2
                MOVE.L      #$80000000,BINNUM       ;AND BINNUM TO 2**31
DONE            STOP        #$2000
                END         START
```

Figure 3-27 A program to convert signed ASCII decimal digits to the equivalent 32-bit binary number.

A program to convert a signed decimal number stored in ASCII code to the equivalent 32-bit binary number is given in Fig. 3-27. In the program, the decimal number to be converted may have up to 10 digits with the most significant digit being stored in the lowest address, labeled INPNUM. The number may be prefixed with a + or − sign and is terminated by a blank character. If the magnitude of the decimal number exceeds $2^{31} - 1$, which is the limit of a 32-bit signed number, an error code ERROR will be set to 1, indicating an overflow, and the result will be set to -2^{31}. To simplify the implementation, the special case of -2^{31}, which has a valid binary representation, is not considered. Furthermore, when an invalid ASCII-coded decimal digit is detected, ERROR will be set to 2.

In the program, multiplying a 32-bit partial sum by 10 is accomplished by using four ADD instructions. This implementation is much faster than double-precision multiplication.

3-8 Decimal Arithmetic Group

As seen in the last figure, the conversion between decimal and binary is time-consuming. In scientific applications, extensive computations are involved, and consequently it is desirable to use binary numbers internally. However, in many business applications, large amounts of data need to be input and output with very little computational activity involved. For such cases, it becomes more efficient to work on numbers in the BCD form because the conversion between BCD and binary can be avoided.

The MC68000 provides three instructions for performing addition, subtraction, and negation with packed BCD numbers. They are the ABCD (add decimal with X flag), SBCD (subtract decimal with X flag), and NBCD (negate decimal with X flag) instructions, summarized in Fig. 3-28. All three instructions are limited to byte operations—i.e., only two BCD digits can be operated on at a time. In order to support multiple-precision operations, which are required in most cases of decimal arithmetic, each instruction includes the extend flag in its operation. For the same reason, the ABCD and SBCD instructions permit memory-to-memory operations provided that both operands are in the predecrement addressing mode.

The same set of decimal arithmetic instructions is used for both signed and unsigned operands. Unlike a signed binary number, a signed decimal member is represented in the 10's complement form. The sign is determined by the most significant digit of a decimal number. If this digit is 5 or greater, the number is considered negative.

In order to compare the decimal arithmetic instructions with their binary counterparts, suppose that the initial conditions in hexadecimal are

$$D1.B = 18, \quad D2.B = 24, \quad \text{and} \quad X \text{ flag} = 0$$

Assuming these conditions before each instruction, the following instructions have the indicated results in hexadecimal

Mnemonic	Size or Postfix	Operand Format	Allowable EA Modes	Operation	Condition Flags N Z V C X
ABCD (Add decimal with X flag)	Byte	Dx,Dy −(Ax),−(Ay)		$Dx_{10} + Dy_{10} + X \rightarrow Dy$ $(SRC)_{10} + (DST)_{10} + X \rightarrow DST$	u * u * *
SBCD (Subtract decimal with X flag)	Byte	Dx,Dy −(Ax),−(Ay)		$Dy_{10} - Dx_{10} - X \rightarrow Dy$ $(DST)_{10} - (SRC)_{10} - X \rightarrow DST$	u * u * *
NBCD (Negate decimal with X flag)	Byte	EA	Data alterable	$0 - (EA)_{10} - X \rightarrow EA$	u * u * *

Figure 3-28 Decimal arithmetic instructions.

Instruction		Result	Instruction		Result
ABCD	D1,D2	D2.B = 42	ADDX.B	D1,D2	D2.B = 3C
SBCD	D1,D2	D2.B = 06	SUBX.B	D1,D2	D2.B = 0C
SBCD	D2,D1	D1.B = 94	SUBX.B	D2,D1	D1.B = F4
		(94 as unsigned decimal or −6 as signed decimal)			
NBCD	D1	D1.B = 82	NEGX.B	D1	D1.B = E8

The program in Fig. 3-29 shows a typical implementation of decimal computations. The program computes

$$X = |X - Y| + Z$$

where each variable stores a 10-digit decimal number. According to Motorola's convention, the two most significant BCD digits are stored in the lowest addressed byte associated with that variable. As a result, a decimal arithmetic operation should begin with the highest address of each operand. Furthermore, the extend flag must be cleared before the first two BCD digits are operated on.

This example also demonstrates that calculations in decimal are inefficient. Normally, binary arithmetic is used unless the conversion between binary and decimal outweighs the computational activity.

```
           ORG      $2000
XX         DC.B     $12,$34,$56,$78,$90    ;DECIMAL 1234567890
YY         DC.B     $44,$55,$66,$77,$88    ;DECIMAL 4455667788
ZZ         DC.B     $00,$11,$22,$33,$44    ;DECIMAL 0011223344
WW         DS.B     5                      ;W = ABS (X - Y) + Z
SIZE       DC.W     5                      ;NO. OF BYTES PER NUMBER
START      MOVEA.W  #XX,A0
           ADDA.W   SIZE,A0
           MOVEA.W  #YY,A1
           ADDA.W   SIZE,A1
           MOVEA.W  #ZZ,A2
           ADDA.W   SIZE,A2
           MOVEA.W  #WW,A3
           ADDA.W   SIZE,A3
           MOVE.W   A3,D0                  ;SAVE A3
           MOVE.W   SIZE,D6                ;USE D6 AS COUNTER
           SUBQ.W   #1,D6                  ;D6 = SIZE - 1
           MOVE.W   D6,D7                  ;SAVE COUNTER
LOOP1      MOVE.B   -(A0),-(A3)            ;LOOP1 MOVES X TO W
ENDLP1     DBF      D7,LOOP1
           MOVEA.W  D0,A3
           MOVE.W   D6,D7
           ADDI.W   #0,D7                  ;MAKE SURE X FLAG IS CLEARED
LOOP2      SBCD     -(A1),-(A3)            ;LOOP2 SUBTRACTS Y FROM W
ENDLP2     DBF      D7,LOOP2
           MOVE.B   (A3),D1
           CMPI.B   #$50,D1                ;IS W < 0?
           BLT.S    PLUS
           MOVEA.W  D0,A3                  ;YES, CONVERT IT TO 10'S COMPLEMENT
           MOVE.W   D6,D7
           ADDI.W   #0,D7                  ;CLEAR X FLAG
LOOP3      NBCD     -(A3)                  ;LOOP3 NEGATES W
ENDLP3     DBF      D7,LOOP3
PLUS       MOVEA.W  D0,A3
           MOVE.W   D6,D7
           ADDI.W   #0,D7
LOOP4      ABCD     -(A2),-(A3)            ;LOOP4 ADDS Z TO W
ENDLP4     DBF      D7,LOOP4
           STOP     #$2000
           END      START
```

Figure 3-29 An example of decimal arithmetic instructions.

3-9 Logical Group

The logical instructions, which include the Boolean operations AND, OR, exclusive-OR, and NOT, are summarized in Fig. 3-30. All the instructions perform bitwise Boolean operations on their operands, which may be bytes, words, or longwords. Except for the NOT instruction, which inverts the bits in the specified operand, every other logical instruction requires a source and a destination operand. It should be noted that compared to the AND and OR instruction, the operand format of the EOR instruction is more restrictive, which does not allow the source to be a memory operand. Boolean operations AND, OR, and exclusive-OR may also be performed on the contents of the condition code register or of the status register. However, the instruction becomes privileged when the status register is specified as the destination.

Among other applications, the AND, OR, or EOR instruction can be used to set, clear, complement, or test bits selectively in the destination operand according to the bit pattern specified as the source operand. Such operations are commonly required in I/O programming for manipulating the contents of the control register or checking the status of an I/O device. In order to illustrate these operations, suppose that operand XYZ initially has 01010110. Then, each of the following operations can be accomplished by the indicated instruction.

Operation	Instruction		Results
Clear bits 0, 2, 5, and 6 in XYZ and leave other bits unchanged.	ANDI.B	#$9A,XYZ	XYZ = 00010010
Set bits 0, 2, 5, and 6 in XYZ and leave other bits unchanged.	ORI.B	#$65,XYZ	XYZ = 01110111
Complement bits 0, 2, 5, and 6 in XYZ and leave other bits unchanged.	EORI.B	#$65,XYZ	XYZ = 00110011
If bits 6, 5, 2, and 0 in XYZ are 0110, branch to LABEL1.	MOVE.B	#$65,D1	D1.B = 01100101
	AND.B	XYZ,D1	D1.B = 01000100
	CMPI.B	#$24,D1	Z flag = 1
	BEQ	LABEL1	

As an example to illustrate logical instructions, let us consider the conversion from ASCII to BCD. In order to use the decimal arithmetic instructions discussed in the last section, operands must be in the BCD form. When decimal numbers are input as ASCII-coded digits, two digits need to be combined into a byte according to the BCD format. This conversion process typically requires logical operations. An implementation is given in Fig. 3-31, which converts a 10-digit decimal number from ASCII to BCD, starting from the most significant digit.

As another example of logical instructions, the program in Fig. 3-32 compares two longword operands, OPRA and OPRB, in parallel, and counts the number of matched bit pairs. This program first performs the logical operation

$$OPRA \oplus OPRB$$

A 0-bit in the result indicates that the two corresponding bits in the operands are

Figure 3-30 Logical instructions.

Mnemonic	Size or Postfix	Operand Format	Allowable EA Modes	Operation	Condition Flags N Z V C X
AND (AND logical)	.B, .W, .L	EA,Dn Dn,EA	Data Memory alterable	$(EA) \wedge Dn \rightarrow Dn$ $Dn \wedge (EA) \rightarrow EA$	* * 0 0 –
ANDI (AND immediate)	.B, .W, .L Byte Word	#I,EA #I,CCR #I,SR[1]	Data alterable	$I \wedge (EA) \rightarrow EA$ $I \wedge CCR \rightarrow CCR$ $I \wedge SR \rightarrow SR$	* 0 0 0 – * * * * * * * * * *
OR (OR logical)	.B, .W, .L	EA,Dn Dn,EA	Data Memory alterable	$(EA) \vee Dn \rightarrow Dn$ $Dn \vee (EA) \rightarrow EA$	* * 0 0 –
ORI (OR immediate)	.B, .W, .L Byte Word	#I,EA #I,CCR #I,SR[1]	Data alterable	$I \vee (EA) \rightarrow EA$ $I \vee CCR \rightarrow CCR$ $I \vee SR \rightarrow SR$	* * 0 0 – * * * * * * * * * *
EOR (Exclusive OR logical)	.B, .W, .L	Dn,EA	Data alterable	$Dn \oplus (EA) \rightarrow EA$	* * 0 0 –
EORI (Exclusive OR immediate)	.B, .W, .L Byte Word	#I,EA #I,CCR #I,SR[1]	Data alterable	$\#I \oplus (EA) \rightarrow EA$ $\#I \oplus CCR \rightarrow CCR$ $\#I \oplus SR \rightarrow SR$	* 0 0 0 – * * * * * * * * * *
NOT (Logical complement)	.B, .W, .L	EA	Data alterable	$(\overline{EA}) \rightarrow EA$	* * 0 0 –

Note: 1. Privileged instructions.

85

```
              ORG      $2000
INPNUM    DC.B     '1234567890'
BCD       DS.B     5
START     MOVEA.W  #INPNUM,A0
          MOVEA.W  #BCD,A1
          MOVE.W   #4,D7
LOOP      MOVE.B   (A0)+,D0        ;D0 = ASCII(I)
          ANDI.B   #$0F,D0         ;D0 = 0000 BCD(I)
          MOVE.B   (A0)+,D1        ;D1 = ASCII(I+1)
          ANDI.B   #$0F,D1         ;D1 = 0000 BCD(I+1)
          ASL.B    #4,D0           ;D0 = BCD(I) 0000
          OR.B     D1,D0           ;D1 = BCD(I) BCD(I+1)
          MOVE.B   D0,(A1)+        ;SAVE 2 BCD DIGITS
ENDLP     DBF      D7,LOOP
          STOP     #$2000
          END      START
```

Figure 3-31 A program to convert an ASCII-coded decimal number to BCD.

```
            ORG      $2000
OPRA      DC.L     $12341234
OPRB      DC.L     $45677654
NUM       DS.B     1
START     MOVE.L   OPRA,D0
          MOVE.L   OPRB,D1
          EOR.L    D1,D0           ;D0 = OPRA EOR OPRB
          CLR.B    D2
          MOVEQ    #31,D7
LOOP      LSL.L    #1,D0           ;SHIFT THE MOST SIGNIFICANT BIT
*                                  ;INTO C FLAG
          BCS.S    ENDLP           ;IF C FLAG = 0,
          ADDQ.B   #1,D2           ;INCREMENT COUNT BY 1
ENDLP     DBF      D7,LOOP
          MOVE.B   D2,NUM
          STOP     #$2000
          END      START
```

Figure 3-32 A program to count the number of matched bit pairs between two arrays.

either both zeros or both ones. Then, the program counts the number of 0 bits in the result by shifting and checking one bit at a time.

3-10 Shift and Rotate Group

The MC68000 instructions for performing shift and rotate operations are summarized in Fig. 3-33. The eight instructions are: ASL (arithmetic shift left), ASR (arithmetic shift right), LSL (logical shift left), LSR (logical shift right), ROL (rotate left), ROR (rotate right), ROXL (rotate left through X flag), and ROXR (rotate right through X flag).

Each instruction uses the same format for specifying the number of shifts (shift count) and the operand to be shifted or rotated. When the destination operand is a data register, the shift count may be given by the lower 6 bits of the specified source data register or as an immediate operand ranging from 1 to 8. If a data register is used to store the shift count, up to 63 shifts may be performed per instruction. The bits in the specified data register to be shifted may be a byte, word, or longword. When the destination is specified as a memory operand, a word shift will be performed with the implied shift count equal to 1.

The eight instructions can be classified in two ways. First, there are the left shift/rotate instructions, which move data bits to the left, and the right shift/rotate instructions, which move bits to the right. Second, there are the shift instructions and the rotate instructions.

For the shift instructions, the destination operand may be shifted logically or arithmetically. During a logical shift, as data bits are shifted out on one end,

Mnemonic	Size or Postfix	Operand Format	Allowable EA Modes	Operation	Condition Flags N Z V C X
ASL (Arithmetic shift left)	.B, .W, .L Word	Dx,Dy #I3,Dy EA	Memory alterable		* * * * *
ASR (Arithmetic shift right)	.B, .W, .L Word	Dx,Dy #I3,Dy EA	Memory alterable		* * * * *
LSL (Logical shift left)	.B, .W, .L Word	Dx,Dy #I3,Dy EA	Memory alterable		* * 0 * *
LSR (Logical shift right)	.B, .W, .L Word	Dx,Dy #I3,Dy EA	Memory alterable		* * 0 * *
ROL (Rotate left)	.B, .W, .L Word	Dx,Dy #I3,Dy EA	Memory alterable		* * 0 * -
ROR (Rotate right)	.B, .W, .L Word	Dx,Dy #I3,Dy EA	Memory alterable		* * 0 * -
ROXL (Rotate left through X flag)	.B, .W, .L Word	Dx,Dy #I3,Dy EA	Memory alterable		* * 0 * *
ROXR (Rotate right through X flag)	.B, .W, .L Word	Dx,Dy #I3,Dy EA	Memory alterable		* * 0 * *

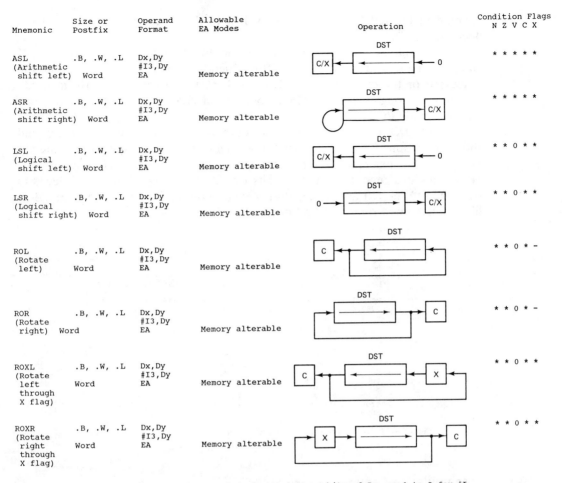

Note: The shift count is in the lower 6 bits of Dx, or 1 to 8 for #I, or 1 for EA.

Figure 3-33   Shift and rotate instructions.

zeros are always shifted in on the other end. The V flag is cleared while the other flags are conditionally set. Logical shifts can be used to isolate bits in the operand.

The arithmetic shift instructions are designed to preserve the sign of the original operand while being shifted. The ASR instruction extends the sign bit after each right shift operation. Therefore, this instruction may be used to divide an operand by 2^N, where N is the shift count. However, when the operand is negative, the ASR may not produce the same result as the quotient yielded from the DIVU instruction. For example, shifting -9 right by two bits yields -3, whereas dividing -9 by 4 using DIVU yields -2. The maximum difference between the two operations is 1. The ASL instruction yields the same shifted result as the LSL instruction. But ASL sets the V flag to indicate an overflow whenever the sign bit has been changed by the left shift operation. Therefore, shifting an operand to the left by N bits is equivalent to the signed multiplication of the operand by 2^N.

The rotate instructions perform circular shift operations. Bits shifted out of an operand are not lost, as in the shift instructions, but are rotated back into the other end of the operand. The ROXL and ROXR instructions perform rotate operations through the X flag. On the other hand, the ROL and ROR instructions do not include the X flag in the circle of rotation.

The ROXL and ROXR instructions are essential in implementing shift and rotate operations for operands with more than 32 bits, as required in some applications. For example, in implementing the algorithm discussed in Sec. 3-7 for performing unsigned division of 64 bits by 32 bits, the 64-bit dividend needs to be shifted to the left as a whole during each iteration. The program in Fig. 3-34 illustrates how to rotate a 64-bit operand by N bits.

```
           ORG      $2000
OPR        DC.L     $12345678,$9ABCDEF0
NSIZE      DC.W     12
START      MOVE.L   OPR,D0
           MOVE.L   OPR+4,D1        ;D0 = b63 b62...b32, D1 = b31 b30...b0,
*                                   ;X = ?
           MOVE.W   NSIZE,D7        ;D7 = NO. OF SHIFTS
           SUBQ.W   #1,D7
LOOP       ROXR.L   #1,D1           ;D0 = b63 b62...b32, D1 = ? b31...b1,
*                                   ;X = b0
           ROXR.L   #1,D0           ;D0 = b0 b63...b33, D1 = ? b31...b1,
*                                   ;X = b32
           ROXL.L   #1,D1           ;D0 = b0 b63...b33, D1 = b31...b1 b32,
*                                   ;X = ?
           ROR.L    #1,D1           ;D0 = b0 b63...b33, D1 = b32...b1,
*                                   ;X = ?
ENDLP      DBF      D7,LOOP
           MOVE.L   D0,OPR
           MOVE.L   D1,OPR+4
           STOP     #$2000
           END      START
```

Figure 3-34 A program to rotate a 64-bit operand to the right N-bit position.

3-11 Bit Manipulation Group

A bit manipulation instruction can check and modify an individual bit in an operand and leave the remaining bits unchanged. Operations that manipulate individual bits are frequently required to update or maintain tables consisting of several fields when each field is implemented by a single bit. The bit manipulation instructions for the MC68000 are summarized in Fig. 3-35.

All four instructions test the specified bit in the destination by copying the complement of that bit to the Z flag, which can then be checked with a following conditional branch instruction. In addition to bit testing, the BCHG (bit test and change), BCLR (bit test and clear), and BSET (bit test and set) instructions also complement, clear, and set the bit being tested, respectively. The BTST (bit test) instruction does not affect the destination operand. Therefore, its destination operand can be specified by any data addressing mode. In BCHG, BCLR, and BSET, the destination operand is restricted to the data alterable addressing modes.

The operand size of a bit manipulation instruction is implied by the destination addressing mode—byte for a memory operand and longword for a data register. The source operand indicates which bit in the destination is to be operated

Mnemonic	Size or Postfix	Operand Format	Allowable EA Modes	Operation	Condition Flags N Z V C X
BCHG (Test bit and change)	Byte or longword	Dn,EA #I,EA	Data alterable	$\overline{\text{DST[bit no.]}}$ -> Z, DST[bit no.]	- * - - -
BCLR (Test bit and clear)	Byte or longword	Dn,EA #I,EA	Data alterable	$\overline{\text{DST[bit no.]}}$ -> Z; 0 -> DST[bit no.]	- * - - -
BSET (Test bit and set)	Byte or longword	Dn,EA #I,EA	Data alterable	$\overline{\text{DST[bit no.]}}$ -> Z; 1 -> DST[bit no.]	- * - - -
BTST (Test bit)	Byte or longword	Dn,EA #I,EA	Data	$\overline{\text{DST[bit no.]}}$ -> Z	- * - - -

Note: Byte for memory destination and longword for data
register destination.

Figure 3-35 Bit manipulation instructions.

on. This bit number can be specified as the contents in a data register or as an immediate value, with 0 corresponding to the least significant bit. The bit operation is performed using the bit number modulo 8 if the destination is a memory operand and modulo 32 if the destination is a data register.

As an example involving bit manipulation instructions, let us consider the implementation of the sieve of Eratosthenes algorithm. This algorithm is a well-known procedure to find all the prime numbers in a given range by elimination. This procedure is often implemented in a high-level language as a benchmark program to compare the performances of different microprocessors or compilers for integer operations and memory accesses.

To explain the sieve algorithm, suppose that we wish to find the prime numbers between 2 and 25. The algorithm begins by listing all integers in this range.

2, 3, 4, 5, 6, 7, 8, 9, 10, 11, 12, 13, 14, 15, 16, 17, 18, 19, 20, 21, 22, 23, 24, 25

Then, crossing out all multiples of 2, the list becomes

2, 3, 4, 5, 6, 7, 8, 9, 10, 11, 12, 13, 14, 15, 16, 17, 18, 19, 20, 21, 22, 23, 24, 25

The same crossing-out process is repeated for the next uncrossed number, which is 3. After crossing out all multiples of 3, we have

2, 3, 4, 5, 6, 7, 8, 9, 10, 11, 12, 13, 14, 15, 16, 17, 18, 19, 20, 21, 22, 23, 24, 25

Repeating the same process with the multiples of 5, and so on, this list becomes

2, 3, 4, 5, 6, 7, 8, 9, 10, 11, 12, 13, 14, 15, 16, 17, 18, 19, 20, 21, 22, 23, 24, 25

The remaining numbers at the end of this process are prime numbers.

To implement the sieve algorithm, each integer can be assigned a 1-bit flag to indicate whether or not that integer has been crossed out. Since 2 is the only even prime number, the memory for storing flags can be reduced by half if only

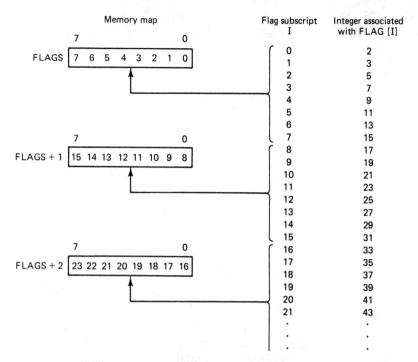

Figure 3-36 Memory map of 1-bit flags.

odd numbers are included. Let FLAG[0] denote the flag associated with 2 and FLAG[I] denote the flag associated with integer $2 \times I + 1$, where $I = 1, 2, 3, 4, \cdots$. Figure 3-36 shows the memory map when the flags are implemented by an array of bytes beginning with FLAGS. It can be seen that the index of the byte and the bit position, where FLAG[I] is stored, can be calculated, respectively, as the quotient and the remainder of I divided by 8.

Based on the sieve algorithm, a pseudocode to find all the prime numbers in the range from 2 to N and return the number of primes and the maximum prime in this range is as follows.

```
Set all flags to 0;
1 → COUNT;
FOR I = 1, number of flags (i.e., N/2)
  DO IF FLAG[I] = 0
    THEN
      COUNT + 1 → COUNT;
      2 × I + 1 → MAXPRI;
      IF MAXPRI ≤ √N
        THEN
          I + MAXPRI → K;
          FOR J = K, number of flags, STEP MAXPRI
            DO 1 → FLAG[J]
        ENDIF
    ENDIF
ENDLOOP;
```

Flag Subscript I	Integer Represented by FLAG[I]	Initial FLAG[I]	Iteration N			
			N = 1 FLAG[I]	N = 2 FLAG[I]	N = 3 FLAG[I]	N = 4 FLAG[I]
0	2	0	0	0	0	0
1	3	0	0	0	0	0
2	5	0	0	0	0	0
3	7	0	0	0	0	0
4	9	0	1	1	1	1
5	11	0	0	0	0	0
6	13	0	0	0	0	0
7	15	0	1	1	1	1
8	17	0	0	0	0	0
9	19	0	0	0	0	0
10	21	0	1	1	1	1
11	23	0	0	0	0	0
12	25	0	0	1	1	1
13	27	0	1	1	1	1
14	29	0	0	0	0	0
15	31	0	0	0	0	0
16	33	0	1	1	1	1
17	35	0	0	1	1	1
18	37	0	0	0	0	0
19	39	0	1	1	1	1
20	41	0	0	0	0	0
21	43	0	0	0	0	0
22	45	0	1	1	1	1
23	47	0	0	0	0	0
24	49	0	0	0	1	1
25	51	0	1	1	1	1
26	53	0	0	0	0	0
27	55	0	0	1	1	1
28	57	0	1	1	1	1
29	59	0	0	0	0	0
30	61	0	0	0	0	0
31	63	0	1	1	1	1
32	65	0	0	1	1	1
33	67	0	0	0	0	0
34	69	0	1	1	1	1
35	71	0	0	0	0	0
MAXPRI =			3	5	7	11
COUNT =			2	3	4	5

Figure 3-37 Trace of the sieve algorithm.

The outer loop searches for the next prime number. Once it is found, the variable count is incremented by 1, the new prime is stored into MAXPRI, and all multiples of MAXPRI are crossed out in the inner loop by setting their associated one-bit flags to 1. Since only the flags for odd numbers are included and the flag associated with MAXPRI is FLAG[I], the subscript of the flag for the first multiple of MAXPRI to be crossed out (i.e., $3 \times$ MAXPRI) is I + MAXPRI. For the next multiple, $5 \times$ MAXPRI, the subscript is I + $2 \times$ MAXPRI, and so on. The contents of the first 36 flags after each of the first four iterations are shown in Fig. 3-37. But, when a prime is greater than $\sqrt{N}$, all its multiples should have already been crossed out during some earlier iterations. The reason is that all the factors of any number less than N cannot be greater than $\sqrt{N}$. Therefore, the inner loop is skipped for any prime that is greater than $\sqrt{N}$.

An MC68000 implementation of the preceding pseudocode is given in Fig. 3-38. In the program, N is 32,767 ($2^{15} - 1$). Therefore, 16,384 (2^{14}) flags are required, which are implemented by using 2048 (2^{11}) bytes.

3-12 Position-Independent Code

A position-independent code is a routine that can be loaded anywhere in memory for execution without adjustment. This feature eliminates the need for the linker to perform program relocation.

```
                ORG     $2000
NUMFLG  DC.W    16384
SQROTN  DC.W    182
FLAGS   DS.B    2048
MAXPRI  DS.W    1
COUNT   DS.W    1
START   MOVE.W  NUMFLG,D7
        LSR.W   #3,D7                           ;D7 = NUMBER OF BYTES TO STORE FLAGS
        SUBQ.W  #1,D7
        MOVEA.W #FLAGS,A0
LOOP1   CLR.B   (A0)+                           ;DO LOOP1 TO SET ALL
ENDLP1  DBF     D7,LOOP1                        ;FLAGS TO 0 (i.e., TRUE)
        MOVEQ   #1,D0                           ;USE D0 AS COUNT FOR PRIMES
        MOVE.W  NUMFLG,D7                       ;D7 = NUMBER OF FLAGS
        SUBQ.W  #2,D7
        MOVEA.W #FLAGS,A0
        MOVEQ   #1,D6                           ;USE D6 AS I
LOOP2   MOVE.W  D6,D5                           ;DO LOOP2 FOR I = 1 TO NUMBER OF FLAGS
        LSR.W   #3,D5                           ;D5 = BYTE INDEX FOR FLAG(I)
        MOVEQ   #7,D4
        AND.W   D6,D4                           ;D4 = BIT POSITION WITHIN THE BYTE
        BTST    D4,0(A0,D5.W)                   ;FLAG(I) = 0?
        BNE     SKPLP3                          ;IF NOT 0 THEN SKIP BODY OF LOOP2
        ADDQ.W  #1,D0                           ;COUNT = COUNT + 1
        MOVE.W  D6,D1                           ;USE D1 AS MAXPRI
        ADD.W   D6,D1
        ADDQ.W  #1,D1                           ;MAXPRI = 2*I + 1
        CMP.W   SQROTN,D1                       ;IF MAXPRI >= SQRT(N)
        BGE     SKPLP3                          ;SKIP LOOP3
        MOVE.W  D6,D2                           ;USE D2 AS K
        ADD.W   D1,D2                           ;K = I + MAXPRI
        MOVE.W  D2,D3                           ;USE D3 AS J
LOOP3   CMP.W   NUMFLG,D3                       ;DO LOOP3 FOR J = K TO NUMFLG
        BGT.S   SKPLP3                          ;STEP MAXPRI
        MOVE.W  D3,D5                           ;D5 = BYTE INDEX FOR J
        LSR.W   #3,D5
        MOVEQ   #7,D4
        AND.W   D3,D4                           ;D4 = BIT POSITION WITHIN THE BYTE
        BSET    D4,0(A0,D5.W)                   ;SET FLAG(J) TO 1 (i.e., FALSE)
        ADD.W   D1,D3
ENDLP3  BR      LOOP3
SKPLP3  ADDQ.W  #1,D6
ENDLP2  DBF     D7,LOOP2
        MOVE.W  D0,COUNT
        MOVE.W  D1,MAXPRI
        STOP    #$2000
        END     START
```

Figure 3-38 Implementation of the sieve algorithm.

Position-independent programming is particularly important in writing certain system or utility routines. Such routines are stored on a disk and are loaded into memory for execution whenever they are needed. Since the available memory space changes dynamically, it is desirable for the supervisor program to be able to load them anywhere it determines without the need for relocation.

As mentioned in Sec. 3-1, there are two types of operand expressions, absolute and relocatable. An absolute address does not change after the program is relocated and therefore is position-independent. On the other hand, a relocatable address is position-dependent. Position-independent code can be achieved by using the program counter relative addressing modes in accessing all relocatable memory operands. In a PC relative addressing mode, the operand address is specified as a distance from the current instruction, which is a constant regardless the program's loading origin.

The MC68000 uses a PC relative addressing mode in all branch instructions and also provides the PC with displacement and PC with index addressing modes in referencing source operands. Figure 3-39 shows how PC relative addressing modes support position-independent programming.

To make a program position-independent, in accessing memory source operands the PC displacement and PC with index modes should be used as substi-

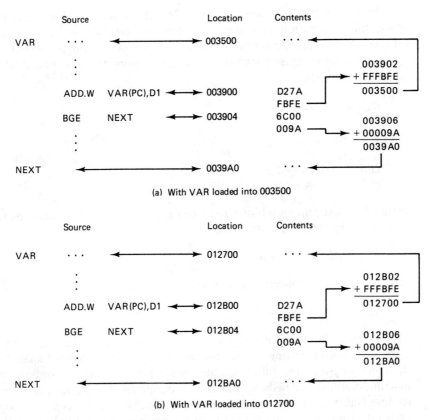

(a) With VAR loaded into 003500

(b) With VAR loaded into 012700

Figure 3-39 Position independence provided by PC relative addressing modes.

tutions for the absolute and address register indirect with displacement modes. For example, in the following instruction sequence:

```
OPERS    DC.W        . . .
         .
         .
         .
         MOVE.W    OPERS,D1
         .
         .
         .
         MOVE.W    OPERS(A1),D2
```

the two MOVE.W instructions should be replaced by

```
MOVE.W        OPERS(PC),D1
```

and

```
MOVE.W        OPERS(PC,A1.L),D2
```

However, the PC relative modes are restricted to accessing source operands. When the destination is a memory operand, position independence can be achieved by loading the actual operand address into an address register and then using the address register indirect mode in accessing that operand. For example, the instruction

```
CLR.W      VAR
```

can be rewritten as

```
LEA        VAR(PC),A1
CLR.W      (A1)
```

Similarly, to set up an address register for the predecrement and postincrement addressing modes, the instruction

```
MOVEA.L    #label,An
```

can be made position-independent by replacing it with

```
LEA        label(PC),An
```

A note should be made here. As mentioned earlier, position-independent code is useful in writing utility routines, which are commonly shared by more than one program in a multiprogramming system. However, in order to be shared in a time-multiplexed fashion, a common routine must not modify itself. (Common routine sharing is discussed further in Sec. 5-6.) In other words, any operand to be used as a destination or a temporary working area should be supplied by the calling program, not included as part of the shared routine. Suppose that the variable VAR in the preceding example is provided by the calling program through a user stack pointed by A6. Then, clearing VAR could be accomplished by the position-independent code

```
VAR        EQU        6
            .
            .
            .
           CLR.W      VAR(A6)
```

where VAR is assumed to be the fourth word from the top of the stack.

Sometimes, operand addresses are stored in memory locations called *operand pointers*. A typical example is the branch table discussed earlier. In order to make the program position-independent, its relocation factor must be added into operand pointers at execution time before the pointers are used. The relocation factor is the loading origin of the program and can be calculated as

Relocation factor = actual address of a memory operand
$$- \text{ relative address of the same operand}$$

This technique is illustrated by the following example, assuming that BEGIN is the first assigned location in the program:

```
BEGIN         .                              ;ORIGIN OF THE PROGRAM
              .
              .

VARX    DC.W    10                           ;RELOCATABLE OPERAND
VARY    DC.W    -5                           ;RELOCATABLE OPERAND
VARZ    DC.W    3                            ;RELOCATABLE OPERAND
              .
              .
              .

ADDRS   DC.L    VARY-BEGIN,VARZ-BEGIN        ;POINTERS TO VARY AND VARZ
              .
              .
              .

        LEA     ADDRS(PC),D1                 ;LOAD D1 WITH THE ACTUAL
                                             ;ADDRESS OF ADDRS
        SUBI.L  #ADDRS-BEGIN,D1              ;SUBTRACT THE RELATIVE
                                             ;ADDRESS OF ADDRS FROM D1
        LEA     ADDRS(PC),A1
        ADD.L   D1,(A1)                      ;ADD THE RELOCATION FACTOR
                                             ;INTO ADDRS
        ADD.L   D1,4(A1)                     ;ADD THE RELOCATION FACTOR
                                             ;INTO ADDRS+4
```

After the instruction sequence is executed, ADDRS will have the correct addresses of VARY and VARZ.

Finally, an example is shown in Fig. 3-40 to convert a given program to position-independent code. This program calculates the sum of a word array ARRAY and stores the result into an operand TOTAL.

```
ARRAY    DC.W      -5,3,0,-10,1,15,12,-6,9,6
SIZE     DC.W      10
TOTAL    DS.W      1
START    MOVEA.L   #ARRAY,A1
         CLR.W     D0
         MOVE.W    SIZE,D7
         SUBQ.W    #1,D7
LOOP     ADD.W     (A1)+,D0
GNDLP    DBF       D7,LOOP
         MOVE.W    D0,TOTAL
         STOP      #$2000
         END       START
```

(a) Position-dependent code

```
ARRAY    DC.W      -5,3,0,-10,1,15,12,-6,9,6
SIZE     DC.W      10
TOTAL    DS.W      1
START    LEA       ARRAY(PC),A1
         CLR.W     D0
         MOVE.W    SIZE(PC),D7
         SUBQ.W    #1,D7
LOOP     ADD.W     (A1)+,D0
ENDLP    DBF       D7,LOOP
         LEA       TOTAL(PC),A2
         MOVE.W    D0,(A2)
         STOP      #$2000
         END       START
```

(b) Position-independent code

Figure 3-40 Example of position independent code.

EXERCISES

1. Trace the sample program in Fig. 3-1 and show the final results in the array ARRAY.

2. Assume that AA and BB are absolute symbols and XX and YY are relocatable symbols. For each of the following expressions, indicate whether the expression is absolute, relocatable, or invalid.

   (a) AA + 5   (b) XX − YY + 5   (c) AA + BB   (d) XX + YY   (e) AA − XX
   (f) YY − AA   (g) AA + BB + XX − YY   (h) XX − AA*2 + BB − YY   (i) YY*2 − XX
   (j) *−AA   (k) *+XX   (l) −AA   (m) −XX   (n) −AA − BB/2

3. Assume that AA and BB are labels. Identify the addressing mode for each of the following operands:

   (a) $100   (b) #$100   (c) AA   (d) #AA + $10 − BB   (e) 4(A1,D2.L)
   (f) AA + $10(A1)   (g) #BB   (h) AA(PC)   (i) $10(PC,A1.L)   (j) −(A2)   (k) (A2)+

4. For each of the following instructions, indicate which of the addressing modes listed next are valid for specifying the EA operand.

   (a) JMP EA   (b) ROL EA   (c) ADD.W EA,Dn   (d) ADDQ.W #I,EA
   (e) OR.W Dn,EA
   (1) Immediate addressing mode.
   (2) Data register direct addressing mode.
   (3) Address register direct addressing mode.
   (4) Address register indirect addressing mode.
   (5) Address register indirect with postincrement addressing mode.
   (6) Address register indirect with predecrement addressing mode.
   (7) Address register indirect with displacement addressing mode.
   (8) Address register indirect with index addressing mode.
   (9) Program counter with displacement addressing mode.
   (10) Program counter with index addressing mode.

5. Give the reason why the memory-to-memory compare instruction uses the postincrement addressing mode but the instruction for performing memory-to-memory subtraction with the X flag uses the predecrement addressing mode.

6. Which of the following are invalid instructions? State the assembly error for each invalid instruction.

(a)	ADD.W	OPRX,OPRY
(b)	MOVE.W	−(A1),(A1)+
(c)	CLR.W	A3
(d)	MOVE.W	OPRX + #4,D1
(e)	MOVE.W	#OPRX + 4,D1
(f)	CLR.W	#8(A1)
(g)	BR	4(A2)
(h)	MOVE.W	OPRX(PC,D2.L),$100(A3)
(i)	LEA	OPRX(A1,D1.W),A1
(j)	LEA	(A1)+,A2
(k)	CLR.W	$100(A2.W,D2.W)
(l)	MOVEQ	#6,OPRX
(m)	ADDQ.L	#6,OPRX
(n)	MOVEQ.B	#6,D2
(o)	SUBQ.L	#12,D2
(p)	SUB.L	#12,D2
(q)	INC.L	D2

7. Show the reserved space and initialized contents in hex generated by the following sequences of directives:

(a)
```
        ORG    $1200
        DC.W   10,−5
        DC.B   $20,0
        DC.L   −$34
```
(b)
```
        ORG    $2000
        DC.W   −$6F,30
        DS.W   5
     AA DC.L   −50,100
        DC.W   AA,BB−CC
     BB DC.B   'MESSAGE',$0D,$0A
     CC DC.B   0
```

8. Verify that the test condition for the relation less or equal is

$$Z + (N \oplus V) = 1$$

and for the relation lower or same is

$$C + Z = 1$$

9. Give three different subtract instructions to subtract 1 from D2.

10. For each instruction, assume the following initial conditions:

Registers	Locations
D1: 01233637	004000:0102
D2: 9090F345	004002:3344
A1: 00004004	004004:5040
A2: 00004008	004006:1111
CCR:00	004008:2222
	00400A:3333

Determine the results, including the condition flags, for each of the following instructions:

(a) ADD.W   −(A1),D2
(b) ADD.B   D2,D1
(c) ADD.L   #FFF0,D2
(d) LEA   4(A1),A3
(e) LEA $1200(PC),A3 (Assume that the instruction is assembled at
                          001250.)
(f) SUB.W   D2,D1
(g) CLR.L   (A1)+
(h) MOVEM.W D1/A1/D2/A2,$4004
(i) MOVEM.W $4000,D1/A1/D2/A2

11. Assume that all operands are signed 16-bit numbers. Write program sequences that will compute the following expressions in binary:

(a) X = Y + Z * 3   (b) X = Y * Z − W + 5
(c) X = Quotient of (Y + 3)/(Z − 2)   R = Remainder
(d) X = Quotient of (Y**3 − Y * 10)/Z   R = Remainder

12. Assuming that OPRX is associated with address 001200 and each of the following instructions is assembled at address 001000, find the machine code for the instructions:

(a) ADDI.W #35,OPRX(A1)   (b) ADD.W   OPRX(PC,D1.L),D2
(c) DIVS   OPRX,D1   (d) DIVS   OPRX(PC),D1
(e) ASL   −(A1)   (f) ASR.W   #5,D1

13. Assuming that NEXT is associated with address 003580 and each of the following instructions is assembled at address 003850, find the machine code for the instructions:

(a) BGT   NEXT   (b) BR   NEXT+4
(c) DBF   D2,NEXT   (d) DBNE D1,NEXT$-$\$12
(e) JMP   NEXT   (f) JMP   NEXT(PC)

14. Assuming that OPRA = 0012 and OPRB = FF12, determine the unsigned and signed products of OPRA multiplied by OPRB. Give your answers in both hexadecimal and decimal forms.

15. Given that D2 = FFFFFF12 and VAR = FFF2, determine the results of the instruction

    DIVS   VAR,D2

16. Given that D2 = 00133456 and VAR = 0121, determine the results of the instruction

    DIVU   VAR,D2

17. Write a program that compares two character strings STG1 and STG2, each having N bytes. Set FLAG to 1 if the two strings are the same; otherwise, set FLAG to 0.

18. Write a program that finds the number of positive nonzero elements and the number of negative elements in the array WDARY of N words. Use POSNUM and NEGNUM to store the counts.

19. Given the instruction sequence

VARS	DC.W	10,3,-5,1,0,-6,7,3,8,-1
START	MOVE.W	#9,D7
	CLR.W	D0
	MOVEA.L	#VARS,A1
LOOP	ADD.W	(A1)+,D0
	CMPI.W	#15,D0
ENDLP	DBLE	D7,LOOP

determine the results including A1, D0, D7, and Z flag after exit from the loop.

20. Write an instruction sequence to compare two 64-bit signed integers, OPRX and OPRY. If OPRX is greater than OPRY, set D7 to 1; otherwise, clear D7.

21. Write an instruction sequence to implement the following flowchart:

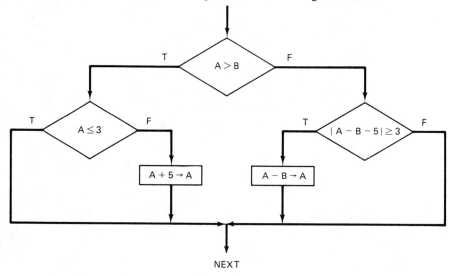

22. Assuming word operands, write an instruction sequence to implement each of the following FORTRAN statements:
    (a) IF (I + J .GT. 7) I = I + J + 2
    (b) IF (I .GT. 6 .OR. I .EQ. J − 2) GOTO 20

23. Implement the following FORTRAN compute goto statement in assembly language.

    GOTO (10, 20, 30, 40) I + K

    This FORTRAN statement jumps to label 10 if I + K = 1, to label 20 if I + K = 2, to label 30 if I + K = 3, and to label 40 if I + K = 4.

24. Write a program that will replace each blank character in a given ASCII character string with a $.

25. Write a program to perform $N \times M$ matrix addition assuming that each element is a 16-bit integer.

26. Write a program to find the transpose of a square matrix assuming that each element is a 32-bit integer.

27. Implement the unsigned double-precision multiplication algorithm given in Sec. 3-7.

28. Implement the unsigned double-precision division algorithm given in Sec. 3-7.

29. Determine the results after the following program is executed:

```
              ORG       $2000
OPR           DC.W      $724E
FLAG          DS.B      1
START         MOVE.W    OPR,D0
              MOVE.W    #7,D7
LOOP          LSR.W     #1,D0
              ROXL.W    #1,D1
ENDLP         DBF       D2,LOOP
              CLR.B     FLAG
              CMP.B     D0,D1
              BNE.S     DONE
              ADDQ.B    #1,FLAG
DONE          STOP      #2000
              END       START
```

30. Seven-segment LED display devices such as the one shown in the following figure are frequently used for displaying numerical data in microprocessor-based instruments. A digit is displayed by sending the device a 7-segment code to light the corresponding LEDs. For example, assuming that segment *a* corresponds to the least significant bit of a 7-segment code, an output of byte 5B will cause digit 2 to be displayed. Write a program that translates a hexadecimal digit given in HEXDGT to the equivalent 7-segment code and stores the result in SEVSEG.

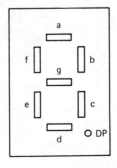

31. Write a program to perform the conversion from binary to ASCII-coded hexadecimal. Assume that the 32-bit unsigned number to be converted is in BINNUM and the resulting 8 hexadecimal digits are to be stored 1 digit per byte beginning at HEXDGT.

32. Write an instruction sequence that will divide an unsigned 32-bit integer stored in register D0 by decimal 10. Store the quotient back to register D0 and the remainder to register D1.

33. Assume that BINNUM has an unsigned 32-bit integer. Write a program that will convert it to the equivalent ASCII-coded decimal number. Use a 5-byte array OUTPUT to store the results with leading zeros being replaced by blank characters.

34. Assume that eight Boolean variables $X_0, X_1, \ldots, X_7$ have been stored in the variable INPUT with X_i corresponding to bit i. Write an instruction sequence to evaluate the Boolean expression

$$f(X_7, X_6, \ldots, X_0) = X_6\overline{X}_3X_2X_0 + \overline{X}_7\overline{X}_5X_1X_0 + X_7X_3X_1$$

and store the result (0 or 1) into FX.

35. Convert the following program segment to position-independent code:

```
ARYX      DC.W       3, -1,5,7,0, -10,8,11,2,6
ARYY      DS.W       10
SIZE      DC.W       10
START     MOVEA.L    #ARYX,A0
          MOVEA.L    #ARYY,A1
          MOVE.W     SIZE,D7
          SUBQ.W     #1,D7
LOOP      MOVE.W     (A0) +,(A1) +
ENDLP     DBF        D7,LOOP
                     .
                     .
                     .
```

4

Development Tools

Once an assembly language program is written and is assembled into machine code, several software development tools can be used to execute and test the program. One method is to use the program as input to a simulator that simulates the execution of each MC68000 instruction. A second method is to execute the program in an MC68000-based microcomputer. Finally, the program can be tested by using an emulator as a substitution for the microprocessor, which is part of a microcomputer development system.

Although the actual means used to execute a program vary from one development tool to the next, they all provide some debugging facilities to assist a user in program testing. Typical debugging aids include those that allow a user to execute any given program portion, to trace each instruction execution, to dump a memory image, and to display the processor's registers. This chapter will discuss some typical development tools and debugging facilities.

4-1 Simulators and Cross Assemblers

Simulators

A simulator program duplicates the exact execution of machine code for the given microprocessor on a different computer. In a simulator, the architecture of the MC68000 is simulated by a block of memory in the host machine. In other words, the PC, SR, register set, and the memory area storing the program to be simulated are all represented by memory locations in the host. Execution of each MC68000 instruction is therefore simulated by several instructions in the host machine. During the simulation, the contents of these memory locations are the same as the register contents would be if the same program were executed in the microprocessor being simulated.

The input to the simulator comes from two sources, one of which is the cross assembler/linker, whose output is the load module. The second input source is the user, whose input consists of the simulation commands. For an on-line system, the user successively enters commands through a terminal and examines the displayed results to determine the next simulation command. Typical simulation commands are those that allow the user to trace program execution, dump memory and register contents, and suspend program execution at given addresses. This interactive environment makes the simulator a valuable debugging tool.

A simulator enables a user to test and debug programs in a computer other than the target microprocessor. In addition to serving as a teaching tool, a simulator also allows software to be developed in parallel with the hardware design during the development of a microprocessor-based project. Since the simulator does not operate in the real time of execution of the target microprocessor, time-dependent programs cannot be completely tested before the hardware has been built. However, the number of elapsed clock cycles of the simulated execution is maintained, from which the actual execution time of a given program portion can be estimated.

Cross assemblers

If an assembly language program is to be executed using a simulator, the program is normally assembled by a cross assembler running in the same host system. The functions performed by a cross assembler are essentially the same as those performed by a self-assembler. These include the translation of mnemonic instructions into machine code, the execution of assembler directives, the detection of syntax errors, and the processing of macros. The difference between the two is that a cross assembler for the MC68000 is executed in a host machine rather than in an MC68000-based system. A cross assembler is written in a high-level language so that it can be run on a variety of host computers. In conjunction with a simulator, the cross assembler enables a designer to develop and test all but the time-dependent software before the hardware has been built.

Since cross assemblers and simulators are available at minimal cost for most microprocessors, they serve as low-cost yet valuable tools for the development of microprocessor software. The user can create and correct the software with an on-line text editor in a time-sharing system. Cross assemblers and simulators for widely used microprocessors, which are designed to run in personal computers, are also available.

The role and usage of a cross assembler in the process of microprocessor software development are depicted in Fig. 4-1. The outputs produced by the cross assembler consist of a listing, which serves as a programming aid, and an object module. One or more object modules can be linked to produce a load module. Some cross assemblers output load modules directly and, therefore, do not require linkers. The listing contains the line number, location, and machine code for each assembled instruction, as well as the source code. In addition, a cross reference table that lists all the symbols defined in the source program along with their

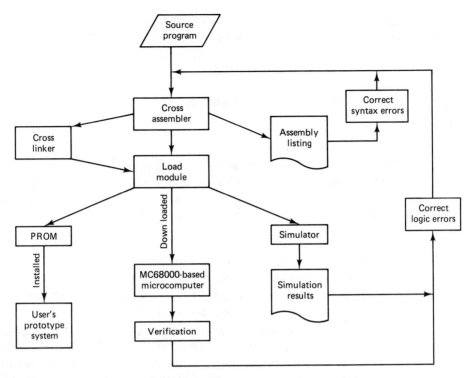

Figure 4-1 Use of cross assemblers and simulators.

addresses is generated. If syntax errors are detected, the types of errors and where they occur are identified so that the source program can be easily corrected and reassembled.

Once the assembler errors have been corrected, the object module may be used as input to a simulator, which simulates the execution of each instruction. Program status, register contents, and memory contents can be displayed under the control of simulator commands. Therefore, logic errors can be detected without executing the load module in the actual microprocessor. The process of correcting errors, reassembling, and testing using the simulator may need to be repeated several times. The object module may also be loaded through direct linkage (i.e., downloading) into a microcomputer so that it can be tested by the actual microprocessor.

If the software to be developed is for a user's prototype system, it needs to be finally installed in the user-designed prototype. After the software has been debugged using a simulator or a microcomputer based on the target microprocessor, it is then integrated into the prototype system by putting it into PROMs and then installing the PROMs in the prototype.

The load module produced by the cross assembler/linker is typically in the ASCII-coded hexadecimal form. In other words, the code consists of the ASCII characters for the hexadecimal digits 0 through 9 and A through F. Because the program may be quite long, a load module is segmented into several records, each containing part of the machine code and a load address. The standard format used by an MC68000 cross assembler and/or linker for generating load modules is the so-called S-record format, which is discussed in Sec. 4-3.

4-2 MC68000 Educational Computer Board (ECB)

Hardware organization

The Motorola MC68000 Educational Computer Board, or simply ECB, is an MC68000-based single-board microcomputer. The board contains necessary logic that is designed to provide an inexpensive tool for executing and testing MC68000 assembly language programs. As shown in Fig. 4-2, the major hardware features included in an ECB are as follows:

1. An MC68000L4 microprocessor operating at the speed of 4 MHz.
2. 16k-byte ROM to store the monitor called TUTOR. The range of the on-board ROM is 008000 to 00BFFF, and addresses from 0000000 to 000007 are also read-only, which are reserved for the reset exception vector.
3. 32K-byte RAM to store the user's program and data. The on-board RAM occupies the addresses from 000008 to 007FFF. However the locations from 000008 to 0003FF are allocated for the exception vector table and the area from 000400 to 0008FF are reserved for use as temporary storage by TUTOR. Therefore the user's program must be loaded into the area from 000900 to 007FFF.
4. Two asynchronous serial interface devices (ACIA) to provide two serial ports. Port 1 is for connection to a CRT terminal as the system console. Port 2 provides a link to a host, typically a development system or fully equipped microcomputer system.
5. An integrated parallel interface and timer device (PI/T). This device provides a parallel port (port 3) for connection to a Centronix type printer. Also provided by this device is a serial interface for an audiocassette recorder.
6. A reset button and an abort button. The reset button is used to initialize the board to the initial state, and the abort button to suspend user program execution and to return control to TUTOR for subsequent command entry.
7. A wire-wrap area of 3.5 square inches. This area allows the user to develop interfaces for specific applications. Through a 46-pin connection area, the user has direct access to most of the MC68000 signal pins.

One-line assembler/disassembler

To simplify program entering and displaying, TUTOR includes a one-line assembler/disassembler as part of the monitor. This simple assembler allows the user to deposit a program directly into memory in assembly language instead of machine code. After a source statement is entered, it is immediately translated to the corresponding machine instruction, which is then stored in memory. Con-

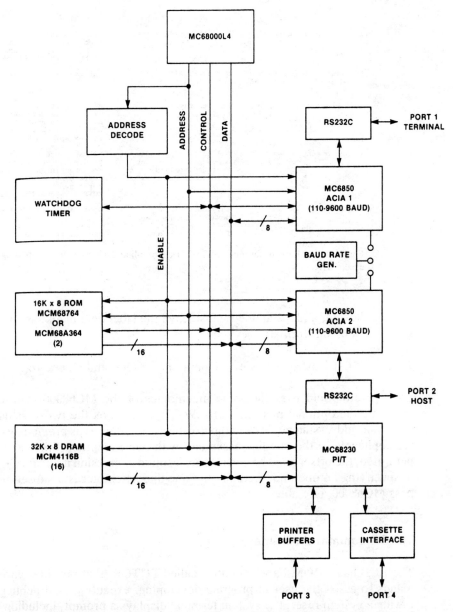

Figure 4-2 Functional block diagram of the ECB. (Courtesy of Motorola, Inc.)

versely, to display a program stored in memory, each machine instruction is translated back (disassembled) to the symbolic form before being displayed.

Since this one-line assembler does not save the source code, its functions are much more restricted than those of a usual two-pass assembler such as the one in Chap. 3. Figure 4-3 lists the major restrictions imposed by this one-line assembler and shows how to get around them. The most notable one is that labels

Function	Restriction	Alternative
1. Storage and data definition directives	Only DC.W is available.	For DC.B and DC.L, use memory deposite command. For DS, skip the number of bytes to be reserved.
2. Directives other than DC and DS such as END, ORG, etc.	Not available.	Not required for TUTOR.
3. Label field	Must be blank, no label is allowed.	An instruction or location is referenced by using an absolute address or expression. For example, BRA $1234
4. Addressing modes	All addressing modes are supported except that no label is allowed in an operand.	Use absolute expression to specify the offset required in an addressing mode. For example, MOVE.W $2000,$3000(A1)
5. Constants	Only decimal (N), hexadecimal ($N) and ASCII ('string') forms are allowed.	Octal and binary numbers can be avoided by converting them to decimal or hexadecimal.

Figure 4-3 Major differences of TUTOR's one-line assembler from a two-pass assembler.

are not allowed, and a statement must leave the label field blank, as shown in the general statement format:

(At least one space)   Operator   Operand,Operand. . .

The operator field uses the same mnemonics of the MC68000 instruction set, including the optional postfixes, .B, .W, .L, and .S, as the two-pass assembler. The same addressing modes and their respective notations as previously discussed are applicable to the one-line assembler with one exception. Since a label is not permitted, the offset must be given as an absolute expression if an offset is required in specifying an operand. Actually the one-line assembler is a subset of the two-pass MC68000 assembler.

TUTOR command summary

The ECB has a ROM-based monitor, called TUTOR, that provides various commands to assist the user in program developing, executing, and debugging. Following a system reset, the system terminal displays a prompt, including the monitor name and version number, as

TUTOR 1.3 >

and waits for a command. After a proper command is entered, a carriage return (CR) causes the command to be processed. Upon command completion, the system returns to TUTOR and displays a prompt indicating that it is ready to accept the next command.

All TUTOR commands along with special function keys are summarized in Fig. 4-4. In describing the command syntax, the following notations are used:

⟨A⟩ indicates that "A" is a parameter

[B] indicates that "B" is optional

A typical command requires some parameters such as memory addresses and data. When a command has more than one parameter, they are separated by one or more spaces. In specifying a parameter, unlike the assembler syntax, a number without a prefix is interpreted as a hexadecimal number. A decimal number must be preceded by a $ sign. For example, the expression

$$7600 + \$40 - 3AB4$$

is evaluated as hexadecimal 7600 plus decimal 40 minus hexadecimal 3AB4.

When an expression is used as an address parameter, an offset is always added to form the physical address. In order to support relocatable code, TUTOR provides eight offset registers, denoted by R0–R7, each of which contains a 24-bit offset. These registers are not actual MC68000 registers, and their contents are used only to modify address parameters in commands. An address parameter can be given as an expression plus an offset such as 160 + R2. If no offset register is given, the expression is automatically added by offset R0. During a system initialization, all offset registers are set to zero. Except for R7, which always remains zero, an offset register can be set to a nonzero value by the command

.R⟨register number⟩ ⟨expression⟩

In running and debugging absolute code, address parameters are to be entered as actual physical addresses. In such cases, no offset register is needed. In addition, offset register R0 should not be modified after being initialized to zero.

Entering a program

A program is entered into the ECB by using the memory-modifying command, which has the form:

MM (or simply M) ⟨address⟩[;⟨options⟩]

If option DI (disassembler/assembler invoke) is chosen, this command displays memory contents in disassembled form and accepts assembly instructions as new contents. Otherwise, data are displayed and entered in the hexadecimal format. After the command and a CR are entered, the addressed byte, word, longword, or instruction, depending on the given option, is displayed followed by a ?. The user may enter the new contents or leave the current content unchanged by not entering anything. This memory-update operation may continue with the next location by entering a CR following the new content. If this command is used to display and modify data, its operation may also continue by opening the next backward location with a ∧ followed by a CR or by reopening the current location with an = followed by a CR. A . followed by a CR terminates the MM command and returns to TUTOR with a > prompt.

Command	Description
BF <address1> <address2> <word> (Block of memory fill)	This command fills memory words starting from <address1> through <address2> with the data word given in <word>.
BM <address1> <address2> <address3> (Block of memory move)	This command moves a memory block starting with <address1> through <address2> to another block beginning at <address3>.
BR [<address>[;<count>]] (Breakpoint set)	This command sets one to eight breakpoints. <address> indicates the location of a breakpoint and <count> specifies a count that is decremented each time the breakpoint is encountered until count = 0. If no parameters are given, the BR command displays all breakpoints.
BS <address1> <address2> <data> [<mask>] (Block of memory search; options: B, W, L)	This command searches memory starting with <address1> through <address2> for the data given in <data>. The optional <mask>, if used, is ANDed to data.
BT <address1> <address2> (Block of memory test)	This command performs a memory test starting with <address1> through <address2> (both are even addresses). If no error is detected, the tested memory block is set to all zeros; otherwise, a message is displayed.
DC <expression> (Data conversion)	This command computes <expression> and shows the result in both hexadecimal and decimal forms.
DF (Display formatted registers)	This command displays all MC68000 registers: D0 - D7, A0 - A6, PC, SR, USP and SSP.
DU[<port number>] <address1> <address2> [<text..>] (Dump memory (S-record))	This command sends out memory contents starting with <address1> through <address2> to <port number> in the S-record format. The optional <text>, if used, is output as part of the header.
GD [<address>] (Go direct)	This command starts program execution from <address> without setting breakpoints. If the optional starting address is not used, execution begins at the address in PC.
GO (or G) [<address>] (Go)	This command starts program execution from <address> until a breakpoint in the breakpoint table is encountered or an exception occurs. If a breakpoint has a count associated, program execution does not stop at the breakpoint until its count reaches 0.
GT <breakpoint address> (Go until breakpoint)	This command sets a temporary breakpoint at <breakpoint address>, and starts program execution at the address in PC until the temporary breakpoint or one with a zero count in the breakpoint table is encountered.
HE (Help)	This command displays all the available commands.
LO[<port number>][;<options>] [=text] (Load (S-records); options: X, -C)	This command loads machine code or data in the S-record format from <port number> to memory. The optional <=text>, if used with port 2, sends a message to that port before loading starts.
MD[<port number>] <address1> [<count>][;<option>] (Memory display; option: DI)	This command displays <count> bytes of memory starting with <address> using <port number>. The optional DI, if present, displays data in the disassembled form. Otherwise, the hexadecimal form is used.
MM (or M) <address> [;<options>] (Memory modify; options: W, L, O, V, N, DI)	This command displays and, if needed, modifies memory content at <address>. The current content after being displayed is replaced by the new data if entered. A CR causes the command to repeat for the next location and a "." terminates the command.
MS <address> <data...> (Memory set)	This command sets memory beginning at <address> with hexadecimal data or ASCII string given as <data...>.
NOBR [<address> <address>....] (Breakpoint remove)	This command removes breakpoints at <address> from the breakpoint table. If no address is given, all breakpoints are removed.
NOPA (Reset printer attach)	This command detaches the parallel printer from the system terminal connected to port 1.
OF (Display offsets)	This command displays the offsets contained in registers R0 - R7.

Figure 4-4 TUTOR commands summary.

Command	Description
PA (Printer attach)	This command logically attaches the parallel printer to the system terminal connected to port 1. Once attached, the printer prints any information that is displayed on the system terminal.
PF[<port number>] (Port format)	This command displays and, if needed, modifies the character format and other parameters of serial port 1 or 2 as specified by <port number>.
TM [<exit character>] (Transparent mode)	This command connects serial ports 1 and 2 together. When <exit character> is entered from port 1, direct connection between ports 1 and 2 is terminated and <trailing character> is sent to port 2.
TR (or T) [<count>] (Trace)	This command traces <count> instructions starting with the address in PC. A CR causes next instruction to be traced.
TT <breakpoint address> (Temporary breakpoint trace)	This command sets a temporary breakpoint at <breakpoint address>, and starts tracing at the address in PC until a breakpoint with a zero count is encountered.
VE[<port number>] [=text] (Verify (S-records))	This command verifies memory contents with the data in the S-record format from <port number>. The optional <=text>, if used, is sent to port 2.
* text.... (Send message)	This command sends <text> to port 2.
.A<register number> [<expression>] (Display/set address register)	This command displays the address register selected by <register number> and, as an option, modifies the content with <expression>.
.D<register number> [<expression>] (Display/set data register)	This command displays the data register selected by <register number> and, as an option, modifies the content with <expression>.
.R<register number> [<expression>] (Display/set relative offset register)	This command displays the relative offset register selected by <register number> and, as an option, modifies the content with <expression>.
.PC [<expression>] (Display/set program counter)	This command displays the program counter and, as an option, modifies the content with <expression>.
.SR [<expression>] (Display/set status register)	This command displays the status register and, as an option, modifies the content with <expression>.
.SS [<expression>] (Display/set supervisor stack pointer)	This command displays the supervisor stack pointer and, as an option, modifies the content with <expression>.
.US [<expression>] (Display/set user stack pointer)	This command displays the user stack pointer and, as an option, modifies the content with <expression>.
(BREAK) (Abort command)	This key aborts any command currently doing console I/O.
(DEL) (Delete character)	This key deletes the last entered character.
(CTRL D) (Redisplay line)	This key redisplays the entire line.
(CTRL H) (Delete character)	This key is equivalent to the DEL key.
(CTRL W) (Suspend output)	This key suspends output to the terminal. Depressing any other key resumes the output.
(CTRL X) (Cancel command line)	This key cancels the entire line.
(CR) (Process command line)	This key causes the command to start.

Figure 4-4 (*continued*)

```
TUTOR  1.3 ) MM 2000;DI
002000    FFFF          DC.W    $FFFF ? DC.W 1
002002    FFFF          DC.W    $FFFF ? DC.W -3
002004    FFFF          DC.W    $FFFF ? DC.W 5
002006    FFFF          DC.W    $FFFF ? DC.W -7
002008    FFFF          DC.W    $FFFF ? DC.W 9
00200A    FFFF          DC.W    $FFFF ? DC.W -11
00200C    FFFF          DC.W    $FFFF ? DC.W 13
00200E    FFFF          DC.W    $FFFF ? DC.W -15
002010    FFFF          DC.W    $FFFF ? DC.W 8
002012    FFFF          DC.W    $FFFF ?
002014    FFFF          DC.W    $FFFF ? MOVE.W #0,D0
002018    FFFF          DC.W    $FFFF ? MOVE.W $2010,D7
00201C    FFFF          DC.W    $FFFF ? SUBQ.W #1,D7
00201E    FFFF          DC.W    $FFFF ? MOVEA.W #$2000,A0
002022    FFFF          DC.W    $FFFF ? CMPI.W #0,(A0)+
002026    FFFF          DC.W    $FFFF ? BLE.S *
002028    FFFF          DC.W    $FFFF ? ADD.W -2(A0),D0
00202C    FFFF          DC.W    $FFFF ? DBF D7,$2022
002030    FFFF          DC.W    $FFFF ? MOVE.W D0,$2012
002034    FFFF          DC.W    $FFFF ? MOVE.B #228,D7
002038    FFFF          DC.W    $FFFF ? TRAP #14
00203A    FFFF          DC.W    $FFFF ?.


TUTOR  1.3 ) MM 2026;DI
002026    6FFE          BLE.S   $002026 ? BLE.S $202C
002028    D068FFFE      ADD.W   -2(A0),D0 ?.

TUTOR  1.3 )
```

Figure 4-5 Example of entering a program with TUTOR.

As an example, assume that a typical assembly language program such as the one given next is to be executed using the ECB.

```
              ORG       $2000
ARY           DC.W      1,-3,5,-7,9,-11,13,-15
SIZE          DC.W      8
SUM           DS.W      1
START         MOVE.W    #0,D0
              MOVE.W    SIZE,D7
              SUBQ.W    #1,D7
              MOVEA.W   #ARY,A0
LOOP          CMPI.W    #0,(A0)+
              BLE.S     ENDLP
              ADD.W     -2(A0),D0
ENDLP         DBF       D7,LOOP
              MOVE.W    D0,SUM
              STOP      #$2000
              END       START
```

Figure 4-5 shows the step-by-step sequence for loading this program into memory. As seen from the figure, several instructions have been modified. Most of them are syntax changes due to the limitations of the one-line assembler. In order to verify program execution, it is necessary to return to TUTOR after the program is completed. This is why the last executable instruction in the program, which is

```
STOP       #$2000
```

is replaced by the two instructions

```
MOVE.B     #228,D7
TRAP       #14
```

This instruction sequence is the exit system call, which causes a clean return to TUTOR without affecting the registers and memory contents of the user program. However, if it is called in a user-mode program, a privilege violation exception will occur.

Before starting program execution, it is desirable to obtain a program listing for verification. This can be accomplished by using the memory display command, which has the format:

MD[⟨port number⟩] ⟨address⟩ [⟨count⟩][;⟨option⟩]

where ⟨port number⟩ is the I/O port of the displaying device, ⟨address⟩ and ⟨count⟩ are, respectively, the beginning address and the size in bytes of the memory block to be displayed, and ⟨option⟩ specifies the display format. For example,

MD3   2000   3A;DI

generates a listing of the program previously entered through the parallel printer, as given in Fig. 4-6. This disassembled listing looks different from the originally entered program because some instructions may have more than one assembly language equivalent. In addition, the disassembler always displays addresses in hexadecimal and everything else in decimal.

Program execution and breakpoints

Execution of a target program is initiated by passing control to the program from TUTOR. When a program has logic errors, an effective way to locate them is to execute the program in portions. By stopping at crucial points and checking intermediate results in registers and pertinent memory locations, the errors can be identified quickly.

To assist in program debugging, TUTOR allows the user to run all or any portion of a program using the breakpoint feature. A breakpoint can be set at any instruction in the program. When the program attempts to execute the instruction at a breakpoint, program execution is suspended and control is returned to TUTOR. Therefore, after a breakpoint is encountered, the user can verify results or even modify register and memory contents before resuming program execution

```
002000    0001FFFD    OR.B     #-3,D1
002004    0005FFF9    OR.B     #-7,D5
002008    0009        DC.W     $0009
00200A    FFF5        DC.W     $FFF5
00200C    000D        DC.W     $000D
00200E    FFF1        DC.W     $FFF1
002010    0008        DC.W     $0008
002012    FFFF        DC.W     $FFFF
002014    303C0000    MOVE.W   #0,D0
002018    3E382010    MOVE.W   $00002010,D7
00201C    5347        SUBQ.W   #1,D7
00201E    307C2000    MOVE.W   #8192,A0
002022    0C580000    CMP.W    #0,(A0)+
002026    6F04        BLE.S    $00202C
002028    D068FFFE    ADD.W    -2(A0),D0
00202C    51CFFFF4    DBF.L    D7,$002022
002030    31C02012    MOVE.W   D0,$00002012
002034    1E3C00E4    MOVE.B   #228,D7
002038    4E4E        TRAP     #14
```

Figure 4-6 Disassembled listing of a sample program.

from the breakpoint. With the BR (breakpoint) command, up to eight breakpoints can be set at any one time.

When a breakpoint is set in a loop, it is sometimes desirable to allow the program to iterate through the loop a certain number of times before being stopped at the breakpoint. This can be accomplished by associating a count with the breakpoint. Each time a breakpoint is encountered, its count is decremented by one, and program execution continues as usual until the count reaches zero. After the count is decremented to zero, program execution will stop each time the breakpoint is encountered.

Using the sample program in this section as an example, Fig. 4-7 illustrates the use of a breakpoint. The command

```
BR      202C;4
```

inserts a breakpoint before the DBF instruction with the initial count set to 4. This will cause program execution to stop on the fifth encounter of the DBF instruction. After a system reset, the status register is initialized to $2700, putting the MC68000 in the supervisor mode. If the target program is to be executed in the user mode, the command

```
.SR      700
```

would be needed to clear the S bit in the status register. For the sample program, although all registers to be used are initialized in the program, it is a good practice

```
TUTOR  1.3 >  BR 202C;4

BREAKPOINTS
00202C     00202C;4

TUTOR  1.3 >  .US 1F00

TUTOR  1.3 >  .SS 1800

TUTOR  1.3 >  GO 2014
PHYSICAL ADDRESS=00002014

AT BREAKPOINT
PC=0000202C SR=2708=.S7.N... US=00001F00 SS=00001800
D0=FFFF0006 D1=FFFFFFFF D2=FFFFFFFF D3=FFFFFFFF
D4=FFFFFFFF D5=FFFFFFFF D6=FFFFFFFF D7=FFFF0004
A0=00002008 A1=FFFFFFFF A2=FFFFFFFF A3=FFFFFFFF
A4=FFFFFFFF A5=FFFFFFFF A6=FFFFFFFF A7=00001800
--------------------00202C     51CFFFF4          DBF.L   D7,$002022

TUTOR  1.3 >  NOBR

BREAKPOINTS

TUTOR  1.3 >  GO
PHYSICAL ADDRESS=0000202C

TUTOR  1.3 >  MD 2012 2
002012     00 1C 30 3C 00 00 3E 38  20 10 53 47 30 7C 20 00   ..0<..>8 .SG0I .
```

Figure 4-7 Example of program execution with a breakpoint.

also to set the user stack pointer and/or supervisor stack pointer to point to the user RAM either by TUTOR commands or as part of the program. This is because a stack pointer, depending on the processor mode, is used implicitly in some instructions such as subroutine calls. In the example, the commands

    .US   1F00

and

    .SS   1800

initialize the user stack pointer to 001F00 and the supervisor stack pointer to 001800.

The next command

    GO (or simply G) 2014

causes program execution to start at location 002014. After the loop in the sample program has been iterated 4 times, execution is suspended at the DBF instruction during the fifth iteration. Upon entering TUTOR at the breakpoint, register contents and the instruction pointed to by the PC are displayed.

Suppose that normal program execution is to be resumed for the remaining program. Then, this requires the

    NOBR

command to remove all the breakpoints currently being set, followed by a GO command without specifying the address parameter, which starts execution from the address in PC. After program execution completes and control returns to TUTOR due to the exit system call, the result in location 002012 corresponding to SUM is checked with an MD (memory display) command.

It is worth mentioning that in this case the DF (display registers) command is not applicable for checking the program results. This command displays the contents of MC68000 registers at the last breakpoint encountered or instruction traced instead of the current contents. If program execution was initiated with a GO command without a breakpoint, after returning to TUTOR via an exit system call, the DF command would display the register contents corresponding to the first instruction being executed in the program.

In addition to GO, there are two other commands that can be used to start user-program execution. One is the GD (go direct) command and the other is the GT (go until breakpoint) command. The GD command, which has the format

    GD [⟨address⟩]

starts executing the target program from the specified address if one is given or from the address in PC. Unlike GO, this command executes the entire target program without recognizing any breakpoints previously set in the BR commands. The GT command has the format

GT ⟨breakpoint address⟩

where the parameter is the address of a temporary breakpoint. This command starts program execution from the address pointed to by PC and sets a temporary breakpoint in addition to those entered in the BR command. Unlike the previously described breakpoint, a temporary breakpoint always has a zero count and is removed when it is encountered.

Program tracing

In program debugging, sometimes it is desirable to check instruction executions one by one. This debugging tool, known as *tracing* or *single-stepping*, is provided by the TR command with the form:

TR (or simply T) [⟨count⟩]

where the optional count specifies the number of instructions to be traced. If it is not entered, the count is assumed to be one.

The TR command executes the specified number of instructions one at a time, beginning from the address in PC. After each instruction execution, all registers are displayed, along with the instruction to be executed next. A CR will cause the next instruction to be traced. By checking registers and/or memory contents before and after an instruction, the user can verify whether that instruction has performed the intended operation or not.

Figure 4-8 shows how to use the trace facility. The command sequence in this example sets PC to 002014, traces the first five instructions, and then resumes usual execution until the target program is completed.

Program patching

Frequently, a program needs to be modified several times before all errors can be corrected. Instead of reentering the entire program each time, changes can be made by directly patching the program in memory. Deleting a sequence of instructions can be done by inserting a branch instruction to skip over the instruction block that needs to be deleted. If only a few instructions are to be skipped, a simple way is to change each word occupied by these instructions to $4E71, which corresponds to the NOP instruction.

Inserting a block of instructions can be accomplished as follows. First, save the instruction at the insertion point and replace it with a branch instruction jumping to the end of the program. Then, append to the program the saved instruction and new instructions, followed by another branch instruction returning to the next instruction in sequence. This is illustrated in Fig. 4-9. The example inserts a block of instructions between the two instructions labeled X and Y.

Of course, deletions and insertions can be made by moving a block of code

```
TUTOR  1.3 > .PC 2014

TUTOR  1.3 > TR
PHYSICAL ADDRESS=00002014
PC=00002018 SR=2704=.S7..Z.. US=00001EFC SS=00001800
D0=FFFF0000 D1=FFFFFFFF D2=FFFFFFFF D3=FFFFFFFF
D4=FFFFFFFF D5=FFFFFFFF D6=FFFFFFFF D7=FFFF0007
A0=00002002 A1=FFFFFFFF A2=FFFFFFFF A3=FFFFFFFF
A4=FFFFFFFF A5=FFFFFFFF A6=FFFFFFFF A7=00001800
--------------------002018    3E382010        MOVE.W  $00002010,D7

TUTOR  1.3 :>
PHYSICAL ADDRESS=00002018
PC=0000201C SR=2700=.S7..... US=00001EFC SS=00001800
D0=FFFF0000 D1=FFFFFFFF D2=FFFFFFFF D3=FFFFFFFF
D4=FFFFFFFF D5=FFFFFFFF D6=FFFFFFFF D7=FFFF0008
A0=00002002 A1=FFFFFFFF A2=FFFFFFFF A3=FFFFFFFF
A4=FFFFFFFF A5=FFFFFFFF A6=FFFFFFFF A7=00001800
--------------------00201C    5347            SUBQ.W  #1,D7

TUTOR  1.3 :>
PHYSICAL ADDRESS=0000201C
PC=0000201E SR=2700=.S7..... US=00001EFC SS=00001800
D0=FFFF0000 D1=FFFFFFFF D2=FFFFFFFF D3=FFFFFFFF
D4=FFFFFFFF D5=FFFFFFFF D6=FFFFFFFF D7=FFFF0007
A0=00002002 A1=FFFFFFFF A2=FFFFFFFF A3=FFFFFFFF
A4=FFFFFFFF A5=FFFFFFFF A6=FFFFFFFF A7=00001800
--------------------00201E    307C2000        MOVE.W  #8192,A0

TUTOR  1.3 :>
PHYSICAL ADDRESS=0000201E
PC=00002022 SR=2700=.S7..... US=00001EFC SS=00001800
D0=FFFF0000 D1=FFFFFFFF D2=FFFFFFFF D3=FFFFFFFF
D4=FFFFFFFF D5=FFFFFFFF D6=FFFFFFFF D7=FFFF0007
A0=00002000 A1=FFFFFFFF A2=FFFFFFFF A3=FFFFFFFF
A4=FFFFFFFF A5=FFFFFFFF A6=FFFFFFFF A7=00001800
--------------------002022    0C580000        CMP.W   #0,(A0)+

TUTOR  1.3 :>
PHYSICAL ADDRESS=00002022
PC=00002026 SR=2700=.S7..... US=00001EFC SS=00001800
D0=FFFF0000 D1=FFFFFFFF D2=FFFFFFFF D3=FFFFFFFF
D4=FFFFFFFF D5=FFFFFFFF D6=FFFFFFFF D7=FFFF0007
A0=00002002 A1=FFFFFFFF A2=FFFFFFFF A3=FFFFFFFF
A4=FFFFFFFF A5=FFFFFFFF A6=FFFFFFFF A7=00001800
--------------------002026    6F04            BLE.S   $00202C

TUTOR  1.3 :> GO
PHYSICAL ADDRESS=00002026
```

Figure 4-8 Program tracing.

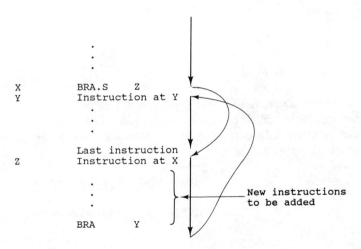

Figure 4-9 Program patching by inserting new instructions at the end of the program.

```
DC.W    1                       ; DC.W    1,-3,5,-7,9,-11,13,-15
DC.W    -3
DC.W    5
DC.W    -7
DC.W    9
DC.W    -11
DC.W    13
DC.W    -15
DC.W    8                       ; DC.W    8
DC.W    ?                       ; DS.W    1
MOVE.W  #0,D0                   ;ASSUME THAT A6 HAS PROGRAM ORIGIN
MOVE.W  $10(A6),D7              ;$10 IS THE RELATIVE ADDRESS OF SIZE
SUBQ.W  #1,D7
LEA     0(A6),A0
CMPI.W  #0,(A0)+
BLE.S   *+4                     ;4 IS THE BRANCH DISTANCE (ENDLP - BLE.S)
ADD.W   -2(A0),D0
DBF     D7,*-$E                 ;-$E IS THE BRANCH DISTANCE (LOOP - DBF)
MOVE.W  D0,$12(A6)              ;$12 IS THE RELATIVE ADDRESS OF SUM
MOVE.B  #228,D7
TRAP    #14
```

Figure 4-10 Relocatable version of the sample program in Fig. 4-6.

upward or downward and by filling the gap with new instructions. However, care must be taken to make sure that instruction operands in the program are modified accordingly to reflect the address changes of all moved instructions and variables.

Relative offset registers

The sample program in this section will execute properly if and only if the program is entered starting at 002000. This is because operands ARY, SIZE, and SVAR are referenced in the program by using the absolute addressing mode. With the index addressing mode, the program can be relocated to a new location, provided that the index register is set to the new origin before execution begins. Figure 4-10 is a relocatable version of the sample program using the one-line assembler syntax. The program assumes that register A6 will be initialized with the actual starting address prior to program execution. Note that to make the program relocatable, it is necessary to replace the instruction

```
MOVEA.W      #ARY,A0
```

with

```
LEA      0(A6),A0
```

Address parameters in the commands to enter, execute, and debug this program can be specified as relative addresses, independent on the physical origin, by using offset registers. For example, the following command sequence will enter and execute this program starting at location 003000.

```
.R6       3000          ;USE R6 FOR OFFSET AND SET IT TO $3000
MM        R6;DI
          .             ;ENTER THE PROGRAM AS SHOWN IN FIG. 4-10


          .

.SS       -800+R6       ;SET SS TO $2800
```

```
.A6        R6              ;SET A6 TO PROGRAM ORIGIN
GO         14 + R6         ;BEGIN EXECUTION FROM THE FIRST INSTRUCTION
MD         12 + R6 2       ;DISPLAY RESULT
```

Should it become desirable to relocate the program to a new origin—for instance, 008050—then the machine code can be moved without any modification by the block move command

```
BM        R6       3A + R6       8050
```

After setting R6 to the new origin 008050 by

```
.R6       8050
```

the same command sequence,

```
.SS        − 800 + R6
.A6        R6
GO         14 + R6
MD         12 + R6 2
```

will execute the program properly starting at the new origin and display the final result.

4-3 S-Records

Program saving and loading

The ECB allows memory contents, which may be code and/or data, to be saved on and reloaded from external storage devices. This facility eliminates the need to key in the program each time it is run. One way is to save the program on a cassette tape. This requires a cassette recorder to be connected to port 4 of the ECB, which has the necessary interface for converting signals between digital and audio forms.

A second way is through a host system to use its mass storage device for saving and loading a program. A typical host could be a fully-equipped development system with a variety of software and hardware resources. Therefore, this method also offers the advantage that a user can utilize the host's software facilities, such as text editor, assembler, and linker, for making program changes. As shown in Fig. 4-11, the host is connected to port 2 of the ECB by a serial link. Each acts as a remote terminal to the other. Transferring a file from host to ECB is called *downloading* and from ECB to host is called *uploading*.

S-records

With either option, memory image is saved and reloaded as an absolute load file consisting of several S-records. In order to transmit an S-record in an asynchron-

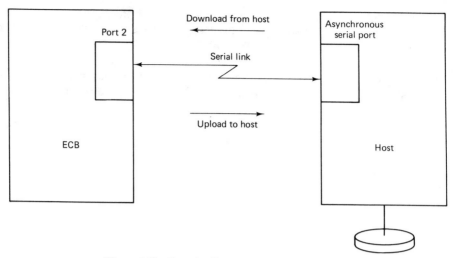

Figure 4-11 Downloading and uploading a program.

ous serial format that uses 7 data bits per character, the record cannot be in the binary form. Instead, each byte of binary data is represented by two ASCII-coded hexadecimal digits in an S-record.

Because a program may be quite long, a load module is segmented into several data records, each containing part of code/data, followed by a termination record. Each record is preceded by two ASCII characters to identify the record type. The possible record types are S0, S1, S2, S3, S5, S7, S8, and S9. For the ECB, a typical S-record file is composed of one or more S1 data records followed by an S9 termination record.

An S1 record has the general format

S1⟨bb⟩⟨aaaa⟩⟨ddd . . . dd⟩⟨xx⟩

where each lowercase letter represents an ASCII-coded hexadecimal digit and angle brackets are added for clarity but are not actually included in the record. The meaning of each field is as follows:

Record type field (S1): Contains two characters indicating the type of this record. The S1 type means a code/data record with a 2-byte load address.

Record length field (bb): Contains two hexadecimal ASCII digits representing the number of bytes (character pairs) in the record excluding the record type and record length fields. Therefore, the number of data bytes in an S1 record may not exceed 252.

Load address field (aaaa): Contains four hexadecimal ASCII digits representing the 16-bit starting memory address at which the code and data in this record are to be loaded. The leftmost digit corresponds to the most significant 4 bits of the load address.

Data field (bbb. . .bb): Consists of actual machine code or data. Again, each byte of binary code/data is encoded in two characters.

Checksum field (xx): Consists of two hexadecimal ASCII digits that are the 1's complement of the sum of all bytes in the record length, load address, and data fields. In other words,

$$xx = 1\text{'s complement of bb} + aa + aa + dd + dd + \cdots + dd$$

This field is provided for error checking during record transfers.

As an example, the S1 record

S1092012FFFF303C00005A

indicates the following:

1. The record is an S1 record with $9 - 2 - 1 = 6$ bytes of data.
2. The starting address to load the code/data is hexadecimal 2012.
3. The code/data field consists of bytes FF, FF, 30, 3C, 00, and 00.
4. The checksum byte is 5A formed as

$$1\text{'s complement of } 09 + 20 + 12 + FF + FF + 30 + 3C + 00 + 00$$

The termination record for a block of S1 records is an S9 record. It has the same format as the S1 record except that an S9 record does not have a data field. The S9 record format is

S9⟨bb⟩⟨aaaa⟩⟨xx⟩

where bb is the record length in bytes and xx is the checksum. The address field, aaaa, contains a 16-bit transfer address, which is to be used as the initial value of PC after the program is loaded. A typical linker would assign the transfer address according to the operand given in the END statement. If no transfer address is specified, this field will be filled with four ASCII zeros. Since the number of bytes in the address and checksum fields is fixed, the record length for an S9 record is always 03.

An S-record module may include an optional S0 record as a header preceding the first data record. An S0 record may contain any character string to identify the module. This record will not actually be loaded into memory, but it simply provides descriptive information on this module.

The record format of the S0 type is

S0⟨bb⟩0000⟨ddd . . . d⟩⟨xx⟩

where bb is the record length in bytes, ddd. . .d is any character string, and xx is the checksum. Since there is no need for a load address, this field is filled with four ASCII zeros. For example, suppose that we wish to include PROGRAM 1 as the header of an S-record module. Then, the first record in the module will be

S00C000050524F4752414D20318A

For an S-record module generated by TUTOR, if no header message is given, the module will include an S0 record with no data field.

Although the MC68000 supports 16M bytes of memory, as previously mentioned the ECB has only 48K bytes of RAM and ROM located at 000000 to 00BFFF. Since any address of the on-board memory can be specified in 16 bits, S-record module produced by TUTOR consists of records of types S0, S1, and S9 only. As an example of an S-record module, consider the program given in Fig. 4-6. If this program is converted to the S-record format without a header message, the resulting module will be as shown in Fig. 4-12. The module begins with an S0 record with no header message, has four S1 records containing the memory image, and is terminated with an S9 record with transfer address zero.

For an MC68000-based system that uses a full 24-bit address to address memory, an S-record module uses S2 and S8 records as code/data and termination records. The formats of S2 and S8 types are same as those of S1 and S9 except that the address field of an S2 or S8 record contains a 3-byte address. Likewise, the record type S3 and S7, which use 4-byte load and transfer addresses, are designed to support 32-bit systems—for example, 68020-based systems.

A module may include an optional S5 record that indicates the number of code/data records (S1, S2, or S3) in the module. An S5 record has no code/data field, and its 2-byte address field is used to specify the code/data record count.

Figure 4-13 summarizes all S-record types. However, TUTOR does not accept records of types S3, S5, and S7, nor does it generate records of types S2, S3, S5, S7, and S8.

```
S0030000FC
(Record type: header; Message: none)

S11320000001FFFD0005FFF90009FFF5000DFFF1D8
(Record type: data; Load address: 2000;
No. of data bytes: 19 - 2 - 1 = 16;
Data bytes to be loaded: 00, 01, FF, ..., F1)

S11320100008FFFF303C00003E3820105347307C5E
(Record type: data; Load address: 2010;
No. of data bytes: 19 - 2 - 1 = 16;
Data bytes to be loaded: 00, 08, FF, ..., 7C)

S113202020000C5800006F04D068FFFE51CFFFF46D
(Record type: data; Load address: 2020;
No. of data bytes: 19 - 2 - 1 = 16;
Data bytes to be loaded: 00, 0C, 58, ..., F4)

S10D203031C020121E3C00E44E4EA5
(Record type: data; Load address: 2030;
No. of data bytes: 13 - 2 - 1 = 10;
Data bytes to be loaded: 31, C0, 20, ..., 4E)

S9030000FC
(Record type: termination; Transfer address: none)
```

Figure 4-12 S-records for the program in Fig. 4-6.

Record Type Field	S0
Description	Header record
Record Length Field	1 ASCII digit pair
Address Field	0000
Data Field	0 - 252 ASCII digit pairs, 0 - 252 characters
Checksum Field	1 ASCII digit pair

S1 Record Format

Record Type Field	S1
Description	Data record with 2-byte load address
Record Length Field	1 ASCII digit pair
Address Field	2 ASCII digit pairs, 16-bit load address
Data Field	1 - 252 ASCII digit pairs, 1 - 252 bytes of code/data
Checksum Field	1 ASCII digit pair

S2 Record Format

Record Type Field	S2
Description	Data record with 3-byte load address
Record Length Field	1 ASCII digit pair
Address Field	3 ASCII digit pairs, 24-bit load address
Data Field	1 - 251 ASCII digit pairs, 1 - 251 bytes of code/data
Checksum Field	1 ASCII digit pair

S3 Record Format

Record Type Field	S3
Description	Data record with 4-byte load address
Record Length Field	1 ASCII digit pair
Address Field	4 ASCII digit pairs, 32-bit load address
Data Field	1 - 250 ASCII digit pairs, 1 - 250 bytes of code/data
Checksum Field	1 ASCII digit pair

S5 Record Format

Record Type Field	S5
Description	Size record
Record Length Field	1 ASCII digit pair
Address Field	2 ASCII digit pairs, number of data records in the module
Data Field	None
Checksum Field	1 ASCII digit pair

S7 Record Format

Record Type Field	S7
Description	Termination record with 4-byte transfer address
Record Length Field	1 ASCII digit pair (05)
Address Field	4 ASCII digit pairs, 32-bit transfer address
Data Field	None
Checksum Field	1 ASCII digit pair

Figure 4-13 Summary of S-record types.

S8 Record Format

Record Type Field	S8
Description	Termination record with 3-byte transfer address
Record Length Field	1 ASCII digit pair (04)
Address Field	3 ASCII digit pair, 24-bit transfer address
Data Field	None
Checksum Field	1 ASCII digit pair

S9 Record Format

Record Type Field	S9
Description	Termination record with 2-byte transfer address
Record Length Field	1 ASCII digit pair (03)
Address Field	3 ASCII digit pair, 24-bit transfer address
Data Field	None
Checksum Field	1 ASCII digit pair

Figure 4-13 (*continued*)

TUTOR commands for saving and loading programs

Saving a program requires the DU (dump) command, which has the form

DU[⟨port number⟩] ⟨address 1⟩⟨address 2⟩[⟨text. . .⟩]

The port number specifies the output device: 2 for the host and 4 for the cassette recorder. The two address parameters define the beginning and ending addresses of the memory block to be saved. The DU command saves the specified memory block by first converting the contents to S-records and then transmitting these records to the specified output port. An optional text string may be included in the output S0 record as a header message. As an example of the DU command, the S-record in Fig. 4-12 was generated by the command

DU3   2000   203A

The command to load a saved program performs the reverse operation: loading an absolute load module in the S-record format to memory after being converted from ASCII to binary. The load command has the form

LO[⟨port number⟩][;⟨options⟩][= ⟨text. . .⟩]

where ⟨port number⟩ is the input port number. This command has three options:

1. ; − C for ignoring the checksum in each S-record
2. ;X for displaying input on the system terminal while loading
3. = ⟨text. . .⟩ for sending a character string to port 2 to request the host to begin downloading

Note that unlike the DU command, LO does not specify beginning and ending addresses because the load address for each data record is included in the input file.

Development Tools   Chap. 4

4-4 Development Systems*

Microcomputer development system

A microcomputer development system provides both software and hardware design aids, from initial program development to debugging the prototype hardware of microprocessor-based systems. In addition to the processor module, other major hardware components of a development system include the following:

Large memory: A development system is run under the control of a rather sophisticated monitor that occupies a considerable amount of memory. To support the system software and to provide the user with enough storage for program development, the main memory of a typical development system is over 512K bytes.

Hard disk: To eliminate the need to key in a program each time it is run, a mass storage device is a necessity. Just as a disk unit is a required part of a large computer system, a hard disk is a standard mass storage device in a development system. The disk is used to store system programs, user programs, and data.

System console: A console provides a means of communication between the user and the system. Typically, a CRT terminal is used as the system console to bring up the system, input commands, and create programs. Results are displayed on the screen at a speed of up to approximately 1000 characters per second (9600 baud).

Printer: A printer is needed to produce a hard copy of the program or data.

PROM programmer: A PROM programmer allows the user to program PROMs through the development system under software control.

Emulator: An emulator is a real-time debugging facility. With the accompanying software, it is an efficient development tool for microprocessor-based hardware development as well as software development.

Logic analyzer: This is a development tool for digital hardware design. It allows a user to monitor several signals simultaneously and to examine the relationships among them.

The operating system for the development system consists of a monitor and a group of system programs stored on a mass storage device. When the system is turned on, the monitor becomes resident in the memory and supervises the operation of the system. The main functions of the monitor are to manage both the hardware and software resources and to provide an interface between the user and the system. The monitor recognizes the user's commands from the system console and then performs the requested tasks by executing the appropriate system routines. In addition, the monitor includes file management routines and I/O handlers. This allows the user to simplify the I/O programming and to create, manipulate, and delete files. The system programs normally include a text editor

* This section has been adapted from *Microcomputers for Engineers and Scientists, 2/E,* © 1987, Glenn A. Gibson/Yu-cheng Liu, by permission of Prentice-Hall, Inc., Englewood Cliffs, New Jersey.

for creating and modifying source programs and other ASCII files, an assembler, one or more interpreters and compilers (typical high-level languages for micro-computers are BASIC, Fortran, C, and Pascal), a linker, and a set of utility routines. Two utility routines that are frequently available are a real-time debugging routine, which is used in conjunction with an emulator, and a routine for controlling a PROM programmer.

All development systems are interactive systems in which commands, source code, and data are entered through a terminal. When interactive processing is employed, the user may add, delete, or change source text by giving the proper commands to the text editor and then, in the case of adding or changing text, typing in the desired text string. The text editor may also be used to store newly created or modified source modules as files on a storage device or recall them from a storage device for further editing.

PROM programmers

A PROM programmer is a device for installing programs into PROM memory chips, and when used with a development system, it may be placed under software control. The front panel of a PROM programmer includes one or more sockets for inserting the PROM chips that are to be programmed or examined. There must be a separate socket for each of the possible PROM pin configurations that may be plugged into the programmer.

The control signals for programming a specific PROM are not TTL-compatible, and they vary, depending on the memory device being programmed. To accommodate these varying electrical requirements, some programmers are built to accept circuit modules that provide customized electrical outputs. Each module is called a *personality card* and provides all the electrical signals needed for programming a given type of memory chip. In addition to personality cards for the various PROMs, a PROM programmer may have a control module that includes a microprocessor. The control module permits a block of data from a development system to be written into a PROM with a single command. A programmer may also include a display for verifying the contents of a PROM. In conjunction with a development system, a typical PROM programmer can perform the following operations:

1. Loading the data to be programmed from a selected input device (disk file or system console) into the memory of the development system
2. Displaying or changing data in the memory of the development system
3. Programming a segment of a PROM with the data that are stored begining at a specified address in the memory of the development system
4. Transferring a block of data in a PROM into memory so that the contents of the PROM may be examined through the system console or used to produce a duplicate PROM
5. Transferring a block of data from a PROM into a disk file
6. Comparing a block of data in a PROM with the contents of a segment of memory (program verification)

Because the contents of an EPROM (erasable PROM) are determined by charge distribution, an external energy source can be used to change its contents to the initial state (i.e., to erase the EPROM). Usually, the external source is ultraviolet light and the initial state is 1. The length of time required to erase an EPROM depends on the type of device and varies from 10 to 50 minutes. EPROM erasers are commercially available and are inexpensive. Once erased, an EPROM can be programmed using a PROM programmer, assuming that the necessary personality card is installed.

Emulators

After the hardware and software have been developed, both are integrated into the prototype system for testing and debugging. At this stage, additional hardware and software are necessary to provide efficient diagnostic features. An emulator in conjunction with a development system can be used to test not only the software but also the hardware of the prototype system. The emulator is substituted for the prototype's microprocessor and executes the microprocessor instructions in the environment of the prototype system under the control of the development system. Therefore, most of the hardware and software resources of the development system can be shared with the prototype system during the debugging stage. A program can be executed step by step while the status is being displayed, just as if the program were being run in the development system. In addition, prototype hardware items such as memory modules, I/O interfaces, and interrupt management logic can be tested and debugged individually by programs stored in the development system. Once the prototype system is completely debugged, the emulator is removed and replaced by the prototype's microprocessor.

Figure 4-14 is a block diagram showing an MC68000 emulator connected to the development system and an MC68000-based prototype system. The emulator consists primarily of an MC68000 microprocessor to emulate the prototype's processor, the control logic needed to trace and monitor the emulation, and the emulator memory, which can be used to store the program to be emulated. In debugging the prototype system, the MC68000 is removed from its socket, and a 64-pin connector, which is attached to the emulator, is substituted for the MC68000. The connector is interfaced to the emulator through a flexible cable and necessary driver circuits. The interface between the development system and the emulator allows the system hardware to be shared by the prototype system and allows the user to control the emulation via the development system. Note that because it has an MC68000 microprocessor, an MC68000 emulator can be operated without being connected to a user's prototype system. This feature facilitates software development even before the user's hardware is available.

Under the software provided with the emulator, the program to be emulated can be stored entirely in the emulator memory or entirely in the prototype's memory or be divided between the two. This allows the user to test the memory modules of the prototype system individually. Also, the peripherals of the development system can be loaned to the prototype system by substituting the I/O ports of the development system for those of the prototype system. Under the

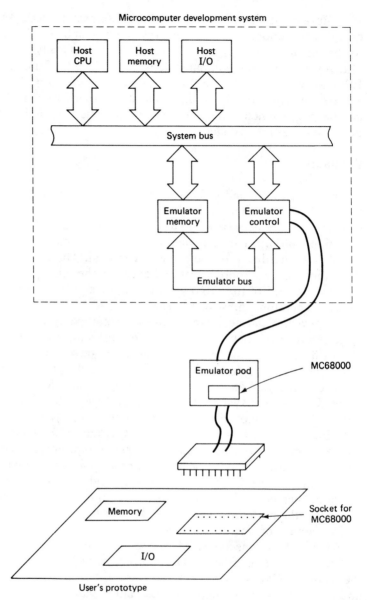

Figure 4-14 Connection of an emulator. Glenn A. Gibson/Yu-cheng Liu, *Microcomputers for Engineers and Scientists, 2/E*, © 1987. Reprinted by permission of Prentice Hall, Inc., Englewood Cliffs, New Jersey.

full-emulation mode, the emulator runs the program stored in the prototype's memory using the prototype's memory and I/O system. All control signals, data, and addresses are supplied by the prototype hardware; consequently, the prototype operates as if its MC68000 were being used.

Emulator commands are available to allow the user to control and monitor the emulation. After an emulation has been terminated, selected portions of its log may be displayed. Among the representative commands of a typical emulator are the following:

1. *Go:* Starts emulation until a break condition is satisfied and allows the user to specify the starting point and breakpoints. A break condition can be specified on address values, data values, and/or bus status.
2. *Step:* Allows the user to single-step through the program from a given starting address.
3. *Trace:* Allows the user to specify the conditions for enabling and disabling trace data collection during real-time and single-step emulation. Trace information includes register contents, memory contents, flags, and input/output pins.
4. *Display:* Displays trace data and emulation conditions. Various forms, including binary, hexadecimal, and symbolic (disassembled), can be chosen for display.
5. *Clock:* Specifies whether the internal clock (the one in the emulator) or an external one (provided by the prototype) is used to run the emulator processor during an emulation.
6. *Memory map:* Displays and declares what user memory is to be accessed and the range of memory to be borrowed from the development system.

Logic analyzers

The role of the logic state analyzer in digital hardware design is as important as that of the oscilloscope in troubleshooting analog circuitry. An oscilloscope may simultaneously display up to four voltage signals as a function of time. However, to debug a digital circuit, normally many signal lines need to be examined at the same time (e.g., all address lines or data lines may need to be monitored while debugging an I/O interface). Also, the exact voltage is often not important; only the state of each signal is of interest. A logic state analyzer simultaneously samples the states of several input channels, typically 16, each time it detects a clock pulse and stores the input states in its internal memory. The sampled input data may then be displayed in a 0/1 format on the screen of the analyzer to provide the user with a snapshot of the circuit activity.

The logic signals to be examined are fed into the logic state analyzer through multiconductor cables and external probes. The probes have high-input impedance to reduce the loading on the circuit being tested. The input signals are sampled under the control of the clock input, either by positive-going transitions or by negative-going transitions. The internal buffer memory allows the analyzer continuously to retain the most recent segment of data. Many analyzers permit the use to select data just before and just after a specific event. This is done by means of triggering. When the incoming data match the trigger conditions or trigger word, the data just before and after this point are frozen in the analyzer's memory. This feature allows the user to analyze the state transition both leading up to and after a preselected input combination. As opposed to a logic state analyzer, a conventional oscilloscope can display the signal only after it has been triggered.

If an analyzer has an internal clock to sample the inputs at a high clock rate and can display several signals as timing waveforms simultaneously, it is called a logic analyzer. The capability to sample data asynchronously and to display the inputs as timing diagrams is useful in debugging handshaking and other control signals. A logic analyzer can also detect unexpected signal spikes. A typical logic analyzer has the ability to record data with frequency up to 200 MHz and to detect spikes as narrow as 5 nanoseconds.

Figure 4-15 illustrates a typical display generated by a logic analyzer. This example shows the actual timing waveforms of sixteen MC68000 pin signals collected from an ECB while executing the tight loop

```
LOOP     ADDQ.B    #1,$2000
         BRA       LOOP
```

This two-instruction loop is stored from locations $002014 through $002019. In this case, the sixteen pin signals being monitored are system clock (CLOCK), address strobe ($\overline{AS}$), read/write (R/$\overline{W}$), acknowledge ($\overline{DTACK}$), upper data strobe ($\overline{UDS}$), lower data strobe ($\overline{LDS}$), lower 5 address bits (A5–A1), and lower 5 data bits (D4–D0). Monitored signals can also be displayed in digital form as state listings or both as timing waveforms and as state listings simultaneously.

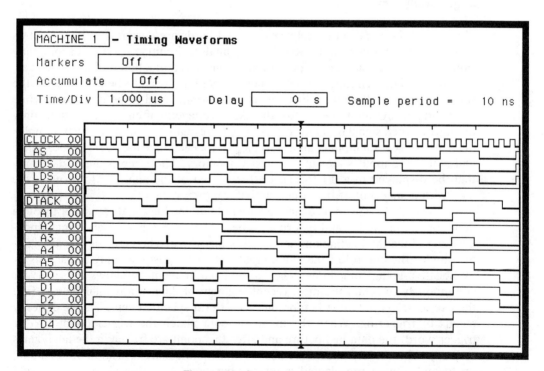

Figure 4-15 Sample display of a logic analyzer.

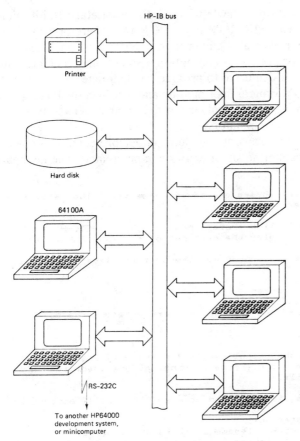

HP-IB bus

Printer

Hard disk

64100A

RS-232C

To another HP64000
development system,
or minicomputer

Figure 4-16 Typical HP64000
development system. Glenn A.
Gibson/Yu-cheng Liu, *Microcomputers
for Engineers and Scientists, 2/E*,
© 1987. Reprinted by permission of
Prentice Hall, Inc., Englewood Cliffs,
New Jersey.

HP64000 development system

An example of microprocessor development systems is the HP64000 system. A
development system manufactured by a microprocessor vendor supports only the
microprocessors designed by the same company. The HP64000 system offered
by Hewlett-Packard is more universal in this respect. It supports the software
and hardware development for most of the commonly used microprocessors, not
just for one microprocessor family made by a particular vendor. Among the microprocessor families it supports are the 8080/8085, 6800/6809, Z80, 8086, M68000,
and Z8000.

Although an HP64000 development station (model 64100A) can operate as
a stand-alone system, up to six of them can be tied together through the high-
speed HP-IB bus to provide for team development. As shown in Fig. 4-16, these
stations can share the hard disk and printer with one station (any one) being
designated as the master station. An HP64000 system may also link to a minicomputer such as an HP3000 or a Digital Equipment Corporation (DEC) VAX or
to another HP64000 system via RS-232-C serial lines.

Each station is based on a Hewlett-Packard's proprietary 16-bit microprocessor and is equipped with 32K ROM and 64K RAM. Therefore, the HP64000 is a multiprocessing system with all stations operating simultaneously except when accessing the hard disk or printer. As an option a station may include a dual 5¼-inch diskette drive or cartridge drive to provide local storage. A station also has a space to plug in a PROM programmer module and has 10 card slots for optional development tools such as a state analyzer, a timing analyzer, software performance analyzer, and various emulators.

Each user can create a separate account, either protected or unprotected. However, within one account no subdirectory can be created. The keyboard has

```
Note that in the parentheses are added comments.   The initial soft
key label line appears as:

edit compile assemble link emulate prom_prog run --ETC--
(--ETC-- key is to display the next set of soft key labels.)

After "assemble" key is depressed, the soft key label appears as:

<FILE>
(File name to be assembled.)

After a filename TEST and "return" key are entered, the soft key
label appears as:

listfile options
(listfile: specify the output device for assembly listing.
 options: allow user to override listing options specified in the
          source file.)

After "listfile" key is depressed, the soft key label appears as:

<FILE> display printer null
(<FILE>: specify a disk filename to store the listing.
 display: display the listing on screen.
 printer: print out the listing.
 null: none.)

After "printer" key is depressed, the soft key label appears as:

options

After "options" key is depressed, the soft key label appears as:

list nolist expand nocode xref
(list: force listing of all lines.
 nolist: force no listing of all lines except errors.
 expand: list all source and macro generated codes.
 nocode: suppress object code generation.
 xref: generate a cross-reference table.)

After "list", "xref" are depressed, the command line appears as:

assemble TEST listfile printer options list xref

After "return" key is depressed, file TEST is assembled, listing is
printed, and the soft key label line returns to its initial state:

edit compile  assemble  link  emulate prom_prog run --ETC--
```

Figure 4-17 An example of using soft keys. Glenn A. Gibson/Yu-cheng Liu, *Microcomputers for Engineers and Scientists, 2E,* © 1987. Reprinted by permission of Prentice Hall, Inc., Englewood Cliffs, New Jersey.

eight soft keys and four function keys in addition to regular alphanumeric and cursor movement keys. The four function keys are CLR LINE, RECALL, CAPS LOCK, and RESET. The CLR LINE key causes the current line to be cleared. This key is useful when aborting a command before it starts to execute. The workstation saves previous commands on a stack. Pressing the RECALL key allows the user to recall the previous command for execution. The RESET key is for returning to the monitor and for holding the display on screen. When it is pressed once, the system pauses and freezes the screen until any key except RESET is depressed. Pressing the RESET key twice causes the termination of current operation and returns to monitor.

The eight soft keys make the HP64000 very easy to use. By using these keys, the user can enter keywords or options in a command with single keystrokes. On the bottom of the screen, there is a soft-key label line that constantly displays all allowable entries. As each soft key is pressed, the soft-key label line changes accordingly to reflect the next expected syntax choices in a command. Therefore, if the user follows the soft-key label line at each step, the resulting command is always free of syntax errors. To illustrate how soft keys are used to enter a command, the actual display of the soft-key label line for an assemble command is shown in Fig. 4-17.

Note that the first line of the source file must identify the microprocessor for which the source code is written. For example, an MC68000 program must include "68000" as the first line. If a sequence of commands is to be executed again and again, a command file can be set up to eliminate much of the required interaction between the user and the system. The command file can be created either by the text editor or by the "log-commands to filename" command. This command saves all further commands to a file designated by the given filename until the "log-commands off" command is entered.

For example, assume that a file COMSEQ is created to include the following lines (comments for each line are given in parentheses):

PARMS &SOURCE	(pass a parameter to command sequence)
assemble &SOURCE listfile printer options list xref	
	(assemble the given program, print a listing and select options)
link	(link)
&SOURCE	(object filename to be linked)
a blank line	(no library files to be linked)
000002000H,000000000H,000000000H	(specify beginning addresses for PROG, DATA, and COMMON areas)
yes	(more object files to be linked)
SUBPROG	(object file name)
a blank line	(no library files to be linked)
000003000H,000000000H,000000000H	(specify beginning addresses for PROG, DATA, and COMMON areas)
no	(no more object files to be linked)
a blank line	(select default options)
&SOURCE	(use parameter as absolute file name)

Then, to assemble any file, TEST, and link it with SUBPROG requires only the command:

```
COMSEQ TEST
```

The HP64000 system provides cross assemblers/linkers and cross Pascal and C compilers for the commonly used 16-/32-bit as well as 8-bit microprocessors. The system does not provide simulators. Therefore, to verify and debug a program, the appropriate emulator must be installed.

One unique software tool provided by the HP64000 is the software performance analyzer. Operated in conjunction with an emulator, this tool is used to analyze the characteristics of the user's software and therby assists the user in optimizing the performance of his software. The software performance analyzer allows the user to measure and display six major program characteristics. Each measurement is displayed in both event count and bar graph forms. The six measurements are as follows:

1. *Program activity:* Displays the processor activities in each of the given (up to 12) modules or program segments. This measurement is valuable in identifying the modules that create the bottlenecks. For example, Fig. 4-18 reveals that Module E is responsible for more than 50% of the CPU activity. Therefore, improving this module would be the most effective way of optimizing the performance of the entire software system.

2. *Memory activity:* Displays memory access activities for given memory regions. It is useful in allocating available memory efficiently.

3. *Module duration:* Displays the time distribution during execution of a selected module or code segment. This indicates to the user whether or not a module is operating within its expected bounds.

EVENT	COUNT	PCNT
MODULE A	475	5%
MODULE B	2000	21%
MODULE C	195	2%
MODULE D	850	9%
MODULE E	4850	51%
MODULE F	1150	12%

Figure 4-18 Sample display of program activities. Glenn A. Gibson/Yu-cheng Liu, *Microcomputers for Engineers and Scientists, 2/E,* © 1987. Reprinted by permission of Prentice Hall, Inc., Englewood Cliffs, New Jersey.

4. *Module usage:* Displays the time distribution between successive accesses to a selected module or code segment. This indicates the intensity of demand for the services of a module. One possible application is in comparing different scheduling policies.

5. *Intermodule duration:* Displays the time distribution of transitions between two selected modules. Transition time is the time between leaving a module and entering the other module.

6. *Intermodule linkage:* Displays the numbers of direct transfers between two selected modules. Up to six pairs of modules may be selected. This measurement reveals the intensity of various program flow paths.

EXERCISES

1. Assume that register A1 is simulated by the 32-bit variable IA1, the N flag by the Boolean variable NF, and memory location I by the 8-bit array element MEMORY(I), and that other condition flags are not simulated. Show a statement sequence in a high-level language, such as Fortran or Pascal, to simulate each of the following MC68000 instructions
   (a) ADD.B   #12,(A1)+   (b) MOVE.B   120, − (A1)
   (c) SUB.B   #10,10(A1)

2. What would each of the following TUTOR commands do?
   (a) BR   2060;4   (b) BR   (c) GO   2100
   (d) GT   2100   (e) MM   2000;W (f) .PC   2100
   (g) BM   2000   3000   5000   (h) TR

3. Give the TUTOR command sequence that will execute the program beginning at 2010 with a breakpoint set at 2120, display memory locations 2000–2010 at the breakpoint, step through the next four instructions, and then resume real-time execution.

4. Assume the initial conditions:
   SR has 0000, A2 has 1504, memory locations 1500–1507 have F0, F1, F2, F3, F4, F5, F6, and F7. Trace each of the following MOVE instructions.
   (a) MOVE.B   − (A2),(A2)+   (b) MOVE.B   (A2)+, − (A2)
   (c) MOVE.B   − (A2), − (A2)   (d) MOVE.B   (A2)+,(A2)+
   Based on the trace results, discuss how each of the MOVE instructions is executed.

5. Consider the program in Fig. 4-6. Assume that the code section in memory block from 2014 through 203A is moved to memory area beginning at 3500. Can this program be executed without any changes at new address 3500? Justify your answer.

6. Consider the program in Fig. 4-6. If the entire program is moved by the command

   BM   2000   203A   3000

   show the necessary changes that must be made to the machine code in order to execute this program from the new address.

7. Explain why the maximum number of code/data bytes per S1 record is 252.

8. Determine the S0 record if the header message is SAMPLE 4.1.

9. Determine the S1 record for the following assembly language program:

```
        ORG     $2000
ABC     DC.W    5, -8,2
STR     MOVE.W  ABC,D0
        ADD.W   ABC+2,D0
        SUBQ.W  #10,D0
        ADD.W   D0,ABC+4
        STOP    #$2000
        END     STR
```

10. Given the following absolute load module

```
S1113000000102030405
S109203C0000
S9030000FC
```

determine the contents of all affected memory locations after this module is loaded. Would a checksum error occur during the loading process?

11. Draw a flowchart of the system routine that is capable of loading an S1 record.

12. List the TUTOR commands that are designed to provide supports for program debugging.

5

Subroutines
and Advanced
Programming Techniques

The programming examples given in preceding chapters are relatively simple. In many cases, a program is much more complex and its resulting code is substantially longer. How to design a program that is easy to implement, debug, and modify becomes increasingly important as the program size grows. The most effective way to achieve this goal is to divide the entire program into several relatively independent modules. Each module is individually implemented as a subroutine, which can be independently tested and debugged. Then, the modules are combined to form the final program.

A subroutine as shown in Fig. 5-1 is a closed-type routine. After a subroutine is executed, the control returns back to the calling routine. In addition to the advantage of providing modularity, a subroutine also allows a single copy of code to be reexecuted at several places in the program, thus reducing programming time and saving memory space.

To implement a subroutine, one must consider three basic elements in addition to the main body of the subroutine:

1. *Control linkage:* Passes control to the subroutine and returns to the next instruction following the call after the subroutine is executed. This requires the return address, which is the content of PC, to be saved upon entering a subroutine and to be retrieved when exiting from a subroutine.

2. *Register saving and restoring:* Saves all registers that are to be modified in a subroutine and restores them before returning to the calling routine.

3. *Parameter passing:* Allows initial data to be passed to and results to be returned from a subroutine.

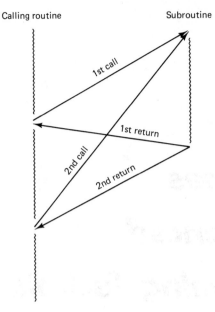

Calling routine   Subroutine

1st call

1st return

2nd call

2nd return

Figure 5-1   Subroutines.

Since the stack plays an important role in implementing each of these, it is necessary to discuss the stack first.

5-1 Stack

A stack is a data structure that can be used to save and restore information in a last-in, first-out (LIFO) fashion. In many occasions, the most recently saved item is the one to be retrieved first. Let us consider the case of nested subroutine calls. For example, routine A calls subroutine B, which in turn calls subroutiine C, in which subroutine D is called. As each call occurs, the return address to routine A is saved first, followed by the return address to subroutine B, and finally the return address to subroutine C. After subroutine D is completed, program control is returned to subroutine C, then to subroutine B, and eventually back to routine A. As shown in Fig. 5-2, this requires that the return address to subroutine C be retrieved first and the saved return address for routine A be retrieved last. A stack enables information to be saved and restored in a LIFO fashion effectively. Most microprocessors provide stack facilities, and the MC68000 is no exception.

Figure 5-3 illustrates how a LIFO stack is implemented using a stack pointer. Initially, a block of memory is reserved for the stack, and the stack pointer points to the high-address boundary of the stack. To save (push) a data word onto the stack, the stack pointer is decremented by 2, and then the data word is moved to the memory location pointed to by the SP. A typical notation for the push stack operation is

Source $\rightarrow$ $-$(SP)

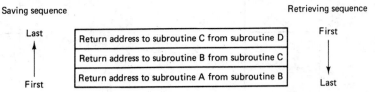

Saving sequence

Retrieving sequence

Last

First

First

Last

| Return address to subroutine C from subroutine D |
| Return address to subroutine B from subroutine C |
| Return address to subroutine A from subroutine B |

Figure 5-2   Order of saving and retrieving return addresses in nested subroutine calls.

Retrieving (popping) the last item from the stack requires exactly the opposite steps. The content at the stack top is moved to the destination, followed by incrementing the SP by the data length. This pop stack operation is typically described by the notation

$$(SP) + \; \to \; Destination$$

The stack pointer always points to the top of the stack, where the last saved item is stored, which is also the first item to be retrieved. As data are pushed, the

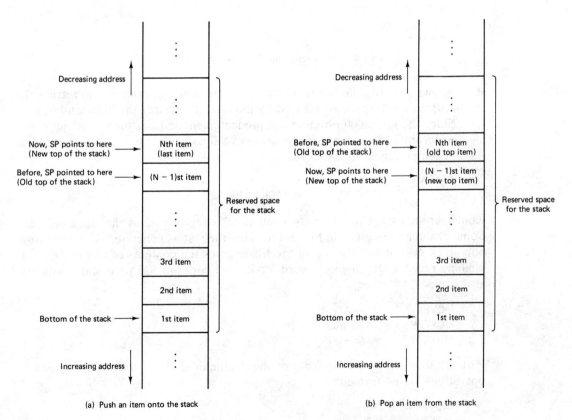

(a) Push an item onto the stack

(b) Pop an item from the stack

Figure 5-3   Saving and restoring data using the stack.

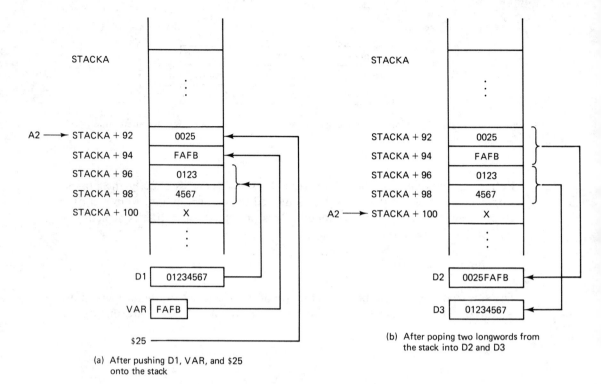

(a) After pushing D1, VAR, and $25 onto the stack

(b) After poping two longwords from the stack into D2 and D3

Figure 5-4 Examples of push and pop operations.

stack grows towards the lower address, and as saved information is retrieved, the occupied stack space is released by moving SP towards the higher address.

Since the MC68000 provides the predecrement and postincrement addressing modes, any address register may serve as a stack pointer to implement a stack. As an example, the two instructions:

```
STACKA      DS.W        50
            MOVEA.L     #STACKA + 100,A2
```

would set up a stack of 50 words using address register A2 as the stack pointer. Some examples are given in Fig. 5-4 to show the results generated from push and pop stack operations. Part (a) of the figure gives the contents of this stack after pushing register D1, memory word VAR, and constant $25 onto stack with instruction:

```
MOVE.L      D1, - (A2)
MOVE.W      VAR, - (A2)
MOVE.W      #$25, - (A2)
```

Part (b) shows the new contents of the destinations if the following pop stack operations are performed:

```
MOVE.L      (A2) + ,D2
MOVE.L      (A2) + ,D3
```

Even though any address register is capable of serving as a stack pointer, register A7 is implicitly used as the stack pointer in some instructions such as subroutine call and return for saving and retrieving certain implied operands.

5-2 Subroutines

Control linkage

Passing program control to and from a subroutine requires special instructions. The MC68000 instructions designed to provide the necessary control linkage between a calling routine and a subroutine are summarized in Fig. 5-5. A subroutine call instruction saves the return address by pushing the content of the PC onto the system stack and then jumps to the subroutine. Similar to unconditional jumps, the MC68000 has two subroutine call instructions.

The general one is the JSR (jump to subroutine) instruction. This instruction allows its operand, which represents the beginning address of the called subroutine, to be specified by any control addressing mode. An example is given in Fig. 5-6 to show the operation performed by a subroutine call:

```
JSR        SUBRT
```

The example assumes that the initial content of SP is 003000 and that the JSR instruction is assembled at location 015000. After executing the JSR instruction, the address of the next instruction following JSR, which is 015004, is pushed to location 002FFC on the stack and the subroutine address is loaded into the PC.

The other subroutine call instruction is the BSR (branch to subroutine) instruction, which—as in the BRA instruction—limits the subroutine address to being specified by the relative addressing mode. An optional postfix .S, if used, forces the instruction to be assembled in a short form using an 8-bit branch distance. Otherwise, in a forward reference 16 bits are used to specify the branch distance.

The last executable instruction in a subroutine is the RTS (return from subroutine) instruction. This instruction pops the top of the system stack to the PC, causing a return to the next instruction following the subroutine call. Since the

Mnemonic	Size or Postfix	Operand Format	Allowable EA Modes	Operation	Condition Flags N Z V C X
JSR (Jump to subroutine)	Unsized	EA	Control	PC -> -(SP); EA -> PC	- - - - -
BSR (Branch to subroutine)	.S or none	DST		PC -> -(SP); DST -> PC	- - - - -
RTS (Return from subroutine)	Unsized	None		(SP)+ -> PC	- - - - -
RTR (Return and restore condition codes)	Unsized	None		(SP)+ -> CCR; (SP)+ -> PC	* * * * *

Figure 5-5 Subroutine-related instructions.

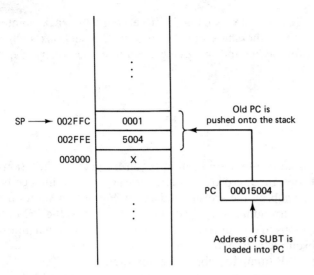

Old PC is
pushed onto the stack

SP → 002FFC | 0001
002FFE | 5004
003000 | X

PC | 00015004

Address of SUBT is
loaded into PC

Figure 5-6 Action caused by the
JSR SUBT instruction.

operands PC and SP are both implied, the RTS instruction has no user-specified operands. The MC68000 also has an RTR (return and restore condition codes) instruction. If the condition codes are saved onto the stack at the beginning of a subroutine, the RTR instruction is used to restore the condition codes and then return to the calling routine.

Saving and restoring registers

Both the calling routine and the subroutine share the same set of registers. In order for the calling routine to continue its execution properly, it is necessary that the subroutine save all registers that are to be modified and restore them before returning to the calling routine.

The most effective way to save and restore registers is with a stack. The following two instructions save and restore, respectively, all registers except A7 using the system stack:

```
MOVEM.L     D0 – D7/A0 – A6, – (SP)
MOVEM.L     (SP) + ,D0 – D7/A0 – A6
```

Since A7 is used to maintain the system stack, this register is automatically updated during a stack operation and therefore should not be saved and restored. Of course, if a subroutine uses few registers, only these registers need to be saved and restored. For example, if only registers D0, D7, A1, and A2 are modified, these registers can be saved and restored by

```
MOVEM.L     D0/D7/A1/A2, – (SP)
```

and

        MOVEM.L   (SP) + ,D0/D7/A1/A2

respectively.

Parameter passing

Although information can be directly passed to and from a subroutine through
registers, application of this method is rather limited due to the size of the register
set. One solution to the problem of parameter passing is to use a memory area
that is directly accessible to both calling routine and subroutine. In Fortran, this
method is used to implement variables defined in COMMON statements. Typically, a common area is employed to pass those parameters that are used frequently during calls to a subroutine.

In most cases, during each call, a different set of parameters is passed to
the subroutine. For each parameter, its address instead of its value is normally
passed to the subroutine. There are two obvious reasons for this. First, when a
parameter is to be used by a subroutine for returning a result, its address must
be made known to the subroutine. Second, if a parameter is an array, only the
beginning address of the array needs to be passed, from which the subroutine is
able to determine the address of each element in the array. Without passing the
array address, it would require the entire array to be passed. Fortran, for example,
allows parameters to be passed to subroutines only by addresses. On the other
hand, Pascal, a structured language, allows a parameter to be passed to a procedure either by address, referred to as a *VAR parameter*, or by value, referred
to as a *value parameter*. Obviously, results cannot be returned from a procedure
through value parameters.

Parameters can be passed through a table defined in the calling routine, with
its address being placed in an address register. As illustrated in Fig. 5-7, the

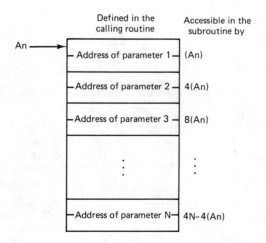

Figure 5-7 Using an address table for
parameter linkage.

subroutine can get the address of any parameter by using this register as an index register and then the value of the parameter if necessary.

Now, we are ready to show a simple example that illustrates the salient points of a subroutine implementation. Suppose that we wish to write a subroutine FIDMAX, which would find the maximum value in a given 16-bit integer array. This subroutine has three parameters: the array to be searched, the number of elements in the array, and the variable indicating where to return the maximum value. Figure 5-8 shows the implementation of subroutine FIDMAX and the instruction sequence that uses FIDMAX to find the maximum element in two arrays, ARRAYA and ARRAYB.

Passing parameters via the stack

Another method to pass parameters is through the system stack. The previous method using a table to pass parameters requires space for a parameter table to be reserved in each calling routine at assembly or compilation time. On the other

```
          ORG       $2000
ARRAYA    DC.W      -9,15,53,35,-15,35,99,57,-22,13
SIZEA     DC.W      10
MAXA      DS.W      1
ARRAYB    DC.W      65,-22,35,11,-77,55,-11
SIZEB     DC.W      7
MAXB      DS.W      1
MAX       DS.W      1
PARTBL    DS.L      3
START     MOVEA.L   #$3000,SP
          MOVE.L    #ARRAYA,PARTBL      ;SET UP A TABLE TO PASS PARAMETER
          MOVE.L    #SIZEA,PARTBL+4     ;ADDRESSES FOR THE FIRST CALL
          MOVE.L    #MAXA,PARTBL+8
          MOVEA.L   #PARTBL,A0          ;A0 = ADDRESS OF PARAMETER TABLE
*
*    CALL SUBROUTINE FIDMAX TO FIND THE MAXIMUM VALUE
*    IN ARRAYA AND STORE IT INTO MAXA
*
          JSR       FIDMAX
*
          MOVE.L    #ARRAYB,PARTBL      ;SET UP A TABLE TO PASS PARAMETER
          MOVE.L    #SIZEB,PARTBL+4     ;ADDRESSES FOR THE SECOND CALL
          MOVE.L    #MAXB,PARTBL+8
          MOVEA.L   #PARTBL,A0
*
*    CALL SUBROUTINE FIDMAX TO FIND THE MAXIMUM VALUE
*    IN ARRAYB AND STORE IT INTO MAXB
*
          JSR       FIDMAX
*
          MOVE.W    MAXA,D0             ;IF MAXB > MAXA
          CMP       MAXB,D0             ;THEN MAX = MAXB
          BGE       STORE               ;ELSE MAX = MAXA
          MOVE.W    MAXB,D0
STORE     MOVE.W    D0,MAX
          STOP      #$2000
*
FIDMAX    MOVEM.L   D0/D7/A1/A2,-(SP)   ;SAVE D0,D7,A1 AND A2 ONTO THE STACK
          MOVEA.L   (A0),A1             ;A1 = ADDRESS OF ARRAY
          MOVEA.L   4(A0),A2            ;A2 = ADDRESS OF ARRAY SIZE
          MOVE.W    (A2),D7             ;D7 = ARRAY SIZE
          MOVEA.L   8(A0),A2            ;A2 = ADDRESS TO STORE THE MAXIMUM VALUE
          SUBQ.W    #2,D7               ;USE D7 AS LOOP COUNTER
          MOVE.W    (A1)+,D0            ;USE D0 TO STORE THE MAXIMUM VALUE
                                        ;INITIALLY, D0 = ARRAY(1)
LOOP      CMP.W     (A1)+,D0            ;THIS LOOP FINDS THE MAXIMUM VALUE
          BGE.S     ENDLP               ;IN THE ARRAY AND STORE IT INTO D0
          MOVE.W    -2(A1),D0
ENDLP     DBF       D7,LOOP
          MOVE.W    D0,(A2)             ;RETURN THE MAXIMUM VALUE
*                                       ;TO THE CALLING ROUTINE
          MOVEM.L   (SP)+,D0/D7/A1/A2   ;RESTORE A2,A1,D7 AND D0
          RTS                           ;RETURN TO THE CALLING ROUTINE
          END       START
```

Figure 5-8 An example of subroutine.

hand, using a stack allows space to be allocated for passing parameters only when it is needed. After the subroutine is executed, the allocated stack space can be released for other uses. Since storage is allocated dynamically during execution time, this method is more memory-efficient. However, the most significant advantage of passing parameters through stack is that it supports the implementation of recursive and reentrant routines. This is because such routines must be pure codes and therefore are not allowed to include alterable locations.

To illustrate parameter passing through the stack, let us reimplement the subroutine FIDMAX in Fig. 5-8. Before calling subroutine FIDMAX, the addresses of three actual parameters are pushed onto the stack with the calling sequence:

```
PEA     ARRAY
PEA     SIZE
PEA     MAX
JSR     FIDMAX
```

After the subroutine is entered and registers D0, D7, A1, A2 are saved by

```
MOVEM.L     D0/D7/A1/A2, – (SP)
```

the system stack appears as shown in Fig. 5-9. Therefore, loading the array address into A1, the array size to D7, and the address for storing the maximum value to

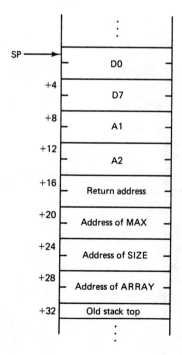

Figure 5-9 Contents of the stack after subroutine FIDMAX is entered.

A2 can be accomplished by

```
MOVEA.L     28(SP),A1
MOVEA.L     24(SP),A2
MOVE.W      (A2),D7
MOVEA.L     20(SP),A2
```

The remaining part of subroutine FIDMAX is the same as the implementation in Fig. 5-8.

Note that after returning from subroutine FIDMAX, the SP does not point to the original location prior to the calling sequence. If the stack space occupied by the parameters is not released, the system stack will continue to grow even though the same subroutine is called each time. Furthermore, in the case of nested calls, the program control cannot be returned properly, thus causing execution errors. To illustrate this point, let us consider the case that routine A calls subroutine B, in which FIDMAX is called. Figure 5-10 depicts the system stack and the stack pointer just after returning to subroutine B upon the completion of FIDMAX. If the SP is not incremented by the size in bytes of the area allocated for parameter passing, then when subroutine B is eventually completed, the return address to routine A would be incorrectly taken from the register save area. Therefore, in the calling sequence, immediately after the

```
JSR       FIDMAX
```

instruction, the following instruction to deallocate the stack is required:

```
ADDA.L      #12,SP
```

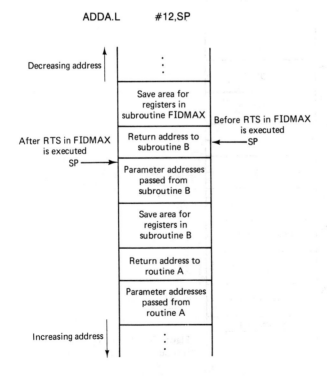

Figure 5-10 Stack in a nested subroutine call.

In the instruction, immediate operand 12 is the total number of bytes used for passing the addresses of parameters ARRAY, SIZE, and MAX.

For this reason, the MC68010 includes a new instruction, RTD, that combines a subroutine return and deallocation of parameters into a single instruction. The RTD instruction has the format

```
RTD       #I16
```

where the immediate operand specifies the number of bytes to be deallocated from the system stack. The instruction first pops the top of stack into PC and then adds the immediate operand into SP. Therefore, the immediate operand should be a *positive* integer corresponding to the total number of bytes used for passing the parameters.

5-3 Multiple-Module Programs

Since the previous example is a very simple one, the subroutine is embedded in the main routine as a single source module. In order for a subroutine to be shared by other users or to be tested independently from its main routine, a subroutine can be implemented as a separate source module. It can then be assembled independently and linked with different routines in which it is called.

The XDEF and XREF directives

When implemented as a separate source module, the subroutine address is not known at the time when the calling routine is assembled or compiled. A pair of directives, XDEF and XREF, is required to resolve such external references. The XREF (external symbol reference) directive has the form

```
XREF       Symbol,Symbol, . . .
```

This directive informs the assembler that each symbol listed in the operand field is defined in another programming module, and the symbol address will be filled in by the linker. Otherwise, since a symbol is referenced but not defined in the current program, an assembly error would occur.

The XDEF (external symbol definition) directive, whose format is

```
XDEF       Symbol,Symbol, . . .
```

specifies each listed symbol as a global symbol that is defined in the current program and may be referenced in other programs. Therefore, any symbol that appears in an XREF directive must be listed as a global symbol in one and only one XDEF directive. On the other hand, a symbol in an XDEF directive may be referenced in several modules and therefore may appear in more than one XREF directive. An example of the correct use of the XDEF and XREF pair is given next.

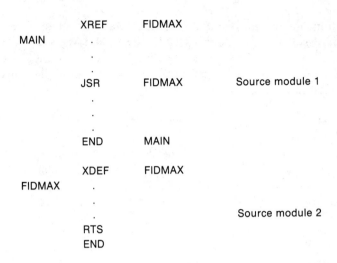

```
            XREF       FIDMAX
  MAIN      .
            .
            .
            JSR        FIDMAX          Source module 1
            .
            .
            .
            END        MAIN

            XDEF       FIDMAX
  FIDMAX    .
            .
                                       Source module 2
            .
            RTS
            END
```

An example of a multiple-module program

A major advantage of a subroutine is that it provides a means for breaking a complex program into several small modules, each being implemented as a subroutine. As opposed to the original program, each module is simpler and hence much easier to design and to debug.

Suppose that we wish to write a program that would scan a given text string and determine the number of occurrences for each word in the string. Assume that a word has no more than 16 characters and that the text string is in capital letters and is terminated with a period. In this program, a word table is to be employed to maintain the occurrence count for each word used. Each entry of this table is allocated 20 bytes. The first 16 bytes store a word, left-justified, and the last byte serves as the occurrence count.

This program is complex enough to justify using a modular approach. Figure 5-11 divides the program into a main routine and three subroutines according to

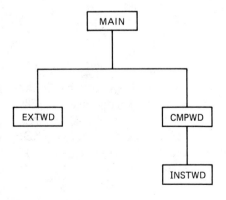

Figure 5-11 An example of breaking a program into several modules.

the major tasks to be performed. The three subroutines are

EXTWD: Searches the character string starting from a given position and returns the first word it has found. This subroutine has three parameters: the array to be searched, the index of the first position to be searched, and the extracted word.

CMPWD: Searches the word table for a given word. If the word is found, its occurrence count is incremented. If it is not found, subroutine INSTWD is called to add this new word to the table. This subroutine has four parameters: the word table, the number of entries in the table, the word to be searched, and the flag to be updated, indicating whether or not a search fails.

INSTWD: Inserts a new word to the word table. This subroutine has three parameters: the word table, the position to be inserted, and the new word.

If we take this approach, the logic flow of the main routine becomes very simple, as shown

```
WHILE  current      character ≠ "."
       DO           call EXTWD to extract the next word;
                    call CMPWD to search the table for
                    the extracted word and update the table


       ENDDO
```

The entire program is implemented in Fig. 5-12. In this example, each routine is implemented as a separate source module, and parameters are passed through the system stack.

```
*          MAIN PROGRAM
*
           XREF     EXTWD,CMPWD
           ORG      $2000
TABLE      DS.B     600                 ;RESERVE A TABLE FOR 30 ENTRIES
NUM        DS.W     1                   ;NO. OF NON-EMPTY ENTRIES, I.E., WORDS
*                                       ;IN TABBLE
WORD       DS.B     17                  ;STORE AN EXTRACTED WORD
TEXT       DC.B     'THIS IS A PROGRAM
           DC.B     'THIS IS AN EXAMPLE.
TXTIND     DS.W     1
MAIN       MOVE.W   #0,NUM
           MOVE.W   #0,TXTIND
           MOVEA.L  #$5000,SP
NEXTWD     PEA      TEXT                ;SET UP PARAMETERS FOR
           PEA      TXTIND              ;CALLING SUBROUTINE EXTWD
           PEA      WORD                ;TO EXTRACT THE NEXT WORD
           JSR      EXTWD
           ADDA.L   #12,SP              ;DEALLOCATE PARAMETERS
           PEA      TABLE               ;SET UP PARAMETERS FOR
           PEA      NUM                 ;CALLING SUBROUTINE CMPWD TO
           PEA      WORD                ;SEARCH THE TABLE FOR THE EXTRACTED
           JSR      CMPWD               ;WORD AND UPDATE THE TABLE
           ADDA.L   #12,SP              ;DEALLOCATE PARAMETERS
           MOVE.W   TXTIND,D0
           MOVEA.L  #TEXT,A0            ;CHECK THE NEXT CHERACTER
*                                       ;IN THE TEXT STRING
           CMPI.B   #'.',0(A0,D0.W)     ;IF END OF STRING IS REACHED, THEN STOP
           BNE      NEXTWD              ;OTHERWISE, EXTRACT THE NEXT WORD.
           STOP     #$2000
           END      MAIN
```

Figure 5-12 An example of multiple-module program.

```
*       SUBROUTINE EXTWD
*
        XDEF    EXTWD               ;       ***************************
EXTWD   MOVEM.L D0/D7/A0/A1/A2,-(SP) ; SP * _____D0_____ *
*                                   ; +4  * _____D7_____ *
*                                   ; +8  * _____A0_____ *
*                                   ; +12 * _____A1_____ *
*                                   ; +16 * _____A2_____ *
*                                   ; +20 *   RETURN ADDRESS   *
*                                   ; +24 * ADDRESS OF NEW WORD *
*                                   ; +28 * ADDRESS OF BEG POS  *
*                                   ; +32 *  ADDRESS OF ARRAY   *
*                                   ;       ***************************
        MOVEA.L 32(SP),A0           ;A0 = ADDRESS OF ARRAY
        MOVEA.L 28(SP),A1           ;A1 = ADDRESS OF BEGIN POSITION
        MOVE.W  (A1),D0             ;D0 = BEGINNING POSITION
        MOVEA.L 24(SP),A2           ;A2 = ADDRESS OF THE NEW WORD
        MOVE.W  #17,D7              ;CLEARR THE ARRAY BEFORE STORING A WORD
LOOP    MOVE.B  #' ',(A2)+
        DBF     D7,LOOP
        MOVEA.L 24(SP),A2           ;A2 = ADDRESS TO STORE THE EXTRACTED WORD
CHECK1  CMPI.B  #'Z',0(A0,D0.W)     ;SEARCH FOR THE BEGINNING OF A WORD
        BLT     SKIP                ;SKIP UNTIL A LETTER IS ENCOUNTERED
        CMPI.B  #'X',0(A0,D0.W)
        BLE     COPY
SKIP    ADDQ.W  #1,D0
        BRA     CHECK1
COPY    MOVE.B  0(A0,D0.W),(A2)+    ;COPY A WORD
        ADDQ.W  #1,D0               ;UNTIL THE END OF
CHECK2  CMPI.B  #'A',0(A0,D0.W)     ;A WORD IS REACHED
        BLT     DONE
        CMPI.B  #'Z',0(A0,D0.W)
        BLE     COPY
DONE    MOVE.W  D0,(A1)             ;UPDATE THE BEGINNING POSITION
        MOVEM.L (SP)+,D0/D7/A0/A1/A2 ;TO BE SEARCHED NEXT TIME
        RTS
        END



*       SUBROUTINE CMPWD
*
        XREF    INSTWD
        XDEF    CMPWD               ;       ***************************
CMPWD   MOVEM.L D0/D1/D7/A0-A3,-(SP) ; SP * _____D0_____ *
*                                   ; +4  * _____D1_____ *
*                                   ; +8  * _____D7_____ *
*                                   ; +12 * _____A0_____ *
*                                   ; +16 * _____A1_____ *
*                                   ; +20 * _____A2_____ *
*                                   ; +24 * _____A3_____ *
*                                   ; +28 *   RETURN ADDRESS   *
*                                   ; +32 * ADDR OF WORD TO SCHED *
*                                   ; +36 * ADDRESS OF NO. OF WORDS *
*                                   ; +40 * ADDRESS OF WORD TABLE *
*                                   ;       ***************************
        MOVEA.L 40(SP),A0           ;A0 = ADDRESS OF THE WORD TABLE
        MOVEA.L 36(SP),A1           ;A1 = ADDRESS OF NO. OF WORDS IN THE TABLE
        MOVE.L  32(SP),D1           ;D1 = ADDRESS OF WORD TO BE SEARCHED
        MOVE.W  (A1),D7             ;D7 = NO. OF WORDS IN THE TABLE
        BEQ.S   NOTEND              ;IF TABLE IS EMPTY, SKIP SEARCH
        SUBQ.W  #1,D7               ;THE FOLLOWING LOOP SEARCHES FOR THE GIVEN
        MOVE.W  #0,D0               ;USE D0 AS INDEX REGISTER
LOOP    LEA     0(A0,D0.W),A3
        MOVEA.L D1,A2
LOOP1   CMPM.B  (A2)+,(A3)+
        BNE.S   NEXTWD
        CMPI.B  #' ',-1(A2)         ;IF THE CURRENT CHARACTER IS A BLANK,
        BEQ.S   FOUND               ;SEARCH IS COMPLETED
        BRA     LOOP1
NEXTWD  ADDI.W  #20,D0              ;INDEX POINTS TO THE NEXT WORD IN THE TABLE
ENDLP   DBF     D7,LOOP
NOTFND  PEA     (A0)                ;PUSH ADDRESS OF WORD TABLE
        PEA     (A1)                ;PUSH ADDRESS OF NO. OF WORDS IN TABLE
        MOVE.L  D1,-(SP)            ;PUSH ADDRESS OF THE NEW WORD
        JSR     INSTWD              ;CALL INSTWD TO INSERT A NEW
*                                   ;WORD INTO THE TABLE
        ADDA.L  #12,SP              ;DEALLOCATE PARAMETERS
        BRA.S   RETURN
FOUND   ADDQ.B  #1,19(A0,D0.W)      ;INCREMENT THE OCCURANCE COUNT
RETURN  MOVEM.L (SP)+,D0/D1/D7/A0-A3
        RTS
        END
```

Figure 5-12 *(continued)*

```
*       SUBROUTINE INSTWD
*
        XDEF    INSTWD              ;       ********************************
INSTWD  MOVEM.L D0-D1/A0-A3,-(SP)   ;    SP *             D0             *
*                                   ;    +4 *             D1             *
*                                   ;    +8 *             A0             *
*                                   ;   +12 *             A1             *
*                                   ;   +16 *             A2             *
*                                   ;   +20 *             A3             *
*                                   ;   +24 *        RETURN ADDRESS      *
*                                   ;   +28 * ADDRESS OF WORD TO BE ADDED *
*                                   ;   +32 *    ADDRESS OF NO. OF WORDS  *
*                                   ;   +36 *    ADDRESS OF WORD TABLE    *
*                                   ;       ********************************
        MOVEA.L 36(SP),A0           ;A0 = ADDRESS OF THE WORD TABLE
        MOVEA.L 32(SP),A1
        MOVE.W  (A1),D0             ;D0 = NO. OF WORDS IN THE TABLE
        ADDQ.W  #1,(A1)             ;UPDATE THE NO. OF WORDS
        MOVEQ.W #20,D1
        MULU    D1,D0               ;D0 IS THE INDEX POINTING TO WHERE THE
*                                   ;NEW WORD IS TO BE ADDED
        SUBQ.W  #1,D1               ;THE FOLLOWING LOOP FILLS THE UNUSED
        LEA     (A0,D0.W),A2        ;SPACES WITH BLANKS
LOOP    MOVE.B  #' ',(A2)+
        DBF     D1,LOOP
        MOVEA.L 28(SP),A3           ;A3 = ADDRESS OF THE WORD TO BE ADDED
        LEA     0(A0,D0.W),A2       ;THE FOLLOWING LOOP COPIES
AGAIN   MOVE.B  (A3)+,(A2)+         ;GIVEN WORD TO THE TABLE
        CMPI.B  #' ',(A3)
        BNE     AGAIN
        MOVE.B  #':',17(A0,D0.W)    ;SEPARATE WORD AND COUNT WITH A ":"
        MOVE.B  #1,19(A0,D0.W)      ;SET INITIAL COUNT TO 1
        MOVEM.L (SP)+,D0-D1/A0-A3
        RTS
        END
```

Figure 5-12 *(continued)*

5-4 Recursive Subroutines

In many cases a formula or algorithm can be defined in terms of itself, or recursively. One commonly used example to illustrate recursion is factorial of N, which for $N \geq 1$ is defined as

$$N! = N \times (N - 1) \times (N - 2) \times \cdots \times 2 \times 1$$

Alternatively, $N!$ can be defined recursively as

$$N! = \begin{cases} N \times (N - 1)! & \text{if } N > 1 \\ 1 & \text{if } N = 1 \end{cases}$$

Any recursive algorithm has an equivalent nonrecursive form. For the example of $N!$, its nonrecursive form is perhaps more straightforward to implement. But in many cases, a recursive algorithm is easier to understand, and the resulting program requires less memory space than the corresponding nonrecursive form. As an example, consider processing a binary tree such as the one given in Fig. 5-13. If the tree is to be traversed in the order of nodes A, B, C, . . . , then the preorder traversal algorithm is best defined recursively as follows:

1. Process the root node. If this node is empty, stop. Otherwise, proceed with Step 2.
2. Traverse the left subtree of the root starting with root = the next node on the left branch from the current root.
3. Traverse the right subtree of the root starting with root = the next node on the right branch from the current root.

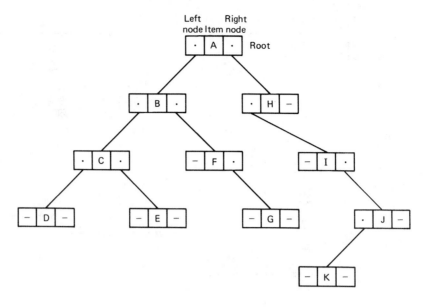

Note: — means empty

Figure 5-13 A binary tree.

In this case, the recursive version is much easier to understand and to implement than the nonrecursive version.

A recursive algorithm can be implemented by a subroutine capable of calling itself, known as a *recursive subroutine*. As an example of recursive subroutine, let us consider factorial of N again. The pseudocode of a recursive subroutine for calculating the factorial of N would look like this:

```
Subroutine   SUBFACT (N, NFACTR)
       IF      N = 1
       THEN NFACTR = 1
       ELSE
               DO     Call SUBFACT (N − 1, NFACTR);
                      NFACTR = N × NFACTR
               ENDDO;
       RETURN
```

Because the subroutine may be called before returning to the previous call, a recursive subroutine must not have any alterable part. In other words, a recursive subroutine must be a pure code that consists exclusively of instructions and constants. Space for storing any temporary results is not allowed to be implemented by static locations such as those defined by the DS and DC directive. Otherwise, the contents of those locations generated in the previous call might be destroyed by the successive calls. This is illustrated in Fig. 5-14, where the content of N for the current call must be preserved during the execution of successive calls. As storage can be allocated dynamically using the stack, in a recursive subroutine the storage required for saving registers, passing parameters, and storing temporary results is provided through the stack. Figure 5-15 shows how to implement the recursive subroutine SUBFACT. In the implementation, N is a 16-bit integer but $N!$ is returned as a 32-bit integer. During each successive call, a stack frame is added which is composed of 22 bytes. The contents of this frame, from the top, are: saved D0, saved D1, saved A1, return address, address of NFACTR, and temporary N (2 bytes). After each return to the previous call, these 22 bytes are released from the stack.

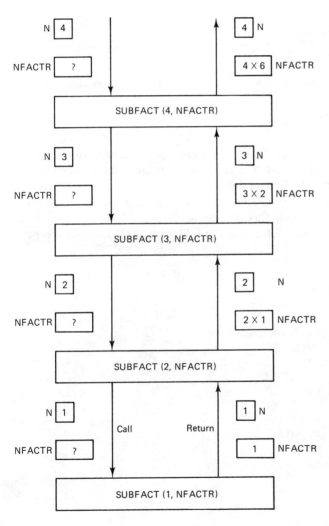

Figure 5-14 An example of recursive subroutine call.

```
                ORG      $2000
N               DC.W     10
NFACTR          DS.L     1
MAIN            MOVEA.L  #$3000,SP
                MOVE.W   N,-(SP)            ;PUSH N ONTO STACK
                PEA      NFACTR             ;PUSH ADDRESS OF N ONTO STACK
                JSR      SUBFACT
                ADDA.L   #6,SP              ;RELEASE 6 BYTES OCCUPIED BY N AND NFACTR
                STOP     #$2000
*
*    SUBFACT IS A RECURSIVE SUBROUTINE TO CALCULATE
*    FACTORIAL OF N USING RECURSIVE CALLS
*
SUBFACT         MOVEM.L  D0/D1/A1,-(SP)
                MOVE.W   20(SP),D0          ;D0 = N
                MOVEA.L  16(SP),A0          ;A0 = ADDRESS TO STORE N!
                CMPI.W   #1,D0
                BEQ.S    DONE
                MOVE.W   D0,D1
                SUBQ.W   #1,D1              ;D1 = N - 1
                MOVE.W   D1,-(SP)           ;PUSH N - 1
                PEA      (A0)               ;PUSH ADDRESS TO STORE (N - 1)! ONTO STACK
                JSR      SUBFACT            ;RETURN (N - 1)!
                ADDA.L   #6,SP              ;RELEASE 6 BYTES OCCUPIED BY PARAMETERS
                MOVE.W   2(A0),D1
                MULU     D0,D1              ;D1 = D0 * LEAST SIGNIFICANT
*                                           ;16 BITS OF (N - 1)!
                MULU     (A0),D0            ;D0 = D0 * MOST SIGNIFICANT
*                                           ;16 BITS OF (N - 1)!
                SWAP     D0                 ;SHIFT D0 TO LEFT BY 16 BITS
                ADD.L    D1,D0              ;D0 = N!
DONE            MOVE.L   D0,(A0)
                MOVEM.L  (SP)+,D0/D1/A1
                RTS
                END      MAIN
```

Figure 5-15   An implementation of the sample recursive subroutine calls.

5-5 Local Variables

For a block-structured high-level language such as Pascal, a procedure may contain local variables and other nested procedures. An inner-level procedure has access to its local variables and those defined in the outer level procedures containing this procedure. Upon completion of a procedure, its local variables are no longer accessible from outside this procedure.

To explain local variables, let us use the following skeleton Pascal program as an example:

```
PROGRAM    MAIN;
  VAR    XX, YY, ZZ: INTEGER;
  PROCEDURE    LEVL1A (Parameters);
   VAR    AA, BB: INTEGER;
   PROCEDURE    LEVL2A (Parameters);
    VAR    CC, DD: INTEGER;
    BEGIN    {LEVL2A}
      . . .
      CC := AA + DD;
      . . .
    END;    {LEVL2A}
   PROCEDURE    LEVL2B (Parameters);
    VAR    EE: INTEGER;
    BEGIN    {LEVL2B}
      . . .
      EE := 3;
      . . .
    END;    {LEVL2B}
```

```
BEGIN    {LEVL1A}
    . . .
    LEVL2A (Actual parameters);
    . . .
    LEVL2B (Actual parameters);
    . . .
END;     {LEVL1A}
BEGIN    {MAIN}
    . . .
    LEVL1A (Actual parameters);
    . . .
END      {MAIN}
```

The scopes of the variables defined in this program are shown in Fig. 5-16. Since variables XX, YY, and ZZ are defined in the main block, they are global variables and are accessible from anywhere in the program. On the other hand, variable EE is local to procedure LEVL2B. This means that variable EE can be accessed only within LEVL2B, and after leaving procedure LEVL2B this variable does not exist any more.

To implement this sample Pascal program, global variables such as XX, YY, and ZZ are defined during compilation time with DC or DS directives. But, as opposed to global variables, spaces for local variables are allocated dynamically during execution time. In other words, local variables should be created only when the procedure in which they are defined is invoked and their storage should be released whenever the procedure is exited. In order to support block-structured languages, the MC68000 provides an instruction pair, LINK and UNLK, for allocating and deallocating storage for local variables using the stack. The two instructions are summarized in Fig. 5-17.

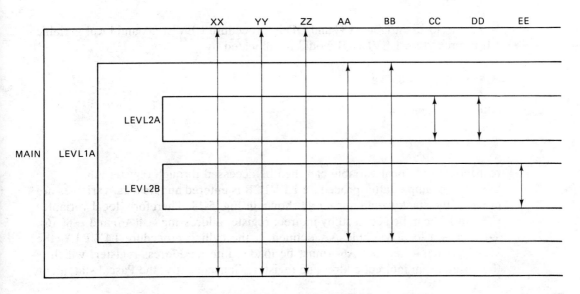

Figure 5-16 Scopes of local variables.

Mnemonic	Size or Postfix	Operand Format	Allowable EA Modes	Operation	Condition Flags N Z V C X
LINK (Link and allocate)	Unsized	An,#I16		An -> -(SP); SP -> An; SP + I16 -> SP	- - - - -
UNLK (Unlink)	Unsized	An		An -> SP; (SP)+ -> An	- - - - -

Figure 5-17 The link and unlink instructions.

The LINK (link and allocate) instruction first pushes the specified address register An onto the stack and copies SP into An. Then, the 16-bit immediate operand is added to the SP. In order to allocate space for local variables, this immediate operand must be a *negative* integer whose magnitude is the size in bytes of the storage to be allocated. In the instruction, operand An is used as a pointer to the area allocated for local variables. As mentioned earlier, inner-level procedures also have access to the local variables defined in outer-level procedures. To accomplish this, it is necessary to keep a link (pointer) to the local area of the procedure that contains the procedure being called. Therefore, before loading An from SP, the LINK instruction saves onto the stack the old An, which is a pointer to the local area of the calling procedure.

The UNLK (unlink) instruction, which uses an address register as its operand, deallocates the storage occupied by local variables. The instruction restores SP from the specified register An and then restores An to its old content from the stack.

Assume that A6 is chosen to implement the pointer to a local area. Then, in implementing the previous sample Pascal program, local variables AA and BB in procedure LEVL1A would be created by

        LINK   A6,# − 8

Likewise, local variables CC and DD in procedure LEVEL2A and local variable EE in procedure LEVEL2B would be allocated by

        LINK   A6,# − 8

and

        LINK   A6,# − 4

respectively. A local variable can then be accessed through register A6.

For example, after procedure LEVL2B is entered and its local variables are created, the stack would appear as shown in Fig. 5-18. Therefore, local variables CC and DD can be accessed by indirect register addressing − 4(A6) and − 8(A6). To access a local variable AA defined in the calling procedure LEVL1A, the saved pointer—i.e., old A6—must be loaded into an address register, which is then used as an indirect addressing register. Consequently, the Pascal statement

        CC := AA + DD

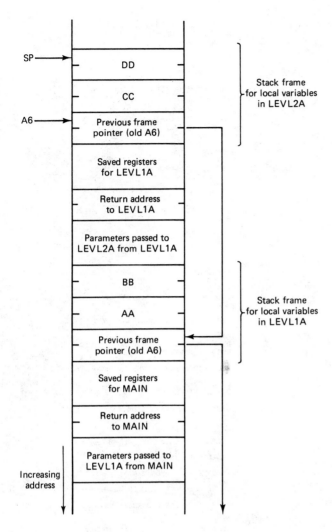

Figure 5-18 Implementation of local variables.

can be implemented as

```
MOVEA.L     (A6),A0
MOVE.L      - 4(A0),D0
ADD.L       - 8(A6),D0
MOVE.L      D0, - 4(A6)
```

Based on this discussion, the sample Pascal program would be complied into the code as shown in Fig. 5-19. Note that the UNLK instruction is designed to deallocate the storage, which is created by a LINK instruction, before returning to the calling procedure. It is still necessary to deallocate the storage used for passing parameters after returning to the calling procedure.

```
LEVL2A    MOVEM.L   D0-D7/A0-A5,-(SP)  ;BEGIN OF PROCEDURE LEVL2A
          LINK      A6,#-8             ;ALLOCATE SPACE FOR LOCAL VARRIABLES
            .                          ;CC AND DD
            .
            .

          MOVEA.L   (A6),A0            ;CC := AA + DD
          MOVE.L    -4(A0),D0          ;     D0 = AA
          ADD.L     -8(A6),D0          ;     D0 = AA + DD
          MOVE.L    D0,-4(A6)          ;     CC = D0
            .
            .
            .

          UNLK      A6                 ;RELEASE SPACE OF CC AND DD
          MOVEM.L   (SP)+,D0-D7/A0-A5
          RTS                          ;END OF LEVL2A
*
LEVL2B    MOVEM.L   D0-D7/A0-A5,-(SP)  ;BEGIN OF PROCEDURE LEVL2B
          LINK      A6,#-4             ;ALLOCATE SPACE FOR LOCAL VARIABLE EE
            .
            .

          MOVEQ     #3,-4(A6)          ;EE := 3
            .
            .
            .

          UNLK      A6                 ;RELEASE SPACE OF EE
          MOVEM.L   (SP)+,D0-D7/A0-A5
          RTS                          ;END OF LEVL2B
*
LEVL1A    MOVEM.L   D0-D7/A0-A5,-(SP)  ;BEGIN OF PROCEDURE LEVL1A
          LINK      A6,#-8             ;ALLOCATE SPACE FOR LOCAL
            .                          ;VARIABLES AA AND BB
            .
                                       ;PUSH PARAMETER ADDRESSES ONTO STACK

          JSR       LEVL2A             ;CALL LEVL2A
          ADDA.L    #N,SP              ;DEALLOCATE SPACE, N = NO OF BYTES
            .                          ;USED BY PARAMETER ADDRESSES
            .
                                       ;PUSH PARAMETER ADDRESSES ONTO STACK

          JSR       LEVEL2B            ;CALL LEVL2B
          ADDA.L    #N,SP              ;DEALLOCATE SPACE, N = NO OF BYTES

            .                          ;USED BY PARAMETER ADDRESSES
            .

          UNLK      A6                 ;RELEASE SPACE OF AA AND BB
          MOVEM.L   (SP)+,D0-D7/A0-A5
          RTS                          ;END OF LEVL1A
*
DATAMA    DS.B      12                 ;RESERVE SPACE FOR GLOBAL VARIABLES
*                                      ;XX, YY AND ZZ
MAIN        .                          ;ENTRY POINT OF MAIN PROGRAM
            .
            .                          ;PUSH PARAMETER ADDRESSES ONTO STACK

          JSR       LEVL1A             ;CALL LEVL1A
          ADDA.L    #N,SP              ;DEALLOCATE SPACE, N = NO OF BYTES
            .                          ;USED BY PARAMETER ADDRESSES
            .
            .

          END       MAIN
```

Figure 5-19 Implementation of the sample Pascal program.

5-6 Multiprogramming Considerations

Multiprogramming

In a multiprogramming environment, the system is shared in a time-multiplexed fashion among several programs. If the current running program is waiting for completion of some other operations, such as input/output, the current program is blocked and the processor switches to the next program. A blocked program is activated again and resumes its execution at a later time. Therefore, improved utilization of the system is achieved by reducing the processor's idle time. Even though a processor can only execute one program at a time, multiprogramming makes it appear that several programs are running simultaneously.

Figure 5-20 graphically demonstrates the chief advantage of multiprogramming systems. Part (a) of the figure shows how two typical programs are executed in a uniprogramming environment. In this example, program 1 begins and continues until I/O is needed (point A); then the I/O is initiated and the processing continues in parallel with the I/O until the processing needs the input data. At this point it must wait until the I/O is completed (point B). When the I/O is finished (point C), the processing is resumed. A similar description applies to points D, E, and F. At the end of process 1, process 2 can begin, and its operation is basically the same as that of process 1.

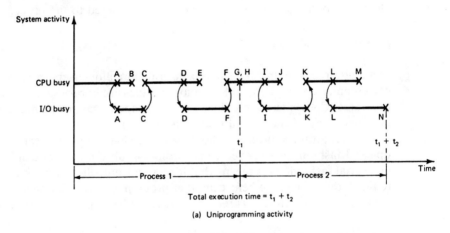

(a) Uniprogramming activity

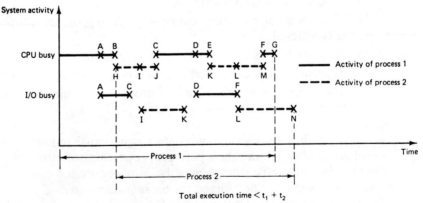

(b) Multiprogramming activity utilizing a single CPU and a single DMA channel

Figure 5-20 Advantage of a multiprogramming versus a uniprogramming system. Yu-cheng Liu/Glenn A. Gibson, *Microcomputer Systems: The 8086/8088 Family, 2/E,* © 1986. Reprinted by permission of Prentice Hall, Inc., Englewood Cliffs, New Jersey.

On the other hand, if multiprogramming is applied, then the activity is as illustrated in Fig. 5-20(b). It is seen that instead of the processor being idle while it is waiting for the I/O of process 1, in a multiprogramming system process 2 can be started and can utilize the processor until it needs to wait for I/O. At that time, if process 1 has finished its I/O operation, it can resume its use of the processor. Thus the overall processing time can be significantly reduced.

When the processor switches from one program to another, it must save the machine status for the current running program so that it can continue this program later. The machine status to be saved consists of the PC, SR, and all data and address registers, including the system stack pointer, which is the USP when each user program is running in the user state. Since program switching is performed by the operating system, the machine status of each program is saved onto the supervisor stack pointed to by the SSP. Figure 5-21 shows the stack image of saved machine status for each program. Before resuming the execution of a blocked program, its saved machine status is copied to the processor.

Reentrant routines

In a multiprogramming system, it is desirable to allow users to share a single copy of a common routine. Typical common routines are library subroutines and system programs. Code sharing provides the advantage of saving memory space because only one copy of the shared routine is stored in memory.

A reentrant subroutine allows it to be shared among users on a time-multiplexed fashion, as opposed to an ordinary subroutine that can be shared only in a serial fashion. This means that for a reentrant subroutine, it is not necessary to finish the subroutine before another program can call the same subroutine. For example, if subroutine X is reentrant, it could be shared in the following manner:

1. Program A calls subroutine X.
2. The processor switches from program A to program B before subroutine X is completed.
3. Program B calls the same copy of subroutine X.
4. Subroutine X is completed and control is returned to program B.
5. The processor switches back to program A, which resumes subroutine X from where it stopped.

As with a recursive subroutine, the principal requirement of a reentrant subroutine is that it must be a pure code, consisting of instructions and constants only. Any temporary storage must be provided by the calling routine. This requirement includes the storage for passing parameters if another subroutine is called within the reentrant routine. This can be accomplished by using a stack pointed to by either the SP or another address register and passing the stack pointer to the subroutine. When the processor switches from one program to the next, it saves the SR and all registers, including the stack pointer. Therefore, each user or program can have its own stack areas. Switching programs causes the content of the stack pointer to change accordingly, pointing to the stack of

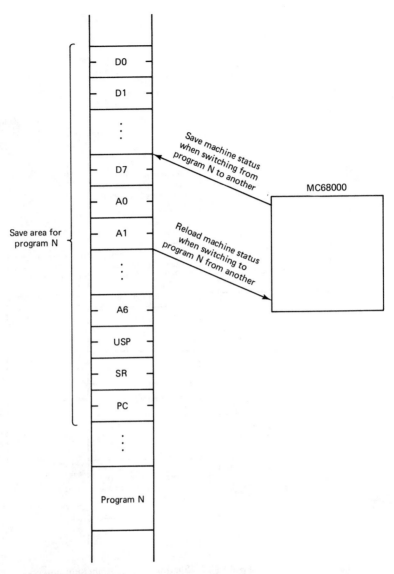

Figure 5-21 Saving and restoring machine status in program switching.

the next program. In this way, as illustrated by Fig. 5-22, the intermediate results generated by the subroutine for the previous program remain intact while the same subroutine is invoked by another program. Since a reentrant routine does not modify itself, it can be stored in ROM, thus providing a protection against being changed unintentionally by users.

   In addition to being pure code, it is desirable for a reentrant subroutine to be position-independent. As mentioned before, a position-independent code can be loaded anywhere in memory for execution without the need for relocation. This flexibility is particularly useful to a reentrant subroutine because it is intended

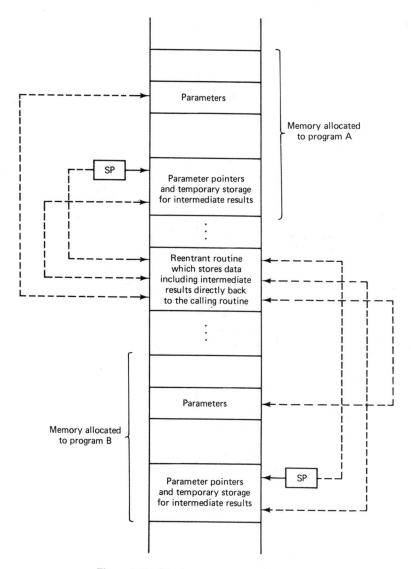

Figure 5-22 Sharing of a reentrant subroutine.

to be shared by more than one program; consequently, it is usually linked dynamically to a calling program at execution time.

Task synchronization

In a multiprogramming system, each program that performs a specific function independently is called a *task*, or *process*. Normally, the time at which a processor switches from one task to another is not a concern to the tasks and would not affect the end results of each task. But, if two tasks are updating—not just using—the contents of a shared memory area, care must be taken to make sure that only one task has access to the shared memory at a time. Otherwise, the results could be erroneous or even unpredictable. Access to a common resource can be controlled by synchronizing the tasks at critical points.

A simple way to explain the need for task synchronization is by an example. Consider a multiprogramming system that handles ticket reservations through two terminals, as given in Fig. 5-23. Both tasks A and B input ticket requests from their respective terminals. Then, each task executes its instruction sequence, X, Y, Z, W, and T, to perform the following. It checks the number of available tickets stored in variable AVAILTIKS, which is accessible to both tasks. If sufficient tickets are available, it issues the requested number of tickets and subtracts the requested number from AVAILTIKS. Otherwise, it ignores the request and waits for the next input.

Depending on the actual sequence of how the processor switches back and forth between the two tasks, the outcomes can be different. Suppose that there are five tickets left, and task A receives a request for four tickets and task B, for three tickets. Then, we have four possible different outcomes:

1. The processor executes statements X, Y, Z, and W of task A and then switches to task B starting from statement X. Since AVAILTIKS has already been updated to 1, task B will not issue any tickets. Eventually, the processor switches back to task A and resumes from statement T. Therefore, four tickets are issued and AVAILTIKS shows 1.

2. The processor executes statements X, Y, Z, and W of task B and then switches to task A starting from statement X. This sequence will yield the results that three tickets are issued and AVAILTIKS shows 2.

3. The processor executes X and Y of task A, switches to task B, and executes X and Y of task B. Since at this point AVAILTIKS has not been changed by task A, task B proceeds with statements W and T. After switching back to task A, its SR and D1 are restored. Since the restored condition code indicates $D1 > 0$, task A also completes its W and T sequence. This causes a total of seven tickets to be issued. In addition, the content of AVAILTIKS is first changed to 2 in task B and then changed to 1 in task A.

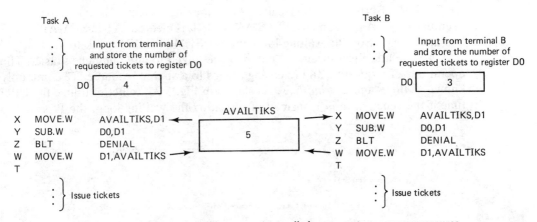

Figure 5-23 An example to illustrate uncontrolled accesses to a common resource.

4. The execution sequence is X and Y of task B; X, Y, Z, W, and T of task A; and then Z, W, and T of task B. Following the same argument in case 3, seven tickets will be issued, and the final content of AVAILTIKS will be 2.

Since the task-switching event is not predictable, sometimes this system works (cases 1 and 2) and sometimes it does not (cases 3 and 4). To resolve this problem, tasks A and B must be synchronized at the critical point X so that only one task is allowed to execute the sequence X through W at a time.

The TAS instruction and synchronization primitives

The TAS (test and set) instruction is specifically designed to simplify task synchronization. As summarized in Fig. 5-24, this instruction can test the current value of a byte operand and set its most significant bit to 1 in a single instruction.

To synchronize tasks the TAS instruction can be used to test and set a software flag, called a *semaphore*, that indicates whether a task has to wait (semaphore = 1) or not (semaphore = 0). For the previous example of the ticket-reservation system, a simple solution to prevent both tasks from updating variable AVAILTIKS simultaneously is as shown:

```
WAIT     TAS        SEMAPHORE
         BNE        WAIT
X        MOVE.W     AVAILTIKS,D1
Y        SUB.W      D0,D1
Z        BLT        DENIAL
W        MOVE.W     D1,AVAILTIKS
         MOVE.B     #0,SEMAPHORE
```

If SEMAPHORE = 0 when the TAS instruction is executed in task A, then SEMAPHORE is set to 1, and meanwhile the Z flag is also set. Even if the processor switches to task B at this point, task B cannot begin with statement X because SEMAPHORE has already been set to 1. This causes task B to repeat the TAS and BNE instruction pair, which does not affect SEMAPHORE, until eventually task A is resumed and SEMAPHORE is cleared. A 0 in SEMAPHORE lets task B exit from its waiting loop and set SEMAPHORE back to 1.

The solution just discussed can be generalized to any number of tasks. The operations of requesting and releasing access to a shared resource are commonly known as the *P* and *V primitives*. As shown in Fig. 5-25, to better utilize the CPU time if the semaphore is 1, instead of repeating the waiting loop, the P primitive

Mnemonic	Size or Postfix	Operand Format	Allowable EA Modes	Operation	Condition Flags N Z V C X
TAS (Test and set)	Byte	EA	Data alterable	(EA) - 0; 1 -> EA[7]	* * 0 0 -

Note: The TAS instruction is executed in a single read-modify-write cycle.

Figure 5-24 The test and set instruction.

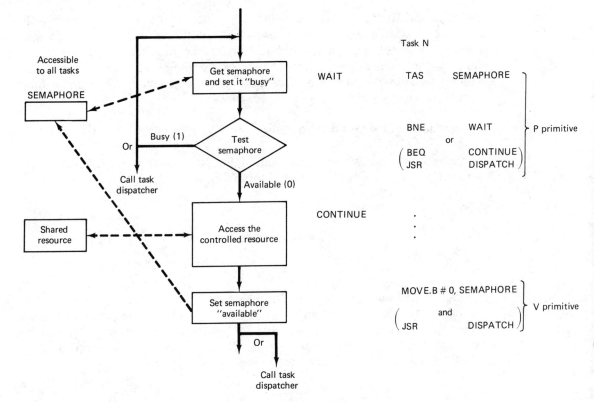

Figure 5-25   P and V primitives.

can call the monitor, which switches the processor to a ready task. Likewise, in the V primitive, the monitor is called to wake up a blocked process associated with the semaphore.

The TAS instruction can be applied to multiple-processor (multiprocessing) systems as well in coordinating access to a common resource. Testing and setting a memory operand requires two bus cycles, a memory read followed by a memory write. In a multiple-processor system, it is possible for another processor to gain the control of the bus between these two cycles and to access the semaphore. To prevent this problem, the TAS instruction uses a special read-modify-write memory cycle, making the test and set a single indivisible operation.

5-7 Macros

A macro is a sequence of statements that—once defined—can be repeated by invoking a single statement within the program. A macro is invoked by a statement calling the macro by name with a list of actual arguments.

As opposed to a subroutine, each time a macro is called, its definition is inserted into the program at that point, with dummy arguments being replaced by actual arguments. This sequence is called a *macro expansion* and is illustrated in Fig. 5-26. After that, the usual assembly process takes place to translate the expanded code into machine instructions. Unlike subroutines, macros do not save memory, but they make a program appear shorter, thus reducing programming time and improving program readability. An assembler that can process macro definitions and perform macro expansions in addition to the usual assembly function is commonly known as a *macro assembler*.

Macro definitions and macro calls

A macro definition, which begins with a MACRO directive and terminates with an ENDM directive, has the general form:

Name   MACRO

.
.   (Prototype code)
.

        ENDM

where Name is the user specified macro name. Dummy arguments may be included in the macro definition to be used as labels, instruction mnemonics, and operands. An argument is designated by a \ (backlash), followed by a digit 0 through 9 or an uppercase letter A through Z. Argument \0 is reserved for the qualifier that may be appended to the macro name.

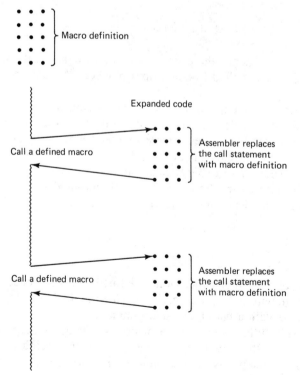

Figure 5-26 Execution of a macro.

Similar to a regular assembly instruction, a macro call has the form

Label	Name.Qualifier	Argument list

where Name is the name of the macro being called, Qualifier is optional for specifying a size postfix, and the arugment list contains the actual arguments separated by commas.

When a macro call is encountered by the macro assembler, the assembler replaces the call statement with the prototype code in the macro definition after substituting the actual arguments for their corresponding dummy arguments. This argument substitution eliminates the need for a parameter linkage at execution time as required by a subroutine. The example in Fig. 5-27 defines a macro SUM for adding two operands and storing the sum into the third operand and shows some typical calls to this macro.

Local labels

A label is often required in a macro. Consider a macro for performing BCD additions, with the operand size being specified as an argument. This macro might be defined as shown in Fig. 5-28(a). When this macro is called, for example, by the statement

```
ADDBCD      #6,ARYA(A5),ARYB(A5)
```

the label LOOP appears in the program after the expansion as shown in Fig. 5-28(b). Any subsequent call for ADDBCD causes LOOP to reappear as a label in

```
SUM        MACRO
           MOVE.\0    \1,D0
           ADD.\0     \2,D0
           MOVE.\0    D0,\3
           ENDM
             .
             .
             .
```

After macro expansion

```
           SUM.L      AA,BB,CC          {    MOVE.L     AA,D0
                                             ADD.L      BB,D0
                                             MOVE.L     D0,CC
             .
             .
             .
LOOP       SUM.W      (A0)+,(A1)+,(A2)+ { LOOP  MOVE.W    (A0)+,D0
                                             ADD.W      (A1)+,D0
                                             MOVE.W     D0,(A2)+
             .
             .
             .
           SUM.L      #$1234,$3000,D7   {    MOVE.L     #$1234,D0
                                             ADD.L      $3000,D0
                                             MOVE.L     D0,D7
             .
             .
             .
```

Figure 5-27 An example of macro definition and macro call.

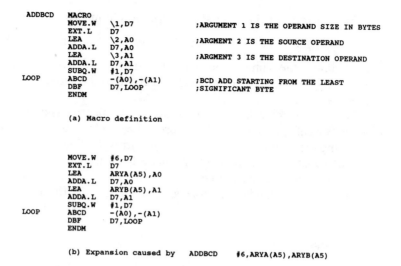

```
ADDBCD    MACRO
          MOVE.W    \1,D7            ;ARGUMENT 1 IS THE OPERAND SIZE IN BYTES
          EXT.L     D7
          LEA       \2,A0            ;ARGMENT 2 IS THE SOURCE OPERAND
          ADDA.L    D7,A0
          LEA       \3,A1            ;ARGMENT 3 IS THE DESTINATION OPERAND
          ADDA.L    D7,A1
          SUBQ.W    #1,D7
LOOP      ABCD      -(A0),-(A1)      ;BCD ADD STARTING FROM THE LEAST
          DBF       D7,LOOP          ;SIGNIFICANT BYTE
          ENDM

          (a) Macro definition


          MOVE.W    #6,D7
          EXT.L     D7
          LEA       ARYA(A5),A0
          ADDA.L    D7,A0
          LEA       ARYB(A5),A1
          ADDA.L    D7,A1
          SUBQ.W    #1,D7
LOOP      ABCD      -(A0),-(A1)
          DBF       D7,LOOP
          ENDM

          (b) Expansion caused by   ADDBCD    #6,ARYA(A5),ARYB(A5)
```

Figure 5-28 An example of need for a local label in a macro.

the same program. This will generate an error during the usual assembly phase because LOOP is defined in more than one place. The above mentioned problem can be resolved by replacing label LOOP with an argument and by using a different actual label for this argument during each call. However, the programmer needs to keep track of which labels have already been used to avoid reusing the same labels. A better solution is to define LOOP as a label local to the macro. A local label is declared by prefixing an @ to the label. Using a local label, the last two instructions in macro ADDBCD should be replaced with

```
@LOOP      ABCD      -(A0),-(A1)
           DBF       D7,@LOOP
```

Each time this macro is called, the assembler attaches a different integer as a suffix to label LOOP during the expansion. As a result, a different label is generated for each expansion.

Macro nesting and recursion

It is perfectly legal for one macro to include a call to another. A macro may even call itself. For a recursive macro, care must be taken to make sure that the expansion will eventually be terminated. Normally this requires the use of conditional assembly directives.

Following is an example of a recursive macro that reserves the number of bytes defined by argument 1 and fills them with the value specified by argument 2.

```
BLKDCB     MACRO
COUNT      SET       \1
           IFGT      COUNT
           DC.B      \2
```

```
COUNT      SET        COUNT-1
           BLKDCB     COUNT,\2
           ENDC
           ENDM
```

In the definition of macro BLKDCB, the

```
COUNT   SET        \1
```

directive assigns symbol COUNT a value specified by argument 1. The IFGT (assemble if greater than) directive is a conditional assembly directive that tests the value associated with COUNT. If the tested value is greater than 0, the assembler reserves a byte with initial value specified by argument 2, reassigns COUNT to COUNT – 1, and expands macro call

```
BLKDCB        COUNT,\2
```

again. If the test fails, all the statements between the IFGT and the ENDC (end of conditional block) directives are skipped, thus terminating the macro expansion. The marcro call

```
BLOCK0        BLKDCB        100,0
```

will be expanded to 100 bytes with preassigned value 0 starting from location BLOCK0. Reserving 50 bytes of constant FF and associating variable BLKFF with the first byte can be accomplished by

```
BLKFF        BLKDCB        50,$FF
```

Conditional assembly directives

A conditional assembly directive such as the one used in the previous example has the general form

```
IFcc        Expression
   .
   .            Range of conditional assembly block
   .
ENDC
```

where cc represents a specified test condition. Based on the evaluation of the given expression and the specified test condition, the block of source code between the IFcc and ENDC directives is to be included or excluded during the assembly process. The possible test conditions are as follows:

IFEQ: Assemble if equal to zero.
IFNE: Assemble if not equal to zero.

IFLT: Assemble if less than zero.

IFGT: Assemble if greater than zero.

IFGE: Assemble if greater than or equal to zero.

IFLE: Assemble if less than or equal to zero.

It is important to understand the difference between a conditional assembly directive and a compare and conditional branch instruction pair. Since a conditional assembly directive is executed at assembly time, it is intended to test the value associated with a symbol (or expression) and therefore cannot be used to test the content of a memory location or register. For example, if ARY is defined as a label, none of the following statements is valid:

```
IFGT    ARY
IFGT    D1 + D2
IFGT    4(A1) − 0(A2,D1.W)
```

EXERCISES

1. Assume that SP = 004000, D0 = 00123456, and D1 = FFEEDDCC, determine the contents of the stack and the stack pointer after D0 and D1 have been pushed onto the stack.

2. Assume that SP = 004000 and that the contents of memory block starting from 004000 through 00400E are 00 11 22 33 44 55 66 77 88 99 AA BB CC and DD. Determine the contents of SP and all affected registers after popping five words from the stack to registers A1, D0.W, and D1.

3. Consider the following sequence of subroutine calls.
   (1) Main routine calls SUB1 with the return address = 001208.
   (2) Subroutine SUB1 calls SUB2 with the return address = 001804.
   (3) Subroutine SUB2 is completed.
   (4) Subroutine SUB1 is completed.
   (5) Main routine calls SUB3 with the return address = 001400.
   (6) Subroutine SUB3 is completed.
   Assume that the SP initially points to 001000, and the only stack activity is due to the calls and returns. Draw a series of diagrams to illustrate the stack at each major point.

4. Reimplement the bubble sort routine given in Fig. 3-19 as a subroutine. Use a parameter table to pass the addresses of parameters ARRAY and NN.

5. Give a typical sequence for calling the subroutine in Exercise 4.

6. Reimplement the routine given in Fig. 3-15, which will find the maximum and minimum values in an array, as a subroutine. Assume that the stack is used for passing addresses of parameters ARRAY, SIZE, MIN, and MAX.

7. Give a typical sequence for calling the subroutine in Exercise 6.

8. Write a subroutine that will search an ASCII string of NUM characters stored in STRING and replace each underscore (_) by a blank space. Assume that parameters NUM and STRING are to be passed via a parameter address table. Also, give a typical calling sequence for this subroutine.

9. Write two subroutines BCDADD and BCDSUB to perform BCD additions and subtractions. Each subroutine has four parameters:

    RESULT: stores the sum or difference
    OPRA: stores the augend or minuend
    OPRB: stores the addend or subtrahend
    SIZE: stores the operand size in bytes

    Assume that the parameter addresses are passed via the stack.

10. Write a main routine that will use the subroutines requested in Exercise 9 to evaluate the expressions:
    (a) X = A + B − C (b) Y = 123 + C + B − A − 87654
    For each expression, the operand size is assumed to be 3 bytes.

11. Write a recursive subroutine to calculate X^N. Assume that operands X and N are words and the result is a longword.

12. Assuming a single processor system, implement the P primitive without using the TAS instruction. Will this implementation work for multiprocessor systems?

13. Consider the example given in Fig. 5-23 to illustrate the problem of uncontrolled access. Suppose the instructions X through W are replaced with the following sequence:

```
X       SUB.W    D0,AVAILTIKS
Y       BGE      T
Z       ADD.W    D0,AVAILTIKS
W       BRA      DENIAL
```

    Will this solve the problem? Justify your answer.

14. Draw a series of diagrams to illustrate the stack for each major point in the program given in Fig. 5-19.

15. Write a macro ABS that will store the absolute value given by argument OPR into argument ANS. Also give three sample calls to this macro and show the expansions resulting from these calls.

16. Write a macro STGCMP that will compare two strings and set a byte flag to 1 if the two strings match and to 0 otherwise. The macro should have four arguments:

    \1: First string to be compared
    \2: Second string to be compared
    \3: Number of bytes in each string
    \4: One-byte variable for the flag

    It is assumed that registers A0, A1, and D7 are to be used in the macro and their contents need not be saved.

17. Show the expansion resulting from each of the following calls to the macro requested in Exercise 16:

    (a) NEXT   STGCMP   ARY1,ARY2,35,FLAG
    (b)   STGCMP   TABLE(A3),$4000,D1,D2
    (c)   STGCMP   0(A3,D3.W),OFFSET(A3,D3.W),SIZE(A3),FLAG(A3)

18. Define two macros DUBADD and DUBSUB to perform 64-bit additions and subtractions. Macro DUBADD adds the first and the second arguments and stores the sum into the third argument. Macro DUBSUB subtracts the first argument from the second and stores the difference into the third.

19. Give an instruction sequence that will use the two macros requested in Exercise 18 to evaluate the expression

$$ANS + AA + BB - CC + DD$$

6

Exception Processing

6-1 Exceptions

Sometimes the processor may temporarily suspend the current program execution in order to respond immediately to certain conditions. This deviation from a normal processing sequence is called an *exception*.

There are many different causes for exceptions, and they can be classified into two general groups, internal exceptions and external exceptions. Figure 6-1 outlines the types of MC68000 exceptions. An exception may be initiated internally in the processor due to an error arising during the execution of an instruction (i.e., divide by zero, invalid address, privilege violation, and invalid op code), the execution of a special instruction (i.e., TRAP, TRAPV, and CHK instructions), or the enabling of the trace mode. An exception may also be initiated externally by sending to the processor a signal from somewhere else in the system. Possible causes for an external exception are a reset signal, a bus error, or an interrupt request from a peripheral device.

In order for the processor to respond properly to the individual exception or to recover from different errors, it is necessary to identify the source during an exception. Each exception is associated with an 8-bit vector number, either generated internally by the MC68000 or supplied externally. This vector number is translated to a memory address, called a *vector address*, by

$$\text{Vector address} = \text{vector number} \times 4$$

The processor can then obtain the beginning address of the service routine to process that particular exception from the calculated vector address.

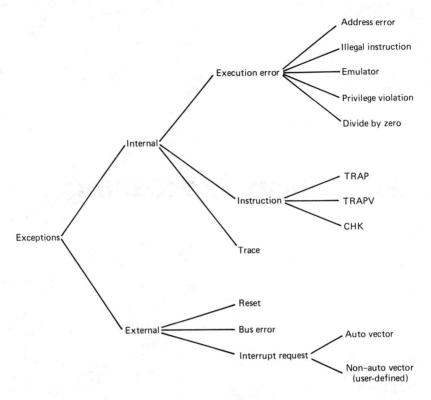

Figure 6-1 Types of MC68000 exceptions.

Figure 6-2 shows the assignment of vector numbers for all exceptions. The first column shows the assigned vector number for each exception. The second and third columns are the associated vector address in decimal and in hexadecimal forms. The fourth column indicates the function code issued by the MC68000 while fetching the contents from that vector address, where SP means the supervisor program space and SD is the supervisor data space. Presumably, the function code can be used by memory management hardware to control unauthorized memory references. The last column lists the exception type associated with a given vector number. Any vector number from 64 through 255 is not preassigned and therefore can be used by a peripheral device for requesting interrupts.

Each exception vector (except reset) uses two words to store the 24-bit beginning address of a service routine for processing the associated exception. The reset vector requires four words because not only the program counter but also the supervisor stack pointer needs to be initialized during a reset.

During an exception, the processor automatically performs an exception sequence in the supervisor mode to start the execution of the service routine. With minor deviations for certain types of exceptions, the general exception sequence consists of the following steps:

1. The current SR, including both the system byte and the condition codes, is saved internally in a temporary register. Then, in the system byte, the su-

Vector Number(s)	Dec	Address Hex	Space	Assignment
0	0	000	SP	Reset: Initial SSP[2]
	4	004	SP	Reset: Initial PC[2]
2	8	008	SD	Bus Error
3	12	00C	SD	Address Error
4	16	010	SD	Illegal Instruction
5	20	014	SD	Zero Divide
6	24	018	SD	CHK Instruction
7	28	01C	SD	TRAPV Instruction
8	32	020	SD	Privilege Violation
9	36	024	SD	Trace
10	40	028	SD	Line 1010 Emulator
11	44	02C	SD	Line 1111 Emulator
12[1]	48	030	SD	(Unassigned, Reserved)
13[1]	52	034	SD	(Unassigned, Reserved)
14[1]	56	038	SD	(Unassigned, Reserved)
15	60	03C	SD	Uninitialized Interrupt Vector
16-23[1]	64	040	SD	(Unassigned, Reserved)
	95	05F		–
24	96	060	SD	Spurious Interrupt[3]
25	100	064	SD	Level 1 Interrupt Autovector
26	104	068	SD	Level 2 Interrupt Autovector
27	108	06C	SD	Level 3 Interrupt Autovector
28	112	070	SD	Level 4 Interrupt Autovector
29	116	074	SD	Level 5 Interrupt Autovector
30	120	078	SD	Level 6 Interrupt Autovector
31	124	07C	SD	Level 7 Interrupt Autovector
32-47	128	080	SD	TRAP Instruction Vectors[4]
	191	0BF		
48-63[1]	192	0C0	SD	(Unassigned, Reserved)
	255	0FF		–
64-255	256	100	SD	User Interrupt Vectors
	1023	3FF		–

NOTES:
1. Vector numbers 12, 13, 14, 16 through 23, and 48 through 63 are reserved for future enhancements by Motorola. No user peripheral devices should be assigned these numbers.
2. Reset vector (0) requires four words, unlike the other vectors which only require two words, and is located in the supervisor program space.
3. The spurious interrupt vector is taken when there is a bus error indication during interrupt processing.
4. TRAP #n uses vector number 32 + n.

Figure 6-2 Exception vector assignment. (Courtesy of Motorola, Inc.)

pervisor (S) bit is set to 1 and the trace (T) bit is cleared. This puts the processor in the supervisor mode and prevents further interruptions caused by tracing while the service routine is executed.

2. The return address is saved by pushing the PC onto the supervisor stack. The return address normally points to the next unexecuted instruction.

3. The saved SR (before S and T bits being modified) is pushed onto the supervisor stack.

4. The processor obtains the vector number, N, associated with the exception and then loads the content at the vector address, $N \times 4$, into the PC. This causes the processor to enter the service routine for processing that exception.

For an interrupt exception, the processor waits until the current instruction is completed and then starts this exception sequence.

To illustrate the exception sequence, suppose that the SSP has 002456 and the instruction

DIVS   #0,D1

is assembled at address 012000. If this divide-by-zero instruction is executed, an exception with vector number 5 will occur. Figure 6-3 shows the registers and the supervisor stack area that are affected during the exception sequence.

Although some similarities exist between a subroutine call and an exception sequence, there are two major differences. First, an exception is always processed in the supervisor mode, whereas a subroutine call does not change the state of the processor. Second, the SR is saved in an exception but not in a subroutine call. This is because some exceptions are initiated by errors and external events,

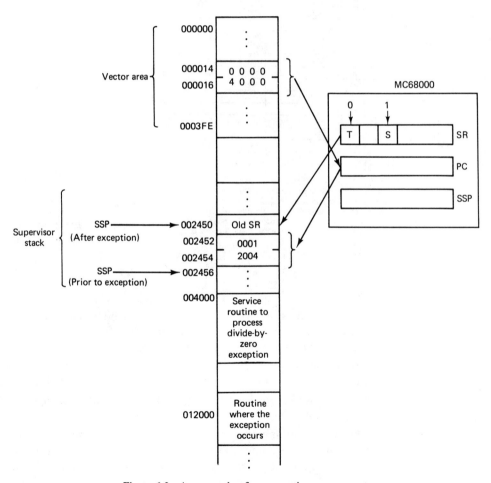

Figure 6-3   An example of an exception sequence.

and therefore it is unpredictable when an exception may occur. If the SR is not saved, the routine where an exception occurs may not be able to continue properly after returning from the exception service routine. An obvious example is that an exception may take place between the two instructions

```
CMP.W    OPR,D1
BNE      NOTEQ
```

In order to branch correctly after returning from the service routine, the condition codes set by the CMP instruction must be preserved.

In order to resume execution of the routine in which the exception occurred, the original SR as well as the return address must be popped from the supervisor stack after the exception service routine is completed. This operation is performed by the privileged RTE (return from exception) instruction defined in Fig. 6-4. Since the RTE instruction restores the original system byte of the SR, it causes the processor to switch back to the user state if this is the original state. As shown in Fig. 6-5, exceptions and the RTE instruction provide a means for transitions between the two processor states. A transition from the supervisor state to the user state can also be made by directly modifying the S bit, but the opposite cannot happen.

Mnemonic	Size or Postfix	Operand Format	Allowable EA Modes	Operation	Condition Flags N Z V C X
RTE (Return from exception)	Unsized	None		(SP)+ -> SR; (SP)+ -> PC	* * * * *

Note: RTE is a privileged instruction.

Figure 6-4 The RTE instruction.

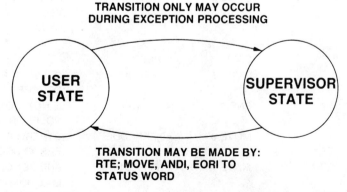

TRANSITION ONLY MAY OCCUR
DURING EXCEPTION PROCESSING

USER STATE   SUPERVISOR STATE

TRANSITION MAY BE MADE BY:
RTE; MOVE, ANDI, EORI TO
STATUS WORD

Figure 6-5 Transitions between user and supervisor states. (Courtesy of Motorola, Inc.)

An exception service routine, unlike a subroutine, uses registers and directly accessible common areas instead of parameter addresses to receive information from and pass results to the interrupted routine. Because some exceptions occur at random points in the interrupted program, for such exceptions it will not be possible to put the parameter addresses in a table or push them onto the stack at the appropriate time. In addition, before an exception occurs, the beginning address of its service routine must be placed in the vector address associated with that exception.

Suppose that we wish to write a service routine for the divide-by-zero exception. Among other things, this service routine would set the variable ERRCODE to 5 and increment the count COUNT5 by one each time a divide-by-zero error occurs. Then the service routine can be implemented as follows:

```
SEREXC5     MOVEM.L     D0 – D7/A0 – A6, – (SP)
            MOVE.W      #5,ERRCODE
            ADDQ.W      #1,COUNT5
                .
                .
                .
            MOVEM.L     (SP) + ,D0 – D7/A0 – A6
            RTE
```

The program where divide-by-zero errors may occur should initialize the common variables ERRCODE and COUNT5 and the exception vector address as outlined next.

```
COUNT5      DS.W        1
ERRCODE     DS.W        1
                .
                .
                .
            MOVE.W      #0,COUNT5        ;INITIALIZE THE ERROR COUNT
            MOVE.W      #0,ERRCODE       ;INITIALIZE THE ERROR CODE
            MOVE.L      #SEREXC5,20      ;INITIALIZE THE EXCEPTION
                                         ;VECTOR ADDRESS FOR DIVIDE
                                         ;BY ZERO
                .
                .
                .
            DIVU        DIVISOR,D1
            CMPI.W      #5,ERRCODE       ;CHECK IF A DIVIDE BY ZERO
                                         ;OCCURRED
            BNE.S       NOERROR          ;IF NOT, CONTINUE AT
                                         ;NOERROR
            MOVE.W      #0,ERRCODE       ;OTHERWISE, CLEAR THE
                                         ;ERROR CODE
            MOVE.W      #$FFFF,D1        ;AND SET QUOTIENT TO THE
                                         ;MAXIMUM POSSIBLE 16-BIT
                .                        ;VALUE
                .
                .
```

6-2 Reset

The MC68000 has a reset pin, $\overline{\text{RESET}}$, to provide a way to start or restart the processor. When this pin is activated, the processor terminates the current program execution and initiates the reset exception sequence. As shown in Fig. 6-6, the reset exception sequence differs from the usual exception sequence in three aspects. Since a reset is intended to restart the system, it does not save the return address and the current SR. Unlike the usual sequence, which affects only the PC, in a reset both the PC and the SSP are initialized from the four-word reset vector at locations 0 through 7. Furthermore, the interrupt mask bits in the SR are set to 7 to ignore all interrupts with a priority 6 or less.

Because a reset is the very first operation to perform after the system is turned on, locations 0 through 7 must be implemented by read-only memory. The contents in locations 0 through 3 are used as the initial value for the system stack pointer, whereas the address stored in locations 4 through 7 points to an initialization routine or monitor, which also must be stored in ROM.

There is also a reset instruction (RESET) designed to reset other components, such as peripheral devices in the system. Sometimes it is desirable to reset these devices to a known condition before starting a new program so that the settings of the devices will not be affected by the previous program. The RESET instruction, which is a privileged instruction, does not affect the processor but sends a signal through the processor's $\overline{\text{RESET}}$ pin. Presumably this pin is connected to other system components for resets. The RESET instruction is defined in Fig. 6-7.

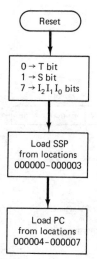

Figure 6-6 Reset exception processing.

Mnemonic	Size or Postfix	Operand Format	Allowable EA Modes	Operation	Condition Flags N Z V C X
RESET (Reset)	Unsized	None		Low -> $\overline{\text{RESET}}$ pin	- - - - -

Note: RESET is a privileged instruction.

Figure 6-7 The RESET instruction.

6-3 Error Exceptions

Address error exception

As mentioned earlier, the MC68000 can access an odd address only as a byte operand. If the processor accesses an odd memory address either for an instruction fetch or for a word or a longword operand reference, an address error exception will occur with vector number equal to 3. Unlike the usual exception sequence, which saves the address of the next instruction to be executed, this exception saves the address of the current instruction that causes the error.

Furthermore, in order to help the service routine diagnose the error, additional information besides the SR and the PC (as in the usual exception sequence) is saved on the supervisor stack. As illustrated in Fig. 6-8, this includes the operation word of the current instruction, the address causing this exception, and

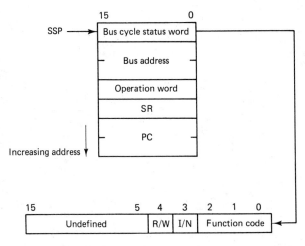

Bit definitions for the bus cycle status word:

R/W indicates data transfer direction:
  1 — Read
  0 — Write

I/N indicates the instruction type:
  1 — Normal instruction, TRAP, TRAPV, CHK or divide-by-zero exception
  0 — Exception other than TRAP, TRAPV, CHK or divide-by-zero

Function code indicates the type of bus cycle. (See Sec. 7-3 for its definition).

Figure 6-8 Stack layout during an illegal address or bus error exception.

the bus cycle status word. This last word reveals the type of the bus cycle in which an illegal address was sent. The information contained in a bus cycle status word includes whether the bus cycle is a read (R/W = 1) or write (R/W = 0); whether this error occurred during an instruction execution (I/N = 1) or not (I/N = 0); and the reference class specified by the function code. The remaining 11 bits of this word are undefined and are reserved for future use. As an example, consider the following instruction sequence:

```
        ORG       $2000
        MOVE.L    #$13100,D1
        MOVEA.L   #$13000,A1
AGAIN   MOVE.W    #0,(A1)
        ADDA.L    #1,A1
        CMPA.L    D1,A1
        BLE       AGAIN
```

During the second iteration through the loop, register A1 would have $13001. As a result, an address error exception will occur while executing the

```
MOVE.W      #0,(A1)
```

instruction. When the exception sequence is completed, the first seven words from the top of stack would appear as

∗∗ 01 00 01 30 01 32 BC 00 09 00 00 20 0A

which can be explained as follows:

∗∗: Is undefined and has no meaning.

01: Indicates that the error occurred in a write bus cycle (R/W = 0) during a normal instruction (I/N = 1) while accessing a data operand in the user mode (function code = 1)

00013001: Is the invalid address.

32BC: Is the operation word of the instruction causing the error, which is

```
MOVE.W      #0,(A1)
```

0009: Is the SR indicating that it is in the user mode and that N = 1 and C = 1 as set by the instruction

```
CMPA.L      D1,A1
```

0000200A: Is the address where the invalid instruction,

```
MOVE.W      #0,(A1)
```

is located.

Bus error exception

During a bus cycle, if the $\overline{\text{BERR}}$ (bus error) input pin is activated by an external logic, a bus error exception will be initiated under certain conditions. (These conditions are discussed in Sec. 7-4.) A bus error exception causes the processor to terminate the current bus cycle and immediately starts an exception sequence. Unlike the usual sequence, the bus error exception saves additional information to help the service routine identify the possible cause and recover from the error. The information that is pushed onto the supervisor stack is the same as that in an address error exception. The vector number assigned to the bus error exception is 2.

Illegal and emulation instructions

During instruction execution, if the fetched operation word is not the first word of any valid MC68000 machine instruction, an illegal instruction exception occurs. For example, consider the instruction sequence:

```
ADDQ.L      #1,D1
MOVE.L      D1,#$123456
   .
   .
   .
```

A syntax would be detected by the assembler due to the invalid destination addressing mode in the second instruction. However, when implemented as

```
ADDQ.L      #1,D1
DC.W        $29C1,$0012,$3456
   .
   .
   .
```

where an invalid machine instruction is inserted as data words, no assembly error will be generated. When this instruction sequence is executed, $29C1 is fetched as the next instruction to be executed after the ADDQ.L instruction is completed. Since $29C1 is interpreted as an instruction to move register D1 to an immediate data, an illegal instruction exception will occur at this point.

The illegal instruction exception follows the usual exception sequence and its vector number is predefined as 4. This exception is designed to detect any unimplemented machine code during execution time. It should be pointed out that some of the unimplemented op codes for the MC68000 are used to define new instructions for later members in the M68000 family.

When the most significant 4 bits of an unimplemented op code is 1010 or 1111, a separate vector number, 10 or 11, respectively, is assigned. Such exceptions, referred to as emulator exceptions, are primary for emulating unavailable instructions. For example, the MC68000 does not have floating-point instructions, but a floating-point package can be designed to perform various floating-point operations implemented by the MC68000 instruction set. The user can invoke this floating-point package through an emulator exception by using DC directives to encode a floating-point instruction beginning with 1010 or 1111. The remaining bits in the machine code can be used to indicate the type of operation to be performed and to specify source and destination operands.

Privilege violation exception

When the S bit in the status register is cleared, the processor is operating in the user mode. During the execution of a privileged instruction, the S bit is examined first. If the processor is in the user mode, this privileged instruction is not executed. Instead, a privilege violation exception is initiated whose vector number is 8. A privilege violation exception has the usual exception sequence except that the saved return address points to the privileged instruction and not to the next unexecuted instruction.

Any instruction that modifies the system byte of the SR is a privileged instruction. In addition, the instruction to move user stack pointer using USP explicitly is priviledged. The following are all the privileged instructions for the MC68000:

AND	#I,SR	(Logical AND immediate to SR)
EOR	#I,SR	(Logical exclusive OR immediate to SR)
OR	#I,SR	(Logical OR immediate to SR)
MOVE	EA,SR	(Move to SR)
MOVE	An,USP	(Move to user stack pointer)
MOVE	USP,An	(Move from user stack pointer)
RESET		(Reset external devices)
RTE		(Return from exception)
STOP		(Stop program execution)

6-4 Trace

When the T bit is set to 1, the MC68000 is in the trace (or single-step) mode. In this mode, the processor automatically initiates a trace exception with vector number equal to 9 after each instruction. Recall that as part of an exception sequence, the processor saves the SR onto the supervisor stack and resets the T bit to 0 prior to entering the service routine. Therefore, the processor is not in the trace mode while executing a trace service routine. Upon completion, the saved SR with the T bit being set is restored, causing the processor to trace the next unexecuted instruction again.

The trace facility is a valuable debugging tool because it allows single-stepping through a program segment. Tracing should be initiated by setting the T bit to 1 and branching to user's code to be traced in a single instruction. This is shown in the following example:

```
MOVE.L    STADR, - (SP)      ;PUSH BEGINNING ADDRESS TO BE TRACED
MOVE.W    #$8700, - (SP)     ;ASSEMBLE A STATUS WORD WITH T = 1
                             ;AND S = 0 ON THE SUPERVISOR STACK
RTE                          ;SET T BIT TO 1 AND TRANSFER CONTROL
                             ;IN A SINGLE INSTRUCTION
```

This example assumes that the processor is currently in the supervisor mode and that variable STADR has the beginning trace address of the user program.

A trace service routine is typically designed in such a way that it allows the user to examine and modify the contents of registers and selected memory locations. This requires that an image of user registers be copied onto the stack and any register modifications be made to this copy, not directly to the registers. Before returning, the registers are restored with the modified values from the stack, allowing the traced program to continue with the modified registers. Figure 6-9 shows a typical stack layout for trace storage. A copy of the registers used by the operating system is also saved if register and memory examine/modify commands are implemented as subroutines. The flowchart in Fig. 6-10 illustrates the major logic to implement register and memory examine/modify commands.

6-5 Trap and Software Exceptions

An exception may be originated directly from program execution, either by normal execution of an exception instruction or by special conditions during instruction execution. These exception instructions are summarized in Fig. 6-11.

Trap

The user can initiate an exception through the software with an instruction, known as a trap instruction. The MC68000 trap instruction has the form

```
TRAP       #I4
```

where I4 is a 4-bit integer in the range of 0 to 15 specifying the lower part of the vector number. This instruction initiates the usual exception sequence with the vector number equal to 32 + I4. Therefore, the vector numbers from 32 to 47 are reserved for the TRAP instruction.

The TRAP instruction can be used to transfer control to routines whose locations in memory are not known by the calling program, thus providing a means of dynamic linkage during program execution. For a typical operating system, this instruction is used to implement supervisor calls, which allow the user program to request various services from the operating system. A different operand in the TRAP instruction can be used for each group of services that the operating system could provide for users.

For example, the TUTOR monitor of the ECB uses

```
TRAP       #14
```

as a supervisor call. The user specifies the function to be performed in the lower byte of register D7. This TRAP instruction passes control from the user program to the TUTOR monitor and starts execution from the address stored in locations $000038–$00003B. The lower 8 bits in register D7 are then interpreted as a function

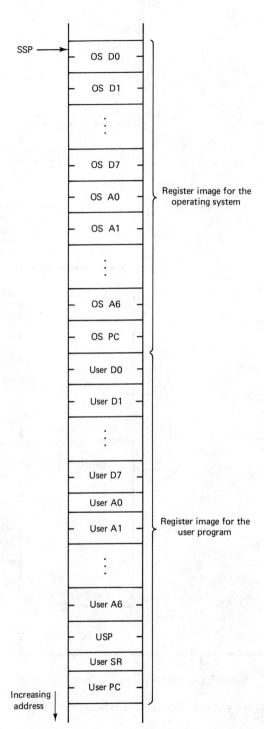

SSP ——▶

OS D0

OS D1

⋮

OS D7

OS A0

OS A1

⋮

OS A6

OS PC

Register image for the
operating system

User D0

User D1

⋮

User D7

User A0

User A1

Register image for the
user program

⋮

User A6

USP

User SR

User PC

Increasing
address

Figure 6-9 Stack layout of trace
storage.

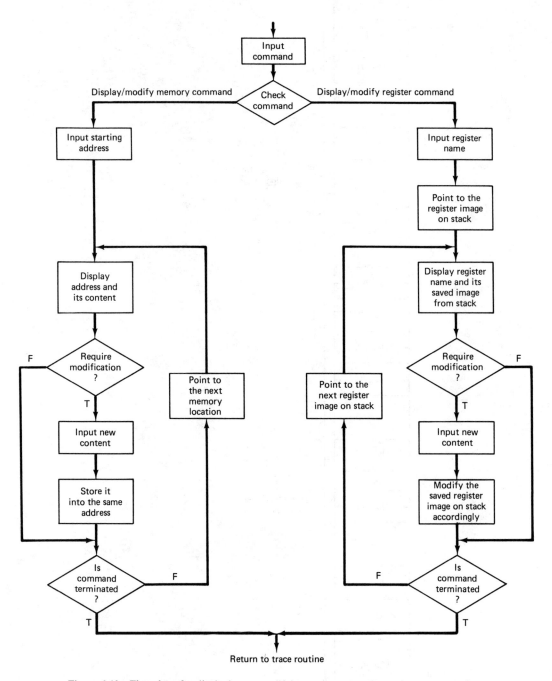

Figure 6-10 Flowchart for displaying or modifying register or memory in a trace routine.

Mnemonic	Size or Postfix	Operand Format	Allowable EA Modes	Operation	Condition Flags N Z V C X
TRAP (Trap)	Unsized	#I4		PC -> -(SSP); SR -> -(SSP); ((32 + I4) x 4) -> PC	- - - - -
TRAPV (Trap on overflow)	Unsized	None		If V = 1 then PC -> -(SSP); SR -> -(SSP); (28) -> PC	- - - - -
CHK (Check register against bounds)	Word	EA,Dn	Data	If Dn.W < 0 or Dn.W > (EA) then PC -> -(SSP); SR -> -(SSP); (24) -> PC	* u u u -

Figure 6-11 The TRAP, TRAPV, and CHK instructions.

number, and the corresponding subroutine is called to perform this function. Figure 6-12 lists the defined functions and their respective function numbers.

Figure 6-13 shows how to invoke a typical system function, GETNUMD, to convert an ASCII-encoded decimal number to its 32-bit binary equivalent. As

FUNCTION	FUNCTION NAME	FUNCTION DESCRIPTION
255	—	Reserved function - end of table indicator.
254	—	Reserved function - used to link tables.
253	LINKIT	Append user table to TRAP 14 table.
252	FIXDADD	Append string to buffer.
251	FIXBUF	Initialize A5 and A6 to 'BUFFER'.
250	FIXDATA	Initialize A6 to 'BUFFER' and append string to buffer.
249	FIXDCRLF	Move 'CR', 'LF', string to buffer.
248	OUTCH	Output single character to Port 1.
247	INCHE	Input single character from Port 1.
246	—	Reserved function.
245	—	Reserved function.
244	CHRPRINT	Output single character to Port 3.
243	OUTPUT	Output string to Port 1.
242	OUTPUT21	Output string to Port 2.
241	PORTIN1	Input string from Port 1.
240	PORTIN20	Input string from Port 2.
239	TAPEOUT	Output string to Port 4.
238	TAPEIN	Input string from Port 4.
237	PRCRLF	Output string to Port 3.
236	HEX2DEC	Convert hex value to ASCII encoded decimal.
235	GETHEX	Convert ASCII character to hex.
234	PUTHEX	Convert 1 hex digit to ASCII.
233	PNT2HX	Convert 2 hex digits to ASCII.
232	PNT4HX	Convert 4 hex digits to ASCII.
231	PNT6HX	Convert 6 hex digits to ASCII.
230	PNT8HX	Convert 8 hex digits to ASCII.
229	START	Restart TUTOR; perform initialization.
228	TUTOR	Go to TUTOR; print prompt.
227	OUT1CR	Output string plus 'CR', 'LF' to Port 1.
226	GETNUMA	Convert ASCII encoded hex to hex.
225	GETNUMD	Convert ASCII encoded decimal to hex.
224	PORTIN1N	Input string from Port 1; no automatic line feed.
223-128	—	Reserved.
127-0	—	User-defined functions.

Figure 6-12 Summary of TUTOR system calls using TRAP #14. (Courtesy of Motorola, Inc.)

```
            ORG       $2000
ASCII       DC.B      '12345'
BINNUM      DS.L      1
START       MOVEA.L   #ASCII,A5        ;POINT A5 AT BEGGIN OF ASCII DIGIT STRING
            MOVEA.L   #BINNUM,A6       ;POINT A6 AT END OF ASCII DIGIT STRING
            MOVE.B    #225,D7
            TRAP      #14
            MOVE.L    D0,BINNUM        ;D0 HAS THE CONVERTED NUMBER
            MOVE.B    #228,D7          ;EXIT CLEANLY TO TUTOR VIA
            TRAP      #14              ;A SYSTEM CALL
            END       START
```

Figure 6-13   An example of using system calls.

shown in Fig. 6-12, the function number corresponding to GETNUMD is 225. In addition to loading 225 into D7, this system call requires three registers to be used for passing parameters and results. Prior to a call, register A5 should point to the ASCII-coded digit string to be converted and register A6 should point to the location following the last digit to indicate the end of the digit string. The resulting 32-bit binary equivalent is returned in register D0.

Another application for the TRAP instruction is to implement breakpoints. By using a breakpoint, the user program stops execution at a specified location and transfers control to the monitor, thus allowing the user to check out registers and memory locations at crucial points in the program. A breakpoint can be set by saving the operation word of the instruction at the specified address and replacing it with a one-word trap instruction. In order to resume execution at the breakpoint after returning, the service routine should include the code to restore the saved operation word and decrement the return address saved on the supervisor stack by 2. Figure 6-14 is an example that illustrates these principles.

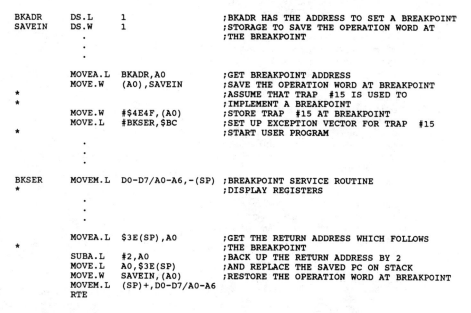

```
BKADR       DS.L      1                ;BKADR HAS THE ADDRESS TO SET A BREAKPOINT
SAVEIN      DS.W      1                ;STORAGE TO SAVE THE OPERATION WORD AT
            .                          ;THE BREAKPOINT
            .
            .

            MOVEA.L   BKADR,A0         ;GET BREAKPOINT ADDRESS
            MOVE.W    (A0),SAVEIN      ;SAVE THE OPERATION WORD AT BREAKPOINT
*                                      ;ASSUME THAT TRAP  #15 IS USED TO
*                                      ;IMPLEMENT A BREAKPOINT
            MOVE.W    #$4E4F,(A0)      ;STORE TRAP  #15 AT BREAKPOINT
            MOVE.L    #BKSER,$BC       ;SET UP EXCEPTION VECTOR FOR TRAP  #15
*                                      ;START USER PROGRAM
            .
            .
            .

BKSER       MOVEM.L   D0-D7/A0-A6,-(SP) ;BREAKPOINT SERVICE ROUTINE
*                                      ;DISPLAY REGISTERS
            .
            .
            .

*           MOVEA.L   $3E(SP),A0       ;GET THE RETURN ADDRESS WHICH FOLLOWS
                                       ;THE BREAKPOINT
            SUBA.L    #2,A0            ;BACK UP THE RETURN ADDRESS BY 2
            MOVE.L    A0,$3E(SP)       ;AND REPLACE THE SAVED PC ON STACK
            MOVE.W    SAVEIN,(A0)      ;RESTORE THE OPERATION WORD AT BREAKPOINT
            MOVEM.L   (SP)+,D0-D7/A0-A6
            RTE
```

Figure 6-14   An example of implementing a breakpoint using a TRAP instruction.

This example assumes that each breakpoint is implemented by

```
TRAP      #15
```

whose machine code is 4E4F. Therefore, the beginning address of the breakpoint service routine is loaded to the vector address $(32 + 15) \times 4 = \$BC$. Upon entering the service routine, since 15 registers are pushed onto the stack, the return address immediately following the breakpoint is saved at the location which is $15 \times 4 + 2 = \$3E$ bytes from the top of the stack.

Trap on overflow

The TRAPV (trap on overflow) instruction initiates a trap if the overflow flag is set to 1. Otherwise, no operation is performed, and execution continues with the next instruction in sequence. The vector number associated with the TRAPV exception is predefined as 7. The TRAPV instruction may be placed following an arithmetic instruction to detect a possible overflow.

CHK instruction

The MC68000 also has an instruction that compares a data register against the specified limit and initiates a trap if the limit is exceeded. This CHK (check register against bounds) instruction has the form

```
CHK       EA,Dn
```

where EA specifies the location of the upper bound and Dn is the data register to be checked. This limit is expressed as a 16-bit 2's complement integer. An exception with vector number 6 occurs if the lower word of data register Dn is less than zero or greater than the given upper bound.

The CHK instruction can be used to ensure that the indices of an array element are within their ranges before that element is accessed. As an example to illustrate this application, let us consider a three-dimensional array of 16-bit integers, $[A_{i,j,k}]$, where $1 \le i \le 5$, $1 \le j \le 7$ and $1 \le k \le 4$. This array along with its index limits can be defined as

```
II          DS.W        1       ;INDEX I
JJ          DS.W        1       ;INDEX J
KK          DS.W        1       ;INDEX K

              .
              .
              .

ILIMIT      DC.W        4       ;RANGE OF I − 1
JLIMIT      DC.W        6       ;RANGE OF J − 1
KLIMIT      DC.W        3       ;RANGE OF K − 1
AA          DS.W        140     ;5 × 7 × 4 WORDS
```

Then, in accessing any element $A_{i,j,k}$, each subscript can be checked to make sure that the subscript is within its range before the address of that element is calculated. With the array being stored as

$$A_{1,1,1}, A_{2,1,1}, \ldots, A_{5,1,1}, A_{1,2,1}, A_{2,2,1}, \ldots, A_{4,7,4}, A_{5,7,4}$$

the address of element $A_{i,j,k}$ is given by

Address of $A_{1,1,1} + 2 \times [(i - 1) + (j - 1) \times$ (range of i)

$$+ (k - 1) \times (\text{range of } i) \times (\text{range of } j)]$$

where ranges of i and j are 5 and 7, respectively. Therefore, the operation

$$A_{i,j,k} \leftarrow 0$$

would be implemented as

```
        MOVE.W      #0,D0
        MOVE.W      KK,D1
        SUBQ.W      #1,D1           ;D1 = K - 1
        CHK         AA - 2,D1       ;ENSURE THAT 0 ≤ K - 1 ≤ 3
        ADD.W       D1,D0           ;D0 = K - 1
        MOVE.W      AA - 4,D2       ;D2 = RANGE OF J - 1
        ADDQ.W      #1,D2
        MULU        D2,D0           ;D0 = (K - 1) × RANGE OF J
        MOVE.W      JJ,D1
        SUBQ.W      #1,D1           ;D1 = J - 1
        CHK         AA - 4,D1       ;ENSURE THAT 0 ≤ J - 1 ≤ 6
        ADD.W       D1,D0           ;D0 = (J - 1) + (K - 1) × RANGE OF J
        MOVE.W      AA - 6,D2       ;D2 = RANGE OF I - 1
        ADDQ.W      #1,D2
        MULU        D2,D0           ;D0 = (J - 1) × RANGE OF I + (K - 1)
                                    ; × RANGE OF I × RANGE OF J
        MOVE.W      II,D1
        SUBQ.W      #1,D1           ;D1 = I - 1
        CHK         AA - 6,D1       ;ENSURE THAT 0 ≤ I - 1 ≤ 4
        ADD.W       D1,D0           ;D0 = INDEX OF A(I,J,K) IN WORDS
        ADD.W       D0,D0           ;D0 = INDEX OF A(I,J,K) IN BYTES
        MOVEA.L     #AA,A0
        MOVE.W      #0,0(A0,D0.W)   ;A(I,J,K) = 0
```

6-6 Interrupts

It is sometimes necessary for the processor to respond to requests from external devices. An interrupt exception is initiated by a request being sent to the processor from a peripheral device. Let us consider the case of inputting data from an input device. Figure 6-15 compares the logic flow of the two approaches, the polling

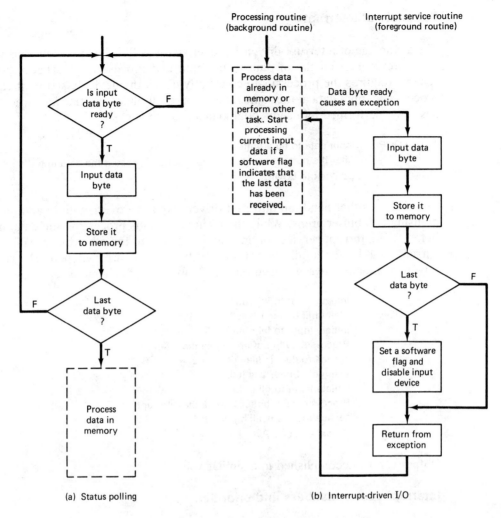

Figure 6-15 Status polling versus interrupt-driven I/O.

scheme and the interrupt-driven scheme. The polling scheme constantly checks the status register of the input device. When the status indicates that a data byte is ready, the processor inputs and stores the data byte into memory and then waits for the next byte by repeating the same process. Obviously, considerable amount of processor time is wasted while polling the status. On the other hand, the interrupt-driven scheme allows the processor to utilize this idle time for performing other tasks. Whenever a data byte is ready for input, the device sends an interrupt request to the processor, causing it to enter the service routine. After the data byte is input and stored in memory by the service routine, the processor returns to the routine where the interrupt occurred and resumes its normal operation until the next interrupt request is received.

Rationale of interrupts

The advantage of interrupt-driven I/O over status polling becomes obvious when there are several blocks of data to be input and processed. Because a polling scheme requires the processor to constantly check the device's status, it cannot process and input data at the same time. As a result, data inputting and processing has to be performed in a sequential manner, as shown:

```
LOOP    Input data to fill a buffer area.
        After the buffer area is full, stop input and process the data in buffer.
        Go back to LOOP.
```

On the other hand, an interrupt-driven input can overlap input and process by using two buffer areas. While the main program is processing the data in one buffer, the interrupt service routine can input data to the other buffer. When the current input buffer is full, the roles of the two buffers are switched. The general flow of the main program based on this double-buffer scheme is as follows.

```
        Initiate input to fill buffer 1.
LOOP    Wait until buffer 1 is full.
        Initiate input to fill buffer 2.
        Process data in buffer 1 while the interrupt
        service routine is filling buffer 2.
        Wait until buffer 2 is full.
        Initiate input to fill buffer 1.
        Process data in buffer 2 while the interrupt
        service routine is filling buffer 1.
        Go back to LOOP.
```

Output can be accomplished in a similar way.

Interrupt vector numbers and priorities

The vector number of an interrupt exception is externally supplied, unlike the exceptions previously described. This is done to enable the processor to indentify which peripheral device issued the received interrupt request. Figure 6-16 illustrates the exception sequence for processing an interrupt request. An interrupt request is initiated from the requesting device by sending a 3-bit interrupt priority level to the processor's $\overline{IPL2}$–$\overline{IPL0}$ pins. A nonzero request level indicates an interrupt request. Therefore, seven priority levels are provided, ranging from 1 to 7 with level 7 being the highest priority. The processor waits until the current instruction is completed before examining the pending request. If the request level is 7 or is higher than the mask level set in the SR, an interrupt acknowledge code is returned to the interrupting device through the processor's FC2–FC0 pins asking for a vector number. Otherwise, the interrupt request is ignored and the processor proceeds by fetching the next instruction in sequence. To identify the request being accepted, the MC68000 also returns the priority level of the accepted request on pins A3 – A1 during an interrupt acknowledge cycle. Since an interrupt

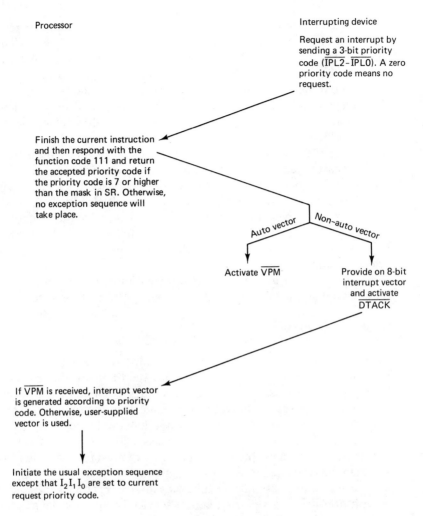

Figure 6-16 Interrupt exception sequence.

with level 7 is always recognized regardless of the processor's mask level, it is commonly known as a *nonmaskable interrupt*. Typically, this type of interrupt is reserved for use by power-failure-detection circuits or other devices that demand immediate attention from the processor.

An interrupting device can supply a vector number using either the auto vector or non-auto vector option. For the auto vector option, the device activates the processor's $\overline{VPA}$ (valid peripheral address) pin, requesting the vector number to be generated internally. The processor automatically generates the vector number according to the received interrupt priority level as

$$\text{Vector number} = 24 + \text{interrupt priority level}$$

Therefore, vector numbers 25 through 31 are reserved for auto vector interrupts starting from priority level 1 through 7, in that order.

If the non-auto vector option is chosen, the interrupting device sends a user-defined 8-bit vector number along with a data transfer acknowledge ($\overline{\text{DTACK}}$) signal to the processor. Even though any 8-bit number is a valid interrupt vector number, the interrupting device should supply one in the range between 64 and 255 to avoid the first 64 reserved vector numbers. Since each interrupting device can have a unique vector number, the non-auto vector scheme allows the system to support more than seven devices when external interrupt management hardware is added.

Once the user-supplied vector is received or an auto vector is generated, the processor begins the usual exception sequence, with one difference. The MC68000 pushes the PC and SR onto the supervisor stack and loads the PC with the address pointed to by the vector number multipled by 4, as in other exception sequences. However, unlike the usual sequence, which does not affect the mask level in the SR, an interrupt sequence raises the mask level to the current request level being served. This prevents the processor from being interrupted by low-priority devices while executing the service routine. Of course, the mask level can be modified to any value in the service routine by software. Several examples on interrupt service routines will be given in Chap. 8 for specific I/O devices.

Nested interrupts

Each interrupt request has a priority so the processor can respond to multiple interrupts on a priority basis and service the one with the highest priority first. High priorities are assigned to high-speed devices so they can receive immediate attention. When several devices issue requests at the same time, external priority management logic will decide which one has the highest priority and then pass that request to the MC68000. The processor also allows the service routine for one device to be interrupted by an interrupt request from a higher-priority device. An example of nested interrupts is given in Fig. 6-17.

The example assumes the following interrupt sequence: Request from device A with priority 5 arrives first; before service routine for device A is completed, request from device B with priority 6 arrives; shortly after that, another request with priority 5 is received from device C. Further assume that the mask level in the main routine is set to 0. Since the mask level in the service routine for device A is 5, which is lower than the priority of the request from device B, device B will be immediately serviced. Even though the request from device C is received in the service routine for device B, the request will not be recognized immediately. Upon returning to the device A service routine, this request will still not be acknowledged because the request priority is not higher than the current mask level. Eventually, the device A service routine will be completed; its RTE instruction restores the mask level back to zero. At this point, service routine for device C will begin.

If a bus error occurs during interrupt processing, the spurious interrupt vector, 24, is taken. The processor then proceeds with the usual exception processing. Another possible error during an interrupt acknowledge cycle is that the vector register of the interrupting device had not been initialized. A device in this case should not respond to an interrupt acknowledge cycle by sending a zero vector.

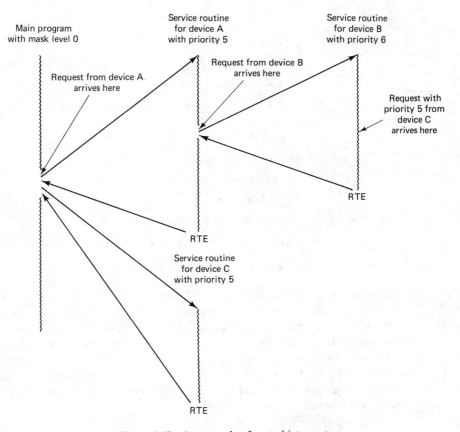

Main program
with mask level 0

Service routine
for device A
with priority 5

Service routine
for device B
with priority 6

Request from device A
arrives here

Request from device B
arrives here

Request with
priority 5 from
device C
arrives here

RTE

RTE

Service routine
for device C
with priority 5

RTE

Figure 6-17 An example of nested interrupts.

Otherwise, a reset exception whose vector is also zero is initiated instead. To avoid this problem, the MC68000 reserves vector number 15 for any uninitialized interrupt vector exception. An I/O interface or device should be designed in a way that if a vector number is not programmed in its interrupt vector register before an interrupt occurs, the device supplies 15 as its interrupt vector number. A typical device having such capability is the MC68000 PI/T (parallel interface and timer). This device is capable of generating interrupt requests for four different sources in the device. If its port interrupt vector register is programmed, the PI/T provides one of four consecutive interrupt vectors during an interrupt, depending on the interrupt source and the vector register content. If this interrupt vector register has not been initialized when the PI/T issues an interrupt request, vector 15 is sent regardless of its interrupt source.

6-7 Multiple Exceptions

It is possible that more than one exception may arise simultaneously. In such cases, the processor responds to multiple exceptions in a priority order. Figure 6-18 lists all exceptions according to their priorities and recognition times. Ex-

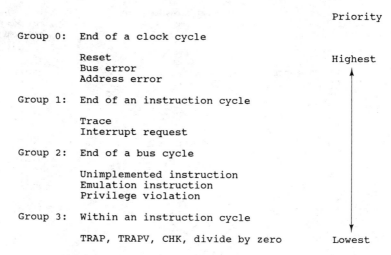

Figure 6-18 Priorities and recognition times of exceptions.

ceptions in group 0 are checked at the end of a clock cycle. These exceptions have higher priorities over others and are processed immediately. The next-highest-priority group includes trace and interrupt, which are recognized at the end of an instruction. Next is group 2, consisting of invalid instruction, emulation instruction, and privilege violation, which are detected after an instruction fetch bus cycle. The TRAP, TRAPV, CHK, and divide-by-zero exceptions are in group 3. These exceptions occur during the instruction execution and have the lowest priority among all.

When a group 0 exception and any exception of lower priority occur at the same time, the one with a higher priority will be initiated and the other one will not be processed. For example, if an address error occurs during a TRAP instruction, then the TRAP exception is aborted and the address error exception starts. If two exceptions not in group 0 occur at the same time, both will be processed, the one with the higher priority first followed by the one with the lower priority. A typical example of this is when an interrupt request arrives during a divide-by-zero instruction. Immediately after entering the service routine for divide-by-zero exception, the interrupt exception is initiated. Upon completion of the interrupt service routine, the processor resumes the service routine for the divide-by-zero error.

EXERCISES

1. Give the necessary instructions to start executing a user-mode program beginning at location 001200 from the supervisor mode.
2. Give the necessary instructions to raise the interrupt mask level to 5 if the current level is below 5.
3. Give the necessary instructions to lower the interrupt mask level to 2 if the current level is above 2.

4. Given the following memory words starting with location 0: 0001 0022 0003 0044 0005 0066 0007 0088 0009 00AA 000B 00CC, determine the starting addresses of service routines for the following exceptions:
   (a) Reset
   (b) Bus error
   (c) Illegal instruction

5. Given that SSP = 004000, SR = 0402, and the contents of the following memory locations are

0000A0	0012
0000A2	0034

   and that the

   TRAP   #8

   instruction is at location 005000, determine the contents of SSP, PC, SR, and the top four words on the supervisor stack after the TRAP instruction is executed.

6. Determine the exception vector and vector address for each of the following exceptions:
   (a) TRAP   #1
   (b) TRAP   #14
   (c) Auto vector interrupt with priority 1.
   (d) Auto vector interrupt with priority 7.
   (e) Non-auto interrupt with priority 1 and a user-supplied vector 5A.

7. What exceptions have a fixed exception vector assigned?

8. How does the MC68000 distinguish an auto vector from a non-auto vector interrupt request?

9. Construct a table to summarize the cause for each type of the MC68000 exceptions.

10. Discuss the chief advantage of using TRAP instructions as opposed to JSR to implement system calls.

11. Could an interrupt request be acknowledged while the processor is executing a trap service routine?

12. For the ECB or the MC68000-based system available to you, find out the starting address of the service routine to process each of the following exceptions:
    (a) Reset (b) Bus error (c) Divide by zero
    (d) Auto vector interrupt with priority 7.
    (e) TRAP   #14

13. Show the necessary instructions to initialize the trace vector. Assume that the trace service routine begins with the instruction labeled as TRACERT.

14. Write a service routine to process address error exceptions. This routine should copy the seven words saved in the supervisor stack during an address error into the memory area starting at $001500, so that these words can be examined with an appropriate monitor command such as DM in TUTOR. After that, the service routine should remove these words from the stack and return control to the monitor. Use an instruction sequence that has an address error to test this service routine.

15. What is the major purpose for having the interrupting device to supply a vector during a non-auto vector interrupt?

16. The ECB has an abort button that, if depressed, generates an auto vector interrupt with priority 7. Write a service routine to replace TUTOR's abort function. This service routine will increment a decimal counter of 2 BCD digits by one each time the abort button is depressed. The initial count is zero, and after reaching 99, the service routine will stop counting and restore TUTOR's abort function.

17. Give an instruction sequence that uses a TUTOR's system call to convert a 32-bit binary stored in BIN to the equivalent ASCII-coded decimal to be stored beginning at ASCII.

7

Bus Operation
and Interface

7-1 Pin Configurations

The MC68000 has a total of 64 pins in the dual-in-line package form. Also available are the 68-pin quad package and grid array types, which include two extra ground pins and two unconnected pins. Figure 7-1 shows the pin assignments of the three package types.

Before discussing how the MC68000 pins are to be connected to other system components, it is necessary to understand their meanings. The following is a summary of the mnemonics and definitions of the MC68000 pins:

Clock (CLK): This input provides the clock signal for the processor.

Address bus (A23–A1): These pins output a word address for memory or I/O device during a bus cycle. Inside the MC68000, an address has 24 bits, but bit 0 is not output. In conjunction with $\overline{\text{LDS}}$ and $\overline{\text{UDS}}$, A23–A1 specify a 24-bit location for a byte or word reference.

Data bus (D15–D0): These bidirectional pins carry the data being transferred to/from the memory or I/O device.

Address strobe ($\overline{\text{AS}}$): An active $\overline{\text{AS}}$ indicates a valid address on the address bus.

Read/Write (R/$\overline{\text{W}}$): This output determines the direction of data transfer. A 1 indicates that the processor is reading data from memory or device, and a 0 specifies a write operation.

Upper data strobe ($\overline{\text{UDS}}$): This output indicates that the upper byte of the data bus (D15–D8) is used for the data transfer.

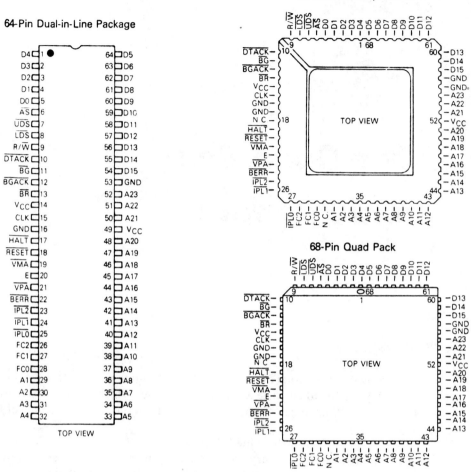

Figure 7-1 Pin assignments. (Courtesy of Motorola, Inc.)

Lower data strobe ($\overline{\text{LDS}}$): This output indicates that the lower byte of the data bus (D7–D0) is used for the data transfer.

Data transfer acknowledge ($\overline{\text{DTACK}}$): A low on this input pin represents an acknowledgement from the addressed memory or I/O device that it has completed the data transfer.

Enable (E): This output is a clock at one-tenth of the incoming CLK frequency, and is used to enable an M6800 type peripheral device for data transfer.

Valid peripheral address ($\overline{\text{VPA}}$): This input is used by the addressed location to indicate that it is an M6800 type peripheral device. If present, the processor uses the enable (E) signal to synchronize data transfer and uses auto vector for interrupt handling.

Valid memory address ($\overline{\text{VMA}}$): In response to an active $\overline{\text{VPA}}$, the processor waits until E is low and then activates $\overline{\text{VMA}}$. This signal indicates to the M6800 type peripheral device that it has been selected for data transfer.

Function code (FC2–FC0): These pins output a 3-bit processor status to provide additional information about the current bus cycle.

Interrupt priority level ($\overline{\text{IPL2}}$–$\overline{\text{IPL0}}$): These input pins are used by an interrupting device to indicate the request priority. An all-low on these pins is interpreted as the highest level, which is 7, whereas an all-high indicates level 0, meaning that no interrupt is requested.

Bus request ($\overline{\text{BR}}$): This input indicates that some other potential bus master, such as a DMA controller, is trying to obtain control of the bus from the processor.

Bus grant ($\overline{\text{BG}}$): This output indicates that a bus request is accepted, and the processor will relinquish bus control at the end of the current bus cycle.

Bus grant acknowledge ($\overline{\text{BGACK}}$): This input is used by the bus-requesting device to indicate that it has become the bus master.

Bus error ($\overline{\text{BERR}}$): This input indicates that a bus error has occurred.

Reset ($\overline{\text{RESET}}$): This is a bidirectional reset pin. As an input pin, the MC68000 can be reset by an external signal. As an output pin, the MC68000 sends out a pulse to reset other system components when executing a RESET instruction.

Halt ($\overline{\text{HALT}}$): A low on this bidirectional pin forces the processor to stop the current operation. This pin is also used by the processor to indicate to external devices that it has stopped.

For a very simple system, the MC68000 can be directly connected to memory and I/O devices. Figure 7-2 shows a complete minimum configuration, illustrating how the fundamental pins can be connected. This configuration, which provides 4K bytes of ROM, 4K bytes of RAM, and a serial interface, is implemented with only 5 LSI devices in addition to the microprocessor.

The two MCM2716 2K × 8 ROM ICs are selected with A13 = 0 and A12 = 0, so the 4K ROM is accessed as memory locations $000000 through $000FFF. The MCM2716 that is connected to pins D0–D7 of the MC68000 corresponds to the odd-addressed bytes and the one connected to pins D8–D15 corresponds to the even-addressed bytes. The 4K RAM provided by two MCM4016 2K × 8 static RAM ICs is accessed with A13 = 1 and A12 = 0 and therefore occupies locations $002000 through $002FFF. The MC6851 is a serial interface device whose internal registers are programmed through two I/O ports. In this design the MC6851 is assigned two consecutive odd addresses, $003001 and $003003. A CRT terminal can be connected to this system through the driver and receiver. Note that since the address from the MC68000 is not fully decoded, there exist many redundant mappings. For example, addresses $XX0000, $XX4000, $XX8000, and $XXC000 all correspond to the same physical ROM location 0.

The complexity of the system bus and the required logic surrounding the microprocessor can vary widely, depending on the system requirements. For the system discussed previously, the bus contains only 13 address lines, and signals are not buffered, thus limiting the number of devices in the system to be very

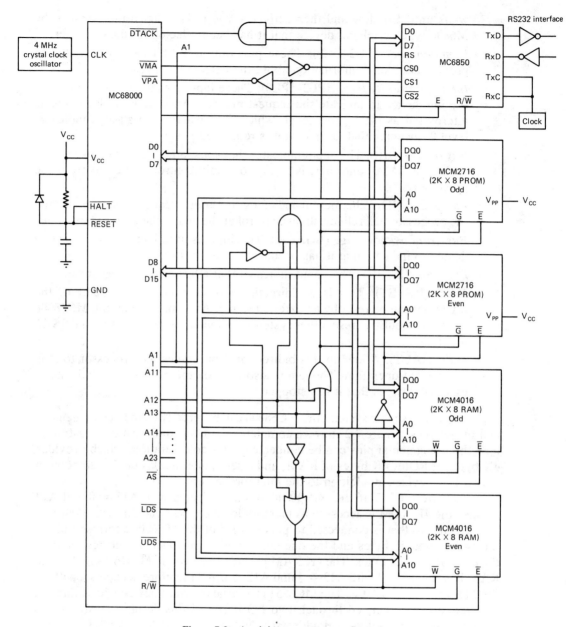

Figure 7-2 A minimum system configuration.

small. In addition, the system does not provide the facility of handling interrupts and DMAs. Although its structure is simple, the application of this configuration is very limited.

In this chapter, we discuss the connections of the MC68000 pins in groups according to their functions, as categorized in Fig. 7-3. In order to understand

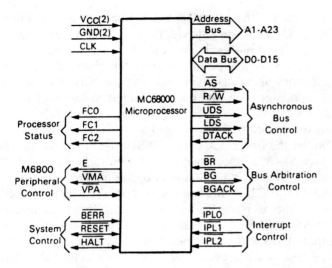

Figure 7-3 Functional groups of MC68000 pins. (Courtesy of Motorola, Inc.)

better the interrelationship among the pin signals, it is necessary to examine the timing of basic bus cycles.

7-2 Bus Cycle Timing

An MC68000 instruction requires one or more bus cycles to execute, and each bus cycle in turn is composed of several clock cycles. The processor needs to fetch the instruction from memory, and additional bus cycles may be required, depending on how many data transfer operations to or from memory are needed. Since the MC68000 is an external 16-bit, internal 32-bit processor, reading or writing a longword from or to memory requires two bus cycles. The following table shows some examples of read and write bus cycles required for fetching and executing various instructions.

Instruction		No. of Read Cycles	No. of Write Cycles
MOVE.L	D2,D3	1	0
MOVE.W	34(A1),D2	3	0
MOVE.B	D3,60(A2)	2	1
ADD.L	56(A3),D4	4	0
ADD.L	D4,56(A3)	4	2
ADDI.W	#$1234,56(A3)	4	1
JMP	XXXX.W	2	0
JSR	XXXX.W	2	2
TRAP	#5	4	3

Note that for the TRAP instruction, the number of read bus cycles includes the fetch of the first instruction word of the trap service routine.

The length of a bus cycle for the MC68000 has a minimum of four clock cycles, denoted by S0/S1, S2/S3, S4/S5, and S6/S7, plus an indeterminate number of wait-state clock cycles. The next bus cycle might not begin immediately after the current one. Since the MC68000 may perform some internal operations after a bus cycle (as in multiplication), there may be an inactive gap between two bus cycles. Therefore, instruction execution times are measured in terms of clock cycles rather than bus cycles.

The timing diagrams for a word read and a word write without a wait state are shown in Fig. 7-4. During the first clock cycle (S0/S1), the processor places an address on address pins A1–A23, specifying the location to be accessed. It also sets the R/W pin initially high to indicate a read operation and sends out a 3-bit function code on pins FC0–FC2. At the beginning of the second clock cycle (S2/S3), the processor asserts the $\overline{AS}$ pin to indicate a valid address and maintains it low for the entire bus cycle. In S2/S3, for a read cycle, the processor maintains the R/W signal high, outputs $\overline{UDS}$ and $\overline{LDS}$, and places data pins D0–D15 into the high-impedance mode. For a write cycle, the processor changes the R/W output to low and places data on D0–D7 and/or D8–D15 according to $\overline{UDS}$ and $\overline{LDS}$. The $\overline{UDS}$ and $\overline{LDS}$ signals are not output until the end of S3. If an acknowledge ($\overline{DTACK}$) is received from the addressed device before S5, the processor proceeds with the fourth clock cycle (S6/S7). In this clock period, the data are latched by the processor for a read operation or by the addressed device for a write operation. Then the processor deactivates $\overline{AS}$, $\overline{UDS}$, and $\overline{LDS}$ signals, enters the first clock cycle (S0/S1), and the data are removed from data pins, thus terminating the bus cycle. The flowchart of this interaction between the processor and addressed device in read and write operations is shown in Fig. 7-5.

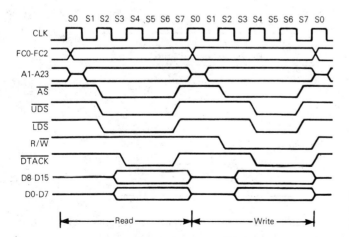

Figure 7-4 Basic bus cycle timing without a wait state. (Courtesy of Motorola, Inc.)

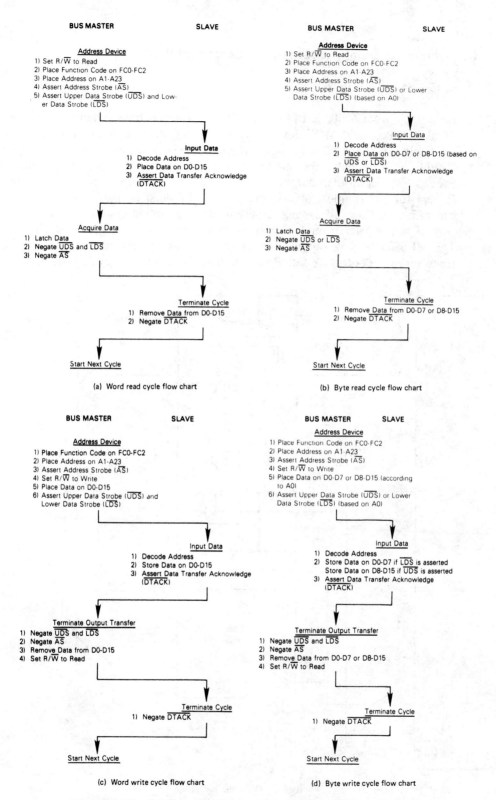

Figure 7-5 Control flow of basic bus cycles. (Courtesy of Motorola, Inc.)

7-3 Connections of Data, Address, and Bus Control Pins

Data bus buffering

Although the MC68000 is TTL-compatible, its outputs have rather limited driving capability like most MOS devices. For example, the maximum sink current for a data pin is rated at 5.3 milliamps, sufficient to be connected to four TTL devices. In addition, to achieve the rated speed, the capacitive load of each pin may not exceed 130 picofarads. Output delays increase for additional capacitive loading. Except for the simplest of systems, a data bus must be buffered to satisfy the capacitive loading and driving requirements of a typical system.

Figure 7-6 is an implementation of data buffering using data transceivers. The MC68000's $R/\overline{W}$ output is inverted and then applied to the T input of the transceiver to control its data flow direction. During a read cycle, T is 0, causing

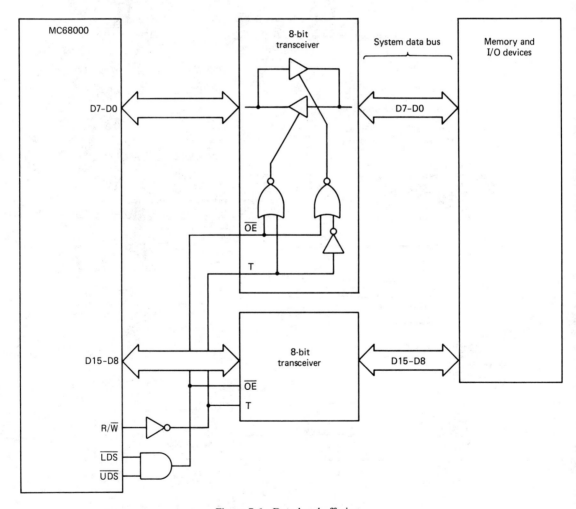

Figure 7-6 Data bus buffering.

the data to flow from the system data bus to the processor. For a write operation, T becomes 1, resulting in a data flow direction from the processor to the system bus. The $\overline{OE}$ input enables the outputs of the transceiver. If $\overline{OE}$ is high, all the data pins of the transceiver are forced into the high-impedance state, so that data cannot flow in either direction, and the processor is logically disconnected from the system data bus. In the figure, this pin is asserted by $\overline{LDS}$ or $\overline{UDS}$. For a system having a DMA device, the $\overline{OE}$ pin is controlled by the complement of the $\overline{BGACK}$ signal from the DMA device. During a DMA cycle, the $\overline{BGACK}$ signal is low, thus logically disconnecting the processor from the system data bus.

For large systems, typically multiple-board systems, it is necessary to add a second level of buffering. Consider the situation that more than one memory module is connected to the bus and each module may consist of a large memory chip array. Including a buffer in each memory module reduces the total load of the system bus. Another reason is that double buffering also reduces the total load seen by devices connected to the system bus. Of course, the second set of transceivers may result in a longer bus cycle time due to the additional delay for access. Figure 7-7 illustrates a double-buffered system. On the device side, at most one pair of transceivers is enabled for data transfer during a bus cycle. Which device and its associated transceivers are to be enabled is selected by a decoder.

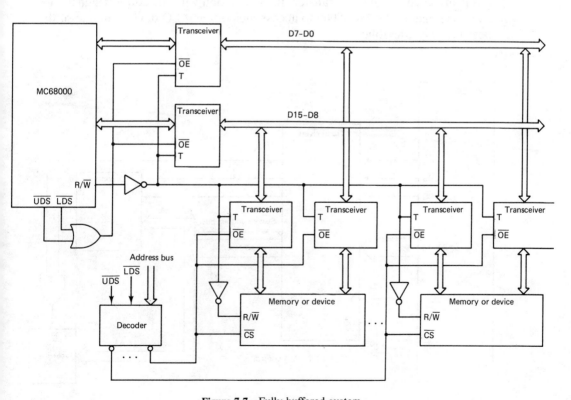

Figure 7-7 Fully buffered system.

Address bus interface

The MC68000 has separate address bus and data bus, thus eliminating the need for address latches. Nevertheless, for the same reason as in data pins, bus buffering is also required for address pins in most systems. In Fig. 7-8, transceivers are used to buffer the address bus with T being grounded. On the device side, the higher portion of the address bus is fed to a decoder generating device-select signals, whereas the remaining address lines are connected to the device for selecting a particular location.

Since more than one device is connected to the system bus, bus contention must be taken into consideration to ensure that only one device is selected at any time. Bus contention occurs when one device is selected before the previous one is deselected. To avoid this problem, the device-select signal generated by an address decoder is conditioned by the $\overline{\text{AS}}$ signal so that all devices are deselected while the address changes.

Although the MC68000 uses 24-bit addresses, it has only 23 address pins, A23–A1, which carry word addresses. In order for the processor to access an even address either as a byte or as a word, it provides two control pins, $\overline{\text{LDS}}$ (lower data strobe) and $\overline{\text{UDS}}$ (upper data strobe). A low on the $\overline{\text{LDS}}$ pin indicates to memory and I/O devices that the lower half of the data bus is to be used in the data transfer. A low on the $\overline{\text{UDS}}$ pin indicates that the upper half of the data bus is involved in the data transfer. In conjunction with the address signals, $\overline{\text{LDS}}$ and $\overline{\text{UDS}}$ enable the MC68000 to access memory and I/O devices in one of three possible ways, as follows:

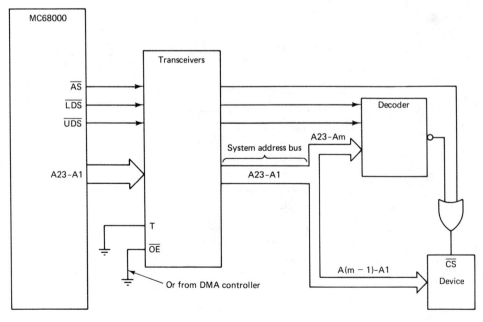

Figure 7-8 Address bus interface.

Operation	Data Lines Used	UDS	LDS
Transfer a byte to or from an odd address	D7–D0	High	Low
Transfer a byte to or from an even address	D15–D8	Low	High
Transfer a word to or from an even adress	D15–D0	Low	Low

As noted before, accessing a word at an odd address is not allowed, and such an attempt causes an invalid address error exception.

Figure 7-9 is a block diagram illustrating how the $\overline{\text{LDS}}$ and $\overline{\text{UDS}}$ signals should be used in the physical implementation of address space. Memory and I/O devices are divided into two banks, each up to 8M bytes. One bank, containing even-addressed bytes, is connected to the upper half of the data bus. The other bank, containing odd-addressed bytes, is connected to the lower half of the data bus. To perform a word transfer, both $\overline{\text{LDS}}$ and $\overline{\text{UDS}}$ are activated. For a byte transfer, either $\overline{\text{LDS}}$ or $\overline{\text{UDS}}$ is activated and the other one is negated, so that only one bank is enabled for transfer. This is necessary to prevent a write operation to one byte from overwriting the content in the other byte within the same word.

Asynchronous bus control

The MC68000 supports two types of bus cycles, asynchronous and synchronous. In an asynchronous bus cycle, the selected memory or I/O device uses a handshaking signal, $\overline{\text{DTACK}}$ (data transfer acknowledge), to indicate to the MC68000 that a data transfer is completed. If the selected memory or I/O device is not capable of transferring data at the maximum processor transfer rate, the device

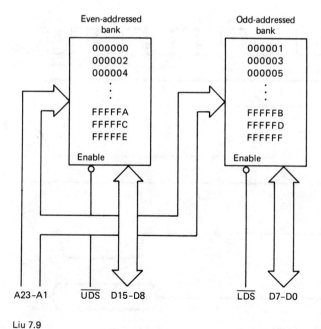

A23–A1 $\overline{\text{UDS}}$ D15–D8 $\overline{\text{LDS}}$ D7–D0

Liu 7.9

Figure 7-9 Physical implementation of the address space.

withholds $\overline{\text{DTACK}}$, and consequently the processor is forced to insert wait states to extend the bus cycle time. This asynchronous nature allows the system to include devices of different speeds and lets the duration of a bus cycle vary, depending on the speed of the selected device. By using asynchronous bus cycles, the system can handle slow devices without penalizing fast devices.

Figure 7-10 illustrates the bus cycle timing of an asynchronous read operation. At the beginning of the bus cycle, the MC68000 sends out function code, address, and control signals. It then waits for the selected device to return the $\overline{\text{DTACK}}$ signal. At the end of state S4, the $\overline{\text{DTACK}}$ pin is checked. If the acknowledge signal is not present, the processor enters the wait state (SW), which has the same bus activity as the S4 and S5 states and can be repeated for any number of times. When the selected device has had sufficient time to complete the transfer, it returns $\overline{\text{DTACK}}$, allowing the processor to proceed from SW to S5. In S6, the processor will latch in the data on the data bus. The processor then terminates the bus cycle in S7 by disabling control signals, address, and function code. A write bus cycle with wait states has a similar timing diagram, except that the $\overline{\text{DTACK}}$ is checked at the end of S6 and wait states are inserted between S6 and S7.

A typical implementation of acknowledge logic is to have the $\overline{\text{DTACK}}$ input normally high. When the selected memory or device receives the bus command, which may be read, write, or interrupt acknowledge, it pulls down the $\overline{\text{DTACK}}$ pin, allowing the processor to terminate the bus cycle. An MC68000-compatible device such as the MC68230 normally has a tristate $\overline{\text{DTACK}}$ output pin, which can be directly connected to the processor's $\overline{\text{DTACK}}$ input pin. For an interface without a $\overline{\text{DTACK}}$ pin (or a memory module) the $\overline{\text{DTACK}}$ signal can be generated

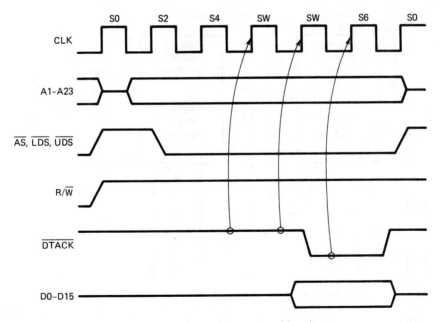

Figure 7-10 Timing of a read bus cycle with wait states.

with minimal external logic. The select signal to enable the interface is applied to a delay logic, whose output is then used as the acknowledge signal. This circuit is known as a wait-state generator and can be implemented with a counter. By switch or jumper settings, the user may choose the number of wait states to be inserted. In order for all the devices' $\overline{\text{DTACK}}$ outputs to be applied to the common $\overline{\text{DTACK}}$ line of the system bus, they should be buffered with open collector or tristate drivers.

One problem with this implementation is that if a device fails to respond or the processor attempts to access nonexistent memory or I/O devices, the system could be kept in an indefinite wait. A time-out logic can prevent this problem. Figure 7-11 is a block diagram showing an acknowledge logic with a time-out circuit implemented by a counter. Since $\overline{\text{AS}}$ becomes low at the beginning of a bus cycle and is kept low until the end of a bus cycle, its complement (AS) is used as the counter-reset signal. If a bus cycle is not terminated in about 16

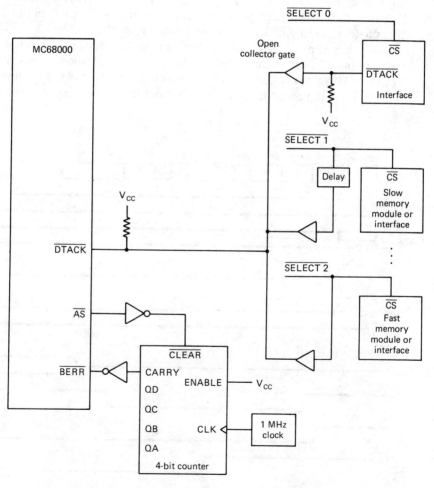

Figure 7-11   Acknowledge and time-out logic.

microseconds in this example, the counter generates a $\overline{\text{BERR}}$ signal, forcing the MC68000 to abort the current bus cycle and then initiate a bus error exception.

Synchronous bus control

In a synchronous bus cycle, the $\overline{\text{DTACK}}$ signal is not used to ensure proper data transfer. Instead, the processor's enable signal (E), which is at a fixed frequency, serves as the synchronization signal to gate the data on or off the data bus. In contrast to an asynchronous bus cycle, the duration of a synchronous bus cycle is close to a constant regardless of the speed of the selected device.

Because the MC6800, the predecessor of the MC68000, uses a synchronous bus, Motorola and some other vendors have designed many synchronous type 8-bit peripherals. The MC6850 ACIA is a typical example. In order to simplify the interface of M6800 peripherals to the MC68000, the MC68000 also includes necessary bus control pins to emulate synchronous bus cycles. In addition to the E pin, the MC68000 has two other pins used only during a synchronous bus cycle. They are the $\overline{\text{VPA}}$ (valid peripheral address) input pin used by an M6800 peripheral to request for a synchronous bus cycle and the $\overline{\text{VMA}}$ (valid memory address) output pin used by the MC68000 to acknowledge the request.

Timing of a synchronous bus cycle for a read operation is illustrated in Fig. 7-12. The MC68000 begins a read cycle as usual by first placing a function code on FC2–FC0 and an address on A23–A1 and then activating $\overline{\text{AS}}$ and $\overline{\text{UDS}}/\overline{\text{LDS}}$

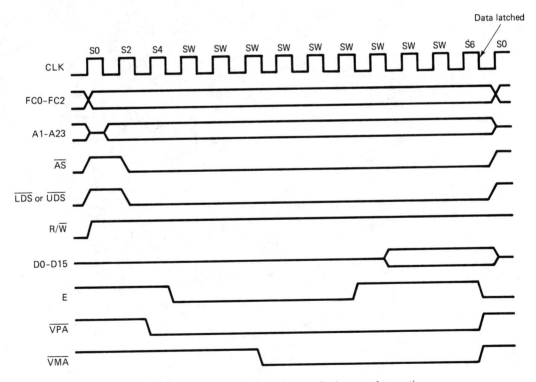

Figure 7-12 Synchronous bus cycle timing for byte read operation.

Bus Operation and Interface   Chap. 7

and setting R/$\overline{\text{W}}$ to read. If the addressed device is an M6800 peripheral, it returns the $\overline{\text{VPA}}$ signal, indicating to the MC68000 that a synchronous bus cycle is in progress. Upon receiving $\overline{\text{VPA}}$, the MC68000 waits until E is low and then activates $\overline{\text{VMA}}$ to select the M6800 peripheral. The selected device uses E as output enable signal and places data on the data bus while E is high. The MC68000 removes data from the data bus at the trailing edge of E and then terminates the current bus cycle by deactivating $\overline{\text{AS}}$, $\overline{\text{LDS/UDS}}$, and $\overline{\text{VMA}}$. A synchronous bus cycle for write operation has similar timing except that the MC68000 keeps the data valid for the entire bus cycle. The frequency of E is only one-tenth of the incoming MC68000 clock frequency, thus allowing 1-MHz peripherals to be used with an 8-MHz MC68000.

Interfacing an M6800 peripheral to the MC68000 can be implemented by following the general block diagram in Fig. 7-13. The decoder's output is conditioned by $\overline{\text{VMA}}$ and $\overline{\text{UDS/LDS}}$ to select the peripheral while the processor's E pin is directly connected to the device's output enable pin. The decoder's output is also fed back to the processor's $\overline{\text{VPA}}$ pin so that when this M6800 device is addressed, the $\overline{\text{VPA}}$ will become low.

Function code outputs

In addition to an R/$\overline{\text{W}}$ bus command, the MC68000 outputs a 3-bit function code (FC2, FC1, FC0) to indicate the type of operand to be transferred during each

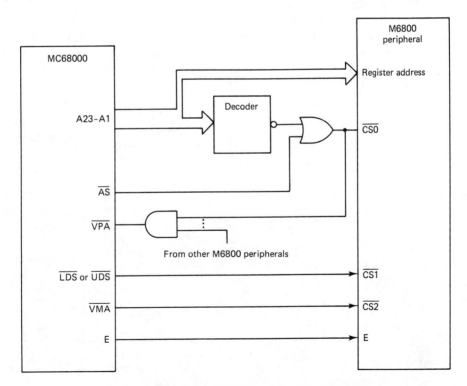

Figure 7-13 Interfacing MC6800 peripherals to MC68000.

bus cycle. An operand type may be user data, user program, supervisor data or supervisor program. A function code is also used to acknowledge any external interrupt request. The function code definition is as follows:

FC2	FC1	FC0	Bus Cycle Type
0	0	0	Undefined, reserved
0	0	1	User data
0	1	0	User program
0	1	1	Undefined, reserved
1	0	0	Undefined, reserved
1	0	1	Supervisor data
1	1	0	Supervisor program
1	1	1	Interrupt acknowledge

If the processor is in the supervisor state or an interrupt exception is taking place, a 1 is output on the FC2 function code pin. Otherwise, FC2 is 0, indicating that the current bus cycle is initiated in the user state. The FC1 function code bit indicates whether a data operand is to be transferred or an instruction or an operand using a PC relative addressing mode is to be fetched. When PC is the address source or reset pointers are fetched, the function code indicates program. On the other hand, the function code indicates data when all operands are written, most operands are read except for PC-related addressing modes, or exception pointers other than reset are fetched.

One usage of the function control outputs is in implementing external interrupt management logic. Note that the MC68000 does not provide a dedicated interrupt acknowledge pin. In order for the interrupting device to supply an interrupt vector number, the function control outputs must be decoded to detect the interrupt acknowledge from the processor. Interrupt management logic is dis-

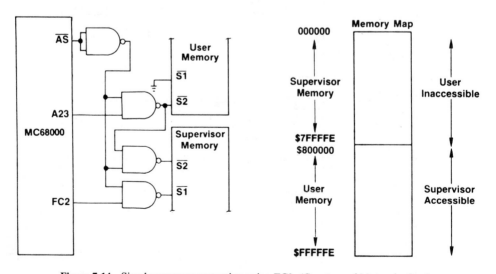

Figure 7-14 Simple memory protection using FC2. (Courtesy of Motorola, Inc.)

cussed in Sec. 7-5. Another potential usage of the function code signals is to provide memory protection.

Consider a typical situation, in which the memory is divided into two regions, one to store the operating system and one to store user's application programs. It is desirable to protect the system memory from being directly referenced by the user while the operating system has access to both system and user memory. This memory protection can be enforced by the logic shown in Fig. 7-14 when the operating system runs in the supervisor state and application programs are executed under the user state. In the example, the range from $000000 to $7FFFFF is the system memory and the range from $800000 to $FFFFFF is the user memory. Since FC2 indicates whether the MC68000 is in the supervisor state (1) or in the user state (0), the system memory is enabled only when FC2 is 1 and A23 is 0. On the other hand, the user memory is enabled whenever the address is between $800000 and $FFFFFF, regardless of the processor state, by using A23 = 1 as the select condition.

7-4 Clock and System Control Circuits

Clock

The maximum clock frequency of an MC68000 varies, depending on its version, as indicated by the speed suffix. For example, the maximum frequency is 8 MHz for the MC68000L8 and 12.5 MHz for the MC68000L12. The letter L indicates the package type of ceramic dual-in-line. Since there are dynamic cells in the MC68000, a minimum frequency is required to retain the internal state. For most versions, the minimum frequency is 4 MHz. Because of the minimum-frequency requirement, single-stepping through bus cycles in hardware debugging is not accomplished by simply stopping the clock. Logic to provide single bus cycles can be implemented using the halt facility, as discussed later.

The clock generator logic can be designed based on a TTL crystal clock oscillator, as shown in Fig. 7-15. The oscillator is an integrated clock generator that contains a quartz crystal and provides the clock output in the TTL level. In

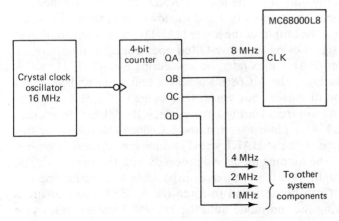

Figure 7-15 Clock generator.

this example, the fundamental clock signal is applied to a frequency divider, supplying clocks of different frequencies required by the MC68000 and other system components.

Reset and halt circuit

The processor must be reset when the system is turned on. During the reset, the MC68000 loads the supervisor stack pointer and the program counter with the contents stored in locations $000000–$000007, sets the status register to interrupt mask level 7, and begins execution at the address in PC. Other registers are not affected by the reset. To cause a power-up reset (i.e., V_{cc} is not initially applied to the MC68000), according to the specifications both the $\overline{\text{RESET}}$ and $\overline{\text{HALT}}$ inputs must be low for at least 100 milliseconds. After $\overline{\text{RESET}}$ and $\overline{\text{HALT}}$ return to high, the reset exception sequence occurs. This requires a circuit that generates a negative-going pulse with sufficient pulse width right after the system is turned on. A typical system also includes a push-button reset logic, allowing the user to restart the MC68000 in an endless loop, runaway, or hang-up situation. Figure 7-16 shows a reset circuit for providing both system power-up and push-button resets.

In this example, the power-up reset signal is generated by the LM555, a typical timing device. Among other applications, this device can be used to produce accurate time delays or oscillation. For our application, the LM555 is configured in the monostable (one-shot) mode. When the system is initially turned on, the trigger input is less than $0.34V_{cc}$. This causes the trigger comparator to set the device's output to high. Since $\overline{Q}$ becomes low, the internal discharge transistor is turned off. This condition allows the external threshold capacitor to charge at an exponential rate determined by the RC time constant. When the threshold input reaches $0.67V_{cc}$, the threshold comparator resets the flip-flop and discharges the threshold capacitor. After the flip-flop has been reset, its output remains low as the system is on. This is because as the trigger capacitor voltage reaches above $0.34V_{cc}$, the flip-flop cannot be set unless the power is turned off.

The push-button reset logic is implemented with two cross-coupled NAND gates. Whenever the switch is depressed, the lower NAND gate is forced to output a 1. This, in turn, causes the output of the upper NAND gate to be 0. Once the switch is released, the upper one returns to 1 and the lower one, to 0. The push-button reset signal, which is the output of the lower NAND gate, is then combined with the power-on reset signal using two wire-ORed open-collector inverters.

Both the $\overline{\text{RESET}}$ and $\overline{\text{HALT}}$ pins must be low during a reset. If $\overline{\text{HALT}}$ is asserted while $\overline{\text{RESET}}$ is high, the MC68000 enters a halt state and stops all activities upon completion of current bus cycle. One usage of the $\overline{\text{HALT}}$ pin is to rerun a bus cycle with a bus error. During a bus cycle, if the MC68000 receives a bus error signal and the $\overline{\text{HALT}}$ pin is asserted, the MC68000 will reexecute this bus cycle and then continue after the $\overline{\text{HALT}}$ signal is removed. If there is no bus error, the MC68000 enters the running mode and proceeds with the next bus cycle when $\overline{\text{HALT}}$ returns to high. This feature makes it possible to execute one bus cycle at a time. A circuit can be designed to force the MC68000 to execute a single bus cycle by entering the run mode until the MC68000 starts a bus cycle

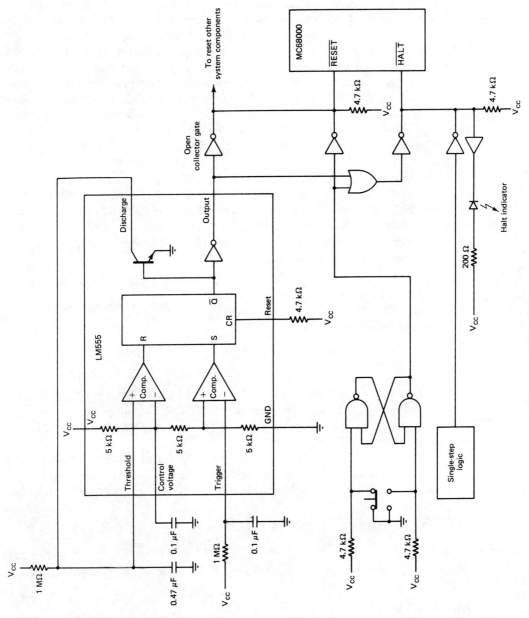

Figure 7-16 Reset circuit.

and then switching back to the halt mode. The facility to single-step bus cycles is a useful hardware debugging tool, as is the instruction trace to software debugging. Implementing a single-step circuit is requested in Exercise 11.

Another design consideration related to the reset operation is the mapping of the reset vector addresses. In order for the system automatically to start execution of a bootstrap loader or a resident monitor whenever the system is reset either manually or by the power-up condition, the contents at the reset vector addresses must be permanently stored. This requires that 8 bytes at locations $000000–$000007 be implemented as a part of ROM. However, other addresses in the lower 1K memory, which correspond to exception vector addresses, should be implemented in RAM to provide flexibility in storing interrupt pointers that vary from one configuration to the next. A solution to this problem is to map addresses $000000–$000007 to high addresses implemented in ROM while assigning low addresses to RAM. An example of the required address decoding logic is given in Fig. 7-17.

The example assumes that the system has 32K RAM occupying the address range of $000008–$007FFF and 32K ROM starting at address $008000. When locations $000000–$000007 are read by the MC68000, ROM responds with the contents in locations $008000–$008007. Therefore, ROM is enabled if the address is in the range of $000000–$000007 and $008000–$00BFFF. To accomplish this, the ROM enable signal is generated based on the condition

$$(A3 = A4 = \cdots = A23 = 0)\cdot(\overline{AS} = 0)\cdot(R/\overline{W} = 1) + (A14 = 0)\cdot(A15 = 1)\cdot$$

$$(A16 = A17 = \cdots = A23 = 0)\cdot(\overline{AS} = 0)\cdot(R/\overline{W} = 1)$$

which is equivalent to

$$[(A3 = A4 = \ldots = A13 = 0) + (A15 = 1)]\cdot(A14 = 0)$$

$$\cdot(A16 = A17 = \ldots = A23 = 0)\cdot(\overline{AS} = 0)\cdot(R/\overline{W} = 1)$$

It should be noted that unlike RAM, a ROM-enable signal need not be conditioned with the $\overline{UDS}$ and $\overline{LDS}$ signals. The reason is that during a byte-read operation, the MC68000 selects the byte from either pins D15–D8 or D7–D0 even though both bytes might be present.

It is necessary to disable the RAM when addresses $000000–$000007 are accessed. Otherwise, both ROM and RAM would be enabled at the same time. To avoid this problem, the RAM-enable signal is generated according to the condition

$$(A3 = A4 = \cdots A14 = 0)\cdot(A15 = 0)\cdot(A16 = A17 = \cdots = A23 = 0)$$

$$\cdot(\overline{AS} = 0)\cdot(\overline{UDS} = 0 + \overline{LDS} = 0)$$

Whether the even, odd, or both banks are to be selected depends on $\overline{UDS}$ and $\overline{LDS}$.

Bus error

The third system control pin is the bus error ($\overline{BERR}$) pin. An input on this pin indicates a bus error. In conjunction with $\overline{DTACK}$ and $\overline{HALT}$, the $\overline{BERR}$ signal determines how the current bus cycle is to be terminated.

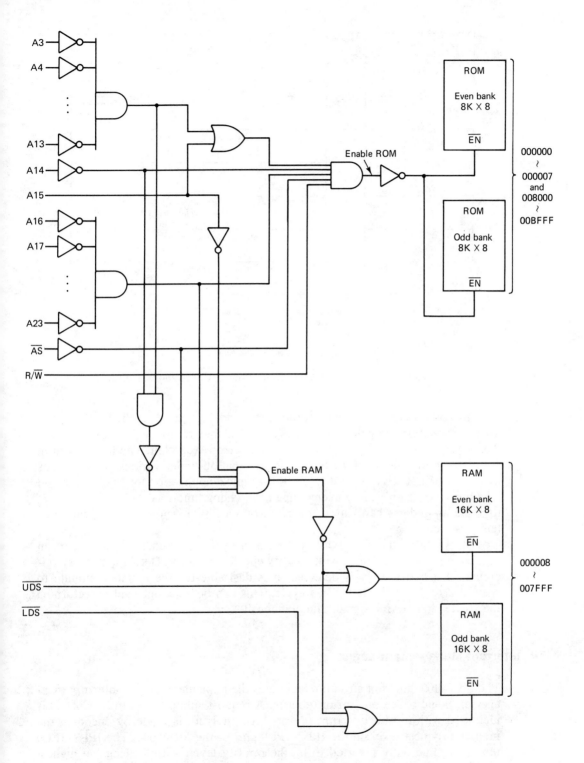

Figure 7-17 Implementing reset vector addresses as ROM locations.

Case No.	Control Signal	Asserted on Rising Edge of State N	Asserted on Rising Edge of State N+2	Result
1	DTACK	A	S	Normal cycle terminate and continue.
	BERR	NA	X	
	HALT	NA	X	
2	DTACK	A	S	Normal cycle terminate and halt. Continue when HALT removed.
	BERR	NA	X	
	HALT	A	S	
3	DTACK	NA	A	Normal cycle terminate and halt. Continue when HALT removed.
	BERR	NA	NA	
	HALT	A	S	
4	DTACK	X	X	Terminate and take bus error trap.
	BERR	A	S	
	HALT	NA	NA	
5	DTACK	NA	X	R9M, T6E, BF4: Unpredictable results, no re-run, no error trap; usually traps to vector number 0. All others: terminate and re-run.
	BERR	A	S	
	HALT	NA	A	
6	DTACK	X	X	Terminate and re-run when HALT removed.
	BERR	A	S	
	HALT	A	S	
7	DTACK	NA	X	Terminate and re-run when HALT removed.
	BERR	NA	A	
	HALT	A	S	

Legend:
N — the number of the current even bus state (e.g., S4, S6, etc.)
A — signal is asserted in this bus state
NA — signal is not asserted in this state
X — don't care
S — signal was asserted in previous state and remains asserted in this state

Figure 7-18 Bus cycle terminations. (Courtesy of Motorola, Inc.)

In addition to the normal termination and halt, as described before, the MC68000 can terminate the current bus cycle and then rerun the cycle or terminate the current bus cycle and then initiate a bus error exception. The table given in Fig. 7-18 shows the resulting bus cycle termination under various combinations of signals BERR, HALT, and DTACK. A typical application for "terminate and take bus error trap" is in implementing a watchdog timer, as shown in Fig. 7-11, to avoid an endless hang-up in the event of accessing a nonexisting location or faulty device.

A typical situation for using the rerun cycle is when an error occurs in accessing memory modules with a parity check capability. During a memory reference, if a parity error is detected, it is desirable for the memory module to request a rerun of the failed bus cycle. This can be accomplished by returning the BERR and HALT signals simultaneously.

7-5 Interrupt Management Logic

The MC68000 interrupt structure facilitates the implementation of interrupt management logic based on a priority basis. A request submitted to the MC68000 is identified with a 3-bit interrupt priority. An interrupt is made by encoding the interrupt request level on the $\overline{IPL2}$–$\overline{IPL0}$ pins of the MC68000. The $\overline{IPL2}$–$\overline{IPL0}$ inputs are internally inverted to be the priority level, with 7 being the highest priority. A zero indicates no interrupt request. If this level is higher than the mask level I2 I1 I0 set in the status register, an interrupt exception processing will begin. Otherwise, the pending request is ignored. However, as noted before, level 7 is a special case that is always recognized.

The following table shows the possible inputs on the $\overline{IPL2}$–$\overline{IPL0}$ pins and the priorities they represent. For each request level, the table also gives the maximum mask level that still allows the interrupt to be recognized.

Interrupt priority level input			Internal interrupt priority level	Maximum mask level to allow the interrupt		
$\overline{IPL2}$	$\overline{IPL1}$	$\overline{IPL0}$		I2	I1	I0
Low	Low	Low	7 (Highest)		Nonmaskable	
Low	Low	High	6	1	0	1
Low	High	Low	5	1	0	0
Low	High	High	4	0	1	1
High	Low	Low	3	0	1	0
High	Low	High	2	0	0	1
High	High	Low	1 (Lowest)	0	0	0
High	High	High	No interrupt request			

In the interrupt exception processing, the processor finishes the current instruction and then sends out an interrupt acknowledge by setting function code pins FC2–FC0 to 111. The mask level is raised to the request level, so that in serving the current interrupt the processor would not be interrupted by requests with equal or lower priorities. In acknowledging an interrupt request, the processor also returns the priority level of the accepted request on address A3–A1. This returned priority level can be decoded to enable the interrupting device for submitting its interrupt vector number to data pins D7–D0.

Since a typical system has several peripheral devices capable of generating interrupt requests, we must consider the possibility that more than one peripheral may issue requests at the same time. External interrupt management logic is therefore required to resolve simultaneous interrupt requests. When two or more devices submit requests at the same time, this logic selects the one with the highest priority level and passes it to the processor.

An example of interrupt management logic to handle up to seven request inputs is given in Fig. 7-19. The example assumes that all seven devices are M6800 peripherals that use auto vector interrupts. A request of an auto vector interrupt is indicated to the processor by asserting its $\overline{VPA}$ input pin. In the acknowledge sequence of an auto vector interrupt, the processor does not input a vector number from the peripheral. Instead, the MC68000 generates a vector number internally, which is the request priority level plus 24. Figure 7-19 uses a priority encoder such as the 74148 to resolve multiple interrupt requests. If one or more of its inputs are asserted, the priority encoder outputs a 3-bit number in the complement form corresponding to the asserted input with the highest priority. This negated request level is applied to the $\overline{IPL2}$–$\overline{IPL0}$ pins. The interrupt acknowledge from the processor is detected by decoding FC2–FC0. Since all interrupts handled are assumed to be the auto vector type in the example, this acknowledge signal is

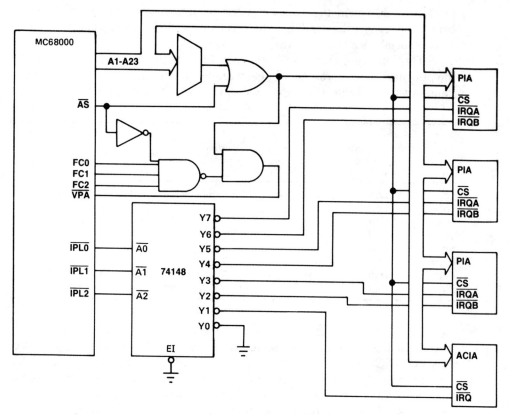

Figure 7-19 Interrupt management logic for multiple M6800 peripherals. (Courtesy of Motorola, Inc.)

applied to the $\overline{VPA}$ pin, causing the MC68000 to start the service routine associated with the interrupting device.

Although the auto vector interrupt provides the advantage of simplicity, it limits the maximum number of devices in the system to seven. The MC68000 also supports a more flexible type of interrupt, the non–auto vector interrupt. Peripherals specifically designed for the M68000 family are based on this type of interrupt structure. During the interrupt acknowledge sequence, the interrupting device is expected to supply an 8-bit vector number. This can be accomplished by decoding the 3-bit request level returned on address lines A3–A1 to generate a signal to select the interrupting device.

Figure 7-20 is a block diagram showing the major logic required to handle both auto vector and non–auto vector interrupts. In the example, priority level 5 is used for non–auto vector interrupts and level 3 for auto vector interrupts. The remaining five request lines can be assigned to either type. As shown in the figure, when a non–auto vector interrupt request is accepted, its respective acknowledge signal is asserted to enable the interrupting device for sending a vector

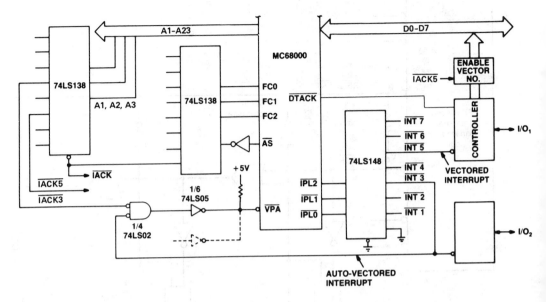

Figure 7-20 Interrupt management logic for both auto and non–auto vector interrupt types. (Courtesy of Motorola, Inc.)

number. If the interrupt request is of the auto vector type, the asserted acknowledge signal enables the $\overline{VPA}$ pin of the MC68000. It is important to note that a vector number can only be sent over D7–D0. Therefore, an 8-bit I/O device using non-auto vector interrupts must be connected to the lower byte of the data bus, i.e., in the odd-addressed bank.

This sample prioritized interrupt management logic can be expanded to handle more than seven interrupt devices. By adding an interrupt controller, such as the one discussed in Sec. 7-7, with all four of its request inputs sharing one request line connected to the priority encoder, up to three additional non–auto vector interrupt devices can be included in the system.

Another alternative for expansion is to have several devices share a request input line to the priority encoder in a daisy-chain fashion, as illustrated in Fig. 7-21. If one or more devices request an interrupt, the corresponding request input to the priority encoder is asserted. Upon the request being accepted, the active-low acknowledge signal ($\overline{IACK}$) propagates through each element on the chain until it encounters the one whose request signal is 1. Then, the acknowledge signal is blocked from propagating to the next lower device. Therefore, the interrupting device that is closest to the interrupt management logic receives an enable signal to place its vector number on the data bus. Other interrupting devices further down the daisy-chain will not receive the interrupt acknowledge even if they have also requested an interrupt. Their requests will not be recognized until the higher-priority device has been serviced.

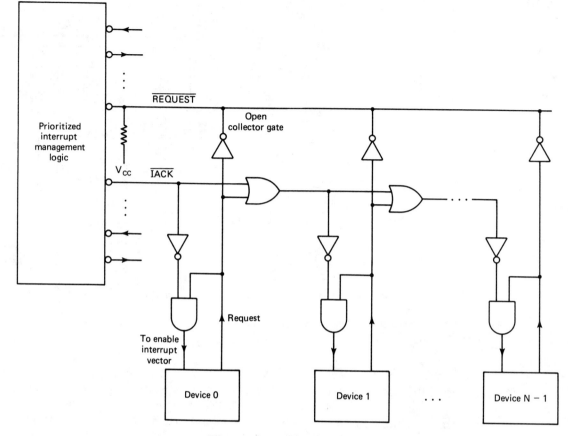

Figure 7-21 Daisy-chain structure.

7-6 DMA Logic

During a bus cycle, the device that initiates the read or write command is the *bus master*, whereas the device responding to the command is the *bus slave*. A processor can act only as a bus master. On the other hand, a memory module is always a bus slave, and so are the interface devices such as the ACIA and PI/T. A DMA (direct memory access) controller has the capability of temporarily gaining control of the bus from the processor. Upon becoming the bus master, the DMA device transfers data directly to or from memory and then relinquishes the bus back to the processor. Unlike interrupts, DMA operations will not affect the processor's instruction execution, except to cause delay for some bus cycles. In programming a DMA controller, it is accessed by the processor as a bus slave like a regular peripheral device.

For supporting DMA devices, the MC68000 provides three bus arbitration pins, $\overline{BR}$ (bus request), $\overline{BG}$ (bus grant), and $\overline{BGACK}$ (bus grant acknowledge). To request control of the bus, the DMA device asserts the $\overline{BR}$ pin low. The MC68000 acknowledges the request by returning the $\overline{BG}$ signal. This indicates that the MC68000 will relinquish the bus as soon as the current bus cycle is completed. When the processor releases the bus, it forces all tristate pins, including address, data, and control outputs, into the high-impedance state. The processor still continues its internal operation unless a bus cycle is needed. Upon receiving $\overline{BG}$, the requesting device waits until the processor has completed its current bus cycle and then asserts the $\overline{BGACK}$ pin, becoming the bus master. The DMA device must keep $\overline{BGACK}$ low as long as it requires the bus. Once the DMA device releases the $\overline{BGACK}$ signal, the processor will regain control of the bus. The timing diagram in Fig. 7-22 shows the handshaking sequence in transferring bus control between the processor and DMA device.

To guarantee valid system operation, upon receiving $\overline{BG}$, the DMA device must wait until $\overline{AS}$ is negated by the processor, indicating the end of a bus cycle, before issuing $\overline{BGACK}$. Furthermore, the requesting device must release $\overline{BR}$ prior to $\overline{BGACK}$ going high. Otherwise, the MC68000 will issue another $\overline{BG}$ acknowledge signal.

A DMA controller specifically designed for the M68000 family includes three corresponding bus access pins, which can be directly connected to the $\overline{BR}$, $\overline{BG}$, and $\overline{BGACK}$ pins of the MC68000. Two such DMA controllers are discussed in Sec. 8-8. However, a general device with DMA capability may provide only two pins for bus access, $\overline{HOLD}$ and $\overline{HLDA}$. Pin $\overline{HOLD}$ is used to issue a bus request to the processor, whereas $\overline{HLDA}$ is used to receive the acknowledge if the bus is granted. In this case, external logic such as that shown in Fig. 7-23 is needed to satisfy the bus request/grant protocol of the MC68000.

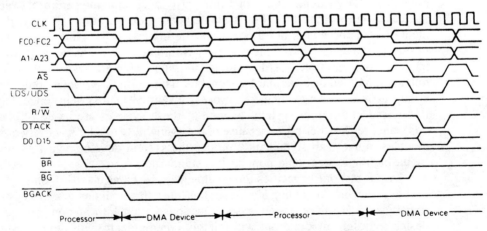

Figure 7-22 Bus arbitration cycle timing. (Courtesy of Motorola, Inc.)

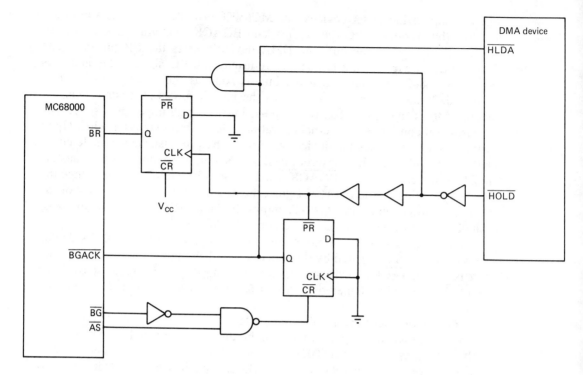

Figure 7-23 DMA logic.

7-7 The VME Bus

We have discussed how the MC68000 pins are to be connected to other components in the system. The signal lines providing communication between two devices comprise the bus. For a single-board configuration, the actual implementation of the bus is not a concern. The number of bus lines used and their positions and exact definitions may vary from one case to the next. However, in implementing multiple-board systems, it is desirable to have interboard communication based on a standard system bus. This permits system modules (printed circuit boards), such as memory, processor, and I/O subsystem, once designed, to be used in different systems as long as these systems are based on the same bus standard. Furthermore, because of the availability of a large variety of system modules, a user can significantly reduce the system development time and cost by basing the system on a popular bus standard.

A bus standard specifies the mechanical as well as electrical characteristics of the system bus, including number of bus lines, line assignments, timing of signal transitions, and driver/receiver specifications. Such information is required to design a system module that will reliably communicate with other modules interfaced to the bus.

Summary of VME bus signals

Motorola proposed the VME bus standard, which has been adopted by a large number of manufacturers making the M68000 family products. The VME bus supports devices of 8-, 16-, and 32-bit data widths and provides three address bus options, 16, 24, and 32 bits. In addition this bus permits the system to have more than one processor, thus providing a multiprocessing capability.

The VME bus standard calls for a total of 192 lines. A PC board is connected to the bus, which is physically implemented on the backplane via two 96-pin connectors, P1 and P2. Connector P1 connects to the primary bus and P2 to the secondary bus. Connector P2 is optional, which is required for expanding the primary bus from 16 data lines to 32 and from 24 address lines to 32. In addition to extra address and data lines, the optional secondary bus provides 64 lines for user-defined I/O functions. Figure 7-24 shows the pin layout of the P1 and P2 connectors. Figure 7-25 lists all VME bus lines and gives the mnemonic, position, and signal description of each line. An asterisk indicates an active low bus signal.

The VME bus lines can be grouped into the following categories: address lines, data lines, control and interrupt lines, bus arbitration lines, and utility lines. The address and data lines are driven by the tristate devices, whereas interrupt request and some other control lines are driven by open-collector devices.

The primary bus has 23 address lines, labeled A01–A23. By including the optional bus, 8 additional address lines, A24–A31, are provided to support up to

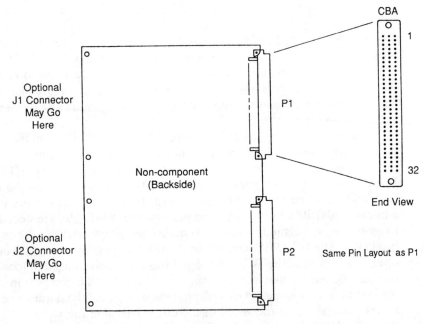

Figure 7-24 PC board reference designations and pin numbering for VME bus standard. (Courtesy of Motorola, Inc.)

SIGNAL MNEMONIC	CONNECTOR AND PIN NUMBER	SIGNAL NAME AND DESCRIPTION
ACFAIL*	1B: 3	AC FAILURE - Open-collector driven signal which indicates that the AC input to the power supply is no longer being provided or that the required input voltage levels are not being met.
IACKIN*	1A: 21	INTERRUPT ACKNOWLEDGE IN - Totem-pole driven signal. IACKIN* and IACKOUT* signals form a daisy-chained acknowledge. The IACKIN* signal indicates to the Eurocard that an acknowledge cycle is in progress.
IACKOUT*	1A: 22	INTERRUPT ACKNOWLEDGE OUT - Totem-pole driven signal. IACKIN* and IACKOUT* signals form a daisy-chained acknowledge. The IACKOUT* signal indicates to the next board that an acknowledge cycle is in progress.
AM0-AM5	1A: 23 1B: 16,17, 18,19 1C: 14	ADDRESS MODIFIER (bits 0-5) - Three-state driven lines that provide additional information about the address bus, such as size, cycle type, and/or DTB master identification.
AS*	1A: 18	ADDRESS STROBE - Three-state driven signal that indicates a valid address is on the address bus.
A01-A23	1A: 24-30 1C: 15-30	ADDRESS bus (bits 1-23) - Three-state driven address lines that specify a memory address.
A24-A31	2B: 4-11	ADDRESS bus (bits 24-31) - Three-state driven bus expansion address lines.
BBSY*	1B: 1	BUS BUSY - Open-collector driven signal generated by the current DTB master to indicate that it is using the bus.
BCLR*	1B: 2	BUS CLEAR - Totem-pole driven signal generated by the bus arbitrator to request release by the current DTB master in the event that a higher level is requesting the bus.

Figure 7-25 VME bus signal identification. (Courtesy of Motorola, Inc.)

4 gigabytes. The address lines are driven by the bus master to specify the word location to be accessed. In conjunction with the address, signals DS0* and DS1* are used to select the upper byte, lower byte, or entire word to be transferred. Along with the address, the master also sends out signal AS*, indicating a valid address, and a 6-bit address modifier (AM0–AM5), indicating the size of the address bus and the cycle type.

There are 16 bidirectional data lines, labeled D00–D15, on the primary bus, only the lower eight of which are used in an 8-bit system. To support 32-bit devices, the optional secondary bus is needed for expanding the data bus by 16 lines (D16–D31). A 32-bit transfer is indicated by an LWORD* signal from the bus master. It should be noted that a 32-bit (longword) transfer can be performed only with addresses divisible by 4. Data transfers on the VME bus are accomplished by handshaking signals in the same manner as described before in the asynchronous bus cycle. The WRITE* signal from the master specifies a read (1) or a write (0) operation, whereas the DTACK* signal from the slave is used to terminate a data transfer. Because a master must wait to be notified of the completion of a transfer, the system may include devices of different speeds and the duration of a bus cycle varies, depending on the speed of the bus master and the slave.

The VME bus supports prioritized non–auto vector interrupts. Seven interrupt request lines, labeled IRQ1*–IRQ7* are provided for a bus master to receive requests, with level 7 being the highest priority. The requesting device decodes the ID returned on A01–A03 and checks the daisy-chained acknowledge

SIGNAL MNEMONIC	CONNECTOR AND PIN NUMBER	SIGNAL NAME AND DESCRIPTION
BERR*	1C: 11	BUS ERROR - Open-collector driven signal generated by a slave. This signal indicates that an unrecoverable error has occurred and the bus cycle must be aborted.
BG0IN*– BG3IN*	1B: 4,6, 8,10	BUS GRANT (0-3) IN - Totem-pole driven signals generated by the Arbiter or Requesters. Bus grant in and out signals form a daisy-chained bus grant. The bus grant in signal indicates to this board that it may become the next bus master.
BG0OUT*– BG3OUT*	1B: 5,7, 9,11	BUS GRANT (0-3) OUT - Totem-pole driven signals generated by Requesters. Bus grant in and out signals form a daisy-chained bus grant. The bus grant out signal indicates to the next board that it may become the next bus master.
BR0*–BR3*	1B: 12-15	BUS REQUEST (0-3) - Open-collector driven signals generated by Requesters. These signals indicate that a DTB master in the daisy-chain requires access to the bus.
DS0*	1A: 13	DATA STROBE 0 - Three-state driven signal that indicates during byte and word transfers that a data transfer will occur on data bus lines (D00-D07).
DS1*	1A: 12	DATA STROBE 1 - Three-state driven signal that indicates during byte and word transfers that a data transfer will occur on data bus lines (D08-D15).
DTACK*	1A: 16	DATA TRANSFER ACKNOWLEDGE - Open-collector driven signal generated by a DTB slave. The falling edge of this signal indicates that valid data is available on the data bus during a read cycle, or that data has been accepted from the data bus during a write cycle.
D00-D15	1A: 1-8 1C: 1-8	DATA BUS (bits 0-15) - Three-state driven bidirectional data lines that provide a data path between the DTB master and slave.
D16-D31	2B: 14-21 2B: 23-30	DATA BUS (bits 16-31) - Three-state driven bi-directional lines for data bus expansion.
GND	1A: 11,15, 17,19 1B: 20,23 1C: 9 2B: 3,12, 22,31	GROUND

Figure 7-25 *(continued)*

signal. If the level of request does not match the level indicated on A01–A03, the current device passes the signal on the interrupt acknowledge in (IACKIN*) line to the next module in the daisy-chain via the IACKOUT* (interrupt acknowledge out) line. Of course, the interrupting module being selected does not pass the acknowledge signal down the daisy-chain. The IACK* from the master is used to start the interrupt acknowledge daisy-chain. Since request signals are open-collector driven and the acknowledge line is organized in a daisy-chained fashion, two or more devices may share a common request line.

In order to support multiprocessor configurations, there are 14 lines designated for bus arbitration. They are typically connected to the bus arbiter in the system controller module, which ensures that only one bus master can have control of the bus at a time. A bus master may request the bus via one of the four request lines (BR0*–BR3*). Each bus request line is driven by an open-collector gate and has a corresponding bus grant line which is daisy-chained (BG0IN*/OUT* through BG3IN*/OUT*). This permits several bus masters to share a common

VME Bus Signal Identification (cont'd)

SIGNAL MNEMONIC	CONNECTOR AND PIN NUMBER	SIGNAL NAME AND DESCRIPTION
IACK*	1A: 20	INTERRUPT ACKNOWLEDGE - Signal from any MASTER processing an interrupt request. Routed via backplane to Slot 1, where it is looped back to become Slot 1 IACKIN* to start the interrupt acknowledge daisy-chain.
IRQ1*-IRQ7*	1B: 24-30	INTERRUPT REQUEST (1-7) - Open-collector driven signals, generated by an interrupter, which carry prioritized interrupt requests. Level seven is the highest priority.
LWORD*	1C: 13	LONGWORD - Three-state driven signal to indicate that the current transfer is a 32-bit transfer.
[RESERVED]	2B: 3	RESERVED - Signal line reserved for future VME bus enhancements. This line must not be used.
SERCLK	1B: 21	A reserved signal which will be used as the clock for a serial communication bus protocol which is still being finalized.
SERDAT	1B: 22	A reserved signal which will be used as the transmission line for serial communication bus messages.
SYSCLK	1A: 10	SYSTEM CLOCK - A constant 16-MHz clock signal that is independent of processor speed or timing. This signal is used for general system timing use.
SYSFAIL*	1C: 10	SYSTEM FAIL - Open-collector driven signal that indicates that a failure has occurred in the system. This signal may be generated by any module on the VME bus.
SYSRESET*	1C: 12	SYSTEM RESET - Open-collector driven signal which, when low, will cause the system to be reset.
WRITE*	1A: 14	WRITE - Three-state driven signal that specifies the data transfer cycle in progress to be either read or write. A high level indicates a read operation; a low level indicates a write operation.

VME Bus Signal Identification (cont'd)

SIGNAL MNEMONIC	CONNECTOR AND PIN NUMBER	SIGNAL NAME AND DESCRIPTION
+5V STDBY	1B: 31	+5 Vdc STANDBY - This line supplies +5 Vdc to devices requiring battery backup.
+5V	1A: 32 1B: 32 1C: 32 2B: 1,13,32	+5 Vdc Power - Used by system logic circuits.
+12V	1C: 31	+12 Vdc Power - Used by system logic circuits.
-12V	1A: 31	-12 Vdc Power - Used by system logic circuits.

| User I/O | 2A: 1-32 2C: 1-32 | Defined by user for I/O applications. |

Figure 7-25 (*continued*)

request line. The master that is granted the bus asserts the BBSY* (bus busy) signal and blocks the grant signal from being propagated to the next module on the same daisy-chain. Control of the bus is not relinquished by the current master until it negates the BBSY* signal.

The bus arbiter, which is part of the system controller, may resolve simultaneous bus requests in one of three options. The priority arbitration option always assigns the bus on a fixed-priority basis, with BR3* being the highest priority level and BR0*, the lowest. With this option, the arbiter also uses the BCLR* (bus clear) line to inform the current bus master that a higher priority request is now pending. This option is useful in implementing hierarchical systems. The round-robin option assigns the bus on a rotating priority basis. In other words, the request line used by the current bus master becomes the one with the lowest priority during the next bus arbitration. This option is typically chosen to implement systems containing multiple masters with equal chances of accessing the bus. The third option, single-level arbitration, honors only requests from the BR3* line and relies on the daisy-chain structure for priority determination.

The utility bus consists of lines to supply powers and timing signals and to provide the system with initialization and diagnostic capability. Included in this group are the lines GND, +5 volts, +5 volts STDBY (+5 volts standby), +12 V, −12V, SYSCLK (system clock), SYSRESET* (system reset), SYSFAIL* (system failure), BERR* (bus error), ACFAIL* (AC failure), SERCLK (serial clock), and SERDAT (serial data). The ACFAIL* line is used to detect and handle power failures. When the AC voltage level drops below a certain level, the power monitor module generates a power-failure signal. This signal causes the user-supplied power-failure-handling logic to generate an interrupt to the bus master, which then saves the current program's vital information onto the disk. After the AC power is restored, the power-failure-handling logic signals the bus master to initiate a power-up sequence. During this sequence, the processor restores the saved information and resumes the execution of the suspended program. Another alternative for handling power failures is to include a standby power source normally provided by batteries. By using the +5-volt dc power supplied via the +5 volt STDBY line, some memory and other modules can remain active during ac power failures for reasonably long periods of time.

The SERCLK and SERDAT lines are reserved for intermodule communications. A module can send a message to an addressed module or to a class of modules in the system. The message is carried in serial form on the SERDAT line, whereas the SERCLK line provides the required timing signal for retrieving the message. These two lines can be used for providing communication between processors, which is frequently required in a multiprocessing system.

Bus interrupt module

Figure 7-26 shows the fundamental structure of a slave module for VME bus–based systems. In addition to the peripheral interface, it includes four major circuits: data bus transceivers, control logic and buffers, address decoder, and interrupt logic. As in a processor module, data bus transceivers are required in a slave module to reduce bus loading in a multiple-board system. The control logic and buffers provide bus drivers to receive control signals such as AS*, and WRITE* and to generate handshaking signals such as DTACK* and BERR*. The address decoder interprets the received address from the processor during a data transfer to determine whether or not this bus module is referenced. If so, the peripheral interface is enabled and the referenced register is selected for data transfer. Otherwise, no action takes place. A detailed discussion of address de-

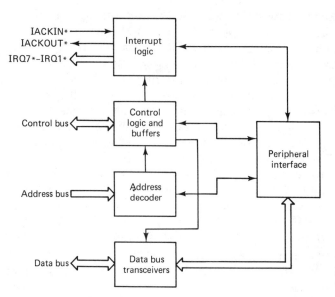

Figure 7-26   Functional block diagram of a VME bus slave module.

coding logic and various peripheral interfaces are given in Chap. 8. The interrupt logic generates interrupt requests for the peripheral interface and to answer interrupt acknowledge signals from the processor module.

In order to be compatible with the protocol of the VME bus, this interrupt logic must be able to: (1) generate interrupt request using request lines IRQ7*–IRQ1*, (2) respond to an interrupt acknowledge bus cycle in both daisy-chain and prioritized configurations, and (3) recognize the priority level of the request currently being accepted by the processor and supply a vector number in the case of a non–auto vector interrupt. Motorola has made available the MC68153 BIM (bus interrupt module) device, designed to simplify the implementation of interrupt logic required on a slave module. The BIM provides the necessary logic for connecting to the interrupt-related VME bus lines and is capable of handling up to four interrupt sources. The interrupt priority level and vector number associated with each of the four interrupt sources can be independently programmed. Figure 7-27 shows the connection of the BIM to the VME bus. The address decoder and data transceivers can be shared with the interface devices on the same module.

The BIM provides four interrupt request pins, $\overline{INT3}$–$\overline{INT0}$. Each $\overline{INT}$ pin can be used by a peripheral device to send an interrupt request by driving it low. There is a separate pair of control and interrupt vector registers associated with each interrupt request pin. The control register can be programmed to enable the interrupt request input and to specify the priority level associated with that request pin. If the interrupt enable bit is cleared, the input from the corresponding $\overline{INT}$ pin will be ignored. An $\overline{INT}$ request input is assigned a priority level from 1 through 7. Upon receiving $\overline{INT}$ inputs that have not been masked, the BIM issues an interrupt request to the processor module by outputting a 0 on one of its seven $\overline{IRQ}$ pins. The $\overline{IRQ}$ pin used to send the request output corresponds to the pending $\overline{INT}$ request with the highest priority level. The vector register associated with

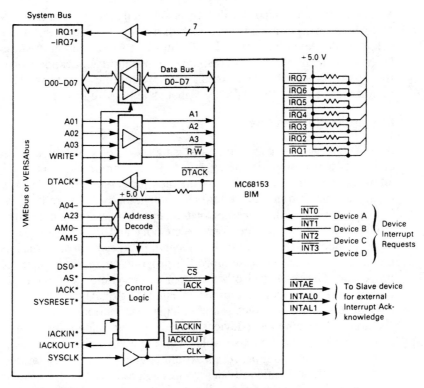

Figure 7-27 Interrupt logic for VME bus interface. (Courtesy of Motorola, Inc.)

each $\overline{\text{INT}}$ pin allows the user to specify an 8-bit vector number to be supplied by the BIM in a non–auto vector interrupt.

During an interrupt acknowledge cycle, the BIM receives an $\overline{\text{IACK}}$ signal, and it also inputs from pins A3–A1 the priority level of the interrupt request being accepted by the processor module. The BIM then checks the daisy-chain serial input ($\overline{\text{IACKIN}}$) signal. If the BIM receives a high $\overline{\text{IACKIN}}$ signal, it takes no action except passing the $\overline{\text{IACKIN}}$ signal to the daisy-chain serial output ($\overline{\text{IACK-OUT}}$) pin. A low $\overline{\text{IACKIN}}$ indicates that an acknowledge cycle is in progress. In this case, the BIM compares the received acknowledge level received from pins A3–A1 with the pending request stored in the device. If a match is found, the BIM blocks the interrupt acknowledge daisy-chain signal by driving its $\overline{\text{IACKOUT}}$ output high. Meanwhile, the BIM outputs the content of the interrupt vector register corresponding to the matched request on data pins D7–D0 and returns a $\overline{\text{DTACK}}$ signal to terminate the interrupt acknowledge cycle. If the BIM has no interrupt request pending at the same level as the received acknowledge, it simply passes the daisy-chain signal to the next device.

The BIM also provides the option for an interrupting slave device to supply its vector number. One typical device capable of sending an interrupt vector number is the MC68230 PI/T. To select this external interrupt acknowledge option for an $\overline{\text{INT}}$ pin, the X/IN (external/internal) bit in its associated control register must be set to 1. Once the device is selected for service, the BIM asserts the $\overline{\text{INTAE}}$ (interrupt acknowledge enable) output, indicating that the two interrupt acknowledge level outputs, INTAL0 and INTAL1, contain the interrupt request level being acknowledged. In response to this interrupt acknowledge, by decoding the INTAL0 and INTAL1 signals the interrupting source sends out its vector number and asserts the $\overline{\text{DTACK}}$ signal as anticipated by the master module.

Bus arbitration module

An effective way of increasing processing power of a system is to have more than one processor module in the system to form a multiprocessor configuration. By allowing concurrent operations, with each processor executing its instructions in parallel, a multiprocessor system can substantially improve its performance.

In a typical multiprocessor system, each processor module—that is, a master module—includes dedicated private memory and I/O devices. These private devices are accessible only to their dedicated processor through the local bus. Local memory is typically used to store the program currently being executed by that processor. The system also has system memory and I/O devices that can be accessed by all processors in the system using the global bus. These shared resources provide the necessary means for passing information between two processors. By having dedicated local devices on each master module, the traffic on the global bus can be kept under a reasonable level. Otherwise, the global bus would become so congested that each processor would have to spend considerable time waiting for the bus, thus significantly degrading each processor's performance. The block diagram in Fig. 7-28 illustrates the overall organization of a multiprocessor configuration, in which each processor has its own local bus.

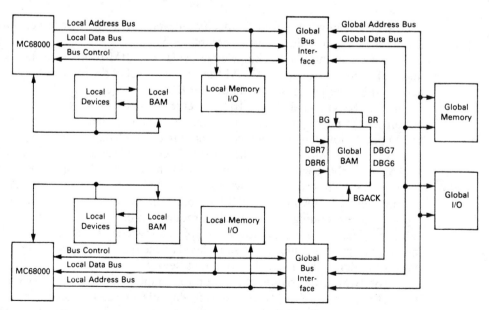

Figure 7-28 A configuration having more than one MC68000. (Courtesy of Motorola, Inc.)

A major consideration facing the implementation of a processor module in a multiprocessor system is the bus arbitration logic. Since more than one processor module has access to the global bus, it is necessary to include a bus arbitration logic in the system to make sure that only one processor module at a time has control of the bus. Simultaneous requests for accessing the global bus can be resolved on a priority basis.

Unlike a DMA controller, which generates a bus request and waits for the bus grant before accessing the bus, a processor does not have the capability of issuing bus requests. Therefore, in a multiprocessor configuration each processor module must include a global bus interface. This logic generates a bus request whenever the associated processor attempts to access the global bus. If the bus is not granted, the processor will enter the wait state until the bus becomes available. The central global bus arbitration logic for the entire system resolves simultaneous bus requests, so that at most one processor module receives the bus grant signal in a bus cycle.

A block diagram illustrating the global bus interface is given in Fig. 7-29. During each bus cycle, the decoder checks the address output by the MC68000 to determine whether the address is a local access or a global access. Typically, the addressing space is partitioned into local and global addresses according to the most significant several bits in the address. As a simple example, consider that the address range $000000–$BFFFFF represents local devices and $C00000–$FFFFFF are shared global addresses. In this case, the decoder needs to check only address bits A23 and A22.

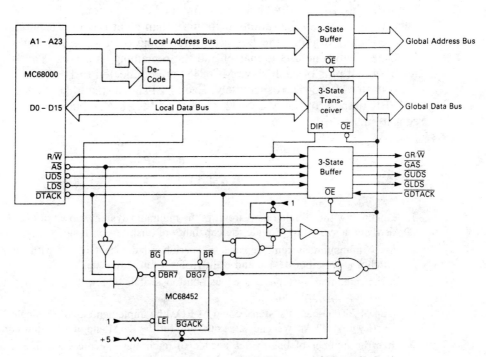

Figure 7-29 Global bus interface. (Courtesy of Motorola, Inc.)

If the address received by the decoder falls into the address range of local devices, the processor proceeds with the bus cycle as usual to access the selected local device. Meanwhile, the output of the decoder disables the tristate global bus interface devices. If a global access is attempted, a request is sent to the MC68452 BAM (bus arbitration module), which serves as the central bus arbiter of the shared global bus. As shown in the figure, signals $\overline{AS}$ and $\overline{DTACK}$ are combined with the output of decoder to generate a $\overline{DBR}$ (device bus request) signal. The $\overline{AS}$ is required to ensure that the address decode signal is valid. The $\overline{DTACK}$ is used to remove the bus request before $\overline{BGACK}$ (bus grant acknowledge) is released. In this configuration, since the MC68452 is the master bus arbiter, its $\overline{BR}$ (bus request) output is connected directly to its $\overline{BG}$ (bus grant) input. If the MC68452 is used to handle several DMA controllers in a single-processor configuration, its $\overline{BR}$, $\overline{BG}$, and $\overline{BGACK}$ pins should be connected to the corresponding pins of the MC68000.

In a global access, an active $\overline{DBG}$ (device bus grant) signal received from the MC68452 enables the tristate global bus interface, thus allowing the processor to begin the transfer. Upon receiving the data acknowledge signal from the global bus, the $\overline{DBG}$ is negated to disable the global bus interface, and the $\overline{BGACK}$ is asserted. Meanwhile, the processor terminates the bus cycle by removing its $\overline{AS}$ signal. This causes the $\overline{BGACK}$ to be removed at the end of every bus cycle, thus allowing the MC68452 to initiate the next arbitration cycle. Since the MC68452 provides eight pairs of $\overline{DBR}$ and $\overline{DBG}$ pins, it can handle up to eight processor modules.

In the preceding connection of the MC68452, its $\overline{LEI}$ (latch enable input) is disabled. This $\overline{LEI}$ pin, which when low latches the request inputs, is used to support cascaded configurations with more than eight bus master modules. In a cascaded configuration, the bus arbitration logic is composed of two or more MC68452s, with one as the master and the remaining as slaves. The $\overline{BR}$ output and $\overline{BG}$ input pins of each slave MC68452 are connected to $\overline{DBR}$ and $\overline{DBG}$ pins of the master MC68452, respectively. Each $\overline{LEI}$ signal should be the logical AND of all $\overline{BR}$ outputs of the MC68452, so that all MC68452s examine their pending request inputs at the same time.

EXERCISES

1. Explain how the simple reset circuit in the minimum system shown in Fig. 7-2 works. Also, add a switch to provide the capability of push-button reset.

2. In the minimum system, replace the peripheral device (ACIA) with eight toggle-switches as an input device and eight LEDs as an output device.

3. In the minimum system, add a push-button switch that will cause an auto vector interrupt if it is pressed.

4. In an MC68000-based system, could its ROM be implemented with a single NK × 16 memory device? Answer the same question for the RAM and justify your conclusion.

5. Give the number of bus cycles needed to fetch and execute each of the following instructions:

(a) ADD.B   VAR,D1
(b) ADD.B   D1,VAR
(c) ADD.L   VAR,D1
(d) ADD.L   D1,VAR
(e) MOVE.L   (A1)+,-(A2)
(f) MOVEM.L   D0-D7,-(A7)
(g) TAS   FLAG

6. Draw a timing diagram for a write bus cycle with two wait states being inserted.

7. Referring to Fig. 4-15, identify each bus cycle and its reference type shown in the timing waveforms.

8. How can an instruction fetch cycle be distinguished from an operand fetch cycle? Assume that PC relative addressing modes are not used.

9. Implement a wait-state generator for a memory module. Through jumper settings, it should be able to cause none, 1, or two wait states.

10. In addition to limiting the access to supervisor memory to the operating system, memory protection can be designed so that a user program (code) is protected from being overwritten by itself or by another user program. Show how this can be implemented. Assume that the memory is divided into three regions: $000000-$7FFFFF for the operating system, $800000-$BFFFFF for user program (code), and $C00000-$FFFFFF for user data. Also, describe how a user program can be initially loaded into memory.

11. Design a simple circuit for providing the single bus cycle stepping function. The circuit should have a two-position switch and a push-button switch. The two-position switch is for selecting the normal run mode or the single bus cycle mode. While in the single bus cycle mode, the user can trace one bus cycle each time by pushing and then releasing the push-button switch.

12. Describe how an interrupt management logic can be implemented with BIMs that can handle up to 15 request lines for non-auto vector interrupts.

13. Could the solution to Exercise 12 be applied to cases in which I/O devices use auto vector interrupts? Justify your answer.

14. Specify the active state for the $\overline{R/W}$, $\overline{LDS}$, and $\overline{UDS}$ pins during the bus cycle in executing the MOVE.W   VAR,D1 instruction.

15. Determine the minimum number of bus cycles that can occur between the time an auto vector interrupt request is recognized and the first instruction in the interrupt service routine is fetched.

16. Summarize the advantages and disadvantages of auto vector interrupts as opposed to non-auto vector interrupts.

17. Show how VME bus lines DS0*, DS1*, and WRITE* should be connected to the MC68000.

8

Input/Output Interface and Programming

An I/O interface or peripheral controller serves as a buffer between the system bus and the peripheral. This is necessary because the protocol used on the system bus is quite different from that adopted by a particular peripheral. The interface is designed to accept and send signals that are compatible with the bus control logic and timing. By using an I/O interface, a peripheral such as a CRT terminal or printer can be designed independently from the bus structure on which it is to be used. To connect the same peripheral to two different bus structures, only the interface must be redesigned.

8-1 Overview of a Peripheral Interface

Figure 8-1 illustrates the general organization of an I/O interface. An interface has several programmable I/O registers that can be directly accessed by the user to control its operation. The data bus buffer provides the interface between the data bus and those I/O registers. Output data to the peripheral, input data from the peripheral, control command, and status information are transferred through the data bus buffer upon execution of input or output instructions by the processor.

    The address decoder accepts the address from the processor to determine whether or not one of the interface registers is referenced. If so, it enables the read/write control logic to access the I/O register being referenced. The read/write control logic manages data transfers between the processor and the I/O registers. It includes the necessary logic to: (1) determine whether an input or output operation is being conducted and direct the data bus buffer to accept output data or control command word from the bus or place input data or status information

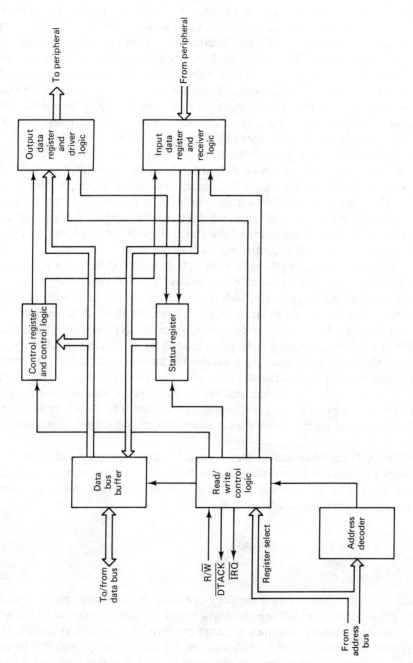

Figure 8-1 Block diagram of an I/O interface.

on the bus; (2) send an acknowledge signal when data have been accepted from or placed on the data bus, thus informing the processor that a transfer has been completed; and (3) send interrupt requests and, if interrupts are non-auto vector type, receive interrupt acknowledgments and send an interrupt vector number.

The data registers in the I/O interface serve as temporary storage for the data being transferred. Two data registers, one for input and the other for output, may be needed if the peripheral is capable of both input and output. Although each can be assigned to a different I/O address (i.e., I/O port), a single I/O address can be shared by both registers because one is read-only, whereas the other is write-only. The control register, which is write-only, can be programmed to specify the operating mode and to enable various functions of the interface. Its associated control logic regulates the flow of data between the peripheral and the system bus, inputs data from or outputs data to the associated peripheral, and converts the data from parallel to the format acceptable to the peripheral, or vice versa. The status register, which is read-only, stores the current status of the device (e.g., input data ready, output data register empty, or errors detected). Sometimes the control register and the status register share the same I/O address and are referred to as the control/status register.

During an input operation, a data byte is received from the peripheral and stored in the input data register by the control logic. A data-ready status is then reported in the status register, which can be examined by the processor. This data byte may then be moved to the processor from the input data register. Also, if the interrupt enable bit in the control register is set, the ready data cause an interrupt request. This allows the processor to input data in the interrupt service routine. Output is performed by a similar but reversed sequence. The processor waits until the output data register is empty. This can be detected either by checking the status register or by recognizing an interrupt. A data byte is then sent and stored in the output data register from the processor. This data byte is transmitted to the peripheral by the control logic whenever the peripheral is ready to accept it.

In an MC68000-based system, an I/O register is accessed as if it were a memory location, an addressing scheme known as *memory-mapped I/O*. For example, testing bit 0 of the status register at location $F0A0 can be accomplished by the instruction sequence

```
WAIT    BTST    #0,$F0A0
        BNE     WAIT
```

which treats the register as a memory operand. As to the processor, there is no distinction between an I/O register and a memory location. Any addressing modes for accessing memory operands are applicable to I/O registers as well. Of course, if an address is assigned to an I/O register, the same address may not be used for a memory location, thus limiting the total size of memory plus I/O registers to 16M bytes. In a typical system, a block of contiguous addresses in the 16M-byte space is normally designated for use by I/O registers.

LSI interface device

The implementation of the interface logic requires many logic gates, flip-flops, registers, and so on. However, several standard LSI interface devices to support the MC68000 have been made available. An interface design is, therefore, significantly simplified by using an LSI interface device as the major component and adding the necessary surrounding logic. The surrounding logic consists of two parts: the interface to the system bus and the interface to the peripheral. The first part is independent of the peripheral and will be examined in the remainder of this section.

The pins of an interface device can be divided into two general groups: one group to be connected to the peripheral and the other to the system bus. The peripheral-related pins vary from one interface device to the next. However, the group of bus-interfacing pins is similar to most devices that are designed to support a particular microprocessor. The bus-interfacing pins typically found in an MC68000-compatible interface device include these:

Dn–D0 (data) pins: These are bidirectional tristate pins to input data from or to output data to the microprocessor. If an interface device has 8 data pins, it is referred to as an 8-bit device; it transfers data to or from the processor 1 byte per bus cycle. Likewise, a 16-bit device has 16 data pins and can communicate with the processor one word at a time. The data pins are enabled only when the device is selected. If not enabled, the data pins will be in their high-impedance state.

$\overline{CS}$ *(chip select) pin:* This input pin, when activated, selects the device and enables the tristate data pins. In some cases, a device may have more than one chip select pin to simplify the address decoding logic required to select the device.

$R/\overline{W}$ *(read/write) pin:* This pin is used to control the direction of data flow through the data pins. A high on this pin indicates that the processor is reading data or status from the device, and therefore enables the data pins for output. On the other hand, a low on this pin enables the data pins for input so that the processor can write data or command to the device.

RSm/RS0 (register select) pins: These input pins are used during a read or write operation to select the internal register that is being accessed. The number of register select pins varies depending on how many programmable registers the device has.

$\overline{DTACK}$ *(data transfer acknowledge) pin:* This output pin is used by the device to inform the processor that it is ready to complete a data transfer. During a write operation, this signal indicates that the device has received the data. Likewise, during a read operation, the device activates this pin, indicating that data are ready for transfer after it places data on the data bus. The MC68000 also supports synchronous data transfers, in which each transfer is carried in a fixed time frame, thus eliminating the need for a $\overline{DTACK}$ handshaking signal. Since the MC6800 adopts a synchronous bus structure, some 8-bit device originally designed for the M6800 family, such as the MC6850, do not have a $\overline{DTACK}$ pin, but they are also compatible with the MC68000.

$\overline{IRQ}$ *(interrupt request) pin:* This output pin is used to issue an interrupt request signal when the device is ready to input data from the processor or when the device has data to be sent to the processor. This pin is to be connected to an interrupt priority management logic.

Some devices may also have a reset pin to reset the device to an initial state.

Connections of an interface device

Figure 8-2 illustrates the major logic of an interface using an LSI device. A typical interface device includes tristate data pins so that they can be connected directly to the data bus. This configuration is applicable for small, single-board systems. For multiboard systems, external transceivers are typically inserted as a data bus buffer to reduce the bus loading. The data transceivers are enabled when the chip select signal becomes active. If they are enabled, they act as drivers during a read operation and receivers during a write operation. Since the data bus of the MC68000 is 16 bits wide, an 8-bit device can be connected either to the lower byte of its data bus or to the upper byte. However, as mentioned before, if an 8-bit device is connected to D15–D8, it cannot support non-auto vector interrupts unless a BIM is used for sending vector numbers.

The address bus interface requires address decoding logic. Because there are many I/O interface modules connected to the system bus and each data, status, or control register on an interface module has a different address, a decoder is required to determine which device is addressed by the current instruction. As shown in Fig. 8-2, the upper part of the address, bits A23–A(m + 2), is applied to an address decoder that determines if the interface device is referenced. The low-order address lines are directly routed to the address pins of the device for selecting an internal register during a read or write operation.

Although an address has 24 bits, the least-significant bit A0 is an internal address bit. Externally, A0 is replaced by signals $\overline{LDS}$ (lower data strobe) and $\overline{UDS}$ (upper data strobe). During a memory or I/O reference, the processor sends out address bits A23–A1 plus $\overline{LDS}$ and/or $\overline{UDS}$. To indicate that a valid address is being sent, the processor also activates the $\overline{AS}$ (address strobe) signal at the same time. When $\overline{UDS}$ is low, it means that an upper byte data transfer is intended, implying A0 = 0. When $\overline{LDS}$ is low, it means that a lower byte data transfer is intended, implying A0 = 1. Therefore, the MC68000 transfers even-addressed bytes over the upper half of the data bus and odd-addressed bytes over the lower half of the data bus. When both $\overline{UDS}$ and $\overline{LDS}$ are low, a 16-bit word is transferred to or from the word address specified by A23–A1.

When an 8-bit device is connected to the upper half of the data bus, as in Fig. 8-2, the chip select logic must be designed so that the device will not be enabled unless $\overline{UDS}$ becomes active. This implementation assigns to the internal registers of the device a block of consecutive even addresses. The lowest address of the assigned block must be divisible by 2^{n+1}, where n is the number of register

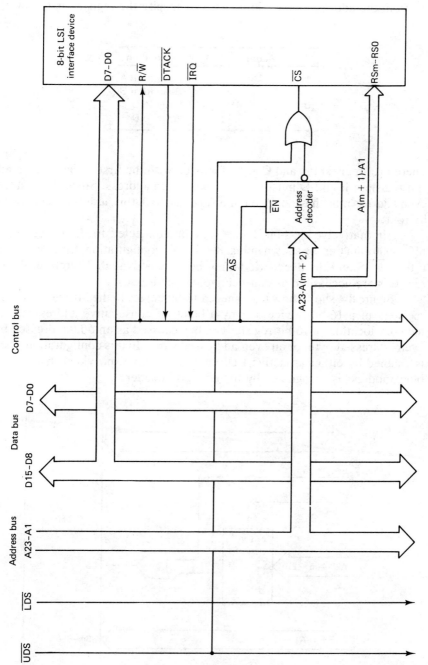

Figure 8-2 Typical 8-bit I/O-interface using an LSI interface device.

select pins. For example, if there are two registers A and B that can be read from and two registers C and D that can be written into, then the R/$\overline{\text{W}}$ signal and bit A1 from the address bus could be used to specify the register as follows:

R/$\overline{\text{W}}$	Address bit A1	Operation
1	0	Read from A
1	1	Read from B
0	0	Write to C
0	1	Write to D

Therefore, registers A and C are referenced with the first assigned even address, and registers B and D must have the next even address. Since the first assigned even address must have both A1 and A0 equal to 0, this address is evenly divisible by four.

Alternatively, an 8-bit device may be connected to the lower byte of the MC68000 data bus, as shown in Fig. 8-3. In this configuration, the device is enabled if both $\overline{\text{LDS}}$ and the decoder's output become activated. Therefore, the internal registers are accessible as consecutive odd addresses.

Figure 8-4 shows how to connect a 16-bit device to the MC68000. The internal registers of a 16-bit device occupy a block of consecutive addresses. Just as a memory location, a 16-bit register can be accessed as an odd-addressed byte, an even-addressed byte, or an even-addressed word. In this configuration, the device is enabled by either an active $\overline{\text{LDS}}$ or $\overline{\text{UDS}}$ or both, provided that the assigned block address is recognized by the address decoder.

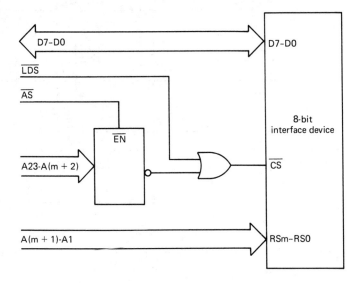

Figure 8-3   Connecting an 8-bit device to the lower byte of the data bus.

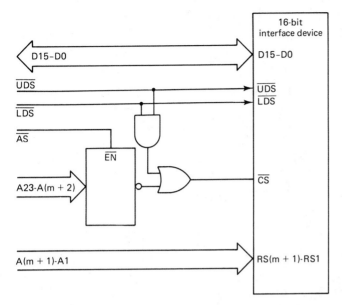

Figure 8-4 Connection of a 16-bit device.

Address decoder

Although address decoding logic can easily be implemented with AND gates, normally binary decoders are used due to two major advantages. First, by using jumpers or switches to select a chip enable signal from the outputs of decoders, the address block assigned to an interface device can easily be modified. Second, when several interface devices reside on one PC board, they can share the same address decoding logic.

Figure 8-5 is an example showing how to design an address decoder. Due to the large size of the MC68000 address bus, the address decoding logic in this example is divided into two stages, each having a 3-to-8 binary decoder. The first binary decoder is enabled when the most significant 8 bits of the received address are 01100000. While being enabled, output $\overline{Y3}$ of this decoder is activated if the next lower 3 bits, A15, A14, and A13, are 011. Therefore, the second binary decoder, which decodes bits A6, A5, and A4 is enabled if the received address falls in the range from $606380 to $6063FF. Each of its eight outputs can then be used as a chip enable signal for one interface device with up to eight programmable registers. The example assumes that devices 0 through 7 require no more than eight locations each and are connected to the lower half of the data bus. For device 0, the RS2–RS0 pins are connected to address lines A3–A1 and the device is accessible as a block of eight consecutive odd addresses beginning at $606381. If a device has fewer than eight registers, a register may be accessed at more than one address resulting from redundant mapping. For instance, the lowest-addressed register of device 2, which has only two programmable registers, can be accessed as location $6063A1, $6063A5, $6063A9, or $6063AD.

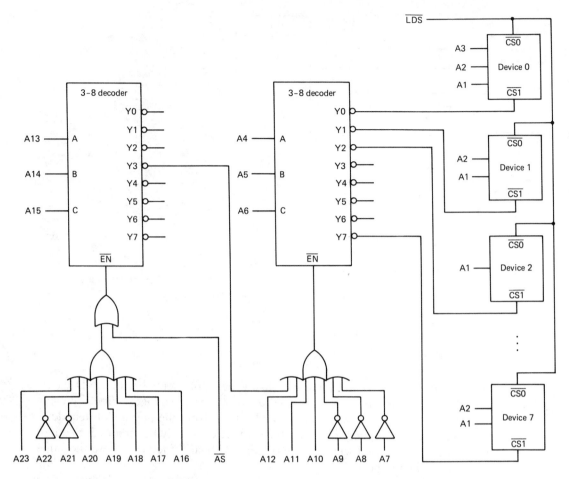

Figure 8-5 Address decoding logic for I/O devices.

8-2 Asynchronous Serial Interface

Asynchronous serial data transmission is typically used for transmitting data between a computer and low-speed peripherals such as CRT terminals. In the asynchronous serial mode, data are transferred one character at a time, with each character being transmitted serially—that is, as a sequence of 0s and 1s. Since the idle gap between two characters may vary, each character is framed with start and stop bits to indicate the beginning and end of a character. The data transfer rate is specified as a baud rate, which is defined as the number of unit intervals per second. In asynchronous serial data transmission, the baud rate is the same as number of bits per second. For a typical terminal, the data rate ranges from 110 baud up to 9600 baud.

Asynchronous serial data format

In asynchronous serial data transmission, each character is transmitted with the following format:

1. *A start bit:* This bit precedes the first data bit indicating the beginning of a character. The start bit is a logical zero, commonly referred to as a *space*.
2. *Seven to eight data bits:* The number of data bits may be either seven or eight, depending on the settings of the interface. The least significant data bit is transmitted first and the most significant bit, last.
3. *An optional even or odd parity bit:* If used, a parity bit is added after the last (i.e., the most significant) data bit. For even parity, the parity bit is set such that the total number of 1s, including itself, is even. For odd parity, the total number of 1s in data and parity bits is odd.
4. *One or more stop bits:* Each character is terminated with one or more stop bits. A stop bit is a logical 1, commonly referred to as a *mark*.

An example of asynchronous data format is shown in Fig. 8-6. The example assumes that an ASCII 1, which is 0110001, is transmitted using the character format of 7 data bits and an odd parity.

Data transmitting and receiving

A serial interface is required in order for a computer to transmit and receive data in the asynchronous serial mode. The transmitter part of the interface has a transmitter data register and a parallel-in, serial-out shift register. Once the processor writes a character to the transmitter data register, the interface automatically sends out the received character using the asynchronous data format. It first sends out a start bit and then shifts out data bits one by one, beginning with the least significant bit. If a parity is chosen, the interface generates and adds a parity bit along with at least one stop bit to the end of the character. After the stop bit(s),

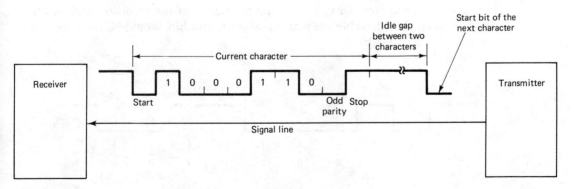

Figure 8-6 Data format of asynchronous serial transmission.

the output remains in the mark state until the interface receives the next character to be sent.

The receiver part of a serial interface has a receiver data register and a serial-in, parallel-out shift register. During a receiving operation, the 1 to 0 transition on the input signal line due to a start bit causes the receiver to sample the incoming signal. The receiver clock is running much faster than the baud rate, typically at 16 times the baud rate, so the sampling point is close to the center of each incoming bit. The receiver samples the incoming signal eight clock pulses after a 1 to 0 transition is detected. Once a valid start bit—that is, logical 0—is recognized, the signal line is sampled after every 16 clock pulses and is shifted into a shift register. The first sampled bit corresponds to the least significant data bit. This data-retrieving mechanism is illustrated in Fig. 8-7. A separate receiver data register is necessary because once a character has been received, the shift register must be made available for the next incoming character. If the character stored in the receiver data register has not been read by the processor before the next character is assembled, an *overrun error* occurs.

When a parity is included, the parity bit is sampled and is compared to the parity bit regenerated by the receiver according to the received data bits. If the two parity bits do not match, a *parity error* is detected. Using a parity bit, any single-bit error can be detected. For a typical LSI interface device, the received parity bit is not actually saved with the data bits into the receiver data register.

After the last data bit or the parity bit, if included, the stop bit is sampled but not stored. If a stop bit is not present—that is, the sampled value is a logical 0—a *framing error* is detected.

The major advantage of asynchronous serial transmission is that a clocking signal is not needed with the transmission. The transmitter and receiver ends use their own clocks, which need not be locked to identical frequency for successful data transmission. Figure 8-8(a) shows that when the receiver clock is running slightly faster than that of the transmitter, the sampling point will drift away from the center of each bit but the character will still be received correctly. Likewise, the receiver clock is permitted to be slower than the transmitter clock as long as it remains within a tolerance. Since each character begins with a start bit, this offset of the sampling point from the center of a data bit will not be accumulated into the next character. Of course, if the frequency of the receiver clock is off by more than the allowable amount, erroneous data bits would be received, as illustrated in Fig. 8-8(b).

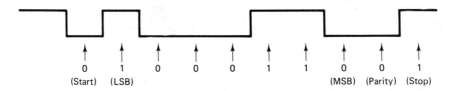

| 0 | 1 | 0 | 0 | 0 | 1 | 1 | 0 | 0 | 1 |
| (Start) | (LSB) | | | | | | (MSB) | (Parity) | (Stop) |

Figure 8-7 Mechanism of sampling the incoming signal.

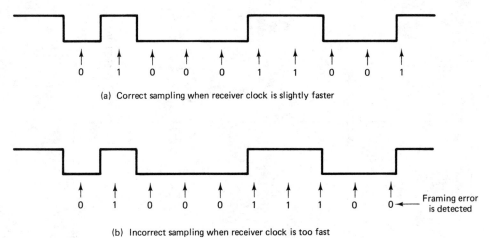

(a) Correct sampling when receiver clock is slightly faster

0   1   0   0   0   1   1   0   0   1

0   1   0   0   0   1   1   1   0   0 ← Framing error is detected

(b) Incorrect sampling when receiver clock is too fast

Figure 8-8 Data sampling when the receiver and transmitter clocks are not identical.

8-3 The MC6850 ACIA

Many peripheral devices are available using asynchronous serial data transfer. To simplify the design of interfacing a processor to a broad spectrum of peripherals, Motorola has made available the MC6850 ACIA (asynchronous communication interface adapter). Although the ACIA was designed as an interface device for the M6800 microprocessor family, it can be used to support the MC68000 as well.

Figure 8-9 gives a block diagram of the ACIA and shows its connection to the MC68000. With the eight data pins being connected to the lower byte of the data bus and address line A1 being connected to the RS (register select) pin, the ACIA is accessed as two consecutive odd addresses. The lower address represents the status and the control registers, and the higher address represents the receiver data and the transmitter data registers. When RS is 0 and the device is selected, either the status register is read (R/$\overline{\text{W}}$ = 1) or the control register is written (R/$\overline{\text{W}}$ = 0). On the other hand, with RS = 1 while the MC6850 is enabled, R/$\overline{\text{W}}$ = 1 will read from the receiver data register and R/$\overline{\text{W}}$ = 0 will write into the transmitter data register.

The ACIA has four chip enable and select pins: E, CS0, CS1, and $\overline{\text{CS2}}$. Having more than one enable and select pin reduces external address decoding and chip select logic. The ACIA is enabled for a read or write operation if and only if E = 1, CS0 = 1, CS1 = 1 and $\overline{\text{CS2}}$ = 0.

Since the ACIA was initially designed to support the M6800 microprocessor family, which uses a synchronous bus, data transfer between the processor and ACIA is synchronized (i.e., controlled) with the enable (E) signal. To be compatible with such M6800 devices, the MC68000 provides control signals for both asynchronous and synchronous bus cycles. In order to distinguish between the

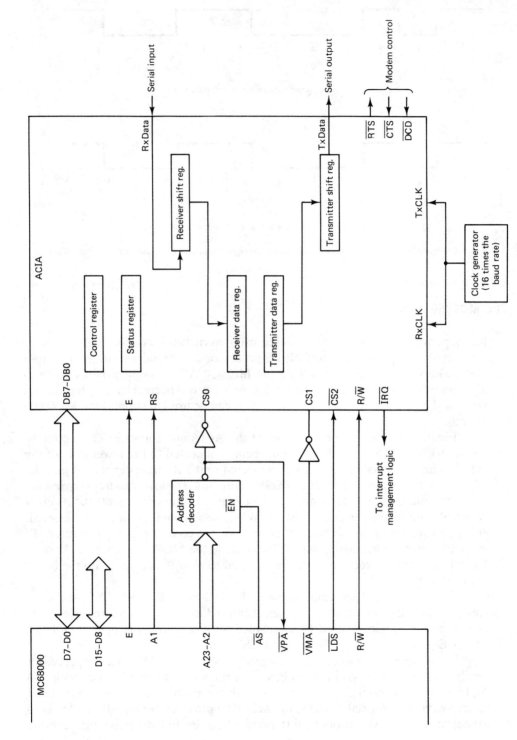

Figure 8-9 MC6850 ACIA.

two bus cycles, once an M6800 peripheral device is addressed, its address decoding logic should return the $\overline{VPA}$ (valid peripheral address) signal to the MC68000 indicating a synchronous bus cycle. If the $\overline{VPA}$ signal is received, the MC68000 will output the $\overline{VMA}$ (valid memory address) signal to select the device for a read or write operation. As shown in Fig. 8-9, the $\overline{VMA}$ and address decoder's signal are internally combined to select the ACIA. After activating $\overline{VMA}$, the MC68000 asserts the E (enable) signal, which enables the ACIA's data pins to move the data to or from the bus. The frequency of the E signal is only one-tenth of the processor clock rate in order to tolerate low-speed devices.

Control register

While the ACIA appears to the processor as two memory locations, internally there are four registers of 8 bits each. The control and transmitter data registers are write-only and the status and receiver data registers are read-only.

The control register determines the operating mode of the ACIA. By programming this register, the user can select the transmission data format and enable the transmitter and receiver interrupts. The bit assignments of the control register are given in Fig. 8-10.

Control bit 7 is used to enable or disable interrupts from the receiver. If this bit is 1, the $\overline{IRQ}$ (interrupt request) pin is asserted whenever the receiver data register is full. The transmitter interrupt enable is controlled by bits 6 and 5. These

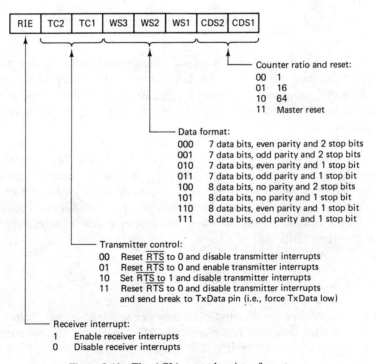

Figure 8-10 The ACIA control register format.

two bits are also used to set the output of the $\overline{\text{RTS}}$ (request to send) pin and to send break characters (continuous logical 0) to the TxData pin.

Bits 4 through 2 determine the number of data bits, either 7 or 8, the number of stop bits, either 1 or 2, and the parity, either even, odd, or none. Note that if a parity is specified, the parity bit will not be stored into data register as part of the received character. Therefore, when a 7 data bit format is chosen, bit 7 in the receiver data register will always be cleared regardless of the parity selection.

Control bits 1 and 0 select the ratio of the receiver clock (RxClk) and the transmitter clock (TxClk) rates to the data transfer rate. Once this divide ratio is chosen, which may be 1, 16, or 64, the transfer baud rate is determined as

$$\text{Incoming (or outgoing) data baud rate} = \frac{\text{frequency of RxClk (or TxClk)}}{\text{clock divide ratio}}$$

Suppose that bits 1 and 0 of the control register are set to 01 and both data receiving and data transmitting use the same baud rate. Then the following table shows the appropriate clock rate of RxClk and TxClk for each of the indicated data transfer rates.

Rate of RxClk and TxClk (in hertz)	Data rate (in baud)
4,800	300
9,600	600
19,200	1,200
38,400	2,400
76,800	4,800
153,600	9,600

A clock generator that can provide these clock rates is shown in Fig. 8-11. The implementation uses two 4-bit counters as a frequency divider to reduce the fundamental frequency, 1.23 megahertz, to the desirable rates. A set of jumpers is included to let the user select one of the clock outputs as the receiver/transmitter clock.

Control bits 1 and 0 are also used to provide a reset for the ACIA. A command with both bits set to 1 will reset the ACIA. In preparation for using the ACIA, a reset command must first be sent to the control register. Then a subsequent command will establish the operating mode for the receiver and transmitter. For example, suppose that the ACIA has addresses $010040 and $010042 and the rate of the receiver and transmitter clocks is selected for 38.4 kilohertz. Then the instruction sequence

```
MOVE.B     #3,$10040
MOVE.B     #$15,$10040
```

will disable interrupts from both receiver and transmitter, select the transmission format of 8 data bits per character with 1 stop bit and no parity, and use 2400 baud as the data transfer rate.

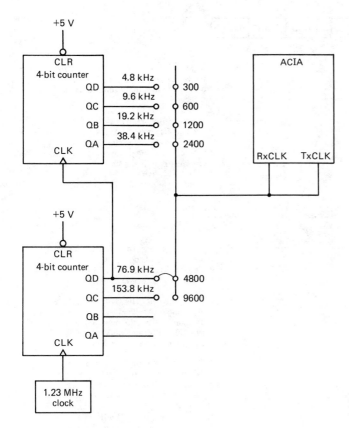

Figure 8-11 Clock generator for the RxClk and TxClk.

Status register

The ACIA indicates its state in a status register, which can be examined under program control. The format of the status register is shown in Fig. 8-12. In a reset, all bits except bit 3 will be cleared.

Status bit 7 indicates whether or not the ACIA is requesting an interrupt via its $\overline{IRQ}$ output pin. Bits 6, 5, and 4 indicate parity, overrun, and framing errors. An error will set the bit corresponding to the error type to 1. Bits 3 and 2 reflect the outputs on the $\overline{CTS}$ (clear to send) and $\overline{DCD}$ (data carrier detect) pins, respectively.

Bit 1 indicates whether the transmitter data register is empty (1) or not (0). Before sending a character to the ACIA, the processor must wait until this bit is set. After writing to the transmitter data register, the ACIA automatically clears this bit and transmits the received character through the TxData pin. Bit 0 indicates whether the receiver data register is full (1) or not (0). The processor can test this bit to determine if the ACIA has received the next character from its RxData pin. Reading the receiver data register causes this bit to be cleared automatically.

The following instruction sequence inputs N characters from the ACIA and

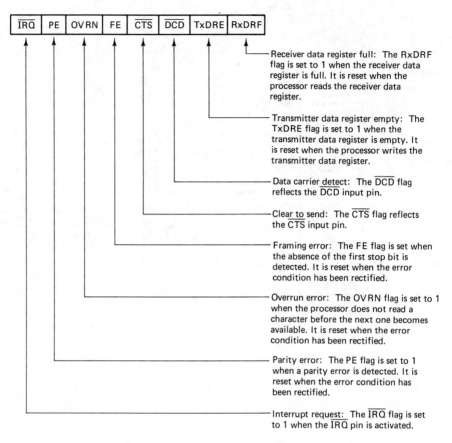

Figure 8-12   The ACIA status register format.

stores them into BUFFER by polling the receiver status bit. The example assumes that the ACIA occupies addresses $010040 and $010042.

```
        MOVE.W    NN,D7
        SUBQ.W    #1,D7
        MOVEA.L   #$10040,A1
        MOVEA.L   #BUFFER,A2
        MOVE.B    #$15,(A1)      ;DISABLE INTERRUPT
WTIN    MOVE.B    (A1),D1        ;READ ACIA STATUS
        ANDI.B    #1,D1          ;TEST RxDRF BIT
        BEQ       WTIN           ;WAIT IF RECEIVER DATA
                                 ;REGISTER IS NOT FULL
        MOVE.B    2(A1),(A2)+    ;READ THE CHARACTER
        DBF       D7,WTIN
```

To output the N characters stored in BUFFER to the terminal connected to the ACIA can be accomplished by

```
              MOVE.W      NN,D7
              SUBQ.W      #1,D7
              MOVEA.L     #BUFFER,A2
WTOUT         MOVE.B      (A1),D1         ;READ ACIA STATUS
              ANDI.B      #2,D1           ;TEST TxDRE BIT
              BEQ         WTOUT           ;WAIT IF TRANSMITTER DATA
                                          ;REGISTER IS NOT EMPTY
              MOVE.B      (A2)+,2(A1)     ;OUTPUT THE CHARACTER
              DBF         D7,WTOUT
```

It is important to point out that in testing a ready status bit, although the two instructions

```
    MOVE.B      (A1),D1
```

and

```
    ANDI.B      #1,D1
```

are equivalent to the bit test instruction

```
    BTST.B      #0,(A1)
```

they cannot be replaced by the logical instruction

```
    ANDI.B      #1,(A1)
```

Because the control register and the status register share the same address, the ANDI.B instruction would read the status, perform a logical AND operation, and then write the result to the control register, not to the status register. This could cause the current operating mode of the ACIA to change. Likewise, a logical or bit set/clear instruction should not be used in lieu of a move instruction for sending a command to a write-only control register.

RS-232C standard

All ACIA pins, including TxData and RxData, are TTL-compatible. Since TTL signals are suitable for traveling over only a short distance, a level converter is needed to convert the TTL type to a type that is more suitable for data transmission. Two major signal standards have been established for transmitting serial data over an extended distance, the 20-milliampere current loop and the EIA RS-232C standards.

The 20-milliampere standard is based on current signals instead of voltage levels. A current flow indicates logical 1 and an absence of current indicates 0. Historically, this standard has been used with teleprinter-type terminals.

Most computer terminals and peripherals using serial interface adopt the RS-232C standard. This standard requires that the space (logical 0) condition be transmitted as a voltage between +5 and +15 volts and the mark (logical 1) condition as a voltage between -5 and -15 volts. For the receiver, signals above $+3$ volts and below -3 volts are interpreted as 0 and 1, respectively.

Converting signals between TTL and RS-232C requires RS-232C line drivers and receivers. Figure 8-13 shows the connections between the ACIA and a terminal. The driver, MC1488, converts the TxData output from TTL to RS-232C and the receiver, MC1489A, converts the received serial signal from RS-232C to TTL for the RxData input.

By means of data communication equipment, data can be transferred between two far-apart systems over the regular voice communication channel, as shown in Fig. 8-14. A computer or terminal that is capable of initiating data transmission and/or receiving data is referred to as *data terminal equipment* (DTE). On the other hand, a modem that merely passes data to or from a communication channel such as phone lines is referred to as *data communication equipment* (DCE). In addition to the electrical characteristic of signal representation, the RS-232C standard also specifies the mechanical interface between the DTE and DCE.

Based on the RS-232C standard, a total of 25 pins or lines are available for connecting the DTE and DCE. The mechanical interface defines the pin position and the meaning of the signal for each pin. The most commonly used 25-pin connector for RS-232C interface is the DB-25 connector. Its pin layout is shown in Fig. 8-15. Pins 1 and 7 are for protective ground and signal ground, respectively. Pin 2 is defined as the transmitted data lead from DTE to DCE and pin 3, as the received data lead from DCE to DTE. Therefore, for a DTE-to-DCE configura-

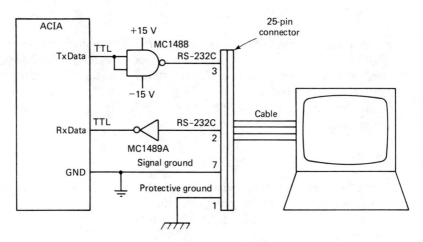

Figure 8-13 Connection between an ACIA and a terminal.

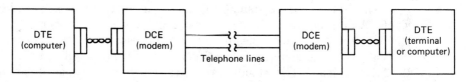

Figure 8-14 General data communication.

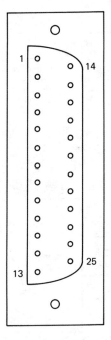

Figure 8-15 Pin layout of a female DB-25 pin connector.

tion, pin 2 of DTE is connected to pin 2 of DCE and pin 3 of DTE to pin 3 of DCE. A terminal or a serial port of a computer can be configured either as a DTE or as a DCE depending on the assignment of pins 2 and 3. When connecting a terminal to a computer with both configured as DTE or both as DCE, the cable must be constructed such that pins 2 and 3 at one end are interchanged. Figure 8-16 shows the interconnections of transmitted data, received data, signal ground, and protective ground for a DTE-to-DCE and a DTE-to-DTE configuration.

Modems

When a serial terminal is close to the computer, they are directly connected with a four-wire cable, and data are transmitted in digital form. However, in order for a computer to transfer data to or from a remote terminal or to access a system providing data base services, it is necessary to transfer data in analog form (tones) using the telephone network. This requires a modem to connect the computer to the telephone network. A modem, which is a shortened form of modulation and demodulation, converts digital data to be transmitted to voice tones and voice tones being received to digital data. For a low-speed asynchronous modem, this conversion is implemented by frequency modulation.

In order to support full-duplex transmission, in which both ends can transmit and receive data simultaneously, the modem at one end is in the originate mode and the other is in the answering mode as shown in Fig. 8-17. A modem uses a separate pair of tones for transmitting data, depending on whether it is in the originate or answering mode. When configured in the originate mode, a modem transmits a logical 1 as a tone of 1270 hertz and a logical 0 as a tone of 1070 hertz and interprets a received signal of 2225 hertz as 1 and 2025 hertz as 0. In the

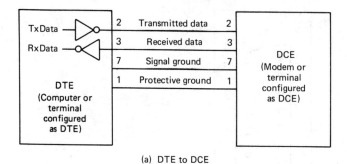

(a) DTE to DCE

(b) DTE to DTE

Figure 8-16 Connection of pins 1, 2, 3, and 7.

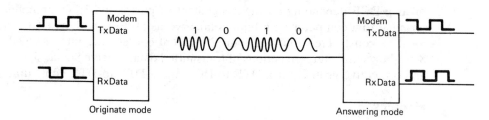

Figure 8-17 Data transmission technique used in low-speed asynchronous modem.

answering mode, a modem converts 1 and 0 to tones of 2225 hertz and 2025 hertz, respectively, and recognizes tones of 1270 hertz as 1 and 1070 hertz as 0.

A typical modem is capable of accepting commands such as answering incoming calls, dialing a specified phone number, and changing operating modes. A command is sent to the modem as a string of characters beginning with special control characters. Therefore, a modem can distinguish a command from regular outgoing data that it received from the transmitted data pin. A modem may also report various status to its DTE through the received data pin.

A typical modem provides 9 pins for connection to an RS-232C serial port. Besides the protective ground, signal ground, transmitted data, and received data pins, the other five pins are for modem control. The following table shows the pin number, EIA (Electronics Industry Association) designation, and signal description of each pin.

Signal name	Pin number	EIA designation	Description
Protective ground (GND)	1	AA	Used to connect the chassis ground of the modem to that of the DTE.
Signal ground (SG)	7	AB	Provides a common ground reference for all other signals between the modem and DTE.
Transmitted data (TD)	2	BA	Used to transfer serial data from the DTE to the modem.
Received data (RD)	3	BB	Used to transfer serial data from the modem to the DTE.
Clear to send (CTS)	5	CB	Indicates that the modem has established a connection with a remote modem and is ready to transmit data.
Data set ready (DSR)	6	CC	Indicates that the modem is connected to the telephone line and is ready for operation.
Data terminal ready (DTR)	20	CD	A signal from the DTE indicating to the modem that the DTE is ready to transmit or receive data.
Data carrier detected (DCD)	8	CF	Used to indicate that the modem has detected carrier signal from the telephone line.
Ring indicator (RI)	22	CE	Indicates that the modem is receiving a ringing signal from the telephone line.

Modem interface

Motorola has made available an LSI interface device, MC68HC51. Basically, this device, like the ACIA, provides an asynchronous serial interface for terminals and modems. However, it provides more functions than the MC6850 and has five modem control pins as opposed to three. Figure 8-18 shows how a modem can be connected to the MC68HC51.

For the processor at the originate end, the sequence of major events involved in establishing a connection to a remote modem, transferring data, and then disconnecting from the telephone network is as follows.

1. Write a control word to the MC68HC51 to turn on its $\overline{\text{DTR}}$ pin. An asserted $\overline{\text{DTR}}$ indicates to the local modem that the processor is ready for data transfer.
2. Check the $\overline{\text{DSR}}$ input by reading the status register of the MC68HC51. If $\overline{\text{DSR}}$ is 1, the modem is not in operating condition.
3. Send a modem command as a character string to the transmitter data register of the MC68HC51 to put the local modem in the originate mode. The modem receives this command from the TD line.
4. Send a modem command as a character string to the transmitter data register of the MC68HC51 to instruct the local modem to dial a phone number. The modem receives this command from the TD line.
5. Wait until the $\overline{\text{CTS}}$ input is on by reading the status of the MC68HC51. If the remote modem answers the call, the originate modem is able to detect

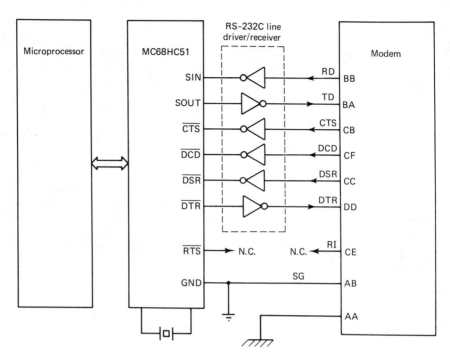

Figure 8-18 Interface of a modem using MC68HC51.

the carrier signal and then assert the $\overline{\text{DCD}}$ pin and maintain the $\overline{\text{CTS}}$ signal activated.

6. The connection is established and data transfer between two DTEs may begin by outputting data to the transmitter data register and inputting data from the receiver data register of the MC68HC51.

7. To terminate a call, the processor at either end can drop the $\overline{\text{DTR}}$ signal, which in turn causes its associated modem to hang up the phone. The modem at the other end will turn off its $\overline{\text{CTS}}$ signal, indicating to its associated processor that the connection is broken.

In the modem connection shown in Fig. 8-18, the RI pin from the modem is not connected because the MC68HC51 does not support this feature. A modem can be programmed to answer calls automatically whenever the phone rings. Even when this automatic answering feature is disabled, the DTE is still able to detect phone ring signals without using the RI signal. This is because a modem can send a ring-detect message to the DTE as data if the phone rings.

The request-to-send ($\overline{\text{RTS}}$) pin of the MC68H51 is not connected in Fig. 8-18. Together with $\overline{\text{DCD}}$, $\overline{\text{RTS}}$ can be used to support half-duplex transmission, in which a modem is allowed either to transmit or receive data but not both simultaneously. An active $\overline{\text{RTS}}$ signal causes a modem to turn on its transmitter, thus generating carrier signals. In a half-duplex environment, before a DTE sends out data, it first asserts the $\overline{\text{RTS}}$ signal. The local modem then checks the $\overline{\text{DCD}}$

signal. If at that time the remote modem has already received its $\overline{\text{RTS}}$ signal and has turned on its transmitter, the local modem should detect the $\overline{\text{DCD}}$ signal and, therefore, not return a $\overline{\text{CTS}}$ signal to DTE. If the $\overline{\text{DCD}}$ is absent, then the local modem returns $\overline{\text{CTS}}$ to its associated DTE and sends out carrier signals. Once the $\overline{\text{CTS}}$ is received, the DTE is allowed to transmit data.

8-4 I/O Programming

Status-polling I/O

Like most other interface devices, the ACIA supports both status-polling and interrupt-driven I/O. In a polling I/O routine, also known as programmed I/O, the ACIA's status is repeatedly checked. A 1 in status bit 0 indicates that the receiver data register has received a character. This bit is cleared automatically when the processor inputs from the receiver data register. In the output case, status bit 1 is set whenever the ACIA is ready to accept the next output character from the processor. A write to the transmitter data register clears this bit.

An example of an I/O routine using status polling is given in Fig. 8-19. The example assumes that an ASCII CRT terminal is connected to the ACIA and that the address assigned to the control/status register is $010040. This program repeatedly inputs a key from the keyboard and echoes it on the screen. If the delete (or rubout) key ($7F) is depressed, the program will erase the previous character from the screen by outputting a sequence of three ASCII characters: $08 (back

```
ACIACS   EQU     $010040              ;ADDRESS OF ACIA CONTROL/STATUS REGISTER
         ORG     $2000
START    MOVEA.L #$5000,SP
         MOVEA.L #ACIACS,A1           ;A1 = ADDRESS OF CONTROL/STATUS REGISTER
         MOVE.B  #3,0(A1)             ;MASTER RESET
         MOVE.B  #$15,0(A1)           ;INITIALIZE ACIA
NEXT     BSR.S   INCHR
         CMP.B   #$7F,D0              ;IS IT A DELETE?
         BEQ.S   DELETE
         CMP.B   #$0D,D0              ;IS IT A CARRIAGE RETURN?
         BEQ.S   CR
         BSR.S   OUTCHR
         BRA     NEXT
DELETE   MOVE.B  #8,D0
         BSR.S   OUTCHR               ;OUTPUT A BACK SPACE
         MOVE.B  #$20,D0
         BSR.S   OUTCHR               ;OUTPUT A SPACE
         MOVE.B  #8,D0
         BSR.S   OUTCHR               ;OUTPUT A BACK SPACE
         BRA     NEXT
CR       BSR.S   OUTCHR               ;OUTPUT A CARRIAGE RETURN
         MOVE.B  #$0A,D0
         BSR.S   OUTCHR               ;OUTPUT A LINE FEED
         BRA     NEXT
INCHR    BTST    #0,0(A1)             ;TEST BIT 0 OF ACIA STATUS REGISTER
         BEQ     INCHR                ;WAIT IF 0
         MOVE.B  2(A1),D0             ;INPUT NEXT CHARACTER
         RTS
OUTCHR   BTST    #1,0(A1)             ;TEST BIT 1 OF ACIA STATUS REGISTER
         BEQ     OUTCHR               ;WAIT IF 0
         MOVE.B  D0,2(A1)             ;OUTPUT NEXT CHARACTER
         RTS
         END     START
```

Figure 8-19 Example of input/output by polling.

space), $20 (blank space) and $08 (back space). If the return key ($0D) is depressed, the program will output a line feed ($0A) in addition to a carriage return ($0D), thus moving the cursor to the left margin of the next line.

Interrupt-driven I/O

Using interrupts eliminates the need for the processor repeatedly to check the ACIA's status. When the receiver has a character to be input by the processor or the transmitter is ready to accept a character from the processor, the ACIA generates an interrupt request if the interrupt facility is enabled. Receiver interrupts can be enabled by setting bit 7 of the control register, and transmitter interrupts can be enabled by setting bits 6 and 5 to 01. However, one interrupt request pin is shared by both the receiver and the transmitter. After an interrupt from the ACIA is received, the processor waits until the current instruction is completed and then initiates an interrupt exception sequence if the priority associated with the received interrupt request is higher than the mask level stored in the processor. This interrupt exception sequence causes the processor to execute a service routine, which reads a character from the receiver data register or writes a character to the transmitter data register.

A sample interrupt-driven I/O program is given in Fig. 8-20. This example inputs a string of characters from the ACIA until a CR or the 80th character is received, whichever occurs first, and then outputs the character string to the ACIA. It is assumed that this assigned interrupt vector is 29 decimal and that the program is executed in the supervisor mode.

In the example, the main routine performs the following major operations:

1. Storing the address of the input service routine, SERIN, into the interrupt vector location 29×4 and initializing the buffer pointer.
2. Enabling the receiver and disabling the transmitter for interrupts and lowering the processor mask level to 0 so that interrupts from the receiver will be processed.
3. Waiting for input to be completed.
4. Replacing the content of the vector address with the address of the output service routine, SEROUT, and initializing the buffer pointer.
5. Disabling the receiver and enabling the transmitter for interrupts.
6. Waiting for output to be completed.

There are two interrupt service routines, SERIN for input and SEROUT for output. The input service routine inputs a character from the receiver data register, stores it into a memory buffer, and updates the buffer pointer and counter. This routine also checks whether the current input character is the last one or not. If it is, the ACIA is disabled from further interrupts and a software flag is set to 1, indicating to the main program that the entire character string has been input. Likewise, the output service routine outputs a character from the memory buffer, updates the buffer pointer, and checks for the end of the character string. After the last character in the string has been output, the output service routine disables

```
INTACI     EQU       29                        ;INTERRUPT VECTOR ASSIGNED TO ACIA
ACIACS     EQU       $010040                   ;ADDRESS OF ACIA CONTROL/STATUS REGISTER
           ORG       $2000
BFPTR      DS.D      1
BUFFER     DS.B      82
COUNT      DC.B      0
FLAG       DC.B      0
START      MOVEA.L   #$5000,SP
           MOVEA.L   #ACIACS,A1                ;A1 = ADDRESS OF CONTROL/STATUS REGISTER
           MOVE.B    #3,0(A1)                  ;RESET ACIA
           MOVE.B    #$95,0(A1)                ;ENABLE RECEIVER INTERRUPTS AND
*                                              ;DISABLE TRANSMITTER INTERRUPTS
           MOVE.L    #BUFFER,BFPTR             ;SET UP BUFFER POINTER
           MOVE.L    SERIN,INTACI*4            ;INITIALIZE ACIA INTERRUPT VECTOR
*                                              ;FOR INPUT SERVICE ROUTINE
           MOVE.B    #0,COUNT                  ;CLEAR COUNT
           MOVE.B    #0,FLAG                   ;CLEAR FLAG
           MOVEA.L   #$5000,SP                 ;INITIALIZE SP
           ANDI      #$F8FF,SR                 ;SET INTERRUPT MASK LEVEL TO 0
WAITIN     TST.B     FLAG                      ;IS INPUT COMPLETED?
           BEQ       WAITIN
           MOVE.L    #BUFFER,BFPTR             ;SET UP BUFFER POINTER
           MOVE.L    SEROUT,INTACI*4           ;INITIALIZE ACIA INTERRUPT VECTOR
*                                              ;FOR OUTPUT SERVICE ROUTINE
           MOVE.B    #0,FLAG
           MOVE.B    #$35,0(A1)                ;ENABLE TRANSMITTER INTERRUPTS
WAITOT     TST.B     FLAG                      ;IS OUTPUT COMPLETED?
           BEQ       WAITOT
           STOP      #$2000                    ;END OF MAIN ROUTINE
*
*   INTERRUPT SERVICE ROUTINE FOR ACIA RECEIVER
*
SERIN      MOVE.L    A2,-(SP)
           MOVEA.L   BFPTR,A2
           MOVE.B    2(A1),(A2)+               ;INPUT THE RECEIVED CHARACTER
           ADDQ.B    #1,COUNT
           CMPI.B    #80,COUNT
           BLT.S     CHKCR                     ;IS IT THE 80TH CHARACTER?
           MOVE.B    #1,FLAG                   ;IF TRUE, INDICATE END OF INPUT
           MOVE.B    #$15,0(A1)                ;DISABLE ACIA FOR FURTHER INTERRUPTS
           MOVE.B    #$0D,(A2)+                ;INSERT CARRIAGE RETURN
           MOVE.B    #$0A,(A2)+                ;INSERT LINE FEED
           ADDQ.B    #2,COUNT
           BRA.S     INRTN
CHKCR      CMPI.B    #$0D,-2(A2)
           BNE.S     INRTN
           MOVE.B    #1,FLAG                   ;INDICATE END OF INPUT
           MOVE.B    #$15,0(A1)                ;DISABLE ACIA FOR FURTHER INTERRUPTS
           MOVE.B    #$0A,(A2)+                ;INSERT LINE FEED
           ADDQ.B    #1,COUNT
INRTN      MOVE.L    A2,BFPTR                  ;SAVE BUFFER POINTER
           MOVEA.L   (SP)+,A2
           RTE
*
*   SERVICE ROUTINE FOR ACIA TRANSMITTER
*
SEROUT     MOVE.L    A2,-(SP)
           MOVEA.L   BFPTR,A2
           MOVE.B    -(A2),2(A1)               ;OUTPUT A CHARACTER
           MOVE.L    A2,BFPTR                  ;SAVE BUFFER POINTER
           SUBQ.B    #1,COUNT
           TST.B     COUNT                     ;COUNT = 0?
           BNE.S     OUTRTN
           MOVE.B    #1,FLAG                   ;INDICATE END OF OUTPUT
           MOVE.B    #$15,0(A1)                ;DISABLE ACIA FOR FURTHER INTERRUPTS
OUTRTN     MOVEA.L   (SP)+,A2
           RTE
           END       START
```

Figure 8-20 Example of interrupt-driven I/O.

ACIA interrupts and sets a software flag to 1. Note that parameter passing between the main routine and an interrupt service routine is through common memory locations, i.e., BFPTR, COUNT and FLAG.

8-5 Parallel Interface and Timer (PI/T)

Peripherals such as A/D and D/A converters and parallel printers transmit several data bits simultaneously, with each bit being transmitted over one signal line. Since data are transferred in parallel, data rates higher than serial transmission are achieved. In a parallel data transfer, handshaking signals are normally used to ensure that the transfer operation is completed properly.

The MC68230 parallel interface and timer (PI/T) is provided to simplify the parallel interface design. The block diagram in Fig. 8-21 shows that this device contains three 8-bit I/O ports, A, B, and C plus a timer. To the microprocessor, the PI/T is an 8-bit device. When its eight data pins, D7–D0 are connected to the lower byte of the data bus, as shown in Fig. 8-22, the device occupies 32 consecutive odd addresses.

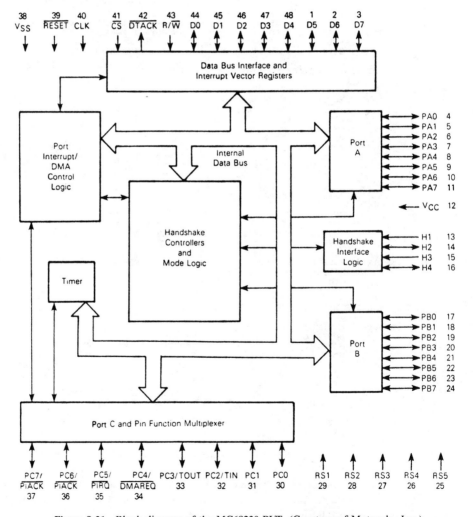

Figure 8-21 Block diagram of the MC68230 PI/T. (Courtesy of Motorola, Inc.)

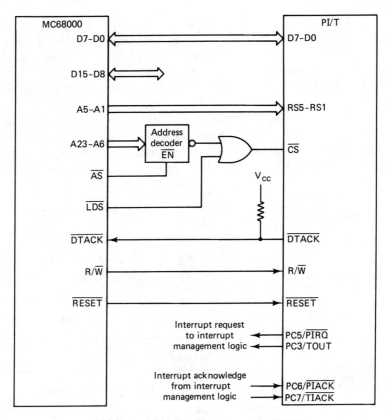

Figure 8-22 Interface of PI/T to the MC68000.

Parallel interface ports

The operating modes of the three parallel ports can be classified in several different ways, as follows:

Bidirectional versus unidirectional: Each I/O port can be independently configured for bidirectional or unidirectional data transfer. As a bidirectional port, the eight I/O pins are used for both input and output. When programmed as a unidirectional port, an I/O pin is used either for input or output depending on its respective direction bit, 0 for input and 1 for output.

8-bit versus 16-bit: Ports A and B can be combined to form a 16-bit parallel port, as opposed to two independent 8-bit ports. In a 16-bit port configuration, port A represents the upper byte and port B represents the lower byte.

Single-buffered versus double-buffered: Data to be output from the PI/T are always buffered—that is, the outgoing data byte is kept in a register until the next byte arrives. Otherwise, data would disappear immediately after the data byte was written to the output port by the processor. In the single-buffered mode, there is one set of latches in the data path. On the other hand, the double-buffered mode uses two sets of latches organized in a first-in, first-out fashion. While the peripheral is moving data from one set of latches, the processor can fill the other set, thus improving the data transfer rate. For input, a port can be double-buffered or unlatched.

Figure 8-23 is a summary of all modes of the parallel ports and control of handshaking pins H1–H4. In a double-buffered input or output operation, a pair of H (handshaking) pins is employed to carry handshaking functions that ensure proper data transfers between the PI/T and the peripheral. Handshaking pins H1

Mode 0 (Unidirectional 8-Bit Mode)
  Port A
    Submode 00 — Pin-Definable Double-Buffered Input or Single-Buffered Output
      H1 — Latches input data
      H2 — Status/interrupt generating input, general-purpose output, or operation with H1 in the interlocked or
          pulsed handshake protocols
    Submode 01 — Pin-Definable Double-Buffered Output or Non-Latched Input
      H1 — Indicates data received by peripheral
      H2 — Status/interrupt generating input, general-purpose output, or operation with H1 in the interlocked or
          pulsed handshake protocols
    Submode 1X — Pin-Definable Single-Buffered Output or Non-Latched Input
      H1 — Status/interrupt generating input
      H2 — Status/interrupt generating input or general-purpose output
  Port B
    H3 and H4 — Identical to port A, H1 and H2

Mode 1 (Unidirectional 16-Bit Mode)
  Port A — Most-Significant Data Byte or Non-Latched Input or Single-Buffered Output
    Submode XX — (not used)
      H1 — Status/interrupt generating input
      H2 — Status/interrupt generating input or general-purpose output
  Port B — Least-Significant Data Byte
    Submode X0 — Pin-Definable Double-Buffered Input or Single-Buffered Output
      H3 — Latches input data
      H4 — Status/interrupt generating input, general-purpose output, or operation with H3 in the interlocked or
          pulsed handshake protocols
    Submode X1 — Pin-Definable Double-Buffered Output or Non-Latched Input
      H3 — Indicates data received by peripheral
      H4 — Status interrupt generating input, general-purpose output, or operation with H3 in the interlocked or
          pulsed handshake protocols

Mode 2 (Bidirectional 8-Bit Mode)
  Port A — Bit I/O
    Submode XX — (not used)
  Port B — Double-Buffered Bidirectional Data
    Submode XX — (not used)
      H1 — Indicates output data received by the peripheral and controls output drivers
      H2 — Operation with H1 in the interlocked or pulsed output handshake protocols
      H3 — Latches input data
      H4 — Operation with H3 in the interlocked or pulsed input handshake protocols

Mode 3 (Bidirectional 16-Bit Mode)
  Port A — Double-Buffered Bidirectional Data (Most-Significant Data Byte)
    Submode XX — (not used)
  Port B — Double-Buffered Bidirectional Data (Least-Significant Data Byte)
    Submode XX — (not used)
      H1 — Indicates output data received by peripheral and controls output drivers
      H2 — Operation with H1 in the interlocked or pulsed output handshake protocols
      H3 — Latches input data
      H4 — Operation with H3 in the interlocked or pulsed input handshake protocols

Figure 8-23 Summary of port mode control of PI/T. (Courtesy of Motorola, Inc.)

and H2 are associated with port A and pins H3 and H4 are with port B. The handshaking functions of H3 and H4 are identical to those of H1 and H2.

The interaction between the H1(H3) and H2(H4) signals in a double-buffered input operation is as follows.

1. The peripheral sends a data byte or word to the input port and then asserts the H1(H3) pin to indicate that data are ready.

2. The asserted H1(H3) signal causes the PI/T to latch the input data and to negate the H2(H4) signal, indicating that the input latch is full. When the H2(H4) signal becomes negated, the peripheral terminates the data transfer by removing the data from the data lines.

3. After the data byte or word being received by the input latch, the PI/T checks the second latch. If empty, the PI/T transfers the data from the input latch to the second latch and then asserts the H2(H4) output. An asserted H2(H4) indicates to the peripheral that the input latch is empty, and therefore the input port is ready to accept the next data byte or word.

4. After the peripheral receives an asserted H2(H4), it may start to send the next data byte/word to the PI/T.

5. If either of the two buffers is full, the processor can remove the received data from the PI/T by reading the port's data register. This is accomplished by polling the port's status register or through an interrupt. Data can also be transferred directly between the PI/T and memory via DMA cycles.

In a double-buffered output operation, handshaking signal H2(H4) indicates that the output latch is full—that is, the PI/T has placed a data byte or word on output data lines. Meanwhile, signal H1(H3) is used by the peripheral to acknowledge receipt of the data byte or word.

An example of using the PI/T as a parallel interface is illustrated in Fig. 8-24. In this example, simple input and output devices are used, which allow data to be input/output in the binary form. Port A is configured as a single-buffered output port and is connected to eight LEDs, which are used as an output device for displaying data bytes. Eight toggle switches are used as an input device for entering data bytes. To provide the required interface for these switches, Port B is configured as a double-buffered input port with the H3 pin connected to a load push-button switch. A more complex example of parallel interface design using the PI/T is given in Sec. 8-6.

The PI/T is programmed through its 23 registers. Figure 8-25 shows the layout of these registers and their formats. Each register has a unique address assigned. Therefore, unlike the ACIA, a control register or status register can be modified with a logical or bit manipulation instruction. Since the PI/T has 5 register select pins, it occupies 32 locations. The unused 9 locations correspond to dummy registers. A read operation from such a register returns a zero byte. In addition, a write operation to any read-only register results in a normal write bus cycle, but the data byte is ignored by the PI/T.

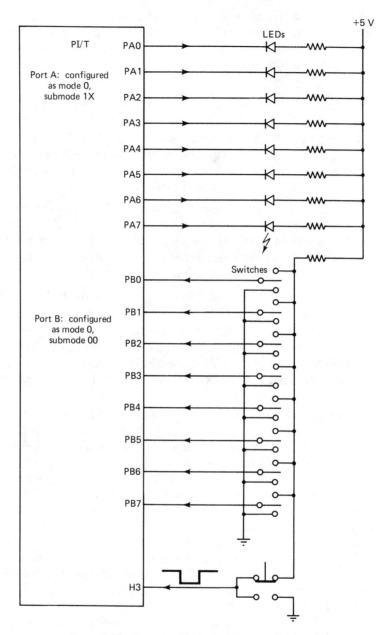

Figure 8-24 Example of using PI/T for parallel interface.

Timer

The timer includes a 24-bit counter and a 5-bit prescaler. When enabled, the counter is decremented by 1 as one of the three events occurs, depending on the operating mode: a rollover of the prescaler from 00 to 1F, an external clock pulse at the TIN pin, or a system clock pulse at the CLK pin. The 5-bit prescaler, designed to reduce a clock frequency by a factor of 32, can be decremented either by the system clock or by the TIN external clock.

Configured as a timer, port C provides three timer-related pins. Pin PC2 becomes the timer input (TIN) pin. This pin serves either as an external clock input pin or as an external run/halt control pin to enable or disable the timer. Pin PC3 becomes the timer output (TOUT) pin, which is used to send an interrupt request or a general-purpose signal when the timer reaches zero. Pin PC7 becomes an input pin to receive the interrupt acknowledge signal, which is required to support non–auto vector timer interrupts.

The operations of the timer are controlled by the timer control register (TCR). Bit 0 is to enable (1) or disable (0) the timer. Bits 2–1 select the timer clock as the CLK system clock with prescaler (00), the CLK system clock with prescaler while TIN = 0 (01), the TIN external clock with prescaler (10), or the TIN external clock without prescaler (11). Bit 3 is not used and is always read as zero. Bit 4 is for zero detection control. When it is cleared, the counter is reloaded from the counter preload register after the counter reaches zero. When it is set, the counter rolls over on a zero detection and then continues counting.

Bits 7–5 specify the possible configurations of the PC3/TOUT and PC7/$\overline{\text{TIACK}}$ pins and control the timer interrupt facility. The six valid settings are

00X: The PC3/TOUT and PC7/$\overline{\text{TIACK}}$ pins act as data pins PC3 and PC7.

01X: the PC3/TOUT pin becomes the TOUT pin, which outputs a square wave while the timer is running. The PC7/$\overline{\text{TIACK}}$ carries the PC7 function.

100: The timer interrupt is disabled. The PC3/TOUT pin becomes the TOUT pin with no output. The PC7/$\overline{\text{TIACK}}$ pin becomes the $\overline{\text{TIACK}}$ pin and its input is ignored.

101: The timer is enabled for non–auto vector interrupts. The PC3/TOUT pin carries the TOUT function for outputting timer interrupt requests. The PC7/$\overline{\text{TIACK}}$ pin carries the $\overline{\text{TIACK}}$ function for receiving interrupt acknowledge signals. Upon receiving a $\overline{\text{TIACK}}$ signal, the content of the timer interrupt vector register (TIVR) is returned as the vector number.

110: The timer interrupt is disabled. The PC3/TOUT pin becomes the TOUT pin with no output. The PC7/$\overline{\text{TIACK}}$ pin carries the PC7 function.

111: The timer is enabled for auto vector interrupts. The PC3/TOUT pin carries the TOUT function for outputting timer interrupt requests. The PC7/$\overline{\text{TIACK}}$ pin carries the PC7 function.

Timer examples

Three examples will be given to illustrate some typical applications of the timer.

The first example is to generate a square wave with a frequency of 2 kilohertz. It is assumed that a system clock of 4 megahertz from the CLK pin is used to run the counter. Since the prescaler is automatically included whenever the system clock CLK is selected, the square-wave output will change from 1 to 0,

5 4 3 2 1	7	6	5	4	3	2	1	0
0 0 0 0 0	Port Mode Control		H34 Enable	H12 Enable	H4 Sense	H3 Sense	H2 Sense	H1 Sense
0 0 0 0 1	a	SVCRQ Select		Interrupt pin function select		Port Interrupt Priority Control		
0 0 0 1 0	Bit 7	Bit 6	Bit 5	Bit 4	Bit 3	Bit 2	Bit 1	Bit 0
0 0 0 1 1	Bit 7	Bit 6	Bit 5	Bit 4	Bit 3	Bit 2	Bit 1	Bit 0
0 0 1 0 0	Bit 7	Bit 6	Bit 5	Bit 4	Bit 3	Bit 2	Bit 1	Bit 0
0 0 1 0 1	Interrupt Vector Number						a	a
0 0 1 1 0	Port A Submode		H2 Control			H2 Int Enable	H1 SVCRQ Enable	H1 Stat Ctrl
0 0 1 1 1	Port B Submode		H4 Control			H4 Int Enable	H3 SVCRQ Enable	H3 Stat Ctrl
0 1 0 0 0	Bit 7	Bit 6	Bit 5	Bit 4	Bit 3	Bit 2	Bit 1	Bit 0
0 1 0 0 1	Bit 7	Bit 6	Bit 5	Bit 4	Bit 3	Bit 2	Bit 1	Bit 0
0 1 0 1 0	Bit 7	Bit 6	Bit 5	Bit 4	Bit 3	Bit 2	Bit 1	Bit 0
0 1 0 1 1	Bit 7	Bit 6	Bit 5	Bit 4	Bit 3	Bit 2	Bit 1	Bit 0
0 1 1 0 0	Bit 7	Bit 6	Bit 5	Bit 4	Bit 3	Bit 2	Bit 1	Bit 0
0 1 1 0 1	H4 Level	H3 Level	H2 Level	H1 Level	H4S	H3S	H2S	H1S
0 1 1 1 0	a	a	a	a	a	a	a	a
0 1 1 1 1	a	a	a	a	a	a	a	a

a Unused, read as zero, data written are ignored.
b Value before $\overline{\text{RESET}}$.
c Current value on pins.
d Undetermined value.
e A write may perform a special status resetting operation.
f Mode-dependent.

Figure 8-25 Register layout of the PI/T. (Courtesy of Motorola, Inc.)

Register Value After RESET (Hex Value)	Accessible	Affected by read	
0 0	R/W	No	Port General Control Register (PGCR)
0 0	R/W	No	Port Service Request Register (PSRR)
0 0	R/W	No	Port A Data Direction Register (PADDR)
0 0	R/W	No	Port B Data Direction Register (PBDDR)
0 0	R/W	No	Port C Data Direction Register (PCDDR)
0 F	R/W	No	Port Interrupt Vector Register (PIVR)
0 0	R/W	No	Port A Control Register (PACR)
0 0	R/W	No	Port B Control Register (PBCR)
b	R/W	f	Port A Data Register (PADR)
b	R/W	f	Port B Data Register (PBDR)
c	R	No	Port A Alternate Register (PAAR)
c	R	No	Port B Alternate Register (PBAR)
d	R/W	No	Port C Data Register (PCDR)
d	R/W^e	No	Port Status Register (PSR)
0 0	R	No	(Null)
0 0	R	No	(Null)

Figure 8-25   (*continued*)

Register Select Bits

5 4 3 2 1	7	6	5	4	3	2	1	0
1 0 0 0 0	TOUT/$\overline{\text{TIACK}}$ Control			Z D Ctrl	a	Clock Control		Timer Enable
1 0 0 0 1	Bit 7	Bit 6	Bit 5	Bit 4	Bit 3	Bit 2	Bit 1	Bit 0
1 0 0 1 0	a	a	a	a	a	a	a	a
1 0 0 1 1	Bit 23	Bit 22	Bit 21	Bit 20	Bit 19	Bit 18	Bit 17	Bit 16
1 0 1 0 0	Bit 15	Bit 14	Bit 13	Bit 12	Bit 11	Bit 10	Bit 9	Bit 8
1 0 1 0 1	Bit 7	Bit 6	Bit 5	Bit 4	Bit 3	Bit 2	Bit 1	Bit 0
1 0 1 1 0	a	a	a	a	a	a	a	a
1 0 1 1 1	Bit 23	Bit 22	Bit 21	Bit 20	Bit 19	Bit 18	Bit 17	Bit 16
1 1 0 0 0	Bit 15	Bit 14	Bit 13	Bit 12	Bit 11	Bit 10	Bit 9	Bit 8
1 1 0 0 1	Bit 7	Bit 6	Bit 5	Bit 4	Bit 3	Bit 2	Bit 1	Bit 0
1 1 0 1 0	a	a	a	a	a	a	a	ZDS
1 1 0 1 1	a	a	a	a	a	a	a	a
1 1 1 0 0	a	a	a	a	a	a	a	a
1 1 1 0 1	a	a	a	a	a	a	a	a
1 1 1 1 0	a	a	a	a	a	a	a	a
1 1 1 1 1	a	a	a	a	a	a	a	a

Figure 8-25 (*continued*)

or vice versa, after $32 \times N$ clock pulses, where N is the programmed value in the preload register. Figure 8-26 shows the timer input and output configuration.

To generate a 2 kilohertz square wave, the initial count N to be programmed into the preload register can be calculated from

$$2 \times 1000 = \frac{4 \times 10^6}{2 \times 32 \times N}$$

Register Value After RESET (Hex Value)	Accessible	Affected by read	
0 0	R/W	No	Timer Control Register (TCR)
0 F	R/W	No	Timer Interrupt Vector Register (TIVR)
0 0	R	No	(Null)
b	R/W	No	Counter Preload Register High (CPRH)
b	R/W	No	Counter Preload Register Mid (CPRM)
b	R/W	No	Counter Preload Register Low (CPRL)
0 0	R	No	(Null)
b	R	No	Count Register High (CNTRH)
b	R	No	Count Register Mid (CNTRM)
b	R	No	Count Register Low ((CNTRL)
0 0	R/W[e]	No	Timer Status Register (TSR)
0 0	R	No	(Null)
0 0	R	No	(Null)
0 0	R	No	(Null)
0 0	R	No	(Null)
0 0	R	No	(Null)

Figure 8-25 (*continued*)

or

$$N = \frac{1000}{32} = 31$$

The timer control register should be initialized as follows:

Bits 7–5: 01X (Use the PC3/TOUT pin to output a square wave.)

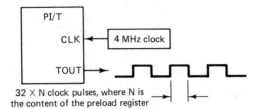

32 X N clock pulses, where N is
the content of the preload register

Figure 8-26 Example of using timer as a square-wave generator.

Bit 4: 0 (After decrementing to zero, the counter starts counting from the initial value.)

Bit 2–1: 00 (Use CLK input with prescaling to run the timer.)

Bit 0: 1 (Enable the timer.)

The following instruction sequence programs the timer preload and control registers, as specified before.

```
PITBAS  EQU      $10001
        MOVEA.L  #PITBAS,A1   ;LOAD BASE ADDRESS OF PI/T TO A1
        MOVE.L   #31,D1       ;SET UP 24-BIT INITIAL COUNT
        MOVEP.L  D1,$24(A1)   ;INITIALIZE 3-BYTE PRELOAD REGISTER
        MOVE.B   #$41,$20(A1) ;SET UP CONTROL REGISTER AND ENABLE TIMER
```

Note that a single

```
        MOVEP.L     D1,$24(A1)
```

instruction is used to load a 24-bit count to the preload register, which consists of three 8-bit registers starting at $26(A1). This instruction also writes the most significant byte of D1 into location $24(A1). However, that location corresponds to a dummy register whose content has no effects on the PI/T operation.

A second example of programming the timer is given in Fig. 8-27(a). The example measures the duration in milliseconds of an external event. The utilization of timer pins is shown in Fig. 8-27(b). At the beginning, the program initializes the preload register to the maximum possible value, $FFFFFF, and sends a command $13 to the timer control register. This command disables timer interrupt, uses TIN input for enabling the timer, and selects the CLK input with prescaler as the clock. Therefore, when the TIN input is 1, the counter is decremented by 1 after every 32 system clock pulses. The timer stops when the TIN input returns to 0.

To detect the end of the external event, the program compares two consecutive readings of the least significant byte of the timer counter. If the two readings are identical, the terminal count N is read from the counter. The event duration can then be estimated as

$$(FFFFFF - N) \times 32 \times 0.25 \text{ microseconds} = \frac{(FFFFFF - N)}{125} \text{ msec}$$

```
PITBAS    EQU      $10001
          ORG      $2000
ELAPS     DS.W     1
START     MOVEA.L  #PITBAS,A1
          MOVE.L   #$FFFFFF,D1
          MOVEP.L  D1,$24(A1)      ;LOAD MAXIMUM COUNT TO PRELOAD REGISTER
          MOVE.B   #$13,$20(A1)    ;ENABLE TIMER, DISABLE TIMER INTERRUPTS
*                                  ;AND USE TIN FOR ENABLING COUNTING
          MOVE.B   #$32(A1),D2     ;READ BITS 7 - 0 OF COUNTER REGISTER
DELAY1    NOP                      ;DELAY AT LEAST 8 MICRO SECONDS
          NOP                      ;BEFORE THE NEXT READ
          NOP
          NOP
          MOVE.B   #$32(A1),D3
          CMP.B    D2,D3           ;COMPARE TWO CONSECUTIVE READINGS
          BNE.S    NEXT1           ;IF NOT EQUAL, TIMER HAS BEGUN COUNTING
          MOVE.B   D3,D2           ;IF EQUAL, READ AGAIN
          BRA      DELAY1
NEXT1     MOVE.B   $32(A1),D2
DELAY2    NOP
          NOP
          NOP
          NOP
          MOVE.B   $32(A1),D3
          CMP.B    D2,D3           ;CHECK TWO CONSECUTIVE READINGS
          BEQ.S    NEXT2           ;TO DETECT END OF COUNTING
          MOVE.B   D3,D2
          BRA      DELAY2
NEXT2     MOVEP.L  $2C(A1),D3      ;READ FINAL COUNT AFTER TIMER STOPS
          SUB.L    #$FFFFFF,D2     ;D2 = D2 - FFFFFF
          NEG.L    D2
          DIVU.W   #125,D5         ;CONVERT ELAPSED TIME TO UNITS OF 0.1 SEC
          MOVE.W   D5,ELAPS
          STOP     #$2000
          END      START
```

(a) Program

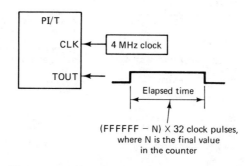

(b) Pin connection

Figure 8-27 Example of using timer for measuring incoming signal.

The third example is designed to illustrate the interrupt facility of the timer. In this example, the timer is programmed to generate an interrupt request periodically at the TOUT pin. It is assumed that the PI/T is wired for non–auto vector interrupt, i.e., the $\overline{\text{TIACK}}$ input pin is connected to the interrupt acknowledge line from the interrupt management logic. Therefore, the vector number INTVEC needs to be programmed into the timer interrupt vector register before the timer is enabled for counting.

For purposes of illustration, a simple timer service routine is included in which the processor clears the TOUT interrupt output and increments a counter, COUNT, by one. Note that in the timer service routine, it is necessary to explicitly remove the interrupt request signal generated by the timer. Otherwise, the service routine would be reentered immediately after returning to the main program. This is different than the ACIA which automatically clears the interrupt request signal whenever its receiver data register is read or transmitter data register is written. The timer interrupt request signal, which is the output of the TOUT pin, stays low once the timer counter is decremented to zero, causing the zero detect status (ZDS) bit to be set. To drive the TOUT to high for removing the interrupt request, the ZDS bit, which is bit 0 in the status register, must be reset to 0. This can be accomplished by writing a 1 to the ZDS bit.

Figure 8-28 shows the entire program and the timer pin configuration of this example. In a typical application, a periodically updated counter can serve as a watchdog timer. For example, in a time-sharing system, a watchdog timer is required to keep track of the amount of time used by each user and determine when to switch from one user to the next.

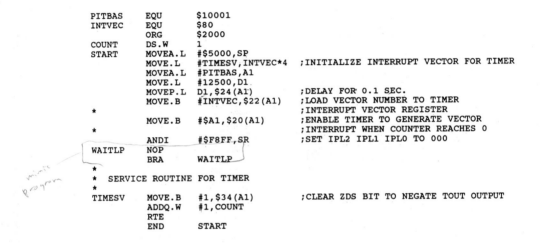

```
PITBAS      EQU       $10001
INTVEC      EQU       $80
            ORG       $2000
COUNT       DS.W      1
START       MOVEA.L   #$5000,SP
            MOVE.L    #TIMESV,INTVEC*4    ;INITIALIZE INTERRUPT VECTOR FOR TIMER
            MOVEA.L   #PITBAS,A1
            MOVE.L    #12500,D1
            MOVEP.L   D1,$24(A1)          ;DELAY FOR 0.1 SEC.
            MOVE.B    #INTVEC,$22(A1)     ;LOAD VECTOR NUMBER TO TIMER
*                                         ;INTERRUPT VECTOR REGISTER
            MOVE.B    #$A1,$20(A1)        ;ENABLE TIMER TO GENERATE VECTOR
*                                         ;INTERRUPT WHEN COUNTER REACHES 0
            ANDI      #$F8FF,SR           ;SET IPL2 IPL1 IPL0 TO 000
WAITLP      NOP
            BRA       WAITLP
*
*    SERVICE ROUTINE FOR TIMER
*
TIMESV      MOVE.B    #1,$34(A1)          ;CLEAR ZDS BIT TO NEGATE TOUT OUTPUT
            ADDQ.W    #1,COUNT
            RTE
            END       START
```

(a) Program

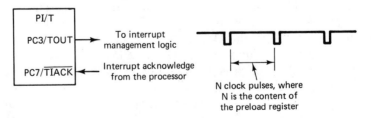

(b) Pin configuration

Figure 8-28 Example of using timer to generate periodical interrupts.

8-6 An Example of Printer Interface

As an example of interface design, this section shows how a PI/T may be used to implement an interface for a parallel printer. In the example, a printer using the standard Centronics control and data signals is assumed.

Hardware configuration

A Centronics-compatible printer has eight data input pins. Data transfer between the interface and printer is accomplished by three handshaking signals, Busy, Strobe, and Acknowledge. When the printer is busy and cannot receive data, the Busy signal is high. For example, if the printer's internal buffer is full, it will assert the Busy signal to stop the interface from sending data. The Strobe signal is a pulsed input signal from the interface, which is used by the printer to input the character from the data pins. After the character is received, the printer returns a negative-going pulse through its Acknowledge pin to indicate that the character has been received and it is ready to accept more data. Figure 8-29 illustrates this Strobe/Acknowledge handshaking operation, which occurs each time a character is transferred.

In addition to a Busy status, the printer also provides three error signals: Error, Paper Out, and Select. All remain active as long as the error conditions exist. The Error signal indicates an error or fault condition. The Paper Out signal indicates that there is no paper, whereas the Select signal goes low when the printer is not on line. There is also a control input, Reset, used to initialize the printer. Among other activities, a Reset pulse causes the printer to clean its internal buffer and returns the print head to the home position.

In this interface design, port A of the PI/T is configured in the 8-bit double-buffered output mode with pins H2 and H1 carrying the Strobe/Acknowledge handshaking function. To support the Busy, Paper Out, and Select signals, bits 2–0 of port B are configured as unlatched input pins. Meanwhile H3 and H4 are programmed as general input/output pins. They are for the Error input and the Reset output. Figure 8-30 shows the connections between the PI/T and the printer with all signals from the PI/T to the printer being buffered.

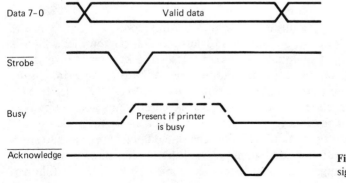

Figure 8-29 Timing of handshaking signals.

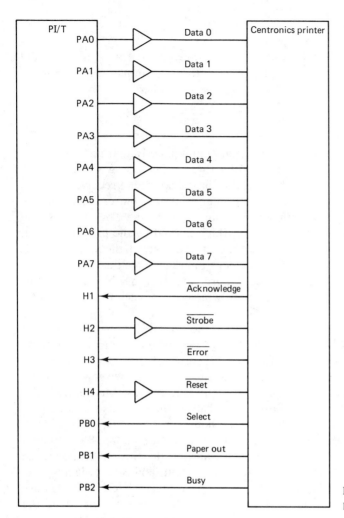

Figure 8-30 Connections between printer and PI/T.

Printer routine

An initialization routine is required to program various control registers in the PI/T to support this interface configuration. The initialization routine, which is given in Fig. 8-31, needs to be called only once after the system is turned on. Once the PI/T is initialized, the user may output data to the PI/T for print. In the initialization routine, the port A data direction register (PADDR) is set to $FF and the port B data direction register (PBDDR) is cleared. This configures port A for output and port B for input.

    Commands are sent to the parallel interface related control registers to specify the appropriate operating mode, submode, and the H pin function for port A and for port B. The settings of these registers and their meanings are as follows:

```
PITBAS    EQU      $10001H              ;BASE ADDRESS OF PI/T
PGCR      EQU      PITBAS               ;PORT GENERAL CONTROL REGISTER
PSRR      EQU      PITBAS+2             ;PORT SERVICE REQUEST REGISTER
PADDR     EQU      PITBAS+4             ;PORT A DATA DIRECTION REGISTER
PBDDR     EQU      PITBAS+6             ;PORT B DATA DIRECTION REGISTER
PCDDR     EQU      PITBAS+8             ;PORT C DATA DIRECTION REGISTER
PIVR      EQU      PITBAS+$A            ;PORT INTERRUPT VECTOR REGISTER
PACR      EQU      PITBAS+$C            ;PORT A CONTROL REGISTER
PBCR      EQU      PITBAS+$E            ;PORT B CONTROL REGISTER
PADR      EQU      PITBAS+$10           ;PORT A DATA REGISTER
PBDR      EQU      PITBAS+$12           ;PORT B DATA REGISTER
PCDR      EQU      PITBAS+$14           ;PORT C DATA REGISTER
PSR       EQU      PITBAS+$16           ;PORT STATUS REGISTER
          ORG      $2000
PTINIT    MOVEM.L  D2/D3,-(SP)
          MOVE.B   #0,PGCR              ;DISABLE H2 AND H4 OUTPUTS
          MOVE.B   #0,PSRR              ;DISABLE INTERRUPT AND DMA
          MOVE.B   #$FF,PADDR           ;ALL PORT A PINS ARE FOR OUTPUT
          MOVE.B   #$79,PACR            ;PORT A IS IN DOUBLE-BUFFERED OUTPUT MODE
          MOVE.B   #0,PBDDR             ;ALL PORT B PINS ARE FOR INPUT
          MOVE.B   #$A8,PBCR            ;PORT B IS IN NONLATCHED INPUT MODE
*                                       ;AND H4 OUTPUT (RESET) IS SET TO LOW
          MOVE.B   #$30,PGCR            ;CONFIGURE PORTS A AND B FOR MODE 0
*                                       ;AND ENABLE H2 AND H4 OUTPUTS
          MOVE.W   #100,D2
DELAY1    NOP                           ;DELAY FOR RESET PULSE WIDTH
          DBF      D2,DELAY1
          BCLR     #3,PBCR              ;SET H4 OUTPUT TO HIGH
          MOVE.W   #2,D2
DELAY2    MOVE.W   #$FFFF,D3
DELAY3    NOP                           ;WAIT FOR PRINTER TO COMPLETE
          DBF      D3,DELAY3            ;ITS RESET OPERATION
          DBF      D2,DELAY2
          MOVEM.L  (SP)+,D2/D3
          RTS
```

Figure 8-31 Initialization routine for the printer interface.

1. The port general control register (PGCR) is programmed to

   00 1 1 0000

   where
   00: Ports A and B are configured in mode 0 (unidirectional 8-bit mode.)
   1: Pins H3 and H4 are enabled.
   1: Pins H1 and H2 are enabled.
   0000: Signals on pins H4–H1 are programmed to be active low.
   In order to enable the PI/T operation properly, the PGCR is written after
   other control registers are programmed, as shown in Fig. 8-31.

2. The port A control register (PACR) is set to

   01 111 0 0 1

   where
   01: Port A is programmed in submode 01. This configures all port A pins in
   the double-buffered output mode when the PADDR is programmed to $FF.

111: The pulsed handshaking signal form is chosen for the H2 pin, and the H2S status bit is always cleared.
0: The H2 interrupt is disabled.
0: The H1 interrupt and DMA are disabled.
1: The H1S status bit is cleared when at least one data latch in port A is full.

3. The port B control register (PBCR) is set to

   10 101 0 0 0

where
10: Port B is in submode 10. This configures all port B pins in the unlatched input mode when the PBDDR is programmed to 0.
101: The output of H4 pin is asserted and the H4S status bit is always zero. Setting bit 3 to 1 will activate the H4 output.
0: The H4 interrupt is disabled.
0: The H3 interrupt is disabled.
0: The H3S status bit is set by an asserted edge of an H3 signal.

4. The port service request register (PSRR) is set to

   0 00 00 000

where
0: This is not used and is always read as 0.
00: The PC4/$\overline{\text{DMAREQ}}$ pin carries the PC4 function and DMA is not used.
00: The PC5/$\overline{\text{PIRQ}}$ and PC6/$\overline{\text{PIACK}}$ pins carry the PC5 and PC6 function, and the non–auto vector interrupt is not used.
000: The interrupt priorities of H1S, H2S, H3S, and H4S are in descending order, beginning with H1S.

The last part of the initialization routine is to reset the printer by sending out a Reset pulse. This is accomplished simply by setting and then clearing bit 3 of the PBCR.

Once the initialization routine is called, the PI/T is ready to receive the data to print. Figure 8-32 gives a sample routine, PTLINE, which prints a given character string based on the status-polling technique. If the printer has an internal buffer, it is necessary to terminate the character string with a line-feed or carriage return in order for the printer to start printing after the character string has been received. In calling routine PTLINE, the user passes the beginning address of the data to print in address register A1 and the 2-byte character count in data register D1. Upon completion, this routine returns a 1-byte status in data register D0. The status is set to 0 if any error is detected from the printer. Otherwise, it is set to 1 to indicate a successful completion.

```
PTLINE      MOVE.L      D2,-(SP)
            TST.W       D1                      ;CHECK CHARACTER COUNT
            BEQ.S       DONE
CHKFLT      BTST        #2,PSR                  ;CHECK H3S STATUS BIT (ERROR SIGNAL)
            BNE.S       ERROR
            MOVE.B      PBDR,D2                 ;INPUT SELECT, PAPER OUT AND BUSY BITS
            ANDI.B      #3,D2                   ;CHECK FOR PAPER OUT ERROR
            CMPI.B      #1,D2                   ;AND SELECT SIGNAL
            BNE.S       ERROR
WAIT        BTST        #0,PSR                  ;CHECK READY BIT
            BEQ         WAIT
PTCHAR      MOVE.B      (A1)+,PADR              ;MOVE NEXT CHARACTER TO PORT A
            SUBQ.W      #1,D1                   ;DECREMENT CHARACTER COUNT
            BEQ.S       DONE
BUSY        MOVE.B      PBDR,D2
            ANDI.B      #4,D2                   ;MONITOR BUSY SIGNAL
            BNE         BUSY
            BRA         CHKFLT
DONE        MOVE.B      #1,D0
            BRA.S       RETURN
ERROR       CLR.B       D0
RETURN      MOVE.L      (SP)+,D2
            RTS
```

Figure 8-32   A sample print routine based on status polling.

Interrupt-driven printer driver

The printer driver routine previously described is based on status polling. An alternative is to design the driver such that an interrupt is used to indicate the readiness of the interface for accepting data to print.

An interrupt-driven driver requires the interrupt vector associated with the printer interface to be set up in the printer initializatin routine. This can be accomplished by including the instruction sequence

```
PITVEC EQU      $88
       MOVE.B   #PITVEC,PIVR
       MOVE.L   #PTSERV, PITVEC*4
       ANDI     #$F8FF,SR
```

The MOVE.B instruction initializes the PI/T interrupt vector register, PIVR. Recalling that port A is used as a data port in this sample interface, its associated vector number must be divisible by four. This is because the PI/T generates an 8-bit vector number, which is the upper 6 bits of the PIVR followed by two 0's if the interrupt is from port A. The MOVE.L instruction loads the beginning address of the printer interrupt service routine into the corresponding vector address, PITVEC $\times$ 4. In this example, the first instruction of the service routine is labeled PTSERV. The ANDI instruction sets the interrupt mask level to 0.

To support non-auto vector interrupts, in the printer initialization routine previously described, the

```
       MOVE.B   #0,PSRR
```

instruction also needs to be replaced with

```
MOVE.B          #$18,PSRR
```

However, the port A interrupt is not enabled unless control bit 1 in the PACR is set to 1. This interrupt should be enabled only when the print data are ready to be sent to the PI/T.

The interrupt-driven printer driver shown in Fig. 8-33 consists of two routines, a setup routine and an interrupt service routine. The setup routine is called

```
*   SETUP ROUTINE
*
STATUS    EQU       $1000
PTDRIV    MOVE.L    D2,-(SP)
          CMPI.B    #2,STATUS          ;IS A PRINT COMMAND IN PROGRESS?
          BEQ.S     RETURN1            ;IF YES, RETURN
          MOVE.B    #2,STATUS          ;SET BUSY FLAG
          MOVE.L    A1,BUFPTR          ;PASS BUFFER POINTER TO SERVICE ROUTINE
          MOVE.W    D1,CHACNT          ;PASS CHARACTER COUNT
          BTST      #2,PSR             ;CHECK H3S STATUS BIT (ERROR SIGNAL)
          BNE.S     ERROR1             ;ERROR IS DETECTED
          MOVE.B    PBDR,D2            ;CHECK FOR PAPER OUT ERROR
          ANDI.B    #3,D2              ;AND SELECT SIGNAL
          CMPI.B    #1,D2
          BNE.S     ERROR1             ;ERROR IS DETECTED
          BSET      #1,PACR            ;ENABLE H1S INTERRUPT
RETURN1   MOVE.L    (SP)+,D2
          RTS
ERROR1    MOVE.B    #1,STATUS          ;SET ERROR STATUS
          MOVE.L    (SP)+,D2
          RTS
*
*   INTERRUPT SERVICE ROUTINE
*
PTSERV    MOVE.L    D2/A1,-(SP)
          MOVE.L    BUFPTR,A1          ;GET BUFFER ADDRESS
          TST.W     CHACNT             ;CHECK CHARACTER COUNT
          BEQ.S     DONE
CHKFLT    BTST      #2,PSR             ;CHECK H3S STATUS BIT (ERROR SIGNAL)
          BNE.S     ERROR2             ;ERROR IS DETECTED
          MOVE.B    PBDR,D2            ;INPUT SELECT, PAPER OUT AND BUSY BITS
          ANDI.B    #3,D2              ;CHECK FOR PAPER OUT ERROR
          CMPI.B    #1,D2              ;AND SELECT SIGNAL
          BNE.S     ERROR2
PTCHAR    MOVE.B    (A1)+,PADR         ;MOVE NEXT CHARACTER TO PORT A
          SUBQ.W    #1,CHACNT          ;DECREMENT CHARACTER COUNT
          BEQ.S     DONE               ;IF ZERO, PRINT IS COMPLETED
          BRA.S     RETURN2
ERROR2    MOVE.B    #1,STATUS          ;SET ERROR STATUS
          BCLR      #1,PACR            ;DISABLE H1S INTERRUPT
          BRA.S     RETURN2
DONE      MOVE.B    #0,STATUS          ;SET DONE STATUS
          BCLR      #1,PACR            ;DISABLE H1S INTERRUPT
RETURN2   MOVE.L    A1,BUFPTR          ;SAVE BUFFER POINTER
          MOVE.L    (SP)+,D2/A1
          RTE
BUFPTR    DS.L      1
CHACNT    DS.W      1
```

Figure 8-33 An interrupt-driven printer driver.

whenever the user has data ready to be printed. The caller passes to the setup routine the beginning address and the character count of the output data. This routine ensures that a printer operation is not already in progress and there are no printer errors. It then enables the printer interrupt and returns to the caller so that other processing may proceed. A memory byte, STATUS, is maintained to indicate the printer status; 0 for completion, 1 for error, and 2 for busy. STATUS is initially cleared in the printer initialization routine. Since this status is updated in the interrupt service routine, it is implemented as an absolute location.

As soon as the setup routine is called, the PI/T generates an interrupt. The interrupt service routine then sends a character to the PI/T. If the current character is the last one in the output data, the service routine sets the completion code and then disables the printer interrupt.

8-7 Multifunction Peripheral Device

To simplify the design and reduce the chip count of a minimum system, Motorola has made available a multifunction peripheral device (MFP), MC68901. The MFP integrates four timers, an 8-bit parallel interface port, a synchronous/asynchronous communication interface adapter, and a 16-source interrupt controller into a single device fabricated in a dual-in-line package with 48 pins. A block diagram of the MC68901 is given in Fig. 8-34. The MFP is interfaced to the MC68000 via eight data pins with asynchronous bus structure. The on-chip peripherals are programmed through 24 registers, organized as shown in Fig. 8-35.

Timers

The MFP contains four 8-bit timers A, B, C, and D, all of which have a prescaler controlled by the clock inputs XTAL1/XTAL2. Timers A and B can be individually programmed in the delay mode, the pulse width measurement mode, and the event-count mode. In the delay mode, the timer counter decrements by 1 each time the number of clock cycles specified by the prescaler have passed. Upon a transition from 01 to 00 in the timer counter, the timer is reloaded from its associated data register and then either outputs a pulse or toggles its timer output pin (TO). A time-out pulse will also cause an interrupt if its interrupt channel is enabled. In the pulse width measurement mode, the timer uses its timer input (TI) as the enable signal. When the TI input is high, the timer counter is decremented as in the delay mode. Therefore, in this mode, the timer can measure the width of the TI signal. In the event-count mode, the prescaler is not used to decrement the timer counter. Instead, the timer is decremented after each 0-to-1 transition on the TI pin, thus allowing the timer to count the number of active transitions.

The operating modes and the prescale values for timers A and B are programmable through their timer control registers TACR and TBCR. Bits 3–0 of

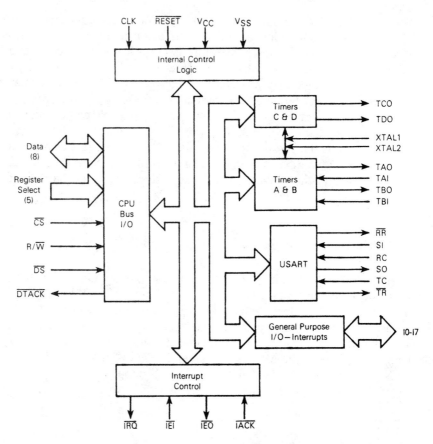

Figure 8-34 Block diagram of the MC68901 MFP. (Courtesy of Motorola, Inc.)

TACR and TBCR define the operating mode and the prescale value as follows

AC3 BC3	AC2 BC2	AC1 BC1	AC0 BC0	Operation Mode
0	0	0	0	Timer disabled
0	0	0	1	Delay mode with prescaler value = 4
0	0	1	0	Delay mode with prescaler value = 10
0	0	1	1	Delay mode with prescaler value = 16
0	1	0	0	Delay mode with prescaler value = 50
0	1	0	1	Delay mode with prescaler value = 64
0	1	1	0	Delay mode with prescaler value = 100
0	1	1	1	Delay mode with prescaler value = 200
1	0	0	0	Event-count mode
1	0	0	1	Pulse width measurement mode with prescaler value = 4
1	0	1	0	Pulse width measurement mode with prescaler value = 10
1	0	1	1	Pulse width measurement mode with prescaler value = 16
1	1	0	0	Pulse width measurement mode with prescaler value = 50
1	1	0	1	Pulse width measurement mode with prescaler value = 64
1	1	1	0	Pulse width measurement mode with prescaler value = 100
1	1	1	1	Pulse width measurement mode with prescaler value = 200

Address						Abbreviation	Register Name
Hex	Binary						
	RS5	RS4	RS3	RS2	RS1		
01	0	0	0	0	0	GPIP	General Purpose I/O Register
03	0	0	0	0	1	AER	Active Edge Register
05	0	0	0	1	0	DDR	Data Direction Register
07	0	0	0	1	1	IERA	Interrupt Enable Register A
09	0	0	1	0	0	IERB	Interrupt Enable Register B
0B	0	0	1	0	1	IPRA	Interrupt Pending Register A
0D	0	0	1	1	0	IPRB	Interrupt Pending Register B
0F	0	0	1	1	1	ISRA	Interrupt In-Service Register A
11	0	1	0	0	0	ISRB	Interrupt In-Service Register B
13	0	1	0	0	1	IMRA	Interrupt Mask Register A
15	0	1	0	1	0	IMRB	Interrupt Mask Register B
17	0	1	0	1	1	VR	Vector Register
19	0	1	1	0	0	TACR	Timer A Control Register
1B	0	1	1	0	1	TBCR	Timer B Control Register
1D	0	1	1	1	0	TCDCR	Timers C and D Control Register
1F	0	1	1	1	1	TADR	Timer A Data Register
21	1	0	0	0	0	TBDR	Timer B Data Register
23	1	0	0	0	1	TCDR	Timer C Data Register
25	1	0	0	1	0	TDDR	Timer D Data Register
27	1	0	0	1	1	SCR	Synchronous Character Register
29	1	0	1	0	0	UCR	USART Control Register
2B	1	0	1	0	1	RSR	Receiver Status Register
2D	1	0	1	1	0	TSR	Transmitter Status Register
2F	1	0	1	1	1	UDR	USART Data Register

NOTE: Hex addresses assume that RS1 connects with A1, RS2 connects with A2, etc. and that DS is connected to LDS on the MC68000 or DS is connected to DS on the MC68008.

Figure 8-35   Register map of the MFP. (Courtesy of Motorola, Inc.)

Bit 4 of the timer control register is used to reset a TO output pin to low, and bits 7–5 are not used.

Timers C and D do not have TI pins, which are required for the pulse width measurement and event-count modes. Therefore, these two timers can be operated only in the delay mode. A typical application is to implement the baud rate generator for the serial communication adaptor by reducing the frequency of the external clock XTAL1/XTAL2 and using the resulting timer outputs TCO and TDO as the receiver and transmitter clocks. Timers C and D share the same control register TCDCR. Bits 6–4 are for programming timer C and bits 3–1 are for timer D. They specify the prescaler values and have the same meaning as bits 2–0 of TACR and TBCR.

USART

The serial interface provided by the MFP supports both asynchronous and synchronous serial data transmissions. This USART (universal synchronous/asynchronous receiver transmitter) operates in the asynchronous mode when the baud rate factor 16 is selected. Its operations are similar to those of the ACIA. If the baud rate factor 1 is selected, this USART operates in the synchronous mode. In the synchronous mode, data sampling is controlled by the clock signal, which is transmitted along with data, thus eliminating the need for the start and stop bits in each character. Data are transmitted as a packet, with one character immediately followed by another. If the next character is not immediately available after the current one has been sent, an underrun error is said to occur. Each packet must include special synchronization characters to indicate the beginning of the packet. The USART has a synchronization character register (SCR) to hold one synchronization character.

The character format is selected independently of the asynchronous and synchronous modes by programming the USART control register (UCR). The definitions of the bits in the control register are as follows:

Bit 7: When this bit is 0, the baud rate factor is 1 and the synchronous mode is selected. When this bit is 1, the baud rate factor is 16 and the asynchronous mode is selected.

Bits 6 and 5: These two bits specify the number of data bits per character, which can be 8 (00), 7 (01), 6 (10), or 5 (11).

Bits 4 and 3: These two bits specify the number of stop bits, which can be none (i.e., synchronous (00)), 1 (01), $1\frac{1}{2}$ (10), or 2 (11).

Bit 2: This bit is used to enable (1) or disable (0) the parity bit.

Bit 1: This bit selects odd (0) or even (1) parity.

Bit 0: This bit is not used.

Unlike the ACIA, which has one status register for both the receiver and transmitter, the USART has a separate receiver status register (RSR) and transmitter status register (TSR). The receiver status register is for reporting various receiver errors and for enabling receiver operations. It contains the receiver buffer full flag (bit 7), the overrun error flag (bit 6), the parity error flag (bit 5), the framing error flag (bit 4), the found/search, or break detect, flag (bit 3), the match/character in progress flag (bit 2), the synchronous strip enable flag (bit 1), and the receiver enable flag (bit 0). Bits 1, 2, and 3 are for detecting and handling of synchronization characters in the synchronous mode. The transmitter status register is for reporting various transmitter errors and for enabling transmitter operations. It contains the transmitter buffer empty flag (bit 7), the underrun error flag (bit 6), the auto-turnaround enable flag (bit 5), the end of transmission flag (bit 4), the break enable flag (bit 3), and the transmitter enable flag (bit 0). Bits 2 and 1 control the transmitter output (SO) while the transmitter is disabled. These two bits put the SO pin in high-impedance state (00), low (01), high (10), or loopback mode (11).

In addition to the serial in (SI), serial out (SO), receiver clock (RC), and transmitter clock (TC) pins, which are typical for a serial communication adapter, the USART also includes two control pins to support DMA operations. The receiver ready (RR) and transmitter ready (TR) output pins reflect the receiver buffer full status and transmitter buffer empty status, respectively, for DMA operations. They can be connected to DMA request input pins of a DMA controller such as the MC68440 to provide block transfer capabilities.

GPIP

The general-purpose interrupt input/output port (GPIP) has eight I/O pins (I7-I0). Each of them can be independently programmed as an input, output, or interrupt request pin. Their functions are programmed through three control registers, the GPIP data register (GPIP), the data direction register (DDR), and the active edge register (AER). Each GPIP pin has an associated bit in these three registers. A data bit is used to output or input data to or from its associated I/O pin. A direction bit defines its associated I/O pin to be an input (0) or output (1) pin. An edge bit defines the interrupt request from its associated I/O pin to be negative-triggered (0) or positive-triggered (1). Whether an I/O pin is enabled for an interrupt request pin is controlled by programming the interrupt controller.

Interrupt controller

The MFP contains an interrupt controller capable of handling up to 16 interrupt sources. Eight of these interrupt sources are external and are input from I7 through I0; the remaining eight are from internal sources. Figure 8-36 shows these interrupt sources and their priority level. Since there are 16 sources, the interrupt controller is programmed through three pairs of 8-bit control registers. Each bit position in a control register pair corresponds to an interrupt channel. The format of a control register pair is shown in Fig. 8-37.

The interrupt enable registers, IBRA and IERB, are used to enable (1) or disable (0) individual interrupt sources. The interrupt-pending registers A and B (IPRA and IPRB) indicate the received interrupt requests from enabled sources. In a polled interrupt system, registers IPRA and IPRB can be read to determine the interrupt source(s) to be serviced and clear the corresponding interrupt pending bit in the service routine. In addition to the interrupt enable registers, there are also a pair of interrupt mask registers, IMRA and IMRB. When a request from an enabled channel is masked, it sets the corresponding interrupt pending bit, but the interrupt controller does not send an interrupt request ($\overline{\text{IRQ}}$) signal to the processor.

Priority	Channel	Description
Highest	1111	General Purpose Interrupt 7 (I7)
	1110	General Purpose Interrupt 6 (I6)
	1101	Timer A
	1100	Receiver Buffer Full
	1011	Receive Error
	1010	Transmit Buffer Empty
	1001	Transmit Error
	1000	Timer B
	0111	General Purpose Interrupt 5 (I5)
	0110	General Purpose Interrupt 4 (I4)
	0101	Timer C
	0100	Timer D
	0011	General Purpose Interrupt 3 (I3)
	0010	General Purpose Interrupt 2 (I2)
	0001	General Purpose Interrupt 1 (I1)
Lowest	0000	General Purpose Interrupt 0 (I0)

Figure 8-36 Priority levels of interrupt sources handled by the MFP. (Courtesy of Motorola, Inc.)

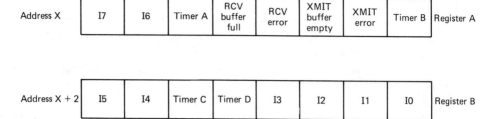

	7							0	
Address X	I7	I6	Timer A	RCV buffer full	RCV error	XMIT buffer empty	XMIT error	Timer B	Register A

Address X + 2	I5	I4	Timer C	Timer D	I3	I2	I1	I0	Register B

Figure 8-37 Format of interrupt control register pairs. (Courtesy of Motorola, Inc.)

There is one interrupt vector register (VR) shared by all 16 interrupt sources. Only the upper four bits of this register are programmable. During an interrupt acknowledge cycle, the interrupt controller outputs an 8-bit vector number, of which the most significant 4 bits are from the interrupt vector register and the remaining 4 bits correspond to the priority level of the request source being selected for service.

In order for the system to include more than one MFP, it has the $\overline{IEI}$ (interrupt enable in) and $\overline{IEO}$ (interrupt enable out) pins to implement a daisy-chained interrupt structure. For a configuration consisting of more than one MFP, the $\overline{IEO}$ output pin of each MFP is connected to the $\overline{IEI}$ input pin of the next lower priority MFP. For the lowest priority MFP, its $\overline{IEO}$ pin is not connected. On the other hand, the $\overline{IEI}$ pin of the highest priority MFP is grounded.

8-8 DMA Controllers

In status-polling or interrupt-driven I/O, the processor participates in the actual data transfer. When a block of data is to be input to or output from memory, this requires several MC68000 instructions for each byte or word transfer, as can be seen in the previous I/O programming examples. Each instruction, in turn, takes one or more bus cycles for execution. For instance, the instruction

        MOVE.W   (A2),(A3)+

requires three bus cycles: fetching the instruction from the memory, reading the source operand pointed by A2, and writing the operand into the destination address. Therefore, previously discussed I/O techniques are adequate only for low-speed peripheral devices.

Direct memory access

Input/output involving a high-speed peripheral such as a disk drive is accomplished by direct memory access (DMA) transfers. During a DMA operation, the actual data transfer is performed by a DMA controller, not a processor. A DMA controller has the necessary logic to steal bus cycles from the processor for data transfer. In addition, a DMA controller contains a memory address pointer and a transfer count register, which are automatically updated after each data item is transferred. Therefore, with DMA, only one bus cycle is required for each data transfer. This not only achieves a high data transfer rate but also releases the processor to perform other tasks.

A DMA controller is capable of being a bus master or a slave. It is in the slave mode when communicating with the processor in setting up a block transfer. During a DMA bus cycle, the controller becomes the bus master to perform a data transfer.

To initiate a DMA bus cycle, the controller sends a request signal to the $\overline{\text{BR}}$ (bus request) pin of the MC68000. The MC68000 waits until the current bus cycle is completed and then returns a grant signal through its $\overline{\text{BG}}$ (bus grant) pin and relinquishes control of the bus. The DMA controller, in turn, responds with a signal to the MC68000's $\overline{\text{BGACK}}$ (bus grant acknowledge) pin, gains the bus control, and initiates a bus cycle to perform the data transfer. After the transfer is completed, the controller returns the bus control back to the processor by deactivating the $\overline{\text{BGACK}}$ signal.

MC68440 DMAC

A typical example of DMA controller is the MC68440, which contains two channels so that two peripheral devices can be serviced simultaneously. Figure 8-38 shows the major connections between the MC68440 and other system components. In order to act as a bus master, a DMA controller must have bus control pins such as R/$\overline{\text{W}}$, $\overline{\text{AS}}$, $\overline{\text{LDS}}$, $\overline{\text{UDS}}$, and $\overline{\text{DTACK}}$, just like the processor. These pins are directly connected to the control lines of the system bus.

The MC68440 uses time-multiplexed address/data bus. A set of 16 pins carries both data bits D15–D0 and address bits A23–A8. Therefore, external data transceivers (74LS245) and address latches (74LS373) are required to connect the MC68440 to the system bus, which has separate data and address buses. This demultiplexing logic is enabled and controlled by four MC68440 signals: $\overline{\text{OWN}}$ (own), $\overline{\text{UAS}}$ (upper address strobe), $\overline{\text{DBEN}}$ (data buffer enable), and $\overline{\text{DDIR}}$ (data direction). In the master mode, the $\overline{\text{OWN}}$ signal becomes activated to enable the external address latches, whereas $\overline{\text{UAS}}$ is used to strobe the upper address bits A23–A8 into the latches. In the slave mode, the MC68440 need not output addresses, and both signals are therefore inactive. The $\overline{\text{DBEN}}$ and $\overline{\text{DDIR}}$ signals control the external data transceivers. $\overline{\text{DBEN}}$ is used as the enable signal, and $\overline{\text{DDIR}}$ controls the data flow direction, high for data flow to the MC68440 and low for data flow to the data bus.

The connection between a peripheral and the MC68440 depends on the transfer type in the DMA cycle, which can be either implicit address or explicit address. The difference between the two is illustrated in Fig. 8-39. In an implicit address transfer, data items flow directly between a device and memory without passing through the controller. Memory responds to the read/write command and the address sent by the controller as if the bus cycle were initiated by the processor.

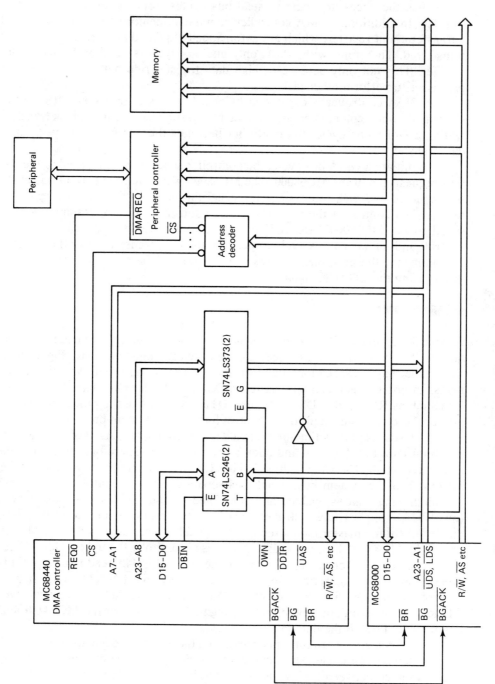

Figure 8-38 Typical system configuration including a DMA controller.

However, selection and control of the device is accomplished through the interface lines directly connected between the device and the controller.

To support this implicit address transfer, the MC68440 provides a separate set of REQ (request), $\overline{ACK}$ (acknowledge), and PCL (peripheral control line) pins for each of the two channels plus the DTC (data transfer complete) and $\overline{DONE}$ (done) pins shared by both channels. The REQ pin is used by a device to request a DMA cycle. The $\overline{ACK}$ pin is used by the controller to indicate that the device should place data on the data bus in a device-to-memory transfer. The PCL pin, which serves more than one purpose, may be programmed for functions such as ready and reload. The DTC pin is used to indicate the end of a DMA cycle. Typically, this signal is used by the device to remove the data from the bus in a memory-to-device transfer. The $\overline{DONE}$ pin is used to indicate the end of the entire block transfer. In a particular application, only some of the interface pins are actually used, depending on the operation mode and the pin configuration of the device.

Note that in a one-cycle data transfer, there may be incompatibility between the 8-bit device and the 16-bit memory. To resolve this problem, a byte-swapping logic (74LS245) is required, as shown in Fig. 8-35(a). When a byte is transferred between an 8-bit device and an even-addressed memory location, this data transceiver is enabled by the $\overline{HIBYTE}$ (high byte) signal from the MC68440, so that the data byte is transferred to or from the even-addressed memory location on data lines D15–D8.

An explicit address data transfer is accomplished by two bus cycles, a read cycle transferring the data from the source to the MC68440 followed by a write cycle transferring the data from the MC68440 to the destination. In a dual-cycle transfer, the peripheral device involved is selected by its address in the same way as the memory. This allows the user to select the peripheral device by software, whereas in a single-cycle transfer the device selection is fixed by hardwiring. In addition, using dual-cycle transfers the MC68440 can move a block of memory from one area to another.

A layout of the MC68440 internal registers is given in Fig. 8-40. There are 17 registers for each of the two channels plus a general control register. Among them, the following registers need to be programmed each time a block transfer is to be initiated:

Memory address register (MAR): This register stores the memory address to be accessed during a DMA cycle. After each transfer, the MAR is incremented to point to the next byte or word.

Device address register. (DAR): This register stores the address of the peripheral device to be accessed during a DMA cycle when an explicit address data transfer is used. For single-cycle data transfers, the DAR need not be programmed, since the peripheral device is implied.

Memory transfer count register (MTCR): This register is initially programmed with the number of bytes or words to be transferred. The MTCR is decremented by 1 after each DMA cycle. When it reaches 0, the block transfer is terminated, a status bit is set, and an interrupt is generated if so programmed.

Sec. 8-8   DMA Controllers

289

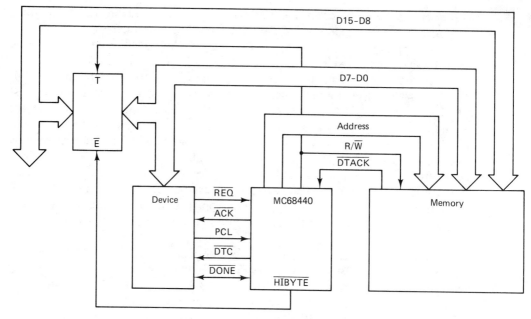

(a) Implicitly addressed device interface

Figure 8-39 Two types of DMA cycles.

Sequence control register (SCR): This register specifies whether the MAR or DAR is to be incremented or should remain constant after each DMA cycle. Since an MC68000-based system uses memory-mapped I/O, by programming this register, the MC68440 can perform memory-to-memory and peripheral-to-peripheral block transfers as well as memory-to-peripheral and peripheral-to-memory transfers.

Operation control register (OCR): This register specifies the transfer direction, the operand size, and the method used to initiate DMA requests. For example, the direction bit (bit 7) indicates whether the data transfer is from device to memory (1) or from memory to device (0).

Channel control register (CCR): This register is used to control the operation of the channel. By writing to the CCR, a block transfer may be initiated, stopped or aborted, and the channel may be enabled to generate an interrupt at the end of a block transfer.

The base transfer count register (BTCR) and base address register (BAR) are used only for a reload or continue operation. In such an operation, the MAR and MTCR are reloaded from the BAR and BTCR, respectively. The channel status register (CSR) and channel error register (CER) reflect the status of a channel operation and report any error that occurred during a DMA cycle.

The remaining registers are normally programmed only once in the initialization routine when the system is turned on. These registers include the general control register (GCR), normal interrupt vector register (NIVR), error interrupt

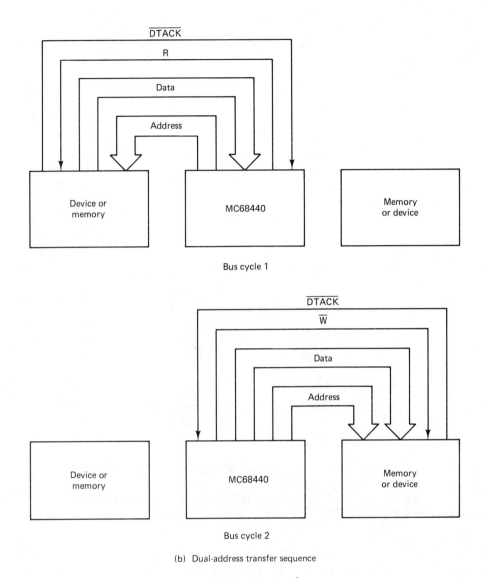

Bus cycle 1

Bus cycle 2

(b) Dual-address transfer sequence

Figure 8-39 (*continued*)

vector register (EIVR), channel priority register (CPR), device control register (DCR), memory function code register (MFCR), and device function code register (DFCR).

Figure 8-41 shows the bit assignments for each of the registers in the MC68440. This figure also gives the offset of memory-mapped location for each register. As an example, to determine the address of a register, assume that the address decoder is designed such that the MC68440 is enabled when the upper 16 bits of the received address are $0FF0. Then the MAR of channel 1 is accessible by the address $0FF000 + $40 + $0C = $0FF04C.

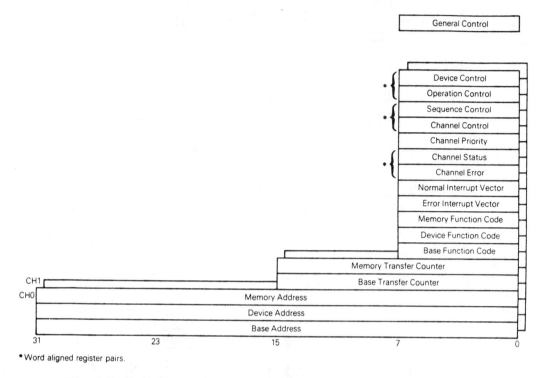

Figure 8-40   Register layout of the MC68440 DMA controller. (Courtesy of Motorola, Inc.)

A typical programming sequence to initiate a block transfer is as follows:

1. Read the channel status from the CSR. If the channel is busy, wait.
2. Write the beginning address of the memory block to be transferred to the MAR.
3. Write the block size to MTCR.
4. Write the address of the peripheral involved in the block transfer to the DAR if explicit address data transfer is to be used.
5. Program the OCR and SCR to select the control options desired such as the transfer direction, operand size, etc.
6. Enable the channel for a block transfer by setting the start channel (STR) bit in the CCR to 1.

Once a block transfer is initiated, the MC68440 takes over the actual data transfer, releasing the processor for performing other tasks. Completion of a block transfer can be detected by polling the CSR or through an interrupt from the MC68440 caused by the end of the block transfer. With two buffer areas, overlapping beween data processing and block I/O based on DMA can be easily achieved.

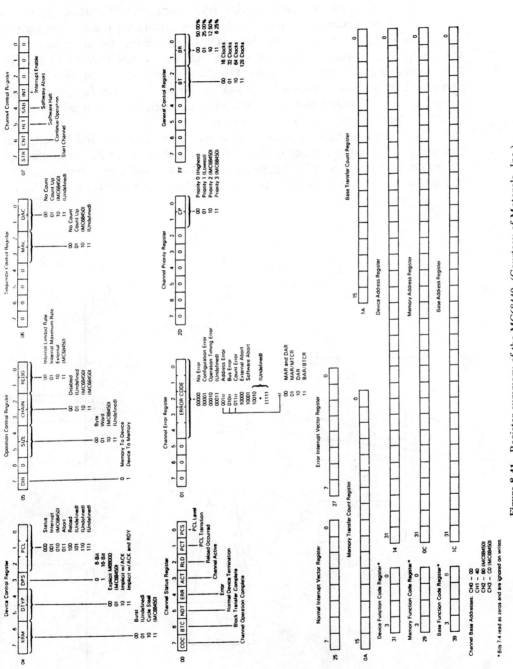

Figure 8-41 Register summary of the MC68440. (Courtesy of Motorola, Inc.)

MC68450 DMAC

Motorola has also made available another DMA controller, the MC68450, which is pin and register compatible with the MC68440, including the bit assignments within the registers. However, the MC68450 has more functional options available. A key difference between the two is that the MC68450 provides four independent channels, versus two in the MC68440. Furthermore, the MC68450 can perform chaining block transfer in addition to single-block transfer and continue operation. In a chaining mode, a single channel operation can transfer several blocks of data between the device and memory.

There are two chaining modes available, array chaining and linked array chaining, illustrated in Figures 8-42 and 8-43, respectively. In the array chaining mode, the processor initially supplies a base address and a base transfer count, instead of the individual memory addresses and memory transfer counts for the

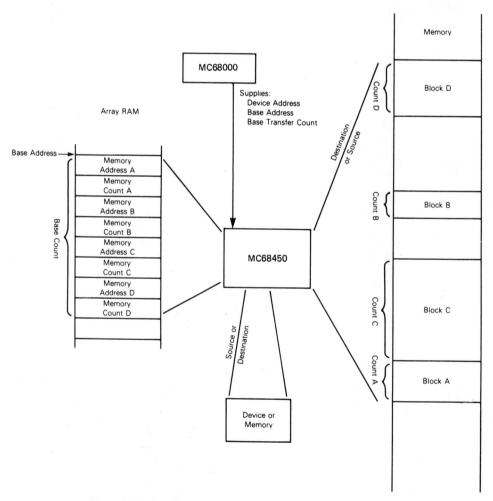

Figure 8-42   Array chaining transfer. (Courtesy of Motorola, Inc.)

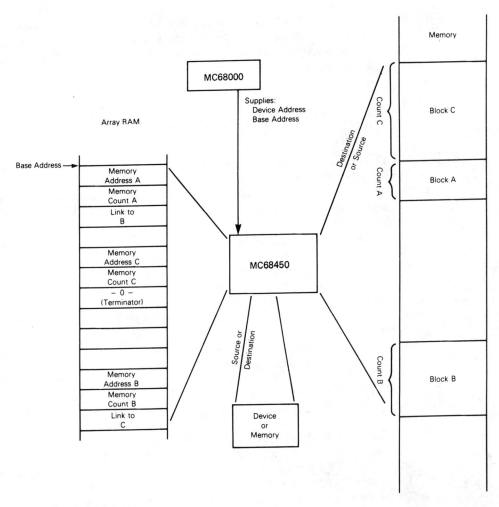

Figure 8-43 Linked array chaining transfer. (Courtesy of Motorola, Inc.)

data blocks to be transferred. The base address points to the beginning address of an array, where the memory address and transfer count for each block transfer are stored in a sequential order. The base transfer count specifies the number of block transfers to be performed, i.e., the number of pairs of memory address and transfer count stored in the array. As each block transfer is completed, the MC68450 automatically reinitializes its MAR and MATC, with the next pair of memory address and transfer count fetched from the array. Then, the base transfer count is decremented and the base address is incremented to point to the next array entry. When the base transfer count reaches 0, the entire channel operation terminates upon the completion of the current block transfer.

The linked array chaining mode differs from the array chaining mode in that each pair of memory address and transfer count need not be physically stored one after another in a contiguous area. Instead, each entry includes a forward pointer, which points to the location where the next pair of memory address and transfer count is stored. This linked array structure provides greater flexibility in inserting or deleting entries. Since the last block to be transferred is indicated by having a zero forward pointer, the processor need not supply the base count in initializing a channel for a linked array chaining transfer.

EXERCISES

1. For a typical large system, both ends of the bus are buffered. Modify Fig. 8-2 such that the data lines connected to the LSI interface are buffered.

2. Assume that an ACIA is accessed as locations $AXXX12 and $AXXX14, where X indicates "don't cares." Show how its bus interface pins should be connected and the required address decoding logic.

3. Assume that incoming data are transmitted at 2400 baud with the data format of 7 data bits per character and no parity, and the baud rate factor of the ACIA is set to 16. Would data be received correctly if the RxClk clock is running at the frequency of 38,700 Hertz? How about at 38,000 Hertz?

4. Assuming the character format of 7 data bits, even parity, 1 start bit, and two stop bits, what is the maximum number of characters that can be transmitted per second at 9600 baud?

5. Assume that 4800 baud rate is to be used for data transmission and the ACIA is initialized by the instruction sequence:

```
MOVE.B      #3,ACIACS
MOVE.B      #$D,ACIACS
```

   (a) Determine the data format to be used for transmission.
   (b) Determine the frequency of the RxClk and TxClk clocks.
   (c) Determine the pulse width of each bit on the RxData and TxData signal lines.
   (d) Draw a timing diagram of the ASCII letter A as being transmitted from the ACIA.

6. Define the three types of errors that the ACIA can detect during data transmission.

7. Write a program to display digits 0 through 9 on a CRT terminal using status polling. Rewrite this program as an interrupt-driven routine.

8. Write a program that would simultaneously display a text string on the screen and input data from the keyboard of the same terminal.

9. Write a program that will input two 2-digit unsigned decimal integers from a CRT terminal and display the 3-digit sum on the same terminal. Assume that two numbers are separated with blanks.

10. Could the ACIA be connected to an interrupt management logic that generates non-auto vector requests to the MC68000?

11. Modify the connection of the ACIA to the MC68000 shown in Fig. 8-9 so that the ACIA is accessed by asynchronous bus cycles rather than synchronous bus cycles.

12. Why is it wrong to enable the receiver interrupt of the ACIA by setting bit 7 of the control register with an OR or BSET instruction?

13. What feature enables a modem to be configured for full-duplex transmission?

14. Assume that the system has two ACIAs, one connected to a CRT terminal and the other to a modem and that the modem has established connection with the remote

station. Write a program such that the system would act as a dumb terminal to the remote station.

15. Assume that eight 8-bit status registers are to be monitored, each of which is connected to a device. Use a PI/T to design the required interface between the bus and these registers.

16. Using a PI/T, design an interface for a 2-digit hexadecimal display constructed with two common anode 7-segment display units. The design should include the connections between the PI/T and the display, and an output routine to display a given 2-digit hexadecimal number.

17. Using a PI/T, design an interface for an 8-digit hexadecimal display constructed with eight common anode 7-segment display units. The design should include the connections between the PI/T and the display and an interrupt-driven display refresh routine. Assume that each display unit is to be refreshed every 8 milliseconds.

18. For the design in Exercise 17 show how the refresh operations can be eliminated by using external data latches.

19. Using the timer of the PI/T as the source of periodical interrupts, write a program that will update the timer after each second and display the time in the form of hh:mm:ss on a CRT terminal.

20. Determine the maximum duration that can be measured in the example given in Fig. 8-27 and show how to extend that limit by a factor of 256.

21. Could the PI/T be connected to an interrupt management logic that generates auto vector requests to the MC68000?

22. Assuming a 5-MHz MC68000-based system, what is the maximum data transfer rate that can be achieved by DMA?

23. Describe the advantages of using dual-cycle DMA transfers as opposed to single-cycle DMA.

9

Memories

Main memory, which is usually referred to simply as memory, is directly accessible to the processor and stores the current program being executed. Main memory may have several modules, with each having its own bus interface logic. A memory module provides a storage segment of 2^M bytes. It can be implemented with several rows of semiconductor memory devices, with each row providing a portion of the storage segment and each device contributing 1 or more bits in each location.

A memory location is accessed through multilevel address decoding as illustrated by the block diagram in Fig. 9-1. The address bits specifying the memory location to be accessed are divided into three groups. The upper group of address bits is decoded to enable one of several memory modules in the system. For reasons of simplicity, only one decoder is shown for generating module select signals. Actually, each memory module includes a module select logic, and all modules receive the address and decode the upper group of address bits at the same time. For the enabled memory module, the middle group of address bits is decoded to select one of several rows of memory devices in the module. Finally, the lower group of address bits are decoded internally inside the selected memory devices to access one of many locations. Since the referenced memory location is accessed entirely through address decoding, the access time is determined by the memory devices used but is independent on the location. In other words, memory locations in a module can be accessed in a random fashion with the same access time.

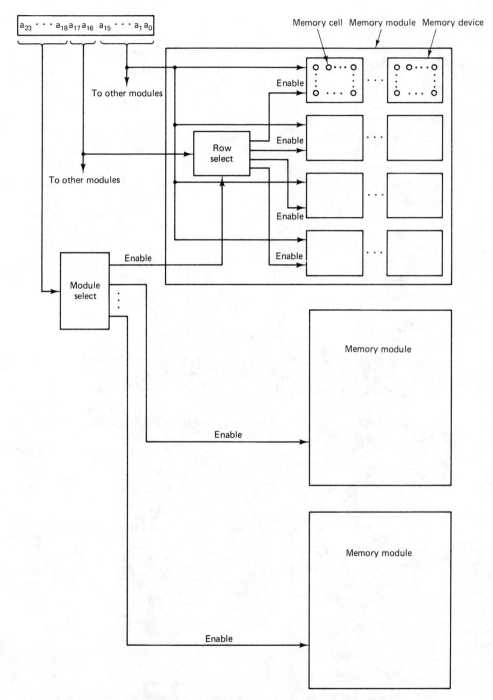

Figure 9-1 Accessing a memory location.

9-1 MOS Memory Devices

Memory devices can be divided into two main categories: read/write memory (RAM) and read-only memory (ROM). RAMs permit read as well as write operations. Since RAMs are volatile, their contents will be lost once the power is turned off. On the other hand, ROMs are nonvolatile devices but allow only read access to the stored data. Therefore, a system typically includes both types of memories, with ROMs storing the permanent portion of the monitor and RAMs storing user programs and data.

The size of a memory device is denoted by $n \times m$, meaning that the device contains n locations with each holding m bits, where n is always a power of 2. Various sizes of RAMs are available, such as $4K \times 1$, $2K \times 8$, $64K \times 1$, $256K \times 1$, and $1M \times 1$. RAMs can be further classified into two categories: static and dynamic, according to the structure of the memory cell.

In memory design, speed, cost, and power consumption are the major issues to be considered. Static RAMs (SRAMs) have the chief advantages of being simple to use and having fast access time. But dynamic RAMs (DRAMs) consume less power, provide higher capacity, and have lower cost per bit. For memory modules of small-to-medium size, typical implementation is with SRAMs. But, for large-size memory with 256K bytes or more, DRAMs are used.

SRAMs

For static memory devices, a flip-flop is used to store each data bit. Figure 9-2 illustrates a six-transistor static memory cell. The data bit is stored according to the states of transistors Q1 and Q2. This cross-coupled transistor pair is such that when one transistor is on, the other is off, and vice versa. A 1 is assigned to the state that exists when Q2 is on and Q1 is off, and a 0 is assigned to the opposite

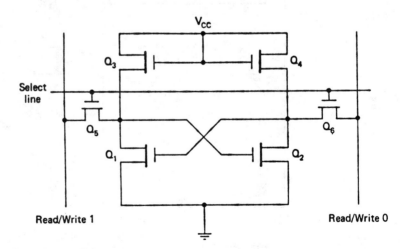

Figure 9-2 Six-transistor static RAM cell. Glenn A. Gibson/Yu-cheng Liu, *Microcomputers for Engineers and Scientists, 2/E,* © 1987. Reprinted by permission of Prentice-Hall, Inc., Englewood Cliffs, New Jersey.

state (Q2 off and Q1 on). The transistors Q3 and Q4 serve as resistors, and Q5 and Q6 act as enable gates. During a write operation, first the cell is selected by raising the voltage level on the select line. When this is done, transistors Q5 and Q6 act as short circuits, so that the read/write 1 line is applied to the gate of Q2 and the read/write 0 line is applied to the gate of Q1. To write a 1 into the cell, a 1 is placed on read/write 1 and a 0 is placed on read/write 0; this causes Q2 to be turned on and Q1 to be turned off. On the other hand, if a 0 is to be written into the cell, a 1 is placed on read/write 0 and a 0 is placed on read/write 1. In either case, once they are set the states of Q1 and Q2 will remain unchanged until the next write operation. The cell can be read simply by applying a voltage to the select line. When this is done, the state of Q1 is applied to the read/write 0 line and the state of Q2 is applied to the read/write 1.

A static RAM device contains an array of memory cells organized in a matrix form and necessary circuits for enabling read or write operation and for selecting the accessed cell. As an example, Fig. 9-3 shows the internal organization of the MCM6641 4K × 1 SRAM device. The device has 4096 cells divided into 64 rows and 64 columns. Six of the address bits are decoded to select one of 64 rows of memory cells. The remaining 6 bits are used as column address inputs to select a column and also, together with the enable ($\overline{S}$) signal, to enable the corresponding I/O circuit for a read or write operation. An I/O circuit permits a stored bit to be

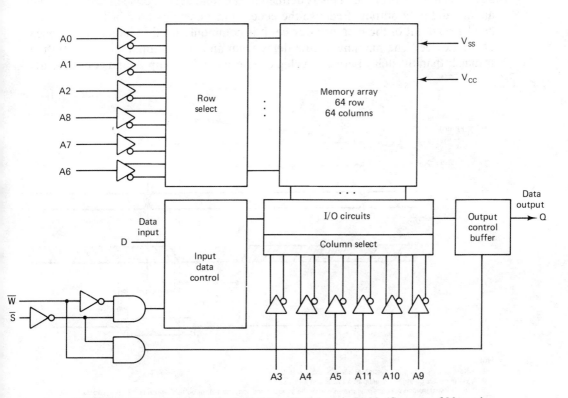

Figure 9-3 Block diagram of the MCM6641 4K × 1 static RAM. (Courtesy of Motorola, Inc.)

output to the data output (Q) pin during a read and to be changed by the input from the data (D) pin during a write. The type of access is specified by the read/write ($\overline{W}$) control input, high for read and low for write. When the $\overline{S}$ control input is high, the device is disabled for read or write and the Q pin is forced into its high-impedance state. Because all the input and output pins are TTL-compatible, no interface between the MOS and TTL signal levels is necessary. Most SRAMs require only a single voltage source of +5 volts.

Memory cycle timing

As with most other digital devices, it is easy to connect memory devices together because they have built-in supporting electronics. However, the timing constraints of the input signals are critical, and the timing requirements vary from one device to another. To ensure proper operation, the control logic in a memory module must provide address inputs and control signals that satisfy the timing parameters as specified by the manufacturer of the memory devices being used. The input timing during a memory read operation is different from the input timing during a memory write operation. Figure 9-4 shows various timing parameters for read and write cycles required by the MCM6641 SRAM.

The most important timing parameter to be considered in selecting a memory device is the access time. This is defined as the time delay between a stable input and a valid data output. Because the access time specifies how fast a data word can be read out of the memory device, it is commonly used to indicate the speed of the device. The maximum time delay from an address input to a data output is longer than the delay between a chip enable and a data output, and consequently

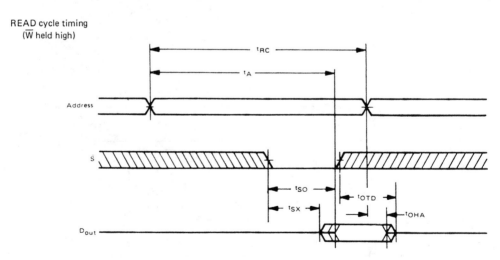

READ cycle timing
($\overline{W}$ held high)

Notes:
1. A Read occurs during the overlap of a low $\overline{S}$ and a high $\overline{W}$.
2. A Write occurs during the overlap of a low $\overline{S}$ and a low $\overline{W}$.
3. If the $\overline{S}$ low transition occurs simultaneously with the $\overline{W}$ low transition, the output buffers remain in a high-impedance state.

Figure 9-4 Timing diagram of the MCM6641 SRAM. (Courtesy of Motorola, Inc.)

WRITE cycle timing (note 3)

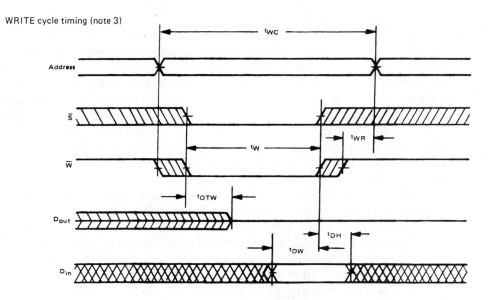

AC OPERATING CONDITIONS AND CHARACTERISTICS
(Full operating voltage and temperature range unless otherwise noted)

Input Pulse Levels...0.8 Volt to 2.0 Volts

Input Rise and Fall Times...10 ns

Input and Output Timing Levels.................................1.5 Volts

Output Load..............................1 TTL Gate and C_L = 100 pF

READ (note 1), WRITE (note 2) cycles

Parameter	Symbol	MCM6641-20 MCM66L41-20 Min	Max	MCM6641-25 MCM66L41-25 Min	Max	MCM6641-30 MCM66L41-30 Min	Max	MCM6641-45 MCM66L41-45 Min	Max	Units
Read cycle time	t_{RC}	200	–	250	–	300	–	450	–	ns
Access time	t_A	–	200	–	250	–	300	–	450	ns
Chip selection to output valid	t_{SO}	–	70	–	85	–	100	–	120	ns
Chip selection to output active	t_{SX}	10	–	10	–	10	–	10	–	ns
Output 3-state from deselection	t_{OTD}	–	40	–	60	–	80	–	100	ns
Output hold from address change	t_{OHA}	50	–	50	–	50	–	50	–	ns
Write cycle time	t_{WC}	200	–	250	–	300	–	450	–	ns
Write time	t_W	100	–	125	–	150	–	200	–	ns
Write release time	t_{WR}	0	–	0	–	0	–	0	–	ns
Output 3-state from write	t_{OTW}	–	40	–	60	–	80	–	100	ns
Data to write time overlap	t_{DW}	100	–	125	–	150	–	200	–	ns
Data hold from write time	t_{DH}	0	–	0	–	0	–	0	–	ns

Figure 9-4 (*continued*)

the former timing figure is normally considered to be the access time. The access time for commonly used SRAMs varies from 35 nanoseconds to 300 nanoseconds.

For a read operation, once the output data are valid, the address input may not be changed immediately to start another read operation. This is because the device needs a certain amount of time, called *read recovery time*, to complete its internal operations before the next memory operation. The sum of the access time and read recovery time is the memory read cycle time. This is the time needed between the start of a read operation and the start of the next memory cycle.

Sec. 9-1   MOS Memory Devices

The memory write cycle time can be similarly defined and may be different from the read cycle time. In addition to the address and chip enable inputs, an active-low write pulse on the $R/\overline{W}$ line and the data to be stored must be applied during the write cycle. The application of the write pulse has two critical timing requirements. First, the address and data must become valid no later than the specified time when the write pulse arrives and must remain stable during the entire write operation. Second, the width of the write pulse, called *write time*, must exceed the specified minimum value. The write cycle time is the sum of address setup time, write time, and write recovery time. Both the read and write recovery times may be zero for some SRAMs, but DRAMs require nonzero recovery times.

In addition to read and write cycles, there is a special memory cycle called read-modify-write, which is often mentioned in memory design literature. Consider the execution of a machine instruction whose destination operand is also one of the source operands (e.g., increment or decrement an operand in memory by 1). During the execution of such an instruction, the contents of a memory location are read out and processed by the CPU, and then the results are stored back into the same memory location. Obviously, this can be achieved using two separate memory reference cycles, a read cycle followed by a write cycle with the address unchanged. However, it is possible to reduce the total memory reference time, which is the sum of the read cycle and write cycle times, by combining them into a single read-modify-write cycle. Except for dynamic RAM, semiconductor memory has nondestructive readout (i.e., the contents of a memory location remain unchanged when it is read). Therefore, only the write recovery time following the read operation and the address setup time for the write operation will be saved. This is a relatively small time savings. Read-modify-write cycles will not be considered in the design examples given in the succeeding sections.

It is important to note that the access time and cycle time discussed in this section are the minimum timing requirements for the memory devices themselves. The access time and cycle time for the memory system as a whole are considerably longer because of the delays resulting from the system bus logic and memory interface logic.

DRAMs

There are several reasons why dynamic RAMs are attractive to memory designers, especially when the memory is large. Three of the main reasons follow:

1. *High density:* For static RAM, a typical cell requires six MOS transistors. The structure of a dynamic cell is much simpler and can be implemented with just one transistor and one capacitor. As a result, more memory cells can be put into a single chip, and the number of memory chips needed to implement a memory module is reduced. A common size for a dynamic RAM chip is 64K $\times$ 1; 1M $\times$ 1 devices are also available.
2. *Low power consumption:* The power consumption per bit of dynamic RAM is considerably lower than that of static RAM. The power dissipation is less than 0.005 milliwatts per bit for dynamic RAM and typically 0.09 milliwatts

per bit for static RAM. This feature reduces the system power requirements and lowers the cost. In addition, the power consumption of dynamic RAM is extremely low in standby mode; this makes it very attractive in the design of nonvolatile memory.

3. *Economy:* Dynamic RAM is less expensive per bit than static RAM. Nevertheless, dynamic RAM requires more supporting circuitry, and therefore there is little or no economic advantage when building a small memory system.

As with static RAMs, the memory on a dynamic memory chip is organized in a matrix formed by rows and columns of memory cells. The simplest type of dynamic RAM cell contains only one transistor and one capacitor, as shown in Fig. 9-5. Whether a 1 or 0 is contained in a cell is determined by whether or not there is a charge on the capacitor. During a read operation, one of the row select lines is brought high by decoding the row address (low-order address bits). The activated row select line turns on the switch transistor Q for all cells in the selected row. This causes the refresh amplifier associated with each column to sense the

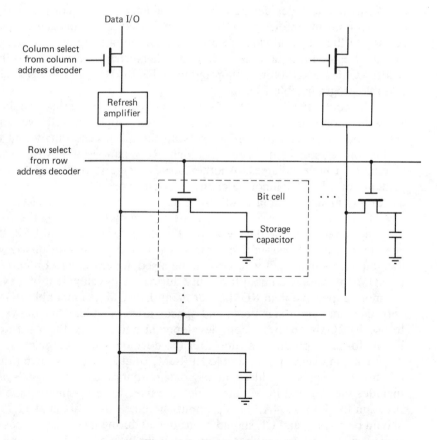

Figure 9-5 Dynamic RAM cell.

voltage level on the corresponding capacitor and interpret it as a 0 or a 1. The column address (high-order address bits) enables one cell in the selected row for the output. During this process, the capacitors in an entire row are disturbed. In order to retain the stored information, the same row of cells is rewritten by the refresh amplifiers. A write operation is done similarly, except that the data input is stored in the selected cell, whereas the other cells in the same row are simply refreshed.

Due to the storage discharge through pn-junction leakage current, dynamic memory cells must be periodically read and restored; this process is called *memory refresh*. The storage discharge rate increases as the operating temperature rises, and the necessary time interval between refreshes ranges from 1 millisecond to 100 milliseconds. When operating at 70°C, a typical refresh time interval is 2 milliseconds. Although in a read or write a row of cells is refreshed, the randomness of memory references cannot guarantee that every word in a memory module is refreshed within the 2-millisecond time limit. This requires extra logic for a memory module implemented with DRAMs to accomplish memory refreshes.

Read-only memory devices

Read-only memory devices permit only read accesses and consequently are used mainly for storing information that does not need to be changed frequently. According to the ways in which information can be initially entered (i.e., in which the ROM can be programmed), read-only memories are divided into three major types: ROM, EPROM (erasable programmable ROM), and E^2PROM (electrically erasable programmable ROM).

The contents of a ROM are permanently specified during its fabrication by a metallization interconnection mask. The user supplies a ROM vendor with the data to be stored and the vendor sets up the mask accordingly and makes the ROMs. Since setup charges are very high, ROMs are used only for systems manufactured in huge volumes. Another disadvantage is that once fabricated, the contents of a ROM cannot be changed. Therefore, if the stored information requires any modification later on, the existing ROMs become useless.

The contents of an EPROM can be altered by first erasing the contents and then reprogramming the device with a PROM programmer. An EPROM is packaged in a standard dual-in-line form, but it has a transparent quartz window so that an ultraviolet light source can be used to erase its contents. Although EPROMs provide maximum flexibility during the development of a system, they are more expensive than ROMs. For many EPROMs, compatible ROM versions with the same pin assignments and speeds are available. This allows a designer to use EPROMs during system development and replace them with compatible ROMs for large production runs after the development is completed.

The pin diagram of a sample EPROM, Intel 2764A, is shown in Fig. 9-6. In addition to the pins for address inputs, data outputs and enable signals, an EPROM includes the V_{PP} and $\overline{PGM}$ pins, which are used for programming the device. To program the Intel 2764A, the V_{PP} input should be maintained at 12.75 volts, $\overline{OE}$ should be 5 volts, and $\overline{CE}$ should be grounded during the entire process. The data to be written and their addresses are input through pins D7 to D0 and A12 to A0

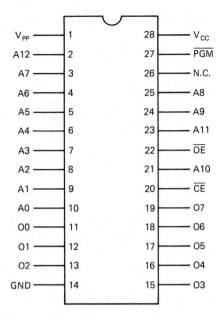

V_{PP} —	1	28	— V_{CC}
A12 —	2	27	— $\overline{PGM}$
A7 —	3	26	— N.C.
A6 —	4	25	— A8
A5 —	5	24	— A9
A4 —	6	23	— A11
A3 —	7	22	— $\overline{OE}$
A2 —	8	21	— A10
A1 —	9	20	— $\overline{CE}$
A0 —	10	19	— O7
O0 —	11	18	— O6
O1 —	12	17	— O5
O2 —	13	16	— O4
GND —	14	15	— O3

Figure 9-6 Pin diagram of Intel 2764 EPROM.

using TTL-level signals. At each address location to be programmed, several 1-millisecond, negative-going TTL program pulses must be applied to the $\overline{PGM}$ input pin.

Altering the contents of an EPROM requires erasing the device with ultraviolet light and reprogramming the entire device with a PROM programmer. Therefore, the device must be physically removed from the host system during a reprogramming operation, a major disadvantage associated with EPROMs.

An electrically erasable programmable ROM (E^2PROM) allows the user to change its contents by writing to the device without removing it from the host system. Furthermore, instead of erasing and then reprogramming the entire device, the E^2PROM erases and alters only the addressed byte during each write operation. To the user, writing to an E^2PROM is the same as writing to a RAM. Nevertheless, an E^2PROM has a very long write cycle time, and only a limited number of write operations can be performed reliably to the same location. A commonly seen figure for this limit is 10,000 write cycles.

An E^2PROM has write ($\overline{WE}$) and ready (RDY) pins to support the write operation. It also integrates data and address registers and necessary erasing and timing logic into the device to simplify its interface to the processor. Upon receiving a write pulse from the processor, the E^2PROM latches the data byte along with the address, thus releasing the bus while performing the write cycle. The device first erases the addressed byte and then writes the latched data into that location. For a typical E^2PROM such as the Intel 2817A, a write cycle may take 10 milliseconds to complete. During the erase and write operations, its RDY remains low to indicate a busy status. For a read reference, the E^2PROM is accessed in the same way as RAM or ROM. However, before a write access, the user must make certain that the E^2PROM is ready. This can be accomplished by polling the ready line via an interface register. Another approach is through interrupts by connecting the RDY pin to one of the interrupt request lines provided by the interrupt management logic.

Because E²PROMs have both the in-circuit programming capability and the nonvolatility advantage, they are ideal for many applications. One application is systems in which the stored data tables or messages require frequent updates. Examples in this area are point-of-sale terminals and electronic digital answering systems. Another application area is microprocessor-controlled instruments whose control options and operating modes can be reconfigured through keypads—for example, data acquisition and display instruments.

9-2 Memory Module Design*

In a microcomputer system, the actual size of the main memory may vary over a wide range, depending on the application. However, the maximum size of the memory is determined by the width of the address bus, which is 16M bytes for MC68000-based systems. To provide greater flexibility, the main memory of a typical system is organized in a modular form. Each memory module is constructed using many memory chips of the same type as basic building blocks to provide a storage segment of 2^M bytes. A memory module also includes its own bus interface logic so that it can be added or removed from the system without affecting other modules.

Each module is assigned to an address range, which is specified by its interface logic. During a memory reference, the address is sent to all memory modules, and only the one that contains that address is activated. Data are then read from or written into the selected memory module. Because each memory module has its own control and bus interface logic, it is easy to include different types of memory in the system. It is also possible to include, in a single system, memory modules of different speeds, thus allowing the cost/speed requirements to be optimized.

SRAM module design

A typical SRAM module can be divided into three functional units: the memory chip array, the control logic, and the bus interface. The block diagram in Fig. 9-7 illustrates the interrelationship among the three functional units.

The memory chip array consists of several identical RAM chips and provides the storage medium. The memory chips are organized in an array consisting of several rows and columns. To provide the desired word length, a row has more than one memory chip, each chip contributing part of the data word. The number of memory locations on each chip and the number of chips in a column determine the capacity of the module in words. The ratio of the memory word length to the number of cells contained in each location on a chip gives the number of chips in each row, and the ratio of the memory capacity in words to the number of locations on each chip gives the number of chips in each column. For instance,

* This section has been adapted from *Microcomputers for Engineers and Scientists, 2/E,* © 1987, Glenn A. Gibson/Yu-cheng Liu, by permission of Prentice-Hall, Inc., Englewood Cliffs, New Jersey.

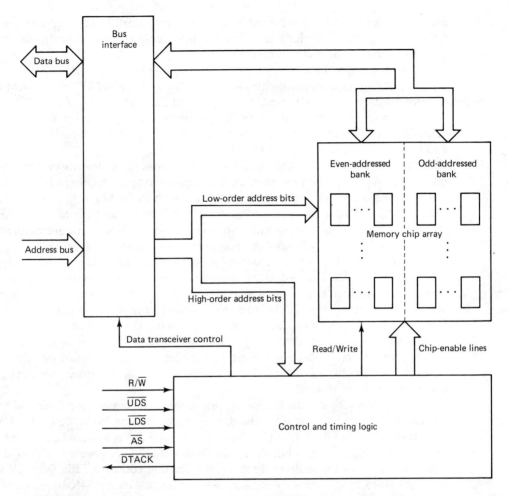

Figure 9-7 Organization of a SRAM memory module.

a 32K × 16 memory module requires a total of 32 4K × 4 RAMs. These chips are arranged in eight rows of four chips each. To provide the same memory capacity would require 128 4K × 1 RAMs, with 16 chips in each row.

A memory module is a bus slave that responds to commands initiated by the processor or a DMA module. The control logic receives a read or write command and then sends the appropriate chip enable and read/write signals to the memory chip array. The high-order address bits are fed to the control logic and are decoded to determine if the memory module is selected. If so, the row that contains that address is enabled, and all others remain disabled. To indicate to the processor that the read or write operation has been completed, a handshaking signal is normally applied to an acknowledge line in the system control bus.

The bus interface logic regulates the direction of data and address flow during memory references. Data are gated from the system bus and sent to the memory chip array during a memory write. For a memory read, data flow is in the opposite direction. The bus interface also receives the address from the bus, and routes the high-order bits of the received address to the control logic to enable a row, while sending the low-order bits to each memory chip to select a particular word from the chips in the enabled row.

As an example for memory module design, suppose that a 16K × 16 memory module is to be implemented with 4K × 4 SRAMs. A typical 4K × 4 SRAM has 12 address input (A11–A0) pins, 4 bidirectional data (D3–D0) pins, a read/write ($\overline{\text{WE}}$) pin, and a chip select ($\overline{\text{CS}}$) pin. To provide a storage capacity of 16K words of 16 bits each, the memory chip array consists of 16 chips organized in four rows and four columns, as shown in Fig. 9-8.

Because a 4K × 4 RAM has 12 bits for address input, the lower 12 address lines (A12–A1) from the bus interface are connected to each chip in the array. A row provides a storage segment of 4K words, with each chip in the row contributing 4 bits. In order to be compatible with MC68000's addressing conversion, the first two columns corresponding to the even-addressed bank are connected to the upper data bus, whereas the remaining two columns corresponding to the odd-addressed bank are connected to the lower data bus. Address bits A13 and A14 together with $\overline{\text{LDS}}$ and $\overline{\text{UDS}}$ are applied to the memory control logic to generate the proper chip enable signal(s). If this module has been assigned to starting memory address 0, the rows correspond to memory segments between locations 0 and 8191, 8192 and 16383, 16384 and 24575, and 24576 and 32767. When the module is selected, only one row is enabled, so that in each column all four corresponding data pins are tied together to contribute just one data bit. The read/write control is connected to every element in the array, which is generated by the control logic.

The control logic, which consists primarily of the decoding circuit and logic to generate the enable signal for the data transceivers and the write enable ($\overline{\text{WE}}$) signal, is shown in Fig. 9-9. Under the assumption that the system has 24 address bits, the most significant 8 bits determine which module is selected. Through the implementation of the address decoder, the starting address of the memory segment provided by the memory module can be assigned to any 64K-byte boundary in the 16M-byte addressing space. An asserted output from the address decoder indicates that the module has been selected and enables the chip enable logic. Address bits A13 and A14 are decoded to enable one row of memory chips in the odd bank, in the even bank, or in both according to the $\overline{\text{LDS}}$ and $\overline{\text{UDS}}$ signals. The module select signal also enables the received read/write signal to be passed to the $\overline{\text{WE}}$ pin of each memory chip. For slow memory it is desirable to generate an acknowledge signal indicating when data are ready during a read cycle or when data have been received during a write cycle. The control logic shown in Fig. 9-9 also provides this feature.

The design of the address and data bus interface is shown in Fig. 9-10. Since low-order address bits A12–A1 are fed to each of the 16 memory chips, they must be buffered to reduce bus loading. If the memory module is intended for a large system, other address bits and control signals such as $\overline{\text{LDS}}$ and $\overline{\text{UDS}}$ should also be buffered. The data bus interface is provided by two octal data transceivers. The $\overline{\text{LDS}}$ and $\overline{\text{UDS}}$ signals conditioned by the module select signal are used to enable the transceivers. The inverted R/W is applied to the direction control (DIR) pin of each transceiver device to specify the data flow direction. For a read, DIR

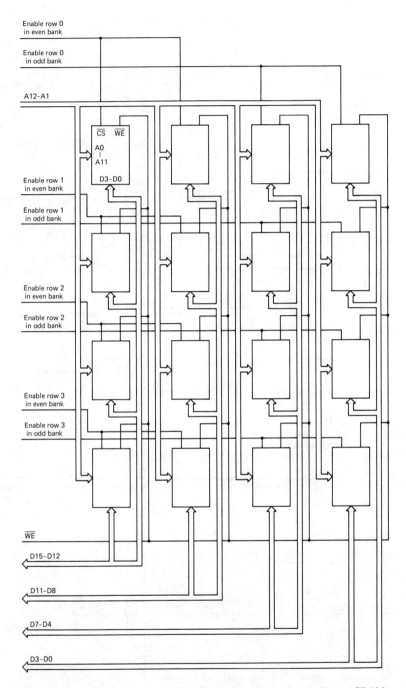

Enable row 0
in even bank

Enable row 0
in odd bank

A12–A1

CS   WE

A0
|
A11

D3–D0

Enable row 1
in even bank

Enable row 1
in odd bank

Enable row 2
in even bank

Enable row 2
in odd bank

Enable row 3
in even bank

Enable row 3
in odd bank

WE

D15–D12

D11–D8

D7–D4

D3–D0

Figure 9-8   16K × 16 memory chip array constructed from 16 4K × 4 SRAMs.

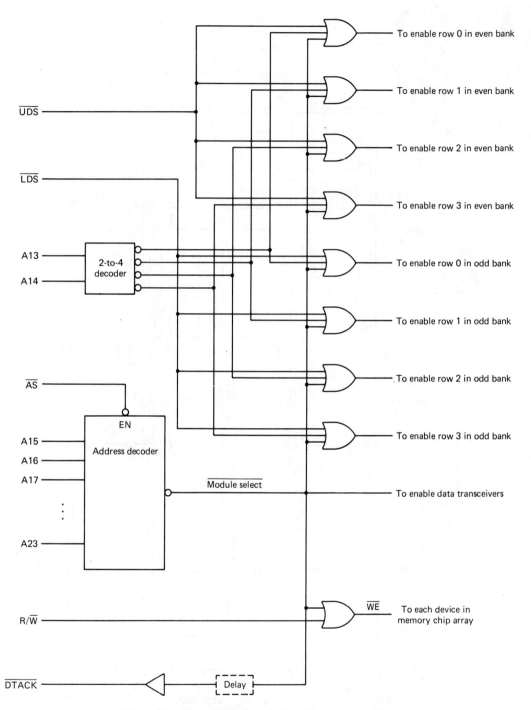

Figure 9-9 Control logic for a 16K × 16 memory module.

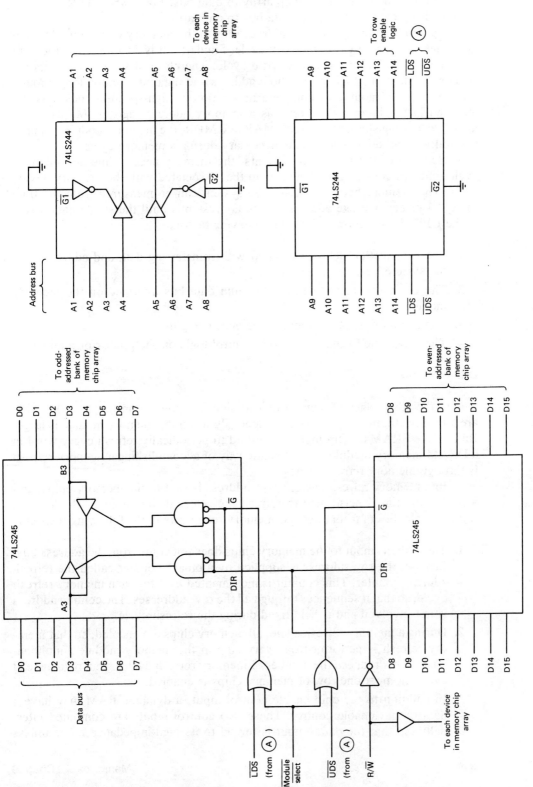

Figure 9-10 Memory interface logic.

is low, so that data flow from chip array to data bus. For a write, DIR becomes high, causing data to flow from data bus to chip array.

As pointed out before, the address sent to the memory chips must be held unchanged during an entire memory cycle. Similarly, it is desirable that the data input be stable during a memory write cycle. Therefore, if the CPU and its associated system bus logic do not hold address and data information long enough for the memory module to complete its operation, high-speed latches must be included in the interface to serve as a memory address register (MAR) and a memory data register (MDR). With MAR and MDR, the memory module can hold the address and data as long as is necessary during a memory cycle.

Because of the interfacing circuits, the memory access time and memory cycle time are considerably longer than that associated with the memory device itself. The memory access time for the system can be measured from the time the CPU places a stable address on the address bus until the stable data arrive at the CPU. It is determined by the following factors:

1. The propagation delay associated with transferring data and addresses on the system bus.
2. The delay due to the address bus and data bus interface on the memory module.
3. The access time of the memory devices being used.
4. The delay due to the system bus control logic on the processor module.

DRAM refresh

Due to the advantages of high-bit density and low-power consumption, DRAMs are attractive to memory designers, especially when the memory module is large. But, unlike SRAMs, extra logic is required to periodically refresh every word in a DRAM memory module. A systematic way of accomplishing a memory refresh is through memory refresh cycles.

In a memory refresh cycle, a row address is sent to the memory chips, and a read operation is performed to refresh the selected row of cells. However, a refresh cycle differs from a regular memory read cycle in the following respects:

1. The address input to the memory chips does not come from the address bus. Instead, the row address is supplied by a binary counter called the refresh address counter. This counter is incremented by 1 for each memory refresh cycle, so that it sequences through all the row addresses. The column address is not involved and is held fixed during the refresh cycle.
2. During a memory refresh cycle, all memory chips are enabled, so that memory refresh is performed on every chip in the memory module simultaneously. This reduces the number of memory refresh cycles. In a regular read cycle, at most one row of memory chips is enabled.
3. In addition to the chip enable control input, a dynamic RAM may have a data output enable control. These two control inputs are combined internally, so that the data output is forced to its high-impedance mode unless

both control inputs are activated. During a memory refresh cycle, the data output enable control is deactivated. This is necessary because all the chips in the same column are selected, and their data outputs are tied together. On the other hand, during a regular memory read cycle, only one row of chips is selected; consequently, the data output enable signal to each row is activated.

Consider a memory module of 16K words implemented by 4K × 1 DRAMs. The memory chip array consists of four rows and sixteen columns. Each chip has 64 rows and 64 columns of memory cells and thus requires 6 bits for the row address and 6 bits for the column address. The block diagram in Fig. 9-11 shows the logic needed to generate the memory refresh address, the chip enable, and

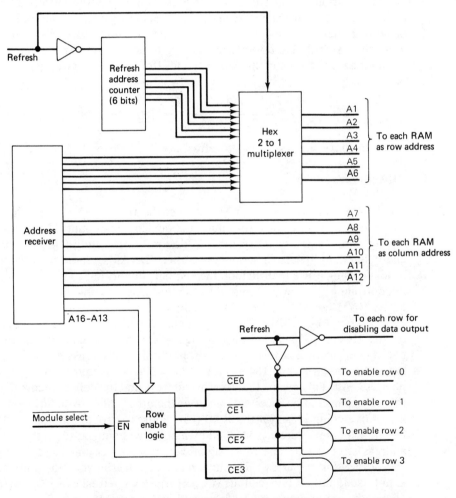

Figure 9-11 Block diagram of a memory refresh address generator. Glenn A. Gibson/Yu-cheng Liu, *Microcomputers for Engineers and Scientists, 2/E,* © 1987. Reprinted by permission of Prentice-Hall, Inc., Englewood Cliffs, New Jersey.

the data output enable signals during a memory refresh cycle. The memory refresh cycle signal, which indicates that a memory refresh is in progress, can be generated by a refresh cycle timing generator on the memory module, an external DMA device, or even the CPU. If the current cycle is a refresh cycle, the 2-to-1 multiplexer selects the row address from the refresh address counter. Otherwise, the row address comes from the address buffer. Assuming that every cell in the chip array must be refreshed within a 2-millisecond time interval, a refresh cycle is required for every $2 \times 10^{-3}/64 = 31.25$ microseconds. At the end of each refresh cycle (i.e., the 1-to-0 transition of the refresh signal), the binary counter is incremented by 1 so that it points to the next row to be refreshed. During a refresh cycle, all chips on the module are enabled for performing a read operation by activating the row enable signals, and the data output of each chip is disabled by deactivating the data output enable signal.

In addition to requiring a refresh logic, there is another disadvantage to using dynamic RAMs. During a refresh cycle, the memory module cannot initiate a read or write cycle until the refresh cycle has been completed. As a result, a read or write request will take up to twice as long to complete if a refresh is in progress. Assuming a cycle time of 400 nanoseconds (for all memory cycles—refresh, read, or write),

$$\frac{64 \times 400 \times 10^{-9}}{2 \times 10^{-3}} \times 100\% = 1.28\%$$

of the memory time is spent on refresh.

DRAM controllers

For high-density dynamic RAM devices, the row address and column address share the same set of pins to reduce the device's pin count. Using such DRAMs further complicates memory module design by including logic for sending row and column addresses in sequence to these DRAMs. Some manufacturers have produced single ICs that include the refresh support logic and other logic needed in controlling the row/column address pins. One example is the Intel's 8203 dynamic RAM controller, which is specifically designed to support Intel's 64K × 1 (2164) and 16K × 1 (2117, 2118) dynamic RAM devices. The block diagrams for the 2164 and 8203 are shown in Fig. 9-12. (The 8203 can operate in one of the two modes according to its 16K/64K pin; only the pin assignments for the 64K mode are shown.) The 2164 has four 128 × 128 cell arrays but only eight address pins, A7–A0. This means that the row address and the column address must share the same pins and be received one after the other. The row address is strobed by a negative-going pulse on the $\overline{\text{RAS}}$ (row address strobe) pin and, with $\overline{\text{RAS}}$ still low, the column address is strobed by a negative-going pulse on the $\overline{\text{CAS}}$ (column address strobe) pin. The most significant row and column address bits specify one of the four cell arrays. During a memory refresh cycle, the address input A7 is not used, and all four cell arrays perform their refreshes simultaneously. This allows the entire device to be refreshed in 128 cycles.

The timing diagrams for the read, write, and refresh-only cycles are shown in Fig. 9-13. For a read cycle, $\overline{\text{WE}}$ must be inactive before the $\overline{\text{CAS}}$ pulse is

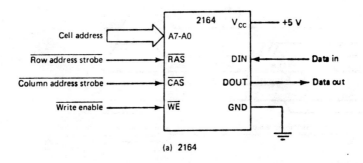

(a) 2164

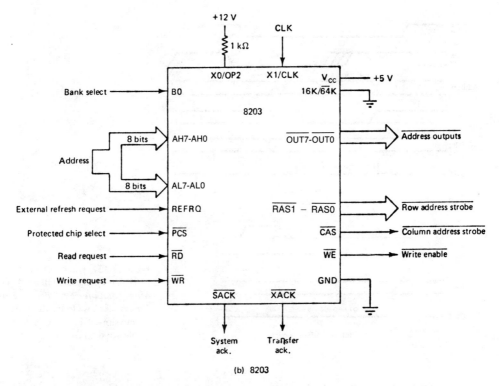

(b) 8203

Figure 9-12 Pin assignments for the 2164 dynamic RAM and its associated 8203 controller. Yu-cheng Liu/Glenn A. Gibson, *Microcomputer Systems: The 8086/ 8088 Family, 2/E,* © 1986. Reprinted by permission of Prentice-Hall, Inc., Englewood Cliffs, New Jersey.

applied and remain inactive until the $\overline{\text{CAS}}$ pulse is over. After the column address is strobed, $\overline{\text{RAS}}$ is raised, and with $\overline{\text{RAS}}$ high and $\overline{\text{CAS}}$ low, the data bit is made available on DOUT. For a write cycle the DIN signal should be applied by the time $\overline{\text{CAS}}$ goes low but after the $\overline{\text{WE}}$ goes low. The write is performed through the DIN pin while $\overline{\text{RAS}}$, $\overline{\text{CAS}}$, and $\overline{\text{WE}}$ are all low. The DOUT pin is held at its high-impedance state throughout the write cycle. For the refresh-only cycle, only the row address is strobed, and the $\overline{\text{CAS}}$ pin is held inactive. The DOUT pin is kept in its high-impedance state.

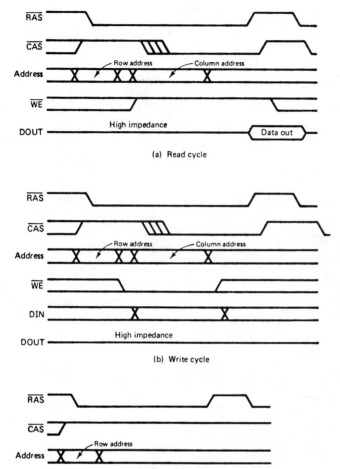

(a) Read cycle

(b) Write cycle

(c) Refresh-only cycle

Figure 9-13 Timing diagrams for the 2164. Yu-cheng Liu/Glenn A. Gibson, *Microcomputer Systems: The 8086/8088 Family, 2/E,* © 1986. Reprinted by permission of Prentice-Hall, Inc., Englewood Cliffs, New Jersey.

The 8203 is designed to output signals whose timing meets the 2164 requirements. The $\overline{OUT7}$–$\overline{OUT0}$ pins provide the properly sequenced row and column addresses, $\overline{RAS1}$–$\overline{RAS0}$ provide the row address strobed for up to two banks of 2164s, and $\overline{CAS}$ and $\overline{WE}$ supply the column address strobe and write enable signals for all the 2164s in the modules. (Note that the addresses output by the 8023 are inverted. This does not cause a problem, but it does mean that all 0s on the address lines will access the cells having row and column address that are all 1s.)

The bank select input B0 determines the $\overline{RAS}$ pin to be activated. Pins AL7–AL0 are used to generate the row address and AH7–AH0 are used for the column address. Normally, the refresh cycle timing is generated inside the 8203, but the REFRQ pin allows the refresh cycles to be initiated by an external source. The module selection is made through the $\overline{PCS}$ pin. It is called the protected chip select pin because once it becomes active, the memory cycle cannot be aborted, even if it immediately returns to its inactive state. The $\overline{RD}$ and $\overline{WR}$ inputs specify whether a memory read or write is to be conducted.

The $\overline{XACK}$ output is a strobe indicating that data are available during a read cycle or that the data have been written during a write cycle. It can be used to strobe data into output latches and to send the ready signal to the processor. The $\overline{SACK}$ output signals the beginning of a memory access cycle; if a refresh cycle is taking place when a memory request is made, the $\overline{SACK}$ signal is delayed until the read or write cycle begins. If the memory device access time is known to be sufficiently low to guarantee that a read or write will be completed in the S4/S5 cycle of the current bus cycle, the $\overline{SACK}$ output may be used as the ready signal instead of the $\overline{XACK}$ output, thus saving wait states that might occur if $\overline{XACK}$ is used.

Either an oscillator must be connected across X0 and X1 or, if OP2 is connected to +12 volts, an external clock signal must be applied to CLK. This signal may come from a bus clock line or a clock in the memory module. Only +5 volts are needed for the mainpower supply, but if the OP2 input is used, a +12-volt supply is required. (REFRQ is actually a dual-purpose pin that can be used for advanced reads, but this feature as well as the read-modify-write cycle will not be considered here).

Figure 9-14 illustrates how an 8203 and thirty-two 2164s could be used to construct a 256K-byte memory module. The memory device array has 16 columns, so that words can be accessed as well as bytes. This requires that the $\overline{LDS}$ and $\overline{UDS}$ bus lines be used in conjunction with the $\overline{WE}$ signal to determine whether only the low-order byte, only the high-order byte, or an entire word is being written.

Another way of reducing the number of chips needed in the support circuitry for dynamic RAM is to put a set of refresh logic on each memory device, thus permitting the device to refresh itself. Such a device is called an integrated RAM or a pseudostatic RAM, and except for memory accesses sometimes being held up by refresh cycles, the device appears to the user to be a static RAM. An example of this approach is the Intel 2186/7, which is an 8K × 8 integrated RAM. The 2186/7 has pin assignments that are essentially the same as for static RAM devices. In particular, it has $\overline{OE}$, $\overline{WE}$, and $\overline{CE}$ pins, which serve the same purposes.

ROM modules

A ROM module is much simpler to implement than a RAM module of the same storage size because ROM devices are characterized by large data widths, typically 4 or 8 bits. This feature reduces the number of devices required in a memory module and optimizes the board design. For example, a 16K × 16 EPROM module required only four 2764s and, as shown in Fig. 9-15, the interconnections are simplified by the absence of write circuitry. The 8-bit tristate data outputs of the two chips in each column are directly tied together in pairs, and only one row is enabled at a time by the chip select control input.

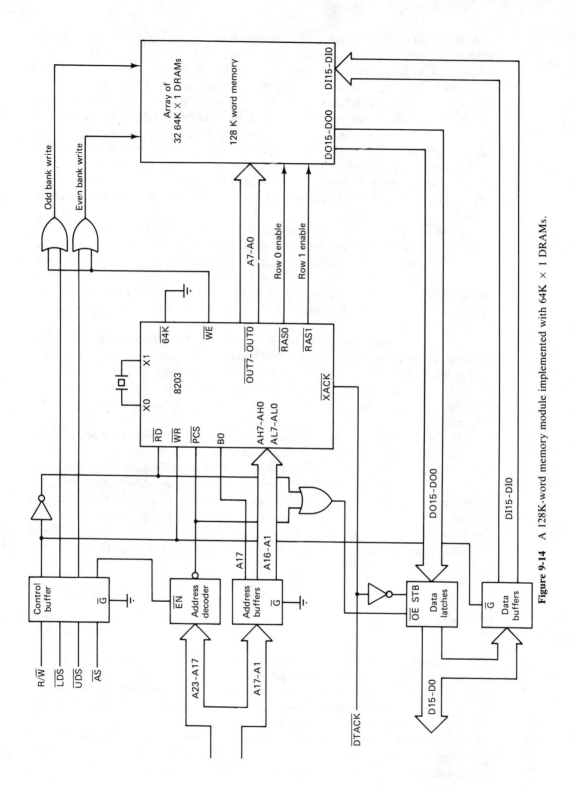

Figure 9-14 A 128K-word memory module implemented with 64K × 1 DRAMs.

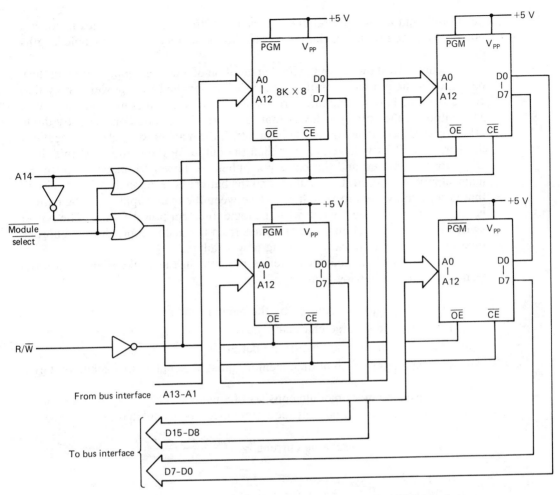

Figure 9-15 Interconnection of four 8K × 8 EPROMs to provide 32K bytes of storage.

Battery backup

One major disadvantage of using MOS RAMs to construct main memory is that the stored information may be lost as a result of even very short power failures. The solution is to provide a backup power supply to support the system if the main supply fails. Because of the cost, normally only part of the memory system is protected from power failure. During a power failure, the status and vital data within the program being executed can be stored in the nonvolatile memory modules; then by restoring this information, the program can continue after the main power is restored.

Some MOS RAMs consume much less power while they are just maintaining information than when they are performing read/write operations. To reduce the drain on the backup power supply during a power failure, the memory module can be forced into a standby mode in which all memory chips are disabled and the stored data are simply retained. Because of this feature, batteries become a practical way to provide backup power for MOS memory over reasonable lengths of time.

Figure 9-16 shows a simple implementation of a power supply with a battery backup. During normal operation, the power is supplied by a power supply that converts an ac line voltage into a regulated dc voltage that is maintained at V_{cc}. The output of the battery is lower than the normal V_{cc}, and consequently diode D1 is forward-biased and diode D2 is cut off. If the main power fails, the capacitor discharges until its voltage is lower than the output of the battery. At this time, D2 is forward-biased and the battery supplies the power to memory. Once the main supply is restored, D2 is cut off and the battery is recharged. A better circuit that is commonly used to switch power between the main supply and the battery is one that uses a power switch with the logic to detect power failure. The power switch is designed such that power comes from the main supply during a normal operation and from the battery during power failure.

The type and number of batteries required in the backup supply are determined by the following factors:

1. The supply current required by the memory modules
2. The battery discharge characteristics
3. The size, weight, and cost of the batteries
4. The maximum length of time memory must be supplied by backup batteries

Because a memory module consists of a memory chip array and supporting logic, the total discharge current requirement can be calculated by

$$\text{Discharge current} = \frac{N_m \times P_m + P_s}{V}$$

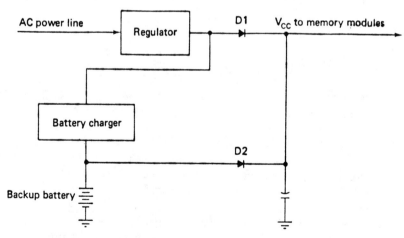

Figure 9-16 Battery backup for a memory power supply. Glenn A. Gibson/Yu-cheng Liu, *Microcomputers for Engineers and Scientists, 2/E,* © 1987. Reprinted by permission of Prentice-Hall, Inc., Englewood Cliffs, New Jersey.

where

N_m = number of memory chips
P_m = power dissipated by each memory chip
P_s = total power dissipated by the supporting logic
V = supply voltage

The required supply current is significantly less if the memory is forced into standby mode during a power failure. Another way to reduce standby power is by using low-power-dissipation CMOS devices for the memory interface and control logic.

The capacity of a battery is rated in terms of ampere-hours at specific discharge currents. However, the ampere-hour rating tends to decrease as the discharge current rating increases. The maximum protection time that can be provided by a backup power source is the ratio of the ampere-hour rating to the discharge current, provided that the discharge current is less than or equal to its rating. For example, assume that a battery has a capacity of 3.2 ampere-hours at a 1-ampere discharge current and that a memory module draws 0.8 ampere. Then the battery can supply the power to the memory module for up to 4 hours. Three such batteries in parallel will be able to provide protection for at least 12 hours.

A desirable feature for a backup battery is a nearly constant output voltage during discharge. Batteries that satisfy this criterion are commercially available in both the rechargeable and nonrechargeable types. Examples of the nonrechargeable type are mercury and silver-oxide batteries, which offer large capacity but small size. Nickel-cadmium and lead-calcium batteries are widely used rechargeable batteries. Although they are considerably larger and heavier than most batteries, the fact that they can be recharged whenever main power is restored is advantageous in some applications.

9-3 Disk Storage

In addition to main memory, a microcomputer has a mass storage or auxiliary storage subsystem. While main memory keeps the currently running program, a mass storage device provides permanent storage for large quantities of programs and data sets organized as files. Unlike the main memory, whose response time is fast and independent of the address being referenced, a mass storage device is much slower because it involves mechanical parts. It is also nonrandom accessible, meaning that data within a data block are accessed sequentially. For this reason, the processor can not directly read or write a particular word in a mass storage device. Instead, an entire data block must be transferred to main memory to be accessed and then the modified data block is stored back to the mass storage device.

Fixed disk

Fixed disks are widely used as mass storage devices in microcomputer systems, which vary in a wide range of capacities and access times. A fixed-disk drive is a sealed package including one or more disks made from aluminum. Each side of a disk is coated with a magnetic substance for storing data. Each disk surface has a read/write head, which keeps a small gap above the disk even during read/write operations. For this reason, a disk platter cannot be removed from the drive and hence is called a fixed disk. It is also known as a hard disk, as opposed to a floppy disk made from flexible Mylar, which is used for a diskette drive.

Figure 9-17 illustrates the structure of a pack of fixed disks. A disk surface is divided into concentric circles called *tracks*. The group of tracks corresponding to the same location on all disk surfaces is called a *cylinder*. A track is further divided into several *sectors*. Data are stored as a string of successive bits in a sector. Between two sectors, there is a gap that marks the beginning of the sector by storing information such as synchronization characters, sector identification, and number of data bytes in the sector. Although the number of tracks per disk is fixed, the number of sectors per track—that is, the size of a sector—can be changed by formatting the disk, a process of writing the identification information to mark the beginning of a sector and a track. Data are read from or written to a disk sector by sector. A typical sector size is 512 bytes.

The disk constantly spins at a high speed, typically 3600 revolutions per minute. To read or write a sector, the drive first advances or retreats the read/write head and positions it on the addressed track. It then waits until the addressed sector is passing the read/write head to begin data transfer. Therefore, the response time is the sum of the access time for positioning the read/write head on the addressed track and the latency time for rotating the sector under the read/write head. A typical average access time is in tens of milliseconds. The average latency time is one-half the revolution time, and it amounts to 8.33 milliseconds at the rotation speed of 3600 revolutions per minute.

The data transfer rate depends on the capacity of the track. For a disk having

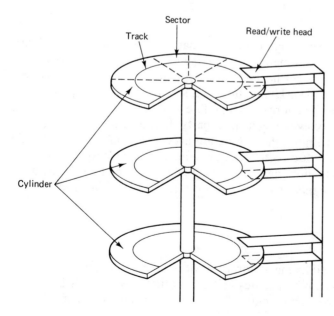

Figure 9-17 Fixed disk drive.

8192 bytes per track, the data rate is approximately

$$\frac{8192 \times 3600}{60} = 491520 \text{ bytes/second}$$

which is equivalent to the transfer time of approximately 0.25 microseconds per bit. Taking into account the gaps, the actual transfer rate becomes approximately 624960 bytes per second, or the equivalent transfer time of 0.2 microseconds per bit.

Disk controller

The interface and control of the disk drive require a disk controller. It can accept commands from the processor to generate disk drive control signals, convert received parallel data from processor to serial MFM-encoded data to be written to the drive, and vice versa, generate CRC (cyclic redundancy check) bytes in writing data to the drive, and check CRC bytes for burst errors in reading data from the drive. Figure 9-18 is a block diagram showing the overall organization of the disk interface and the major signals between a disk controller and a disk drive.

Data sent between the controller and the disk drive are encoded according to the MFM (modified FM) rules, with a data bit being preceded with a clock pulse. In reading data from the disk drive, external logic is required to separate data bits from clock pulses. This is implemented by a phase-locked-loop (PLL) circuit, which constantly tracks the frequency of the incoming signal and locks an oscillator to that frequency. In writing data to the disk drive, the disk controller outputs MFM data along with compensation and synchronization signals. The external write logic adds the delay to the MFM data that is needed to compensate the difference between an inner and an outer track.

In addition to the read data and write data, the disk drive accepts several control inputs from and sends several status outputs to the disk controller. Typical control signals are as follows:

Drive selects: Selects the drive to be accessed.
Direction: Specifies the advance direction of the read/write head, inward or outward.
Step: Advances the read/write head to another track.

Typical status bits from the disk drive include:

Write fault: Indicates an error at the disk drive.
Track 0: Indicates the read/write head is on track 0 (outermost track). This information is required to identify the position of the read/write head.
Index: Indicates the beginning of a track.
Ready: Indicates that the drive is ready.
Seek complete: Indicates that the read/write head has settled and that a read or write can be made.

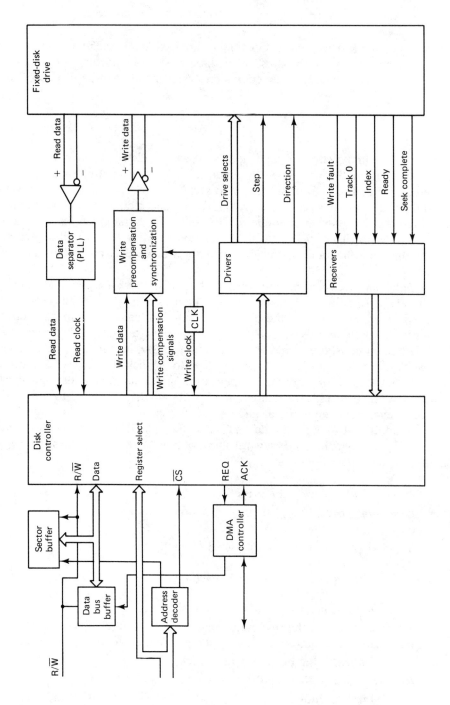

Figure 9-18 Disk drive interface.

Since the data transfer rate is very high, it is not possible to send data byte by byte between the processor and the controller in reading or writing the drive. In a simple configuration, data can be transferred through a DMA controller. To improve the performance, the interface may include a sector buffer, as shown in Fig. 9-18, which allows a sector of data to be stored temporarily before being written to the drive, or vice versa. Further enhancement can be achieved with a look-ahead cache memory. By reading the next sector ahead, access time can be eliminated in accessing the sectors in a sequential fashion. Same savings can be achieved in writing several sequential sectors.

Another method for improving disk performance is by sector interleaving, which assigns logical sectors in nonsequential order. For example, to provide a two-way interleaving, a 32-sector track could be formatted as logical sectors in the sequence: 0, 16, 1, 17, 2, 18, 3, 19, 4, 20, 5, 21, 6, 22, 7, 23, 8, 24, 9, 25, 10, 26, 11, 27, 12, 28, 13, 29, 14, 30, 15, 31. Interleaving provides a delay between logically sequential sectors, which allows the user to process the current sector and then decide if the next sector should be read. For applications where several sectors need to be accessed in sequence, this reduces the chance that the next sector passes over the read/write head, thus causing a one-revolution delay.

Disk accessing

The disk drive is accessed by programming the controller. Typical controller commands includes the following:

Read sector: This command reads one or more sectors of data from the disk. If the read/write head is not positioned in the track where the addressed sector is located, this command automatically performs a seek first.

Write sector: This command writes one or more sectors of data to the disk. Similar to read sector, an implied seek may be initiated by the command.

Restore: This command moves the read/write head to track 0. It is typically used to initialize the drive.

Seek: This command positions the read/write head over the specified track. It is used to overlap seek operations with multiple drives in order to reduce access times. However, a read sector or write sector command does not have to be preceded by a seek command.

Format: This command writes the formatting information to a track. It is used to format a disk.

Each controller command may require several I/O instructions to complete. This is because a command may have several parameters to be sent to the controller, and its status register needs to be read to determine if the command is completed. Moreover, to transfer data to or from a disk, the physical track numbers, where data are stored or are to be written, are required. Since a disk keeps a large number of files, a file management system is required as part of the operating system to manage the disk space to maintain a directory and to find out where a given file is stored. To assist a user in accessing the disk, this software system provides several system routines. Among other things, these routines can be called to perform the following functions:

Open a file: Searches the disk directory for the named file so that the system knows where the file is located on the disk. If the named file is a new file, an entry is created in the directory and disk space is allocated.

Read data from a file: Reads a specified number of bytes from a sector in a file that has already been opened and transfers the data to user-specified memory area. As one of the parameters, the user specifies the sector number to be read relative to the beginning of the file. The file management software translates this logical sector number into physical sector address.

Write data into a file: Writes a specified number of bytes from user area into a given logical sector in a file that has already been opened.

Close a file: Updates the identification information of the file in the directory such as file length and data of access.

Delete a file: Removes a file from the directory.

EXERCISES

1. Summarize the advantages and disadvantages of DRAMs as opposed to SRAMs.
2. For a 64K-byte memory in an MC68000-based system, determine the configuration of the chip array in terms of the numbers of memory chips in each row, in each column, and in the entire module using $16K \times 1$ RAMs. Repeat for $8K \times 4$ RAMs.
3. A typical $1K \times 4$ static RAM is shown in the following figure. Assuming 16-bit data bus, design a 4K-byte memory chip array using this device.

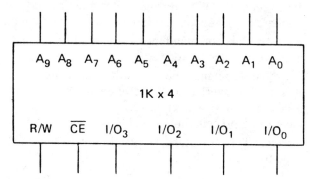

Glenn A. Gibson/Yu-cheng Liu, *Microcomputers for Engineers and Scientists, 2/E,* © 1987. Reprinted by permission of Prentice-Hall, Inc., Englewood Cliffs, New Jersey.

4. Assume that the 64K chip array designed in Exercise 2 is assigned to the memory segment 256K to 310K. Construct the address decoding and row enabling logic (using $16K \times 1$ RAMs).
5. Suppose that only $8K \times 8$ RAM devices are available. How many such devices are required to implement an 8K-byte memory module for an 8-bit, for a 16-bit, and for a 32-bit microprocessor?

6. Assume that a 32K-byte memory module is assigned to the memory segment from 128K to 160K. Determine the inputs A12 through A1 and all chip enable signals to the memory chip array shown in Fig. 9-8 for each of the following addresses received by the module in memory word references.
   (a) $018A04
   (b) $02600A
   (c) $021EEE
   (d) $022000
   (e) $03EEA0
7. Construct the necessary control logic for the 32K-byte EPROM module in Fig. 9-15. Assume that this module occupies the memory segment from 128K to 160K.
8. Why is it not necessary to include $\overline{\text{LDS}}$ and $\overline{\text{UDS}}$ signals in the EPROM enabling logic shown in Fig. 9-15?

10

The MC68010, MC68020, MC68030, and MC68040

To upgrade a popular microprocessor, its manufacturer normally makes improvements on the existing architecture and adds new features instead of adopting an entirely different architecture. With this approach, the manufacturer can develop and maintain a family of upwardly compatible microprocessors. The newly developed microprocessor supports the same basic instruction set and the programming model in the user mode of the previous family members. A user's object code written for an early member in the family can be executed on the new microprocessor without changes. Therefore, the new family member can maintain user code compatibility with the earlier members while providing higher speed and better performance. Figure 10-1 summarizes the new improvements made on each member in the M68000 microprocessor family.

One major design goal for a new microprocessor is to increase its speed. This can be accomplished to a certain degree by using improved device technology so that the processor can operate at a higher clock rate. However, as the existing device characteristics approach their physical limits, architectural enhancements become necessary to improve the performance further. For the M68000 microprocessor family, such performance-oriented enhancements made on later members include the following:

1. Extending the data bus from 16 bits to 32 bits: This increases the bus transfer rate, thus reducing the time in fetching instructions and accessing longword memory operands.

2. Using pipelined internal structure: This provides parallel processing capability inside the processor and therefore reduces the average instruction execution time.

330

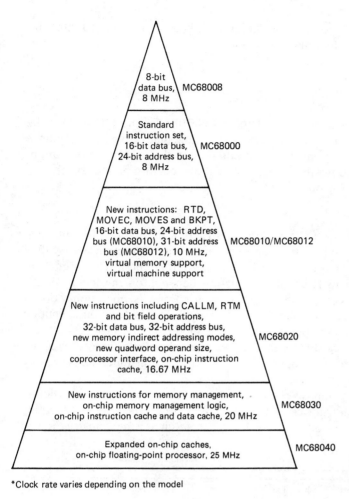

Inside the pyramid, from top to bottom:

8-bit data bus, 8 MHz — MC68008

Standard instruction set, 16-bit data bus, 24-bit address bus, 8 MHz — MC68000

New instructions: RTD, MOVEC, MOVES and BKPT, 16-bit data bus, 24-bit address bus (MC68010), 31-bit address bus (MC68012), 10 MHz, virtual memory support, virtual machine support — MC68010/MC68012

New instructions including CALLM, RTM and bit field operations, 32-bit data bus, 32-bit address bus, new memory indirect addressing modes, new quadword operand size, coprocessor interface, on-chip instruction cache, 16.67 MHz — MC68020

New instructions for memory management, on-chip memory management logic, on-chip instruction cache and data cache, 20 MHz — MC68030

Expanded on-chip caches, on-chip floating-point processor, 25 MHz — MC68040

*Clock rate varies depending on the model

Figure 10-1 Enhanced features of the M68000 family.

3. Including an on-chip cache: By keeping portions of recently used code and data in the processor, a cache memory can reduce average instruction fetch and memory access time.

In addition to speed improvements, some new features have been added to advanced models in the M68000 family to facilitate the implementation of multiprogramming and multiprocessing systems. They include 32-bit address bus, virtual memory support, coprocessor interface, and new instructions. This chapter will examine these enhancements. An introduction to cache memory and virtual memory is given in Chap. 12.

Although their concepts are not new, many of the enhancements, such as 32-bit data and address buses, cache memory, virtual memory management, and pipelined internal structure, were found only in main frames and super minis just a few years ago. This is because a large amount of logic is required to implement such features. As the VLSI technology advanced, more and more circuits could be placed on a single-chip device, and therefore it became possible to integrate these advanced features into a microprocessor.

10-1 MC68010 Enhancements

The major architectural enhancement of the MC68010 over the MC68000 is the capability to support virtual memory and virtual machine. Some performance improvements have also been made. Most notable are the loop mode operation, two new instructions, and flexible allocation of the exception pointer block.

Loop mode operation

The process for a processor to execute an instruction can be divided into two phases, instruction fetch and instruction execution. The instruction is first read from memory using the address stored in the program counter. The number of memory cycles required to fetch the instruction depends on the length of the instruction. Once the processor receives the instruction, its operation word is decoded, and then the specified operation is performed. This instruction-execution time varies depending on the operand addressing mode and the instruction type. For example, moving a register to another register takes little time to execute, whereas multiplying a memory operand into a register consumes considerably more time.

An effective way to improve speed performance is to overlap instruction fetch and execution, as illustrated in Fig. 10-2. While the processor is executing the current instruction, its bus control logic can fetch the next instruction in

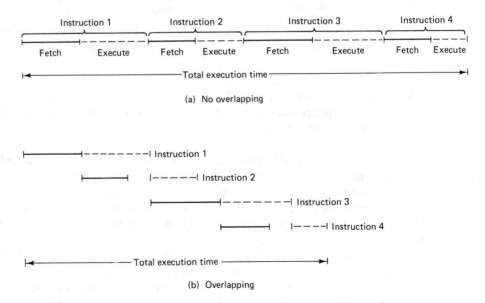

Figure 10-2 Performance improvement by overlapping instruction fetch and execution.

sequence and place it in an instruction queue at the same time. Upon the completion of the current instruction, the next instruction is already in the processor ready to be executed unless the current instruction is jump related. In the case of a jump instruction, the already prefetched instruction is discarded and the next instruction fetch begins after the jump is executed. But instructions are executed in sequence most of the time, and the sequential pattern is broken only when a control instruction is executed. Because of this characteristic, overlapping of instruction fetch and execution can result in significant speed improvement.

The MC68000 has a two-word instruction queue, which can hold two instruction words while decoding the current operation word. Therefore, up to two one-word instructions can be prefetched. The MC68010 further improves this prefetch mechanism to include the loop mode operation. To explain the loop mode, let us consider the following instruction sequence as an example:

```
        LEA        SOURCE, A0
        LEA        DEST,A1
        MOVE.W     #99,D0
AGAIN   MOVE.W     (A0) + ,(A1) +
        DBF        D0,AGAIN
```

When this is executed by the MC68000, it refetches the MOVE.W and DBF instructions for each loop iteration because DBF is a branch instruction. Actually both instructions can be kept in the queue until looping is completed. The MC68010 has the ability to detect such a tight three-word loop and eliminate unnecessary memory cycles for fetching the same two instructions repeatedly. Whenever a DBcc instruction is encountered, the MC68010 checks if the offset is -4 or not—that is, whether or not the loop is composed of three words—and if the target instruction is loopable or not. If both conditions are satisfied, the MC68010 enters the loop mode, in which it simply repeats the two instructions until the exit condition is met. Note that if the target instruction has more than one word, for example,

```
    MOVE.W      CONST,(A2) +
```

it cannot be executed in the loop mode. This is because the MC68010 instruction queue is not large enough to hold both a DBcc and this 2- or 3-word MOVE.W instructions.

Enhancements on exception processing

In the user mode, the MC68010 has the same programming model as the MC68000. However, in the supervisor mode, the MC68010 has three additional registers: vector base register (VBR), source function code register (SFC), and destination function code register (DFC). Both SFC and DFC are 3-bit alternate function code registers that specify the function code outputs (FC2–FC0) in accessing source and destination, respectively. The two registers are used by programs running in the supervisor mode to access addresses in the user data and program spaces when control of memory access is enforced by external memory management logic.

The vector base register is used to determine the location of the exception pointer table in memory. Unlike the MC68000, in which all exception vectors must be in the range from 0–4095, the MC68010 may allocate any memory block for an exception pointer table. The VBR provides the beginning address of the current exception pointer block. During an exception, the vector base address plus 4 times the associated vector number, either generated internally or supplied externally, is used as the vector address. This feature allows an MC68010-based system to have several exception pointer tables.

Another change in exception handling is that during an exception, the MC68010 saves either 4 words in the short format or 29 words in the long format. Figure 10-3 shows the information saved in each format. The short format corresponds to the one used by the MC68000 and is for typical exceptions. The long format is used in an address or bus error exception. In the long format, not only the return address and status register but also the processor's internal data latches and bus buffer registers are saved. This improvement allows the MC68010 to

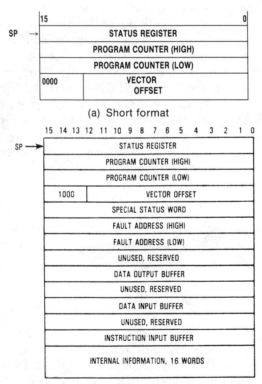

NOTE: The stack pointer is decremented by 29 words, although only 26 words of information are actually written to memory. The three additional words are reserved for future use by Motorola.

(b) Long format

Figure 10-3 Exception stack frames of the MC68010. (Part (b) Courtesy of Motorola, Inc.)

continue the instruction, which causes the error, thus providing the capability to implement virtual memory. The format type is indicated by the most significant 4 bits in the fourth word of an exception stack frame, 0000 for short format and 1000 for long format. When the return from exception (RTE) instruction is executed, the format field is checked in order to determine the number of words in the stack to be restored. This maintains software compatibility with the MC68000. In a case that the format is neither 0000 nor 1000, the MC68010 initiates a format error exception using vector number 14.

New instructions

The MC68010 has four more instructions than the MC68000. Figure 10-4 summarizes these new instructions. The RTD (return and deallocate parameters) instruction is used to return from a subroutine when parameters are passed through the stack. For several reasons, as discussed in Sec. 5-2, it is desirable to use the stack for passing parameters to a subroutine. The MC68000 uses the RTS instruction to return to the calling routine. In this case, after returning from the called subroutine, the calling routine must deallocate the stack space occupied by the parameters with the instruction

     ADDA.L   #LENGTH,SP

The RTD instruction combines the RTS instruction and the stack deallocation operation into a single instruction. The instruction has an immediate operand, which should be the number of bytes used in passing the parameters. After the return address is restored from the stack, this number is added into SP to release the stack space occupied by the parameters.

The MOVEC (move control register) instruction, which is a privileged instruction, moves the content of the specified control register to or from a data or address register. This instruction is necessary to program the new control registers, SFC, DFC, and VBR. The MOVES (move address space) is also a privileged instruction. This instruction moves the source operand from a general register to a location within the address space specified by the DFC register. It can

Mnemonic	Size or Postfix	Operand Format	Allowable EA Modes	Operation	Condition Flags N Z V C X
RTD (Return and deallocate parameters)	Unsized	#I16		(SP) -> PC; SP + 4 + I16 -> SP	- - - - -
MOVEC (Move control register privileged)	Longword	Rc,Rn Rn,Rc		Rc -> Rn Rn -> Rc	- - - - -
MOVES (Move address space privileged)	.B, .W, .L	Rn,EA EA,Rn	Alterable Memory	Rn -> DST[DFC] SRC[SFC] -> Rn	- - - - -
BKPT (Break point)	Unsized	#I3		Execute break point acknowledge bus cycle; Trap as illegal instruction.	- - - - -

Figure 10-4 New MC68010 instructions.

also move the source operand from a location within the address space specified by the SFC register to a general register. As mentioned before, with an external memory management unit, memory protection can be implemented using the function code output associated with each address. For such a system, the MOVES instruction allows the MC68010 to access user's space in the supervisor mode. In addition to the two new privileged instruction, the previously present instruction, MOVE from SR, has been changed to be a privileged instruction. This is necessary to provide virtual machine support.

The last new instruction is the BKPT (breakpoint) instruction. This instruction causes a trap using vector number 4 and is designed to implement software breakpoints. The instruction has an immediate operand, which can be a value from 0 to 7, thus allowing up to 8 breakpoints to be encoded.

Virtual memory support

Both the MC68010 and MC68000 use a 24-bit address bus, which limits maximum memory size as well as maximum program size to 16M bytes. But the MC68010 provides the necessary support to implement virtual memory using external memory management logic. With virtual memory, the system appears to the user to have 16M bytes regardless of the amount of physical memory actually provided by the system. Thus, the system can run programs whose sizes are larger than the available amount of memory. The MC68012, which is an improved version of the MC68010, extends the address bus from 24 bits to 31 bits, and therefore provides a virtual memory space of 2 gigabytes.

The MC68010 virtual memory support is provided by its capability of suspending an instruction execution during an address error and then resuming the faulted instruction later on. Using an external memory management unit, a bus error exception can be initiated whenever a logical address is not currently mapped to physical memory. As mentioned earlier, during a bus error exception, the MC68010 stores its entire machine state on the supervisor stack. It then loads the PC using exception vector 8 and starts to execute the bus error exception handler in which the page fault can be fixed. Upon completion of the bus error exception handler, an RTE instruction is executed, which restores the MC68010 state from the stack, reruns the faulted bus cycle, and continues the suspended instruction.

This mechanism of handling bus error exception also provides support for virtual machine, which allows the MC68010 to emulate another machine. This is because I/O registers and machine registers can be simulated in memory as virtual registers. An access to such a register will cause a bus error exception, and the function of the register can be emulated by the exception handler software.

Bus structure

As can be seen from Fig. 10-5, the MC68010 maintains the same bus structure of the MC68000. However, the MC68012 model has 30 address pins instead of 23. This extends the memory range from 8 megawords (or 16M bytes) to 1 gigaword (or 2G bytes). It should be noted that these address pins are labeled A1 through A29 and A31, and address pin A30 is not present.

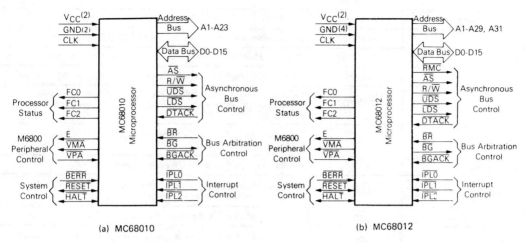

Figure 10-5 MC68010/MC68012 pins divided in functional groups. (Courtesy of Motorola, Inc.)

The MC68012 also has a new output pin, $\overline{RMC}$ (read modified cycle). This pin is used to indicate that the current bus operation is an indivisible read-modify-write cycle. One typical situation of having such a bus cycle occurs during the execution of the TAS instruction. The purpose of the $\overline{RMC}$ signal is to prevent other bus masters from gaining the control of the system bus during a read-modify-write cycle in a multiprocessor configuration.

10-2 MC68020 Extensions

Bus enhancements

Substantial changes on the bus structure have been made to the MC68020. Figure 10-6 summarizes the pin definitions of the MC68020. Unlike the MC68000, which supports both synchronous and asynchronous bus cycles, the MC68020 performs all data transfers using asynchronous bus cycles. Due to its improved bus control logic, a normal read or write bus cycle—that is, one without wait states—is shortened to three clock cycles, S0/S1, S2/S3, and S4/S5, from four cycles as in its predecessors. If neither $\overline{DSACK0}$ nor $\overline{DSACK1}$ (data strobe acknowledge) signal is recognized by the beginning of state S3, wait states are inserted with increments of one clock cycle to accommodate slow devices. Once $\overline{DSACK0}$ or $\overline{DSACK1}$ is received, the MC68020 enters cycle S4/S5, in which it latches incoming data for a read operation or removes data from data pins for a write operation and then terminates the current bus cycle.

A major architectural enhancement made on the MC68020 is that the data bus is expanded to 32 bits from 16 bits as used in previous M68000 family members. This improvement allows the MC68020 to transfer a longword in one bus cycle, thus increasing the speed of the system. A system may have a mixture of byte-,

Signal name	Mnemonic	Function
Address bus	A0–A32	32-bit address bus used to address any of 4,294,967,296 bytes.
Data bus	D0–D31	32-bit data bus used to transfer 8, 16, 24, or 32 bits of data per bus cycle.
Function codes	FC0–FC2	3-bit function code used to identify the address space of each bus cycle.
Size	SIZ0/SIZ1	Indicates the number of bytes remaining to be transferred for this cycle. These signals, together with A0 and A1, define the active sections of the data bus.
Read-Modify-Write cycle	$\overline{RMC}$	Provides an indicator that the current bus cycle is part of an indivisible read-modify-write operation.
External cycle start	$\overline{ECS}$	Provides an indication that a bus cycle is beginning.
Operand cycle start	$\overline{OCS}$	Identical operation to that of $\overline{ECS}$ except that $\overline{OCS}$ is asserted only during the first bus cycle of an operand transfer.
Address strobe	$\overline{AS}$	Indicates that a valid address is on the bus.
Data strobe	$\overline{DS}$	Indicates that valid data is to be placed on the data bus by an external device or has been placed on the data bus by the MC68020.
Read/Write	$R/\overline{W}$	Defines the bus transfer as an MPU read or write.
Data buffer enable	$\overline{DBEN}$	Provides an enable signal for external data buffers.
Data transfer and size acknowledge	$\overline{DSACK0}/\overline{DSACK1}$	Bus response signals that indicate the requested data transfer operation is completed. In addition, these two lines indicate the size of the external bus port on a cycle-by-cycle basis.
Cache disable	$\overline{CDIS}$	Dynamically disables the on-chip cache to assist emulator supprt.
Interrupt priority level	$\overline{IPL0}$–$\overline{IPL2}$	Provides an encoded interrupt level to the processor.
Autovector	$\overline{AVEC}$	Requests an autovector during an interrupt acknowledge cycle.
Interrupt pending	$\overline{IPEND}$	Indicates that an interrupt is pending.
Bus request	$\overline{BR}$	Indicates that an external device requires bus mastership.
Bus grant	$\overline{BG}$	Indicates that an external device may assume bus mastership.
Bus grant acknowledge	$\overline{BGACK}$	Indicates that an external device has assumed bus mastership.
Reset	$\overline{RESET}$	System reset.
Halt	$\overline{HALT}$	Indicates that the processor should suspend bus activity.
Bus error	$\overline{BERR}$	Indicates an invalid or illegal bus operation is being attempted.
Clock	CLK	Clock input to the processor.
Power supply	V_{cc}	+5 volts ± 5% power supply.
Ground	GND	Ground connection.

Figure 10-6 MC68020 pin definitions. (Courtesy of Motorola, Inc.)

word-, and longword-organized devices and memory modules. A 32-bit (longword-organized) device or memory module uses the entire data bus D31–D0. However, a 16-bit device must be connected to the upper word of the data bus, which is D31–D16, and an 8-bit device can be connected only to the most significant byte of the data bus, that is, D31–D24.

In order for the MC68020 to transfer an operand to or from a device whose physical bus width is different than the operand size, the processor uses dynamic bus sizing to determine the actual bus width. During each bus cycle the device indicates its bus width to the MC68020 by returning the $\overline{\text{DSACK1}}$ and $\overline{\text{DSACK0}}$ signals. The two acknowledge signals are also used to inform the MC68020 whether the current data transfer has been completed. The possible encodings of $\overline{\text{DSACK1}}$ and $\overline{\text{DSACK0}}$ are 00 for 32-bit port, 01 for 16-bit port, 10 for 8-bit port, and 11 for not ready; that is, a wait state is to be inserted.

To begin a transfer cycle, the MC68020 always assumes the device to be 32 bits wide. After the current bus cycle is completed, by examining $\overline{\text{DSACK1}}$ and $\overline{\text{DSACK0}}$ the MC68020 knows the actual port size of the device and therefore can initiate subsequent bus cycles to transfer the remaining bytes in the operand if necessary.

For example, in reading a longword operand, the MC68020 reads 32 bits from the data bus. If the device is 32 bits wide, the MC68020 keeps the 32 data bits and continues. If the device responds that it is a 16-bit device, the MC68020 keeps the 16 valid data bits and then runs another bus cycle to obtain the other 16 data bits. An 8-bit data port is handled similarly but with four bus cycles. Note that $\overline{\text{DSACK1}}$ and $\overline{\text{DSACK0}}$ indicate the device port size and not the transfer size. For example, a 32-bit device always responds a 32-bit port size regardless of whether the bus cycle is a byte, word, or longword transfer.

Unlike the previous M68000 family members, which require a word operand to have an even address, the MC68020 allows a word or longword operand to begin at an odd address. This feature significantly simplifies the programming of peripheral devices because the user need not worry about the physical data width of the device. For example, in an MC68000-based system, an 8-bit device must be assigned either consecutive even addresses or consecutive odd addresses. Because of this restriction, two consecutive registers cannot be accessed as a word. The same device, when connected to the MC68020, occupies a block of consecutive addresses, and therefore its internal registers can be programmed as a byte, word, or longword just as if they were memory locations.

To transfer data to or from a misaligned location requires extra bus cycles. For each bus cycle, the MC68020 indicates the operand size—that is, the number of remaining operand bytes to be transferred, with the SIZ1 and SIZ0 outputs. The size indications may be 01 (byte), 10 (word), 11 (3-byte), or 00 (longword) depending on the device width and operand alignment. As an example, transferring a longword, OP0 OP1 OP2 OP3, to or from an odd address in a 32-bit wide device or memory module requires two bus cycles. The MC68020 first transfers byte OP0 on D7–D0 to the odd address with SIZ1 SIZ0 = 01. Then, in the next cycle it transfers OP1 on D31–D24, OP2 on D23–D16, and OP3 on D15–D8 to the next even address with a SIZ1 SIZ0 = 11. Should the same operand be transferred to an odd address X in a 16-bit device or memory module, three transfer bus cycles would occur: (1) OP0 on D23–D16 to the beginning odd address X, (2) OP1 on D31–D24 and OP2 on D23–16 to the next even address X + 1, and (3) OP3 on D31–D24 to address X + 3. The following table lists all possible transfers and their required bus cycles for word-organized devices and memory modules.

Activity	Bus Cycle	SIZ1	SIZ0	A2	A1	A0	Activity on Data Bus	
							D31–D24	D23–D16
Transfer a longword OP0 OP1 OP2 OP3 to or from an even address	1	0	0	X	0	0	OP0	OP1
	2	1	0	X	1	0	OP2	OP3
Transfer a longword OP0 OP1 OP2 OP3 to or from an odd address	1	0	0	0	0	1	XX	OP0
	2	1	1	0	1	0	OP1	OP2
	3	0	1	1	0	0	OP3	XX
Transfer a word OP0 OP1 to or from an even address	1	1	0	X	X	0	OP0	OP1
Transfer a word OP0 OP1 to or from an odd address	1	1	0	X	0	1	XX	OP0
	2	0	1	X	1	0	OP1	XX
Transfer a byte OPB to or from an even address	1	0	1	X	X	0	OPB	XX
Transfer a byte OPB to or from an odd address	1	0	1	X	X	1	XX	OPB

The MC68020 supports only asynchronous bus cycles in which the $\overline{\text{DS}}$ (data strobe) and $\overline{\text{DTACK1}}/\overline{\text{DTACK0}}$ are used as handshaking signals to ensure proper data transfer. In interfacing a word- or longword-organized device, the correct byte data strobe must be generated so that only the relevant portion of the data port or memory bank(s) is enabled. The required byte-enable signals UD and LD for a given bus cycle are a function of the size bits SIZ1 SIZ0 and the least significant two address bits A1 A0. This is different than the MC68000, which outputs $\overline{\text{UDS}}$ and $\overline{\text{LDS}}$ but not A0. From the preceding bus activity table for 16-bit ports, we can generate UD and LD in an MC68020-based system by decoding A0, SIZ1, and SIZ0. Figure 10-7 gives Karnaugh maps for UD and LD, based on which we have

$$\text{UD} = \overline{\text{A0}}$$

$$\text{LD} = \text{A0} + \overline{\text{SIZ0}} + \text{SIZ1}$$

Of course, the UD and LD are to be combined with $\overline{\text{DS}}$ and also outputs of address decoding (or memory module selecting) logic if necessary to enable the odd-addressed or even-addressed bank or both.

For a longword-organized device, there are four byte-enable signals to be generated: UUD (upper upper data byte), UMD (upper middle data byte), LMD

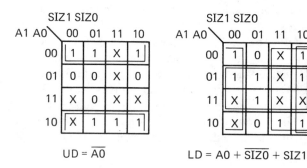

Figure 10-7 Karnaugh maps for UD and LD.

(lower middle data byte), and LLD (lower lower data byte). Although much more complex, the process for deriving Boolean expressions for these signals are similar. By first determining the bus activity table, we can obtain the following Boolean expressions for the four byte-enable signals:

$$UUD = \overline{A0} \cdot \overline{A1}$$

$$UMD = \overline{A1} \cdot \overline{SIZ0} + \overline{A1} \cdot A0 + \overline{A0} \cdot SIZ1$$

$$LMD = \overline{A0} \cdot A1 + \overline{A1} \cdot \overline{SIZ0} \cdot \overline{SIZ1} + \overline{A1} \cdot SIZ0 \cdot SIZ1 + A0 \cdot \overline{A1} \cdot \overline{SIZ0}$$

$$LLD = A0 \cdot SIZ0 \cdot SIZ1 + \overline{SIZ0} \cdot \overline{SIZ1} + A0 \cdot A1 + A1 \cdot SIZ1$$

Figure 10-8 shows the necessary logic to generate byte data-enable signals for 16-bit as well as for 32-bit devices. Note that for 8-bit devices, $\overline{DS}$ is sufficient because only 1 byte can be transferred per bus cycle.

In addition to size, $\overline{DTACK}$, and expanded address and data pins, the MC68020 has several new control pins designed primarily for asynchronous bus control, interrupt control, and emulator control. These new pins are

$\overline{ECS}$ *(external cycle start):* This output pin is asserted during the S0 state of each bus cycle to indicate that the MC68020 may be starting a bus cycle.

$\overline{OCS}$ *(operand cycle start):* This pin has the same output signal as $\overline{ECS}$ except that it is asserted only during the first bus cycle of an operand transfer or instruction fetch.

$\overline{DS}$ *(data strobe):* This pin outputs a low to indicate that the MC68020 is ready to input data in a read cycle or has output valid data in a write cycle. The $\overline{DS}$ signal can be used by the selected device to gate data onto the bus in a read operation and to strobe data off the bus in a write operation.

$\overline{DBEN}$ *(data buffer enable):* This pin provides an enable signal to data bus buffers.

$\overline{IPEND}$ *(interrupt pending):* This output pin is asserted when the received interrupt priority level $\overline{IPL2}-\overline{IPL0}$ is 7 (i.e., nonmaskable) or is higher than the current interrupt mask level I2–I0.

$\overline{AVEC}$ *(auto vector):* This input pin is used to indicate to the MC68020 that the interrupt is an auto vector interrupt. It serves the same purpose as the $\overline{VPA}$ signal in auto vector interrupts for the MC68000.

$\overline{CDIS}$ *(cache disable):* This output pin allows an emulator to force the MC68020 to fetch all instructions from the bus by disabling the internal instruction cache.

Hardware enhancements

In addition to the 32-bit data bus, several other hardware enhancements have been made to the MC68020 to improve its speed. First, a 256-byte instruction cache is added. This allows more instructions to be kept in the processor and therefore substantially reduces its average instruction fetch time. Furthermore, with an instruction cache, the external bus activity is reduced. The reduced bus

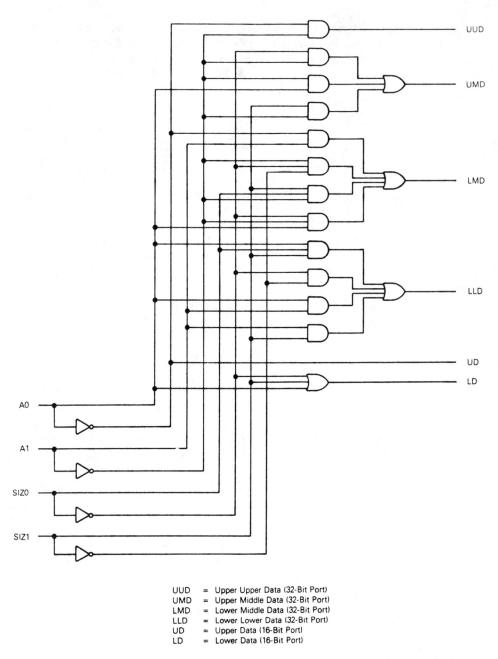

UUD = Upper Upper Data (32-Bit Port)
UMD = Upper Middle Data (32-Bit Port)
LMD = Lower Middle Data (32-Bit Port)
LLD = Lower Lower Data (32-Bit Port)
UD = Upper Data (16-Bit Port)
LD = Lower Data (16-Bit Port)

Figure 10-8 Byte data select generation for 16- and 32-bit ports. (Courtesy of Motorola, Inc.)

utilization by the MC68020 makes the bus more accessible to other bus masters such as a processor and DMA controller. This advantage is particularly significant for multiple-processor systems in which main memory is shared by more than one processor. Second, the MC68020 uses a three-stage pipelined internal structure. This allows up to three consecutive instructions to be fetched, decoded, and executed simultaneously. The MC68020 also has more than one ALU, which allows data manipulation and address calculation to occur at the same time. Third, the MC68020 has a 32-bit barrel shifter, which uses combinational logic to perform shifting. Unlike a conventional shift register, which shifts 1 bit per clock cycle, a barrel shifter can shift multiple bits simultaneously. As a result, it performs high-speed shift operations and makes the shift time independent of the shift count. For example, a typical 31-bit shift instruction requires as few as 6 clock cycles for the MC68020, whereas executed by the MC68000, the operation requires $6 + 2 \times 31 = 68$ clock cycles. Fourth, the coprocessor interface circuit has been integrated into the MC68020. With the coprocessor interface hardware, the communication between the host processor and the coprocessor is automatically handled by the MC68020. This eliminates the need for having I/O instructions to access the coprocessor interface registers and consequently reduces the time required to execute a coprocessor instruction. Finally, a new SP, interrupt stack pointer, has been added to simplify task switching. The already-present supervisor stack pointer, SSP, becomes the master stack pointer, which is used for task-related exceptions. When an interrupt exception occurs, the interrupt stack pointer is the active system stack pointer used for saving the return address. This feature allows the MC68020 to keep two separate stacks, one for the current running task and the other for interrupt routines. Since the stack for the current running task is not disturbed by regular interrupts, it becomes easier to switch from the current task to the next one in a multiprogramming environment.

New addressing modes

The MC68020 uses a 32-bit address bus in contrast to the 24-bit address bus used by the MC68000. This extends the maximum memory space from 16M bytes to 4G bytes. Furthermore, the MC68020 has a total of 18 addressing modes for specifying data operands; whereas the previous M68000 processors have only 12 addressing modes. Figure 10-9 compares the addressing modes of the MC68020 to those of the MC68000/MC68010. As can be seen, extensions made on addressing modes include scaled index, larger displacements, and memory indirect addressing modes.

When an index register is used, the index can be not only a word or longword, as in the MC68000, but it also can be multiplied by a scale factor. An index scale factor may be 1, 2, 4, or 8, so that an index can be used to specify an offset in bytes, words, longwords, or quadwords. The multiplication by a scale factor is used in the address calculation and the original index value remains unchanged in the index register.

The general format for specifying an index is

Xn.SIZE*SCALE

where Xn represents the register (data or address) to be used as the index register, SIZE indicates the index size (which can be W for word or L for longword), and SCALE specifies the scale factor of 1, 2, 4, or 8. To illustrate the flexibility

Addressing Mode	MC68000/MC68010 Syntax	MC68020/MC68030 Syntax
Register Direct		
Data register direct	Dn	Dn
Address register direct	An	An
Register Indirect		
Address register indirect	(An)	(An)
Address register indirect with postincrement	(An)+	(An)+
Address register indirect with predecrement	-(An)	-(An)
Address register indirect with displacement	D16(An)	(D16,An)
Register Indirect with Index		
Address register indirect with index (8-bit displacement)	D8(An,Xn.SIZE)	(D8,An,Xn.SIZE*SCALE)
Address register indirect with index (16-bit or 32-bit base displacement)	No	(BD,An,Xn.SIZE*SCALE)
Memory Indirect		
Memory indirect postindexed	No	([BD,An],Xn.SIZE*SCALE,OD)
Memory indirect preindexed	No	([BD,An,Xn.SIZE*SCALE],OD)
Program Counter Indirect with Displacement	D16(PC)	(BD,PC,Xn.SIZE*SCALE)
Program Counter Indirect with Index		
PC indirect with index (8-bit displacement)	D8(PC,Xn.SIZE)	(D8,PC,Xn.SIZE*SCALE)
PC indirect with index (16-bit or 32-bit base displacement)	No	(BD,PC,Xn.SIZE*SCALE)
Program Counter Memory Indirect		
PC memory indirect postindexed	No	([BD,PC],Xn.SIZE*SCALE,OD)
PC memory indirect preindexed	No	([BD,PC,Xn.SIZE*SCALE],OD)
Absolute		
Absolute short	XXX.W	(XXX).W
Absolute long	XXX.L	(XXX).L
Immediate	#Expression	#Expression

Figure 10-9 MC68020/MC68030 extensions on addressing modes.

provided by scaled indexing, let us consider this example: array AA stores a sequence of single-precision real numbers, and the index for the *i*th element is in data register D0. In order to add the *i*th element into the data register FP1 of the floating-point coprocessor, a typical instruction sequence based on the MC68000 addressing modes would be as follows:

```
LSL.W      #2,D0
LEA        AA,A0
FADD.s     0(A0,D0.W),FP1
```

On the other hand, for the MC68020, this instruction sequence can be replaced by

```
LEA        AA,A0
FADD.S     (0,A0,D0.W*4),FP1
```

Should the array consist of double-precision real numbers, the same operation can be accomplished by changing the scale factor from 4 to 8:

```
FADD.D     (AA,D0.W*8),FP1
```

The second improvement on existing addressing modes is to allow larger displacements for indexed addressing modes. For the previous M68000 microprocessors, the size of a displacement is limited to 8-bit in any indexed mode and 16-bit in the indirect register mode. Because of this limitation, to process an array residing in high addresses it is necessary first to load the beginning array address into an address register. The MC68020 allows a base displacement (BD) to be used in an indexed mode, whose size may be either 16 or 32 bits.

In addition to the flexibilities on indexes and displacements, the MC68020 has four memory indirect addressing modes, which were not available in its predecessors. For a memory indirect addressing mode, the effective address calculated from the displacement, address register, and an optional index is used as the location to obtain the address of the operand rather than the operand itself. The assembler notation for indicating an indirect address in memory is [EA]. Figure 10-10 illustrates the four memory indirect addressing modes: memory indirect postindexed, memory indirect preindexed, PC memory indirect postindexed, and PC memory indirect preindexed.

Memory indirect modes are very efficient in accessing memory operands when a table consists of operand addresses rather than their values. Consider the example in Fig. 10-11. The example assumes that the addresses of two word arrays are passed to a subroutine through the stack. In the subroutine, suppose that the ith word in one array is to be interchanged with its counterpart in the other array. Then this can be implemented by the following three instructions, with D1 having the index i:

```
MOVE.L      ([OFFSET,SP],D1.W*2,0),D0
MOVE.L      ([OFFSET+4,SP],D1.W*2,0),([OFFSET,SP],D1.W*2,0)
MOVE.L      D0,([OFFSET+4,SP],D1.W*2,0)
```

New instructions

Seventeen new instructions have been added to the MC68020 instruction set. These new instructions, which are designed primarily to support advanced high-level languages and multiprocessing systems, are summarized in Fig. 10-12.

Among the new instructions is a group of instructions to perform various bit field manipulation operations. Unlike typical MC68000 instructions, which operate on bits, bytes, words, or longwords, a bit field instruction can manipulate a string of consecutive bits with a variable length from 1 to 32 bits. The BFCHG (bit field change) instruction complements the bits in the specified bit field. The BFCLR (bit field clear) instruction tests the bit field and then clears the bit field to all 0s and the BFSET (bit field set) instruction tests and sets the bit field to all 1s, respectively. The BFTST (bit field test) instruction tests the bit field to set the N and Z flags but does not modify the field. The remaining four instructions use a data register as an operand, in addition to the bit field operand. The BFEXTS (bit field extract signed) and BFEXTU (bit field extract unsigned) extract a value from the bit field, store it into Dn, and perform sign or zero extension to 32 bits. The BFFFO (bit field find first one) instruction scans the bit field, starting with the most significant bit, and stops when a 1 bit is encountered. The offset of that nonzero bit is then stored into the destination Dn. Finally, the BFINS (bit field insert) instruction is used to insert a value from the low-order bits of the specified Dn to the destination bit field.

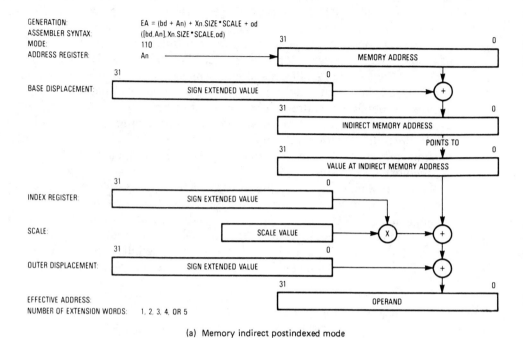

(a) Memory indirect postindexed mode

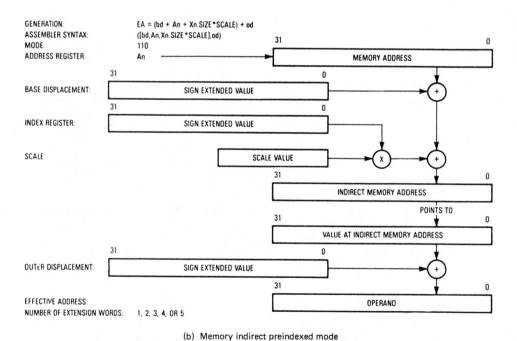

(b) Memory indirect preindexed mode

Figure 10-10 Memory indirect addressing modes. (Courtesy of Motorola, Inc.)

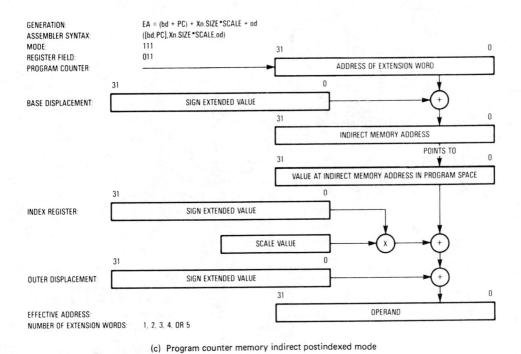

GENERATION: EA = (bd + PC) + Xn.SIZE*SCALE + od
ASSEMBLER SYNTAX: ([bd,PC],Xn.SIZE*SCALE,od)
MODE: 111
REGISTER FIELD: 011
PROGRAM COUNTER:

EFFECTIVE ADDRESS:
NUMBER OF EXTENSION WORDS: 1, 2, 3, 4, OR 5

(c) Program counter memory indirect postindexed mode

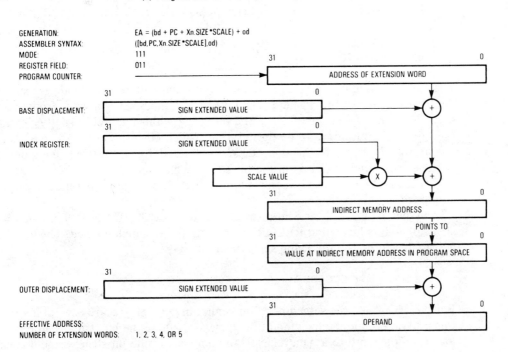

GENERATION: EA = (bd + PC + Xn.SIZE*SCALE) + od
ASSEMBLER SYNTAX: ([bd,PC,Xn.SIZE*SCALE],od)
MODE: 111
REGISTER FIELD: 011
PROGRAM COUNTER:

EFFECTIVE ADDRESS:
NUMBER OF EXTENSION WORDS: 1, 2, 3, 4, OR 5

(d) Program counter memory indirect preindexed mode

Figure 10-10 (*continued*)

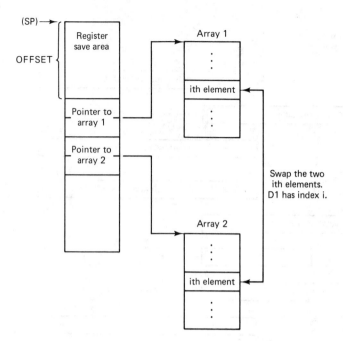

Figure 10-11 Example of using memory indirect modes.

Illustrated in Fig. 10-13, a bit field operand is specified in three components as

EA{OFFSET:WIDTH}

The EA component, which can be any general data addressing mode, specifies the base location of the bit field. The OFFSET component is a value from -2^{31} to $2^{31} - 1$ specifying the offset of the bit string within the field. The beginning position of the bit string to be operated on, which corresponds to the most significant bit, is therefore the sum of EA and OFFSET. The WIDTH component specifies the number of bits in the bit string, which may be from 1 to 32. Both OFFSET and WIDTH can be constants specified by immediate operands or values contained in data registers.

As an example of bit field instructions, suppose that the last 19 bits in a bit string of 40 bits located at RECORDS (A1) are to be complemented. This can be accomplished by the following single instruction:

BFCHG   (RECORDS,A1){#40 − 19:#19}

For the MC68000, the same operation would, in general, require several instructions: to determine the location of the longword where the bit string is stored, to load that longword to a data register, to complement the bit string using a mask corresponding to the relevant bit positions, and to store that data register back to memory.

There are several important applications of bit field instructions. One is to

Instruction	Mnemonic	Operand Format	Operation
Bit field change	BFCHG	EA(OFFSET:WIDTH)	$\overline{\text{Field}}$ -> Field
Bit field clear	BFCLR	EA(OFFSET:WIDTH)	0s -> Field
Bit field extract signed	BFEXTS	EA(OFFSET:WIDTH),Dn	Field -> Dn; Sign extended
Bit field extract unsigned	BFEXTU	EA(OFFSET:WIDTH),Dn	Field -> Dn; Zero extended
Bit field find first one	BFFFO	EA(OFFSET:WIDTH),Dn	Scan for first non-zero bit in field; Offset -> Dn
Bit field insert	BFINS	Dn,EA(OFFSET:WIDTH)	Dn -> Field
Bit field set	BFSET	EA(OFFSET:WIDTH)	1s -> Field
Bit field test	BFTST	EA(OFFSET:WIDTH)	Test field and set N and Z flags accordingly
Compare and swap with operand	CAS	Dm,Dn,EA	If (Dm) = (EA) then Dn -> EA else EA -> Dm
Compare and swap with operand	CAS2	Dm1:Dm2,Dn1:Dn2, (Rn1):(Rn2)	If (Dm1) = (DST1) pointed by Rn1 then If (Dm2) = (DST2) pointed by Rn2 then Dn1 -> DST1 and Dn2 -> DST2 else DST1 -> Dm1 and DST2 -> Dm2
Call module	CALLM #I8,EA (MC68020 only)		Current module state -> -(sp); (EA) -> Module state
Check register against bounds	CHK2	EA,Rn	If Rn < Lower bound (at EA) or Rn > Upper bound (at EA + size) then TRAP

Figure 10-12 New MC68020/MC68030 instructions.

Compare register against bounds	CMP2	EA,Rn	Set Z and C flags according to Rn < Lower bound (at EA) or Rn > Upper bound (at EA + size)
Pack	PACK	-(Ax),-(Ay),#I16 Dx,Dy,#I16	Source (two unpacked BCD bytes) + I16 (adjustment) -> Destination (one packed BCD byte)
Return from module	RTM (MC68020 only)	Rn	(SP)+ -> module state
Trap on condition	TRAPcc	None or #I16 or #I32	If cc then TRAP
Unpack BCD	UNPK	-(Ax),-(Ay),#I16 Dx,Dy,#I16	Source (one packed BCD byte) + I16 (adjustment) -> Destination (two unpacked BCD bytes)

Figure 10-12 (continued)

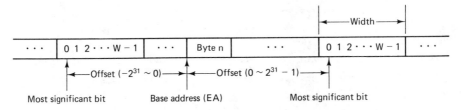

Figure 10-13 Bit field data format.

implement variables of various lengths in some advanced high-level languages. For example, in C, an integer variable can be defined to contain several fields, each of which can be accessed independently. Another typical application is in bit-mapped graphics, which require a tremendous amount of bit field manipulations to control the darkness and color of each pixel in generating a display.

The MC68000 can perform BCD additions, subtractions, and negations, with each data byte having two packed BCD digits. Two new instructions, PACK and UNPACK, have been added to the MC68020 to facilitate the conversion between packed BCD and ASCII or EBCDIC decimal digits. The remaining new instructions are designed to support array range checking, modular-programming, and multiprocessing.

The MC68000 has a CHK instruction for bound checking. Although the upper bound to be check in this instruction can be any value, the lower bound is always zero. The MC68020 adds two instructions, CHK2 and CMP2, which perform variable bound checking and allow not only the upper bound but also the lower bound to be any byte, word, or longword integer. The lower bound is taken from the location specified by EA and the upper bound from EA plus the operand length. The difference between the two instructions is that after bound checking, the CMP2 instruction sets only the condition code, whereas the CHK2 instruction will additionally cause a trap if a bound is exceeded.

To assist in modular programming, the MC68020 has added an instruction pair: CALLM (module call) and RTM (return from module). The CALLM instruction creates a module frame on top of the stack and saves the current module state in that frame. A module state contains module control information, including access level, data area pointer, and arguments. The RTM instruction restores the previous module state from the stack frame and returns to the calling module. For a configuration that uses an MC68851 for memory management, a change of the access level due to CALLM or RTM will cause the memory management unit to verify that the change is valid. This enforces access control to a module based on the access level assigned to the module. The following illustrates a typical sequence in calling a module:

```
DESCRIPTOR  Directives              ;define the descriptor of the module to be
                                    ;called
            .
            .
            .
            PEA      ARGLIST        ;Push the address of an argument list onto the
                                    ;stack
```

Instruction	Improvement
Bcc.L, BRA.L, BSR.L	Supports 32-bit displacements in addition to 8-bit and 16-bit displacements.
CHK.L	Supports 32-bit operands in addition to 16-bit operands.
CMPI	Supports program counter relative addressing modes.
DIVSL.L, DIVUL.L	Supports 64-bit by 32-bit divisions in addition to 32-bit by 16-bit operations.
EXTB.L	Supports byte to longword extension in addition to byte to word and word to longword extensions.
LINK.L	Supports 32-bit displacements in addition to 16-bit displacements.
MULS.L, MULU.L	Supports 32-bit by 32-bit multiplications in addition to 16-bit by 16-bit operations.
TST	Supports program counter relative addressing modes.

Figure 10-14 MC68020/MC68030 enhancements of existing instructions.

```
MOVE.L   LISTCNT, - (SP)      ;Push the argument count onto the stack
MOVE.L   LISTLEN, - (SP)      ;Push the number of bytes in the argument list
                             ;onto the stack
CALL     #12,DESCRIPTOR      ;Pass 12 bytes to the called module
```

The two compare and swap instructions, CAS and CAS2, are designed to support multiprocessing systems. Both instructions use the read-modify-write cycle as in the TAS instruction to compare two operands and swap a third operand, depending on the result of the comparison. The difference between the CAS and CAS2 is that the latter compares two operand pairs and updates two operands, whereas the former can perform this compare-and-swap operation only on one pair of operands.

In addition to the new instructions, several previously existing instructions have been enhanced on the MC68020. One enhancement is to allow 32-bit operands for certain instructions in which only 8- and 16-bit values were used on the MC68000. Another enhancement is to allow 32-bit displacements to be used in branch-related instructions. Figure 10-14 summarizes the MC68020 improvements on existing instructions.

10-3 The MC68030

The major improvement of the MC68030 from the MC68020 is the addition of a data cache and a memory management unit. Both processors use 32-bit data bus and address bus. As shown in Fig. 10-15, the MC68030 retains most of the MC68020's pins for address, data, and bus control. Since there is little difference in the bus structure, an existing design of the MC68020 configured with a memory management unit MC68851 can be upgraded to an MC68030 with minor changes, which can be accomplished with an adaptor board.

Signal name	Mnemonic	Function
Function codes	FC0–FC2	3-bit function code used to identify the address space of each bus cycle.
Address bus	A0–A31	32-bit address bus used to address any of 4,294,967,296 bytes.
Data bus	D0–D31	32-bit data bus used to transfer 8, 16, 24, or 32 bits of data per bus cycle.
Size	SIZ0/SIZ1	Indicates the number of bytes remaining to be transferred for this cycle. These signals, together with A0 and A1, define the active sections of the data bus.
Operand cycle start	$\overline{\text{OCS}}$	Identical operation to that of $\overline{\text{ECS}}$ except that $\overline{\text{OCS}}$ is asserted only during the first bus cycle of an operand transfer.
External cycle start	$\overline{\text{ECS}}$	Provides an indication that a bus cycle is beginning.
Read/Write	$\text{R}/\overline{\text{W}}$	Defines the bus transfer as an MPU read or write.
Read-Modify-Write cycle	$\overline{\text{RMC}}$	Provides an indicator that the current bus cycle is part of an indivisible read-modify-write operation.
Address strobe	$\overline{\text{AS}}$	Indicates that a valid address is on the bus.
Data strobe	$\overline{\text{DS}}$	Indicates that valid data is to be placed on the data bus by an external device or has been placed on the data bus by the MC68030.
Data buffer enable	$\overline{\text{DBEN}}$	Provides an enable signal for external data buffers.
Data transfer and size acknowledge	DSACK0/DSACK1	Bus response signals that indicate the requested data transfer operation is completed. In addition, these two lines indicate the size of the external bus port on a cycle-by-cycle basis.
Cache inhibit in	$\overline{\text{CIIN}}$	Prevents data from being loaded into the MC68030 instruction and data caches.
Cache inhibit out	$\overline{\text{CIOUT}}$	Reflects the CI bit in ATC entries or a transparent translation register; indicates that external caches should ignore these accesses.
Cache burst request	$\overline{\text{CBREQ}}$	Indicates a miss in either the instruction or data cache.
Cache burst acknowledge	$\overline{\text{CBACK}}$	Indicates that accessed device can operate in burst mode.
Interrupt priority level	$\overline{\text{IPL0}}$–$\overline{\text{IPL2}}$	Provides an encoded interrupt level to the processor.
Interrupt pending	$\overline{\text{IPEND}}$	Indicates that an interrupt is pending.
Autovector	$\overline{\text{AVEC}}$	Requests an autovector during an interrupt acknowledge cycle.
Bus request	$\overline{\text{BR}}$	Indicates that an external device requires bus mastership.
Bus grant	$\overline{\text{BG}}$	Indicates that an external device may assume bus mastership.
Bus grant acknowledge	$\overline{\text{BGACK}}$	Indicates that an external device has assumed bus mastership.
Reset	$\overline{\text{RESET}}$	System reset.
Halt	$\overline{\text{HALT}}$	Indicates that the processor should suspend bus activity.
Bus error	$\overline{\text{BERR}}$	Indicates an invalid or illegal bus operation is being attempted.
Synchronous termination	$\overline{\text{STERM}}$	Bus response signal that indicates a port size of 32 bits and that data may be latched on the next falling clock edge.
Cache disable	$\overline{\text{CDIS}}$	Dynamically disables the on-chip cache to assist emulator support.
MMU disable	$\overline{\text{MMUDIS}}$	Dynamically disables the translation mechanism of the MMU.
Microsequencer status	$\overline{\text{STATUS}}$	Status indication for debug purposes.
Pipe refill	$\overline{\text{REFILL}}$	Indicates when the instruction pipe is beginning to refill.
Clock	CLK	Clock input to the processor.
Power supply	V_{cc}	+5 volt ± 5% power supply.
Ground	GND	Ground connection.

Figure 10-15 MC68030 pin definitions. (Courtesy of Motorola, Inc.)

Bus structure

The most noticeable improvements on the bus structure are that the MC68030 provides three different data transfer bus cycles: asynchronous, synchronous, and burst read cycles. An asynchronous bus cycle is performed in the same fashion as in the MC68020. It is accomplished by using handshaking signals $\overline{DS}$, $\overline{DSACK0}$, and $\overline{DSACK1}$, in a minimum of three clock cycles. If the $\overline{DSACK}$ signals are not received by state S3, wait states are inserted to lengthen the bus cycle. The actual amount of data being transferred, which may be 8, 16, or 32 bits, is determined dynamically in each bus cycle by $\overline{DSACK0}$, $\overline{DSACK1}$, SIZ0, and SIZ1.

A synchronous bus cycle has a minimum of two clock cycles, S0/S1 and S2/S3, and is terminated by the $\overline{STERM}$ (synchronous termination) signal rather than $\overline{DSACK0}$ and $\overline{DSACK1}$. However, it can be lengthened by delaying $\overline{STERM}$ to insert wait states in one clock cycle increments between S2 and S3. The $\overline{STERM}$ indicates to the MC68030 that the bus slave is a 32-bit device and the bus cycle is to be terminated on the next falling clock edge. During a read cycle, it indicates that the selected device has placed valid data on the data bus. During a write cycle, it indicates that the device has received the output data.

Synchronous bus cycles proceed as follows:

S0: The MC68030 outputs $\overline{ECS}$ (and $\overline{OCS}$ if asserted) to indicate the beginning of a bus cycle. It places a valid address on A31–A0 and function code on FC2–FC0 and drives $R/\overline{W}$ low if the bus cycle is a write. It also sends out 00 as the SIZ1 and SIZ0 outputs to indicate a 32-bit transfer.

S1: The MC68030 asserts $\overline{AS}$ to indicate a valid address and $\overline{DS}$ to enable the external device for data strobe. Meanwhile, the external device decodes the valid address.

S2: The MC68030 asserts $\overline{DBEN}$ to enable external data buffers. During a write cycle, it also places valid data on D31–D0 pins. The addressed device latches data from the data bus during a write cycle or places valid data during a read cycle. The device asserts $\overline{STERM}$ when it has successfully latched the data from or has placed the data to the data bus. If the MC68030 does not receive the $\overline{STERM}$ input, wait states are inserted until $\overline{STERM}$ is recognized. Once $\overline{STERM}$ is recognized, the MC68030 latches the data during a read cycle.

S3: The processor terminates the bus cycle by negating $\overline{AS}$, $\overline{DS}$, and $\overline{DBEN}$. The addressed device negates $\overline{STERM}$ and removes its data during a read cycle.

Burst cycles are for filling the MC68030 on-chip instruction and data caches, and therefore only read cycles can be performed in the burst mode. With burst cycles, the MC68030 can read a block of four longwords with as little as one clock cycle per longword transfer. To perform burst filling, the addressed device must be a 32-bit port that terminates bus cycles with the $\overline{STERM}$ signal. The MC68030 initiates burst filling by asserting the $\overline{CBREQ}$ (cache burst request) output. The addressed device responds to $\overline{CBREQ}$ by asserting the $\overline{STERM}$ and the $\overline{CBACK}$

(cache burst acknowledge) signals. When the MC68030 receives $\overline{\text{STERM}}$ and $\overline{\text{CBACK}}$, it maintains $\overline{\text{AS}}$, $\overline{\text{DS}}$, R/$\overline{\text{W}}$, address, function code, and size outputs in their current states and latches a longword from the data bus after each clock cycle while $\overline{\text{STERM}}$ remains asserted. This burst operation continues until the entire block is transferred as indicated by the negated $\overline{\text{STERM}}$ and $\overline{\text{CBACK}}$.

In addition to the previously mentioned $\overline{\text{STERM}}$, $\overline{\text{CBREQ}}$, and $\overline{\text{CBACK}}$ pins, the MC68030 has five more new pins not available in the MC68020. These pins are for cache and emulator control, and their functions are as follows:

$\overline{\text{CIIN}}$ *(cache inhibit input):* This input prevents instructions and data from being loaded into the on-chip caches.

$\overline{\text{CIOUT}}$ *(cache inhibit output):* This output reflects the setting of the CI (cache inhibit) bit in the on-chip memory management unit.

$\overline{\text{REFIL}}$ *(pipeline refill):* This output indicates that the MC68030 is beginning to refill its internal instruction pipeline. A pipeline refill is caused by having to break sequential instruction execution to handle nonsequential events such as jumps and exceptions. In order for an emulator to trace the instruction execution sequence, it needs this information to simulate the instruction pipeline.

$\overline{\text{STATUS}}$ *(internal microsequencer status):* This output identifies various microsequencer activities by being asserted for different numbers of clock cycles. Among the reportable status information are normal instruction boundaries, pending exceptions, and various errors. This pin has the same application as the $\overline{\text{REFIL}}$ pin.

$\overline{\text{MMUDIS}}$ *(MMU disable):* This input disables the on-chip memory management unit for performing logical to physical address translation. It is also used by the emulator.

Memory management logic

The MC68030 includes a simplified version of the MC68851 memory management unit (MMU). By integrating the memory management logic into the processor chip, we can not only reduce the device count of the system but also the delay caused by the address translation by eliminating the time of passing signals to an external MMU.

The concept and principle of this on-chip MMU are the same as the MC68851, which is discussed in Sec. 12-3. Like the MC68851, this on-chip MMU provides logical to physical address translations, supports implementation of virtual memory based on the demanded page scheme, and allows eight different page sizes, ranging from 256 to 32K bytes.

On-chip caches

The MC68030 has two on-chip caches of 256 bytes each, one for instructions and one for data. With separated instruction and data caches and with each cache having its own control circuit and internal bus, the processor can perform as many as three accesses to memory and I/O devices simultaneously. This allows the MC68030 to take full advantage of its parallel processing capability. Consider the following situation. Due to the pipelined internal structure, the MC68030 may be executing the current instruction

```
MOVE.W      D2,IOREG
```

and at the time decoding the next fetched instruction

```
ADD.W       ([0,A0,D1.W*2],0),D0
```

and fetching a third instruction. If this third instruction is in the instruction cache and the operand address pointed by [0,A0,D1.W*2] is in the data cache, the MC68030 would be able to output D2 to the external device as required in the first instruction, fetch the source operand address for the second instruction, and load the third instruction into the instruction pipe, all simultaneously.

New registers

Although the MC68030 keeps the user programming model unchanged from previous M68000 family microprocessors, several new registers have been added due to the addition of memory management unit. All new registers are control registers and can be programmed only in the supervisor mode.

In addition to the two alternate function code registers (DFC and SFC) and vector base register (VBR) added to the MC68010 and the interrupt stack pointer (ISP), cache control register (CACR), and cache address register (CAAR) of the MC68020, the MC68030 has added six control registers. They are the CPU root pointer register (CRP), the supervisor root pointer register (SRP), the translation control register (TC), two independent transparent translation control registers (TT0 and TT1), and the MMU status register (MMUSR). These new registers are used to control and provide status information for the on-chip memory management logic.

New instructions

The MC68030 supports all MC68020 instructions except the CALLM and RTM instructions due to the different memory protection mechanism used by the MC68030. Since the memory management unit becomes part of the MC68030, it has four new instructions to program the MMU. The new instructions are: PFLUSH (flush entry in ATC), PLOAD (load an entry into ATC), PMOVE (move to/from MMU registers), and PTEST (test a logical address). They are compatible with the corresponding MC68851 instructions. However, unlike an MC68851 instruction, which requires the coprocessor interface to execute, an MC68030 MMU instruction executes within the CPU just like other CPU instructions and, consequently, is much faster. These new instructions are all privileged and are summarized in Fig. 10-16.

Parallel processing

The performance of the MC68040 is much enhanced by using concurrent processing while still maintaining user object-code compatibility with all earlier members in the M68000 microprocessor family. As long as a program written for an earlier microprocessor in the family is intended to run in the user mode, the same program can be executed in the MC68040 without any modifications, or without even being reassembled. However, this upward compatibility does not exist for the supervisor mode because the MC68040 handles some exceptions differently and its supervisor programming model has made some changes.

A simplified block diagram of its internal structure is given in Fig. 10-17. As shown in the figure, the MC68040 adopts an architecture which has a high degree of parallelism. First, the instruction decode and execution logic is highly pipelined. It is divided into six stages so that instruction fetch, instruction decode, effective address calculation, memory operand fetch, operation execution, and result storing of several consecutive instructions may be performed simultaneously. As a result, most simple MC68000 instructions can be executed at the rate of 1 instruction per clock cycle once the pipeline is filled. For the initial 25-MHz version of the MC68040, this translates to 20 million instructions per second. Second, the MC68040 expands the on-chip memory management logic to two units, one for instruction fetch and one for data access, from only one unit in the MC68030. Having separate instruction and data memory management units permits the MC68040 to perform logical to physical address translations for instruction fetch and operand access in parallel, thus shortening the execution time.

Instruction	Mnemonic	Operand Format	Operation
Flush entry in ATC	PFLUSHA		Invalidate all ATC entries.
	PFLUSH	FC,#MASK	Invalidate all ATC entries for a selected function code.
		FC,#MASK,EA	Invalidate the page descriptor for a specified address entry in each selected function code.
Load an entry into ATC	PLOADR	FC,EA	Load the page descriptor for the specified address entry into the ATC.
	PLOADW	FC,EA	
Move MMU registers	PMOVE	MRn,EA	Move the selected MMU register (MRn) to the destination (EA)
		EA,MRn	or the source to the selected
	PMOVEFD	EA,MRn	MMU register. For PMOVEFD, the source is moved to MRn and the FD bit is set to disable flushing the ATC.
Test a logical address	PTESTR	FC,EA,#LEVEL	Search ATC and the translation tables up to a selected level for
		FC,EA,#LEVEL,An	the page descriptor specified by
	PTESTW	FC,EA,#LEVEL	EA and FC, and use its status to
		FC,EA,#LEVEL,An	set the MMU status register. If An is present, the physical address of the last fetched descriptor is loaded into An.

*All instructions are privileged.

Figure 10-16 New MC68030 instructions.

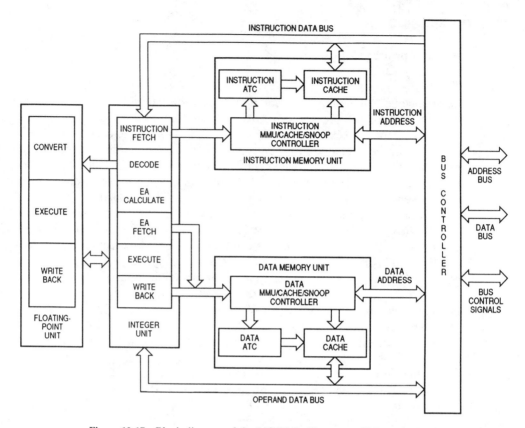

Figure 10-17 Block diagram of the MC68040. (Courtesy of Motorola, Inc.)

Third, the two separate instruction and data caches have been expanded to 4K bytes each from the MC68030's 256-byte caches. A larger on-chip cache increases the chance of cache hits and more significantly, reduces the traffic on the system bus. Finally, in addition to the integer execution unit, the MC68040 has included a floating-point execution unit which can execute the basic floating-point instructions of the MC68881/MC68882 FPCP. Both integer and floating-point execution units can operate independently and in parallel. This floating-point execution unit is also implemented as a pipeline with three stages: convert, execute, and write back. Although slower than integer execution, at 25-MHz clock rate, the MC68040 can achieve the rate of 3.15 million floating-point operations per second (Mflops).

Bus structure

The MC68040 retains the basic bus structure of the MC68020 and MC68030. It uses synchronous bus interface and keeps both 32-bit address and data buses and many of the familiar bus control signals. Because of its expanded 4K-byte instruction and data caches, the MC68040 can achieve a much higher cache hit ratio compared to the MC68030. As a result, in most cases, main memory is accessed by the MC68040 in the block form to transfer information between main memory and its caches. This is the reason that the MC68040 is primarily designed to operate efficiently in the burst mode and main memory should be designed to support burst cycles.

In the burst mode, four consecutive longwords (16 bytes) are transferred in five clock cycles, C1 through C5. During clock cycle C1, the MC68040 sends out the beginning address, the R/W̄ signal, and other bus transfer control signals. The beginning address is aligned to a 16-byte (line) boundary that address bits A3–A0 are zero. During each of the subsequent clock cycles that are controlled by the BCLK (bus clock), the memory sends or receives a longword and internally increments address bits A3 and A2 pointing to the next longword.

Since data transfers between caches and external memory employ efficient burst cycles, only occasionally is there a need for conventional single byte, word, and longword bus cycles. Typically such occasions include accesses to noncacheable data, read-modify-write accesses (TAS and CAS instructions), and writes to write-through pages. Although the MC68040 can transfer single byte, word, or longword in a nonburst mode, it does not support dynamic bus sizing as does the MC68020/MC68030. Therefore, only 32-bit memory and devices can occupy contiguous locations. Normally, an 8-bit device is connected to the least significant byte (D7–D0) and a 16-bit device connected to the least significant word (D15–D0) of the 32-bit data bus so that their interrupt vector number can be sent over D7–D0. Each nonburst data transfer cycle requires two clock cycles. During the first clock cycle, the processor sends out address, R/W̄, and other control signals. During the second clock cycle, the selected device latches data from or places data onto the data bus and asserts T̄Ā (transfer acknowledge signal) to terminate the transfer.

The pin definitions of the MC68040 are summarized in Fig. 10-18. In addition

Signal Name	Mnemonic	Function
Address Bus	A31–A0	32-bit address bus used to address any of 4 Gbytes.
Data Bus	D31–D0	32-bit data bus used to transfer up to 32 bits of data per bus transfer.
Transfer Type	TT1,TT0	Indicates the general transfer type: normal, MOVE16, alternate logical function code, and acknowledge.
Transfer Modifier	TM2,TM0	Indicates supplemental information about the access.
Transfer Line Number	TLN1,TLN0	Indicates which cache line in a set is being pushed or loaded by the current line transfer.
User Programmable Attributes	UPA1,UPA0	User-defined signals, controlled by the corresponding user attribute bits from the address translation entry.
Read/Write	R/W̄	Identifies the transfer as a read or write.
Transfer Size	SIZ1,SIZ0	Indicates the data transfer size. These signals, together with A0 and A1, define the active sections of the data bus.
Bus Lock	L̄ŌCK	Indicates a bus transfer is part of a read-modify-write operation, and that the sequence of transfers should not be interrupted.
Bus Lock End	L̄ŌCKE	Indicates the current transfer is the last in a locked sequence of transfers.

Figure 10-18 MC68040 pin definitions. (Courtesy of Motorola, Inc.)

Signal Name	Mnemonic	Function
Cache Inhibit Out	$\overline{\text{CIOUT}}$	Indicates the processor will not cache the current bus transfer.
Transfer Start	$\overline{\text{TS}}$	Indicates the beginning of a bus transfer.
Transfer in Progress	$\overline{\text{TIP}}$	Asserted for the duration of a bus transfer.
Transfer Acknowledge	$\overline{\text{TA}}$	Asserted to acknowledge a bus transfer.
Transfer Error Acknowledge	$\overline{\text{TEA}}$	Indicates an error condition exists for a bus transfer.
Transfer Cache Inhibit	$\overline{\text{TCI}}$	Indicates the current bus transfer should not be cached.
Transfer Burst Inhibit	$\overline{\text{TBI}}$	Indicates the slave cannot handle a line burst access.
Data Latch Enable	DLE	Alternate clock input used to latch input data when the processor is operating in DLE mode.
Snoop Control	SC1,SC0	Indicates the snooping operation required during an alternate master access.
Memory Inhibit	$\overline{\text{MI}}$	Inhibits memory devices from responding to an alternate master access during snooping operations.
Bus Request	$\overline{\text{BR}}$	Asserted by the processor to request bus mastership.
Bus Grant	$\overline{\text{BG}}$	Asserted by an arbiter to grant bus mastership to the processor.
Bus Busy	$\overline{\text{BB}}$	Asserted by the current bus master to indicate it has assumed ownership of the bus.
Cache Disable	$\overline{\text{CDIS}}$	Dynamically disables the internal caches to assist emulator support.
MMU Disable	$\overline{\text{MDIS}}$	Disables the translation mechanism of the MMUs.
Reset In	$\overline{\text{RSTI}}$	Processor reset.
Reset Out	$\overline{\text{RSTO}}$	Asserted during execution of a RESET instruction to reset external devices.
Interrupt Priority Level	$\overline{\text{IPL2}}$–$\overline{\text{IPL0}}$	Provides an encoded interrupt level to the processor.
Interrupt Pending	$\overline{\text{IPEND}}$	Indicates an interrupt is pending.
Autovector	$\overline{\text{AVEC}}$	Used during an interrupt acknowledge transfer to request internal generation of the vector number.
Processor Status	PST3–PST0	Indicates internal processor status.
Bus Clock	BCLK	Clock input used to derive all bus signal timing.
Processor Clock	PCLK	Clock input used for internal logic timing. The PCLK frequency is exactly 2X the BCLK frequency.
Test Clock	TCK	Clock signal for the IEEE P1149.1 Test Access Port (TAP).
Test Mode Select	TMS	Selects the principle operations of the test-support circuitry.
Test Data Input	TDI	Serial data input for the TAP.
Test Data Output	TDO	Serial data output for the TAP.
Test Reset	$\overline{\text{TRST}}$	Provides an asynchronous reset of the TAP controller.
Power Supply	V_{CC}	Power supply.
Ground	GND	Ground connection.

Figure 10-18 (*continued*)

to the 32-bit data and 32-bit address buses, the remaining pins can be divided into the following functional groups:

1. Transfer attributes (TT1–TT0, TM2–TM0, TLN1–TLN0, UPA1–UPA0, R/$\overline{\text{W}}$, SIZ1–SIZ0, $\overline{\text{LOCK}}$, $\overline{\text{LOCKE}}$, and $\overline{\text{CIOUT}}$) to provide bus cycle type, data size, and other information signals for the bus transfer.
2. Bus transfer control signals ($\overline{\text{TS}}$, $\overline{\text{TIP}}$, $\overline{\text{TA}}$, $\overline{\text{TEA}}$, $\overline{\text{TCI}}$, and DLE) to provide bus master control outputs as well as responses from bus slave to control the bus transfer.
3. Bus arbitration signals ($\overline{\text{BR}}$, $\overline{\text{BG}}$, and $\overline{\text{BB}}$) to support configurations with multiple bus masters.
4. Processor control signals ($\overline{\text{CDIS}}$, $\overline{\text{MDIS}}$, $\overline{\text{RSTI}}$, and $\overline{\text{RSTO}}$) to reset the system and disable on-chip MMUs and caches.
5. Bus snoop control signals (SC1–SC0 and $\overline{\text{MI}}$) to maintain cache coherence in multiprocessor configurations. Cache coherence problem is explained in Sec. 12-2.
6. Interrupt control signals ($\overline{\text{IPL2}}$–$\overline{\text{IPL0}}$, $\overline{\text{IPEND}}$, and $\overline{\text{AVEC}}$) to support both auto vector and non-auto vector interrupt types.
7. Status and clocks (PST3–PST0, BCLK, and PCLK) to support emulation by providing internal execution unit status and to provide timing inputs for the processor.
8. Test signals (TCK, TMS, TDI, TDO and $\overline{\text{TRST}}$) to provide interfacing signals for the external TAP (test access port) for board testing.

Addressing modes, data types, and instruction set

The MC68040 retains the same 18 addressing modes of the MC68020/MC68030. They include the 12 addressing modes common to all members in the M68000 family, plus the 4 memory indirect addressing modes and the 2 index sizing and scaling options that have been added to the MC68020.

The MC68040 supports all the data formats provided by any members in the M68000 family plus the new 16-byte data format. Because the MC68040 extends its instruction set to include floating-point arithmetic operations, it also includes all real data types supported by the MC68881/MC68882 FPCP. The only exception is the packed decimal real (P) type, which represents a floating-point number in the BCD form with a total of 96 bits. In summary, the data types supported by the MC68040 are:

1. Bit, BCD, byte integer, word integer, and longword integer common to all processor members in the family.
2. Bit field and quad-word integer, which are new additions to the MC68020/MC68030.
3. 16-byte data type, which is used only in the new MOVE16 instruction.
4. Single-precision real (S), double-precision real (D), and extended-precision real (X), which are supported by the MC68881/MC68882.

Mnemonic	Description
ABCD	Add Decimal with Extend
ADD	Add
ADDA	Add Address
ADDI	Add Immediate
ADDQ	Add Quick
ADDX	Add with Extend
AND	Logical AND
ANDI	Logical AND Immediate
ASL, ASR	Arithmetic Shift Left and Right
Bcc	Branch Conditionally
BCHG	Test Bit and Change
BCLR	Test Bit and Clear
BFCHG	Test Bit Field and Change
BFCLR	Test Bit Field and Clear
BFEXTS	Signed Bit Field Extract
BFEXTU	Unsigned Bit Field Extract
BFFFO	Bit Field Find First One
BFINS	Bit Field Insert
BFSET	Test Bit Field and Set
BFTST	Test Bit Field
BRA	Branch
BSET	Test Bit and Set
BSR	Branch to Subroutine
BTST	Test Bit
CAS	Compare and Swap Operands
CAS2	Compare and Swap Dual Operands
CHK	Check Register Against Bounds
CHK2	Check Register Against Upper and Lower Bounds
*CINV	Invalidate Cache Entries
CLR	Clear
CMP	Compare
CMPA	Compare Address
CMPI	Compare Immediate
CMPM	Compare Memory to Memory
CMP2	Compare Register Against Upper and Lower Bounds
*CPUSH	Push then Invalidate Cache Entries
DBcc	Test Condition, Decrement and Branch
DIVS, DIVSL	Signed Divide
DIVU, DIVUL	Unsigned Divide
EOR	Logical Exclusive OR
EORI	Logical Exclusive OR Immediate
EXG	Exchange Registers
EXT, EXTB	Sign Extend
*FABS	Floating-Point Absolute Value
*FADD	Floating-Point Add
FBcc	Floating-Point Branch
FCMP	Floating-Point Compare
FDBcc	Floating-Point Decrement and Branch
*FDIV	Floating-Point Divide
*FMOVE	Move Floating-Point Register
FMOVEM	Move Multiple Floating-Point Registers
*FMUL	Floating-Point Multiply
*FNEG	Floating-Point Negate
FRESTORE	Restore Floating-Point Internal State
FSAVE	Save Floating-Point Internal State
FScc	Floating-Point Set According to Condition
*FSQRT	Floating-Point Square Root

Mnemonic	Description
*FSUB	Floating-Point Subtract
FTRAPcc	Floating-Point Trap-On Condition
FTST	Floating-Point Test
ILLEGAL	Take Illegal Instruction Trap
JMP	Jump
JSR	Jump to Subroutine
LEA	Load Effective Address
LINK	Link and Allocate
LSL, LSR	Logical Shift Left and Right
MOVE	Move
*MOVE16	16-Byte Block Move
MOVEA	Move Address
MOVE CCR	Move Condition Code Register
MOVE SR	Move Status Register
MOVE USP	Move User Stack Pointer
*MOVEC	Move Control Register
MOVEM	Move Multiple Registers
MOVEP	Move Peripheral
MOVEQ	Move Quick
*MOVES	Move Alternate Address Space
MULS	Signed Multiply
MULU	Unsigned Multiply
NBCD	Negate Decimal with Extend
NEG	Negate
NEGX	Negate with Extend
NOP	No Operation
NOT	Logical Complement
OR	Logical Inclusive OR
ORI	Logical Inclusive OR Immediate
PACK	Pack BCD
PEA	Push Effective Address
*PFLUSH	Flush Entry(ies) in the ATCs
*PTEST	Test a Logical Address
RESET	Reset External Devices
ROL, ROR	Rotate Left and Right
ROXL, RORX	Rotate with Extend Left and Right
RTD	Return and Deallocate
RTE	Return from Exception
RTR	Return and Restore Codes
RTS	Return from Subroutine
SBCD	Subtract Decimal with Extend
Scc	Set Conditionally
STOP	Stop
SUB	Subtract
SUBA	Subtract Address
SUBI	Subtract Immediate
SUBQ	Subtract Quick
SUBX	Subtract with Extend
SWAP	Swap Register Words
TAS	Test Operand and Set
TRAP	Trap
TRAPcc	Trap Conditionally
TRAPV	Tap on Overflow
TST	Test Operand
UNLK	Unlink
UNPK	Unpack BCD

*MC68040 additions or alterations to the MC68030 and MC68881/M68882 instruction set.

Figure 10-19 MC68040 instruction set summary. (Courtesy of Motorola, Inc.)

The MC68040 has a total of 120 instructions with 20 new instructions. The MC68040 instruction set is summarized in Fig. 10-19. The two new privileged instructions, CINV (invalid cache entries) and CPUSH (push then invalidate), are for providing maintenance functions in managing the instruction and data caches.

The only user integer instruction being added is the MOVE16 (move 16 bytes block) instruction which copies 16 consecutive bytes from the line boundary specified by source to the destination line address. This operation is performed with a burst read from the source followed by a burst write to the destination. The source and destination can be specified on the following five formats.

```
MOVE16      (Ax) + ,(Ay) +
MOVE16      XXX.L,(An)
MOVE16      XXX.L,(An) +
MOVE16      (An),XXX.L
MOVE16      (An) + ,XXX.L
```

A typical application of the postincrement-to-postincrement mode is to provide fast memory block copy. Using absolute long addressing mode for the source performs fast memory block initialization operation.

The MC68040 has a floating-point execution unit which is a simplified version of the MC68881/MC68882 coprocessor (FPCP). The MC68040 can directly execute 18 of the 47 instruction types in the FPCP instruction sets. The remaining 29 instruction types must be implemented by software. In order to simplify the emulation implementation, the MC68040 provides a special unimplemented floating-point instruction exception which is different from regular unimplemented F-line instruction exception. A floating-point instruction exception generates a type $2 stack frame while a regular unimplemented F-line instruction exception is identified by a type $0 stack frame. Packed decimal real (P) numbers must be emulated also. This data type is emulated through an unimplemented data type exception.

EXERCISES

1. Use a table to compare the differences of MC68000, MC68010, MC68020, and MC68030. The comparison should include data bus width, maximum possible memory size, new registers, and new instructions.

2. Assume that an ACIA is to be used in an MC68020-based system. Show the connections of the ACIA to the data, DS, DACK0, and DACK1 bus lines.

3. Assume that a memory module consisting of four byte-organized memory banks is to be interfaced to the MC68020. Show its connections to the data, DS, DACK0, DACK1, UUD, UMD, LMD, and LLD bus lines.

4. Which of the two processor characteristics limits the maximum virtual space size, address register size, or number of address pins?

5. Does the 2-word instruction queue of the MC68000 reduce the bus utilization?

6. Use an example to illustrate how an on-chip cache of one processor may improve the throughput of another processor in a multiprocessor configuration sharing a common bus.

7. Assume the following initial conditions:

```
00102000:  00  10  20  38  00  10  20  39  00  10  20  3A  00  10  20  3B
00102010:  00  10  20  3C  00  10  20  3D  00  10  20  3E  00  10  20  3F
00102020:  00  10  20  40  00  10  20  41  00  10  20  42  00  10  20  43
00102030:  00  10  20  44  00  10  20  45  00  10  20  46  00  10  20  47
00102040:  00  10  20  60  00  10  20  5F  00  10  20  5E  00  10  20  5D
00102050:  00  10  20  5C  00  10  20  5B  00  10  20  5A  00  10  20  59
00102060:  00  10  20  58  00  10  20  57  00  10  20  56  00  10  20  55
00102070:  00  10  20  54  00  10  20  53  00  10  20  52  00  10  20  51
A1:  00100000    D1:00000020
```

Show the effective address and value of the memory operand specified in each of the following instructions:

(a) MOVE.B   D1,([8,A1],D1.W*1,32)
(b) MOVE.B   D1,(8,A1,D1.W,32)
(c) MOVE.W   D1,([8,A1],D1.W*2,0)
(d) MOVE.W   D1,(8,A1,D1.W*2,0)
(e) MOVE.W   D1,([8,A1,D1.W*2],0)
(f) MOVE.L   D1,([8,A1],D1.W*4,4)
(g) MOVE.L   D1,([8,A1,D1.W*8],4)

8. Assuming the same initial condition as given in Exercise 7, show the result after each of the following bit field instructions is executed:

(a) BFCHG   (30,A1){$24,$12}
(b) BFINS   D1,(30,A1){$24, −8}
(c) BFCLR   (30,A1){−8,$12}
(d) BFEXTS   (30,A1){−8, −$12}

9. Write an instruction sequence to implement the following: Set bit 3 in byte ARRAY + 3 to 1 if bit 1 in byte ARRAY or bit 5 in byte ARRAY + 1 is 1; otherwise, clear bit 3 in byte ARRAY + 3. Assume that bit 0 corresponds to the least significant bit in a byte.

10. Which two MC68020 instructions are not available in the MC68030 and why?

11. Construct a cross-reference table to show all the data types supported by the M68000 family. For each data type, list its size in bits and supporting processors.

11

Floating-Point Coprocessors

The MC68000 is a general-purpose microprocessor whose arithmetic instructions are for binary fixed-point arithmetic operations that are applicable to numbers in a relatively small range. For scientific and engineering applications, numbers are frequently represented in the floating-point format. A number X is specified in the mantissa and exponent parts as

$$(-1)^S M \times B^E$$

where S is the sign, M the mantissa, E the exponent, and B the base for the floating-point representation. By moving the radix point in the mantissa and adjusting the exponent accordingly, a floating-point number always retains the most significant digits of X. For example, in scientific notation, the number 123,000,000 would be represented as 1.23×10^8 and 0.000000123 would be given as 1.23×10^{-7}. This allows extremely large numbers as well as extremely small numbers to be representable in the floating-point format.

Performing an arithmetic operation with floating-point numbers can be broken down to a sequence of integer arithmetic operations on the mantissa parts and the exponent parts of the two involved floating-point numbers. To simplify the discussion, let us use decimal arithmetics in the following illustration. Consider the floating-point addition

$$6.21 \times 10^1 + 5.1 \times 10^{-1}$$

which is performed as

$$(6.21 + 0.051) \times 10^1 = 6.261 \times 10^1$$

In general, this requires four major steps:

Step 1. *Subtraction of exponents:* Compare the two exponents and subtract the smaller one from the larger one. In this example, the result is $1 - (-1) = 2$.

Step 2. *Alignment of mantissas:* Adjust the decimal point position in the mantissa of the smaller number so that both mantissas are aligned by the decimal point. This can be implemented by shifting the mantissa of the smaller number to the right by the number of digits that is the difference of two exponents obtained from Step 1. In this example, 5.1 is shifted to the right by two decimal digits.

Step 3. *Addition of mantissas:* Add the two aligned mantissas to form the mantissa of the sum. In this example, the result is $6.21 + 0.051 = 6.261$. The exponent of the larger number is used as the exponent of the sum.

Step 4. *Postnormalization of result:* Adjust the decimal point position in the mantissa and increment or decrement the exponent accordingly so that the result is normalized. In the normalized form, the integral part must be a single nonzero digit. In this example, no adjustment is needed. Should a result be 12.34×10^1, after the postnormalization it would become 1.234×10^2.

Clearly, a floating-point arithmetic operation can be implemented with integer arithmetic instructions by processing the mantissa parts and the exponent parts separately. But this software emulation is slow, and emulation routines are complex. In order to provide fast computations of floating-point numbers, Motorola made available floating-point coprocessors, which include floating-point arithmetic instructions that implement floating-point arithmetic operations in hardware. As a comparison, adding two double-precision real numbers can be performed in as little as 10 microseconds with a floating-point instruction, whereas the same operation executed in the MC68000 instructions requires hundreds of microseconds. A floating-point coprocessor also provides special instructions to perform frequently used scientific functions such as square root, trigonometry, and logarithm.

11-1 MC68881/MC68882 FPCP

Two models of floating-point coprocessor (FPCP), MC68881 and MC68882, are available to provide members in the M68000 family with floating-point processing capabilities. The two models are fully compatible and can be physically interchanged. The only difference between the two is the enhanced performance of the MC68882, which can execute more than one floating-point instruction simultaneously and can perform faster conversion of memory operands to the internal data format.

The FPCP is specially designed to perform arithmetic operations efficiently. It can operate on data of integer and floating-point types, with lengths ranging from 2 to 12 bytes. The instruction set not only includes various forms of addition, subtraction, multiplication, and division but also provides many useful functions, such as taking the square root, exponent, tangent, and so on. As an example of computing power, the FPCP can multiply two 64-bit real numbers in about 71 clock cycles and calculate a square root in about 107 clock cycles. The FPCP provides a simple and effective way to enhance the performance of systems based on the members of the M68000 family, particularly when an application is primarily computational in nature.

The FPCP can neither fetch its own instructions nor load or store memory operands. Therefore, it must operate with a processor in the M68000 family as the host. When configured with the MC68000 or MC68010 microprocessor, the FPCP is interfaced as a peripheral processor, and interaction between the MC68000/MC68010 and the FPCP must be handled by software. For later members in the family, such as the MC68020 and MC68030, the FPCP can be connected as a coprocessor. In such a coprocessor configuration, the communication between the host and FPCP is handled entirely by hardware, thus significantly reducing the amount of programming required.

FPCP's data types

The FPCP can operate on memory operands of seven different data types: byte integer (B), word integer (W), longword integer (L), single-precision real (S), double-precision real (D), extended-precision real (X), and packed decimal string real (P). The number of bytes, format and approximate range of each of these data types are shown in Fig. 11-1. In memory, the most significant byte of a number is always stored in the lowest address.

The three integer formats are identical to those of the M68000 family. However, the FPCP always interprets an integer operand as a signed integer in 2's complement and converts it to extended-precision real format before performing a floating-point arithmetic operation.

All three binary real formats consist of three fields: sign of the number (S), the biased exponent (E), and the fraction (F). The real number represented by these fields is formed as

$$X = (-1)^S 2^{E - \text{bias value}} \times 1.F$$

For the single-precision real format, the valid range of the biased exponent is $0 < E < 255$ with the bias value $= 127$. Consequently, the numbers that can be represented are from $\pm 2^{1-127}$ to $\pm 2^{254-127}$, approximately $\pm 1 \times 10^{-38}$ to $\pm 3 \times 10^{38}$.

The maximum biased exponent—that is, all 1s in this field—is reserved to represent infinity, or "not a number" (NAN). When the biased exponent field has all 1s, a fraction of all zeros represents an infinity and a fraction of a nonzero bit pattern represents an NAN. At the other extreme, the minimum biased exponent—that is, all 0s in this field—is used to represent $+0$ (all 0s with a $+$ sign), -0 (all 0s with a $-$ sign), or a denormalized number. When the biased exponent field has all 0s, a fraction of all zeros represents the real number 0.0, and a fraction of a nonzero bit pattern represents a denormalized number. A denormalized number is a result that causes an underflow and has leading 0s in the fraction even after the exponent is adjusted to its smallest possible value. NANs and denor-

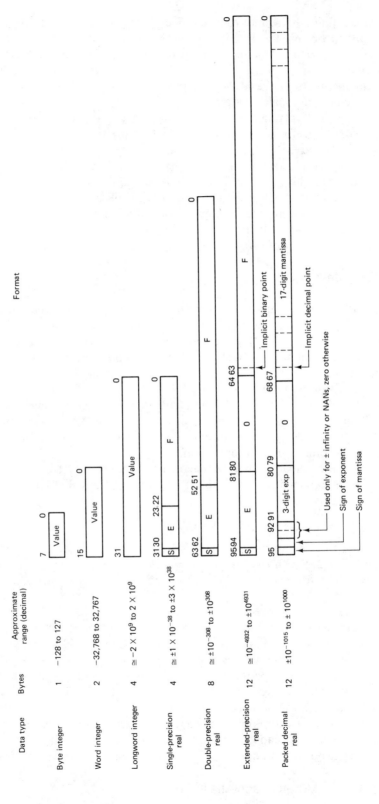

Figure 11-1 Data formats for the FPCP.

malized numbers are normally used to indicate overflows and underflows, respectively, although they may be used for other purposes also.

The double-precision real format has 11 exponent bits and 52 fraction bits. As in the single-precision format, the first nonzero bit in the mantissa is implied and not actually stored. The range of representable nonzero quantities is extended to approximately $\pm 10^{-308}$ to $\pm 10^{308}$. The FPCP internally stores all numbers in the extended-precision real format, which uses 15 bits for the exponent and 64 bits for the mantissa. Unlike the single-precision and double-precision real formats, the most significant bit in the mantissa is actually stored. A primary reason for using the extended-precision real format for internal data storage is to reduce the chances for overflows and underflows during a series of calculations that produce a final result that is within the required range. For example, consider the calculation:

$$D = (A*B)/C$$

where A, B, C, and D are in the single-precision real format. The multiply operation may yield a result that is too large to be represented in the single-precision real format, but yet the final result, after the division by C, may still be within the valid range. The 15-bit exponent of the extended-precision real format extends the range of valid numbers to approximately $\pm 10^{\pm 4932}$. Therefore, for most applications the user need not worry about overflows and underflows in the intermediate calculations.

In addition to the three binary real data formats, the FPCP also accepts a floating-point data format using decimal digits, referred to as the packed decimal real data format. A decimal real format stores real numbers in a three-field decimal format that resembles scientific notation. Therefore, this format is particularly desirable in applications that involve inputting or outputting real numbers in decimal form. The packed decimal real data format consists of a 24-digit decimal string. The string has a 3-digit base 10 exponent, a 17-digit base 10 mantissa, and two separate sign bits for exponent and mantissa. All decimal digits are in the packed BCD form, and the entire number has 12 bytes. As an example, the number 5.23 E-2 has the following representation in the packed decimal real format:

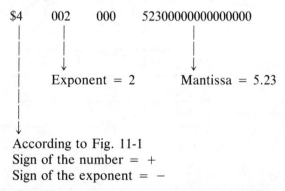

According to Fig. 11-1
Sign of the number = +
Sign of the exponent = −

Programming model

Figure 11-2 shows the FPCP register set. There are eight floating-point data registers, denoted by FP0–FP7. Like the D0–D7 registers of the host processor, they

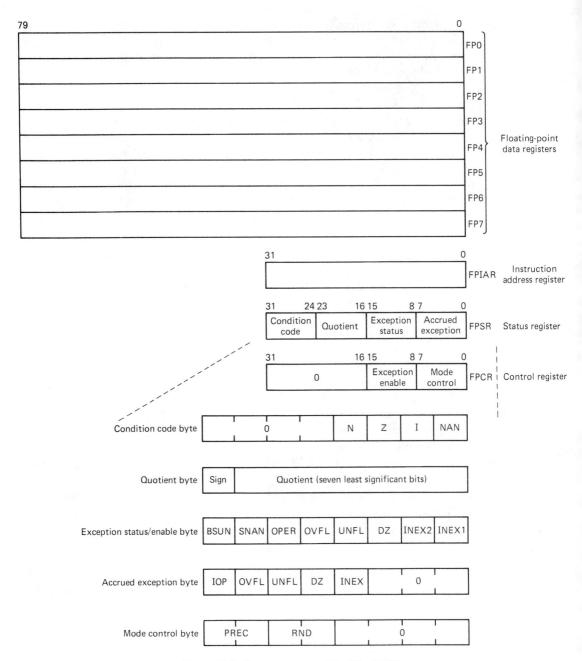

Figure 11-2 Programming model of the FPCP.

are general-purpose registers for holding data operands. Because in most cases numbers are internally stored in the extended-precision real format, each floating-point data register has 80 bits. The 32-bit instruction address register stores the address of the current floating-point instruction being executed. During an exception initiated by the FPCP, this address is useful in locating the instruction that caused the exception.

The status register stores the condition code for certain instructions and reports various errors. It has 32 bits divided into 4 bytes. The condition code byte indicates four conditions, negative (N), zero (Z), infinity (I), and not a number (NAN), that can be tested by conditional branch instructions. The quotient byte is set only in the modulo (FMOD) or remainder (FREM) instruction. For such an instruction, the remainder is stored in a data register, and the least significant part of the quotient can be found in this byte. In some applications, the quotient might also be needed in a modulo operation—for example, in determining the quadrant of a circle for a given angle.

The exception status/enable byte of the status register reports eight error types, which can cause an exception if their respective enable bits are set in the control register. The bit definitions of the exception byte are as follows.

INEX1 (inexact decimal input): A packed decimal real operand cannot be converted exactly to the extended-precision real format; that is, roundoff has been performed. For example, this bit will be set when 3E-1 is used as a source operand.

INEX2 (inexact operation): An operation produces an inexact result, for example, as in 2.0 divided by 3.0. Both INEX1 and INEX2 are normally used only for applications where exact results are required.

DZ (divide by zero): An attempt is made to divide an operand by zero.

UNFL (underflow): An underflow occurs in the exponent of the result; that is, the biased exponent is too small.

OVFL (overflow): An overflow occurs in the exponent; that is, the biased exponent is too large.

OPERR (operand error): An invalid operand is used, such as, square root of a negative number or arcsine of a number greater than 1.

SNAN (signaling not a number): This bit indicates that an operand is not a number, which is useful in handling user-defined data types.

BSUN (branch/set on unordered): A noncompatible condition is present— that is, NAN status bit = 1—when executing a FBcc, FDBcc or FTRAPcc instruction.

The accrued exception byte contains the five error bits required to be compatible with the IEEE standard for trap disabled operation. The IOP (invalid operation) is a combined status bit of BSUN, SNAN, and OPERR, and the INEX (inexact) is a combination of INEX1 and INEX2.

Although the FPCP recognizes eight error types, each error type may be individually masked from causing an exception by clearing the corresponding enable bits to 0 in the control register. If disabled, the error will not cause an exception. Instead, the FPCP will perform a standard response and then proceed with the next instruction in sequence. In particular, the inexact errors, for which the standard response is to return the rounded result, should be disabled for floating-point arithmetics because for most applications precision errors will occur most of the time. Inexact errors need to be handled only in special situations.

The control register is also a 32-bit register. However, its most significant 16 bits are not currently being used but are reserved for future expansions. The remaining 16 bits are divided into the exception enable and the mode control bytes. The exception enable byte has the same layout as the exception status byte of the status register. Setting an enable bit to 1 allows the FPCF to initiate an exception whenever the corresponding exception status bit becomes 1. The control byte is for specifying the options of rounding (RND) and precision (PREC). The bit definitions are given next.

PREC bits:
00 means 64-bit precision.
01 means 24-bit precision.
10 means 53-bit precision.
11 is reserved.

RND bits:
00 means round to nearest integer.
01 means round toward 0, that is, truncation.
10 means round toward $-\infty$.
11 means round toward $+\infty$.

11-2 Instruction Set and Programming

The FPCP has 47 instructions, which can be divided into four groups according to their functions: data transfer, arithmetic, comparison and program control, and transcendental. A typical instruction accepts one or two input operands, performs the operation and then places the result in the destination. In most cases, the destination operand must be a floating-point register. Since the FPCP relies on the host processor for accessing memory operands, if a memory operand is permitted in the instruction, its effective address can be specified with any addressing mode of the host processor.

Many instructions allow more than one format to specify their operands. The valid options for operand sizes depend on the selected operand format. As an example, consider the FABS (absolute value) instruction, which converts the input operand to an extended-precision real number and stores its absolute value in the destination floating-point data register. This instruction allows the following three forms:

```
FABS.Size      EA,FPn
```

where the size postfix may be B, W, L, S, D, X, or P.

```
FABS.X         FPm,FPn
```

and

FABS.X   FPn

In the first form, any data addressing mode supported by the host processor may be used to specify the input operand, including a host's data register. The data format of the input operand may be byte integer (.B), word integer (.W), longword integer (.L), single-precision real (.S), double-precision real (.D), extended-precision real (.X), or packed decimal real (.P). When both operands are floating-point data registers, as in the second form, the size postfix must be .X because the content of a floating-point data register in most cases is in extended-precision form. For an instruction that requires only one input operand, such as the FABS, the same data register may be used for both source and destination, as shown in the third form. To simplify the description of instruction operation, we use SRC to indicate the first operand in the instruction. Therefore, SRC represents EA in the first form, FPm in the second form, and FPn in the third form, and the operation of instruction FABS can be described as

$$|(SRC)| \rightarrow FPn$$

for all three forms.

Data transfer group

There are seven instructions in the data transfer group, as shown in Fig. 11-3. The FMOV instruction allows the user to move an operand to or from a floating-point data register, and if an external operand is used, its data type may be any of the seven forms.

The FPCP has an internal ROM that stores 22 commonly used constants such as π, e, 0.0, 1.0, $\text{Log}_e 2$, $\text{Log}_e 10$. The user can load these constants into data registers as needed for operations by using the move constant ROM (FMOVECR) instruction. Unlike most other instructions, the input operand of this instruction is a 7-bit number specifying the offset of the constants in ROM to be loaded. The available constants and their offsets are

Constant	π	$\text{Log}_{10}2$	e	$\text{Log}_2 e$	$\text{Log}_{10}e$	0.0	$\text{Log}_e 2$	$\text{Log}_e 10$
Offset	$00	$0B	$0C	$0D	$0E	$0F	$30	$31

Constant	1.0	10	10^2	10^4	10^8	10^{16}	10^{32}	10^{64}
Offset	$32	$33	$34	$35	$36	$37	$38	$39

Constant	10^{128}	10^{256}	10^{512}	10^{1024}	10^{2048}	10^{4096}
Offset	$3A	$3B	$3C	$3D	$3E	$3F

In a subroutine call or exception processing, the internal data and control registers of the FPCP need to be saved and restored as for the host processor. For this reason, the data move instruction group includes the move multiple registers (FMOVEM) instruction, which saves a specified list of floating-point data

Mnemonic	Size or Postfix	Operand Format	Allowable EA Modes	Operation
FMOVE (Move data register)	.B, .W, .L, .S, .D, .X, .P .X .B, .W, .L, .S, .D, .X .P .P	EA,FPn FPm,FPn FPm,EA FPm,EA{Dn} FPm,EA{#k}	Data Data alterable Data alterable	(SRC) -> FPn FPm -> EA
FMOVE (Move control register)	.L .L	EA,FPcr FPcr,EA	All Alterable	(EA) -> control register Control register -> EA
FMOVECR (Move constant ROM)	.X	#ccc,FPn		ROM constant -> FPn
FMOVEM (Move multiple data registers)	.X .X .X .X	Reg List,EA Dn,EA EA,Reg List EA,Dn	Control alterable or -(An) Control or (An)+	Data registers -> EA (EA) -> Data registers
FMOVEM (Move multiple control registers)	.L .L	Reg List,EA EA,Reg List	Alterable All	Control registers -> EA (EA) -> Control registers
FRESTORE (Restore internal state)	Unsized	EA	Control or (An)+	(EA) -> Internal state (Privileged)
FSAVE (Save internal state)	Unsized	EA	Control alterable or -(An)	Internal state -> EA (Privileged)

Figure 11-3 FPCP data movement instructions.

or control registers to memory or restores them from memory. In addition, the FPCP supplies a pair of privileged instructions, FSAVE and FSTORE, for saving and restoring its entire machine state to and from memory. This allows the FPCP to be used with the host processor in a virtual memory system. Just as for the host processor, during a page fault, the internal state of FPCP must be saved so that the current floating-point instruction can be continued after the fault being fixed. It requires 184 bytes of memory to save the entire state for the MC68881 and 216 bytes for the MC68882.

Arithmetic group

The FPCP has the instructions for performing the basic floating-point arithmetic operations, addition, subtraction, multiplication, and division. Each instruction requires two input operands, and the result is always stored in the second operand, which must be a data register. The first operand may have any data format and may be a data register or an external operand. It is automatically converted to the extended real form before performing the arithmetic operation, except for the FSGLMUL and FSGLDIV instructions. These two instructions perform single-precision multiply and divide operations and therefore are much faster than the FMUL and FDIV instructions.

In addition to the basic arithmetic operations, the FPCP provides instructions to calculate the square root, adjust the scale values using the power of 2, perform modulo division, round real values to integer values, extract the exponent and fraction, take the absolute value, and change the sign. Most of these instructions require only one input operand. Figure 11-4 summarizes the arithmetic instructions.

Comparison and program control group

Figure 11-5 summarizes the comparison and program control instructions. The compare and test instructions perform a subtract operation and then set the floating-point condition codes N, Z, I, and NAN accordingly. These condition codes can be tested in a conditional branch instruction (FBcc) or a decrement and conditional branch (FDBcc) instruction. In these instructions the cc specifier selects the floating-point condition that causes a branch. Some sample test conditions are EQ (equal), NE (not equal), GT (greater than), GE (greater than or equal), LT (less than), LE (less than or equal), GLE (greater, less, or equal; i.e., NAN = 0), and NGLE (not comparable; i.e., NAN = 1). Note that in executing a conditional branch instruction, the FPCP merely checks its floating-point condition code settings. It is the host processor that performs the branch if the selected condition is true.

Also included in this group are the FNOP (no operation) and FTRAPcc (trap conditionally) instructions. Similar to the TRAPcc of the MC68020 and MC68030, the FTRAPcc causes the host processor to initiate an exception with the vector number equal to 7 when the selected condition is met. The optional 16- or 32-bit immediate operand is for passing parameters to the exception handler.

Transcendental group

In addition to arithmetic instructions, the FPCP has a group of transcendental instructions, which are summarized in Fig. 11-6. These instructions provide fast calculations for trigonometric, inverse trigonometric, hyperbolic, inverse hyperbolic, logarithmic and exponential functions, which are common but time-consuming.

Although each instruction in this group requires only one input operand, a source and a destination may be specified. The operation is performed on the source operand, and the result is stored in the destination, which must be a floating-point data register. When the source is not a floating-point register, any data format may be used, and the source operand is converted to extended-precision format before the operation is performed.

Programming examples

Two examples are given to illustrate FPCP programming. It is assumed that the FPCP is connected to an MC68020 or MC68030 as a coprocessor. In this configuration, since interactions between the FPCP and the host processor are handled by the coprocessor interface hardware of the host, a program requiring floating-point instructions can be written in a superset of instructions composed of the MC68020 and the FPCP instructions.

Mnemonic	Size or Postfix	Operand Format	Allowable EA Modes	Operation
FADD (Add)	.B, .W, .L, .S, .D, .X, .P .X	EA,FPn FPm,FPn	Data	(SRC) + FPn -> FPn
FSUB (Subtract)	.B, .W, .L, .S, .D, .X, .P .X	EA,FPn FPm,FPn	Data	FPn - (SRC) -> FPn
FMUL (Multiply)	.B, .W, .L, .S, .D, .X, .P .X	EA,FPn FPm,FPn	Data	(SRC) * FPn -> FPn
FDIV (Divide)	.B, .W, .L, .S, .D, .X, .P .X	EA,FPn FPm,FPn	Data	FPn / (SRC) -> FPn
FSGLDIV (Single precision divide)	.B, .W, .L, .S, .D, .X, .P .X	EA,FPn FPm,FPn	Data	FPn / (SRC) -> FPn (Single precision)
FSGLMUL (Single precision multiply)	.B, .W, .L, .S, .D, .X, .P .X	EA,FPn FPm,FPn	Data	(SRC) * FPn -> FPn (Single precision)
FNEG (Negate)	.B, .W, .L, .S, .D, .X, .P .X .X	EA,FPn FPm,FPn FPn	Data	-(SRC) -> FPn
FABS (Absolute value)	.B, .W, .L, .S, .D, .X, .P .X .X	EA,FPn FPm,FPn FPn	Data	|(SRC)| -> FPn
FSQRT (Square root)	.B, .W, .L, .S, .D, .X, .P .X .X	EA,FPn FPm,FPn FPn	Data	$\sqrt{(SRC)}$ -> FPn
FGETEXP (Get exponent)	.B, .W, .L, .S, .D, .X, .P .X .X	EA,FPn FPm,FPn FPn	Data	Exponent of (SRC) -> FPn
FSCALE (Scale exponent)	.B, .W, .L, .S, .D, .X, .P .X	EA,FPn FPm,FPn	Data	FPn * $2^{(\text{integer of (SRC)})}$ -> FPn
FGETMAN (Get mantissa)	.B, .W, .L, .S, .D, .X, .P .X .X	EA,FPn FPm,FPn FPn	Data	Mantissa of (SRC) -> FPn

Figure 11-4 FPCP arithmetic instructions.

Mnemonic	Size or Postfix	Operand Format	Allowable EA Modes	Operation
FINT (Integer part)	.B, .W, .L, .S, .D, .X, .P .X .X	EA,FPn FPm,FPn FPn	Data	Integer of (SRC) -> FPn
FINTRZ (Integer part, round to 0)	.B, .W, .L, .S, .D, .X, .P .X .X	EA,FPn FPm,FPn FPn	Data	Integer of (SRC) -> FPn (Round to 0)
FMOD (Modulo remainder)	.B, .W, .L, .S, .D, .X, .P .X	EA,FPn FPm,FPn	Data	FPn mod (SRC) -> FPn
FREM (Remainder)	.B, .W, .L, .S, .D, .X, .P .X	EA,FPn FPm,FPn	Data	Remainder of FPn / (SRC) -> FPn

Figure 11-4 (*continued*)

Mnemonic	Size or Postfix	Operand Format	Allowable EA Modes	Operation
FBcc (Branch conditionally)	.W, .L	DST		If cc then DST -> PC
FCMP (Compare)	.B, .W, .L, .S, .D, .X, .P .X	EA,FPn FPm,FPn	Data	FPn - (SRC)
FDBcc (Decrement and branch conditionally)	Unsized	Dn,DST		If cc then Dn - 1 -> Dn If Dn ≠ 1 then DST -> PC
FNOP (No operation)	Unsized			None
FScc (Set Conditionally)	Byte	EA	Data alterable	If cc then FF -> EA else 00 -> EA
FTRAPcc (Trap conditionally)	None .W, .L	None #Data		If cc then TRAP
FTST (Test)	.B, .W, .L, .S, .D, .X, .P .X	EA FPn	Data	(SRC) - 0

Figure 11-5 FPCP compare and program control instructions.

Mnemonic	Size or Postfix	Operand Format	Allowable EA Modes	Operation
FSIN (Sine)	.B, .W, .L, .S, .D, .X, .P .X .X	EA,FPn FPm,FPn FPn	Data	Sin (SRC) -> FPn
FCOS (Cosine)	.B, .W, .L, .S, .D, .X, .P .X .X	EA,FPn FPm,FPn FPn	Data	Cos (SRC) -> FPn
FTAN (Tangent)	.B, .W, .L, .S, .D, .X, .P .X .X	EA,FPn FPm,FPn FPn	Data	Tan (SRC) -> FPn
FSINCOS (Sine and cosine)	.B, .W, .L, .S, .D, .X, .P .X	EA,FPc:FPs FPm,FPc:FPs	Data	Sin (SRC) -> FPs Cos (SRC) -> FPc
FASIN (Arc sine)	.B, .W, .L, .S, .D, .X, .P .X .X	EA,FPn FPm,FPn FPn	Data	Sin^{-1} (SRC) -> FPn
FACOS (Arc cosine)	.B, .W, .L, .S, .D, .X, .P .X .X	EA,FPn FPm,FPn FPn	Data	Cos^{-1} (SRC) -> FPn
FATAN (Arc tangent)	.B, .W, .L, .S, .D, .X, .P .X .X	EA,FPn FPm,FPn FPn	Data	Tan^{-1} (SRC) -> FPn
FSINH (Hyperbolic sine)	.B, .W, .L, .S, .D, .X, .P .X .X	EA,FPn FPm,FPn FPn	Data	Sinh (SRC) -> FPn
FCOSH (Hyperbolic cosine)	.B, .W, .L, .S, .D, .X, .P .X .X	EA,FPn FPm,FPn FPn	Data	Cosh (SRC) -> FPn
FTANH (Hyperbolic tangent)	.B, .W, .L, .S, .D, .X, .P .X .X	EA,FPn FPm,FPn FPn	Data	Tanh (SRC) -> FPn
FATANH (Hyperbolic arc tangent)	.B, .W, .L, .S, .D, .X, .P .X .X	EA,FPn FPm,FPn FPn	Data	Tanh^{-1} (SRC) -> FPn
FTWOTOX (2 to the x power)	.B, .W, .L, .S, .D, .X, .P .X .X	EA,FPn FPm,FPn FPn	Data	$2^{(SRC)}$ -> FPn
FTENTOX (10 to the x power)	.B, .W, .L, .S, .D, .X, .P .X .X	EA,FPn FPm,FPn FPn	Data	$10^{(SRC)}$ -> FPn

Figure 11-6 FPCP transcendental instructions.

FETOX (e to the x power)	.B, .W, .L, .S, .D, .X, .P .X .X	EA,FPn FPm,FPn FPn	Data	$e^{(SRC)}$ -> FPn
FETOXM1 (e to the x power - 1)	.B, .W, .L, .S, .D, .X, .P .X .X	EA,FPn FPm,FPn FPn	Data	$e^{(SRC)} - 1$ -> FPn
FLOG2 (Log base 2)	.B, .W, .L, .S, .D, .X, .P .X .X	EA,FPn FPm,FPn FPn	Data	$Log_2(SRC)$ -> FPn
FLOG10 (Log base 10)	.B, .W, .L, .S, .D, .X, .P .X .X	EA,FPn FPm,FPn FPn	Data	$Log_{10}(SRC)$ -> FPn
FLOGN (Log base e)	.B, .W, .L, .S, .D, .X, .P .X .X	EA,FPn FPm,FPn FPn	Data	$Log_e(SRC)$ -> FPn
FLOGNP1 (Log base e of X + 1)	.B, .W, .L, .S, .D, .X, .P .X .X	EA,FPn FPm,FPn FPn	Data	$Log_e[(SRC) + 1]$ -> FPn

Figure 11-6 (*continued*)

The first example is to solve the quadratic equation

$$ax^2 + bx + c = 0$$

and store the first root in REAL1 and IMAG1 and the second root in REAL2 and IMAG2. All values are in the single-precision format, and for real roots, IMAG1 and IMAG2 are set to 0. A typical implementation is given in Fig. 11-7.

The second example is a subroutine to convert an unsigned decimal number to double-precision format. The subroutine has three parameters: a 16-digit string giving the integral part of the decimal number to be converted, a 16-digit string giving the fractional part, and an 8-byte array to store the converted binary real number. It is assumed that both integral and fractional parts are supplied in the packed BCD format with the integral part filled by leading zeros and the fractional part filled by trailing zeros. For instance, 123000.000456 would be stored with the integral part having 00 00 00 00 00 12 30 00 and the fractional part having 00 04 56 00 00 00 00 00. As shown before, it is not difficult to convert an ASCII decimal digit string to this packed BCD form.

Figure 11-8 gives an implementation of this decimal-to-real conversion subroutine, with parameter addresses being passed via the stack. As with the host processor, it is necessary to save and restore the FPCP data registers that might be modified in the subroutine. It is important to mention that the content of an 80-bit floating-point data register requires 12 (not 10) memory bytes to save. After register saving, the integral and fractional parts are separately converted to packed real format and then to binary real format. The two resulting real numbers are then added together to form the binary real number equivalent to the original decimal number.

```
AA          DC.S      1.25E2
BB          DC.S      -3.12E1
CC          DC.S      -9.0E-1
REAL1       DC.S      1
IMAG1       DC.S      1
REAL2       DC.S      1
IMAG2       DC.S      1
START       FMOVE.S   BB,FP0          ;LOAD B TO FP0
            FMUL.S    BB,FP0          ;FP0 = B * B
            FMOVE.S   AA,FP1          ;LOAD A TO FP1
            FMUL.S    CC,FP1
            FMUL.S    #4.0,FP1        ;FP1 = 4 * A * C
            FMOVE.S   AA,FP2
            FADD.X    FP2,FP2         ;FP2 = 2 * A
            FSUB.X    FP1,FP0         ;FP0 = B * B - 4 * A * C
            FTST.X    FP0             ;B * B - 4 * A * C < 0?
            FBLT      COMPLEX         ;YES, CALCULATE COMPLEX ROOTS
REALRT      FSQRT.X   FP0             ;NO, CALCULATE REAL ROOTS
            FNEG.S    BB,FP3          ;LOAD -B TO FP3
            FADD.X    FP0,FP3
            FDIV.X    FP2,FP3         ;FP3 = (-B + √B̅ ̅*̅ ̅B̅ ̅-̅ ̅4̅ ̅*̅ ̅A̅ ̅*̅ ̅C̅ )/(2 * A)
            FMOVE.S   FP3,REAL1       ;STORE FIRST REAL ROOT
            FMOVECR   #$0F,FP4        ;LOAD 0.0 TO FP4
            FMOVE.S   FP4,IMAG1       ;SET IMAGINARY PART OF FIRST ROOT TO 0.0
            FNEG.S    BB.FP3
            FSUB.X    FP0,FP3
            FDIV.X    FP2,FP3         ;FP3 = (-B - √B̅ ̅*̅ ̅B̅ ̅-̅ ̅4̅ ̅*̅ ̅A̅ ̅*̅ ̅C̅ )/(2 * A)
            FMOVE.S   FP3,REAL2       ;STORE SECOND REAL ROOT
            FMOVE.S   FP4,IMAG2       ;SET IMAGINARY PART OF SECOND ROOT TO 0.0
            BRA.S     DONE
COMPLEX     FABS.X    FP0
            FSQRT.X   FP0
            FDIV.X    FP2,FP0         ;FP0 = √|̅B̅ ̅*̅ ̅B̅ ̅-̅ ̅4̅ ̅*̅ ̅A̅ ̅*̅ ̅C̅|/(2 * A)
            FMOVE.S   FP0,IMAG1       ;STORE IMAGINARY PART OF FIRST ROOT
            FNEG.X    FP0
            FMOVE.S   FP0,IMAG2       ;STORE IMAGINARY PART OF SECOND ROOT
            FNEG.S    BB,FP3
            FDIV.X    FP2,FP3         ;FP3 = -B/(2 * A)
            FMOVE.S   FP3,REAL1       ;STORE REAL PART OF FIRST ROOT
            FMOVE.S   FP3.REAL2       ;STORE REAL PART OF SECOND ROOT
DONE        FNOP
            STOP      #$2000
            END       START
```

Figure 11-7 Example of computing two roots of quadratic equation.

380

```
          XDEF      BCDTORL                   ;SAVE REGISTERS OF HOST PROCESSOR
BCDTORL   MOVEM.L   A0/A1,-(SP)               ;SAVE DATA REGISTER OF FPCP
          FMOVE.X   FP0,-(SP)                 ;A0 = ADDRESS OF BCD STRING OF
          MOVE.L    24(SP),A0                 ;INTEGRAL PART
*                                             ;A1 = ADDRESS TO STORE PACKED REAL NUMBER
          LEA       PACKED,A1                 ;ASSEMBLE ALL MANTISSA BCD DIGITS EXCEPT
          MOVE.L    (A0)+,4(A1)               ;THE MOST SIGNIFICANT DIGIT
          MOVE.L    (A0)+,8(A1)               ;SIGN = 0, EXP = 16, MS DIGIT = 0
          MOVE.L    #$00160000,(A1)           ;CONVERT INTEGRAL PART FROM
          FMOVE.P   (A1),FP0                  ;PACKED BCD REAL TO BINARY REAL
*
          MOVE.L    28(SP),A0                 ;A0 = ADDRESS OF BCD STRING
*                                             ;OF FRACTIONAL PART
          MOVE.L    (A0)+,4(A1)               ;ASSEMBLE ALL MANTISSA BCD DIGITS EXCEPT
          MOVE.L    (A0)+,8(A1)               ;THE MOST SIGNIFICANT DIGIT
          MOVE.L    #0,(A1)                   ;SIGN = 0, EXP = 0, MS DIGIT = 0
          FADD.P    (A1),FP0                  ;CONVERT FRACTIONAL PART FROM
*                                             ;PACKED BCD REAL TO BINARY REAL AND
*                                             ;ADD IT TO INTEGRAL PART
          MOVE.L    32(SP),A0                 ;A0 = ADDRESS TO RETURN RESULT
          FMOVE.D   FP0,(A0)                  ;RETURN CONVERTED REAL NUMBER
          FMOVE.X   (SP)+,FP0                 ;RESTORE DATA REGISTER OF FPCP
          MOVEM.L   (SP)+,A0/A1               ;RESTORE REGISTERS OF HOST PROCESSOR
          RTD       #12                       ;RETURN AND DEALLOCATE PARAMETERS
PACKED    DS.B      12                        ;TEMPORARY AREA FOR STORING
*                                             ;PACKED BCD REAL NUMBER
          END
```

Figure 11-8 Sample subroutine involving floating-point instructions.

11-3 Interface of the FPCP

The FPCP, which lacks memory-accessing capabilities, relies on the host processor to fetch instructions and to calculate effective memory addresses and load or store memory operands. In loading a memory operand, the host processor reads the operand from memory and then writes it to the FPCP. Storing an operand to memory from the FPCP is performed in a similar but reverse sequence. The host processor communicates with the FPCP through a set of coprocessor interface registers (CIRs) provided by the FPCP.

Connecting the FPCP as a coprocessor

When the host processor is an MC68020 or MC68030, which has coprocessor interface hardware, the communication between the host processor and the FPCP is handled automatically by hardware without any software intervention. In doing so, coprocessor interface registers are not accessed as memory locations, as with peripheral devices. Instead, the MC68020 (or MC68030) sends out a 3-bit coprocessor identification and a 5-bit register selection code, as shown in Fig. 11-9. Bits A19-A16 are 0010 to indicate a coprocessor reference. Along with this address for specifying a coprocessor interface register, the host processor outputs the function code 111 on FC2–FC0 so that the address will not be interpreted as a memory location. Therefore, the chip-enable signal for selecting the FPCP should be generated by decoding signals FC2–FC0, A19–A16, and A15–A13, as shown in Fig. 11-10.

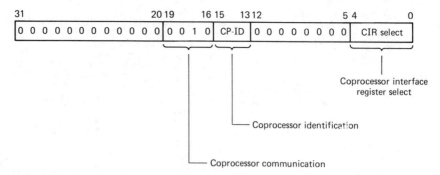

Figure 11-9 Address format for accessing a coprocessor interface register.

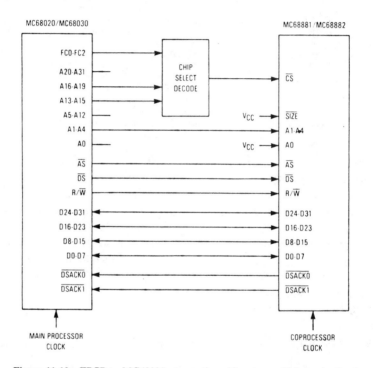

Figure 11-10 FPCP to MC68020 connection. (Courtesy of Motorola, Inc.)

Figure 11-10 also shows the connections of other FPCP pins in an MC68020/MC68030-based configuration. The $\overline{\text{SIZE}}$ (size) pin together with the A0 pin specify the data bus width, which may be 8 bits ($\overline{\text{SIZE}}$ = low), 16 bits ($\overline{\text{SIZE}}$ = high, A0 = low), or 32 bits ($\overline{\text{SIZE}}$ = high, A0 = high). In the example, both pins are connected to V_{cc}, configuring the FPCP to operate over a 32-bit data bus. The $\overline{\text{DS}}$ (data strobe) pin is connected to the $\overline{\text{DS}}$ output pin of the host processor. During a write operation, the host processor sends out data on D31–D0 pins and activates its $\overline{\text{DS}}$ pin to indicate valid data. The two data transfer and size acknowledge ($\overline{\text{DSACK0}}$ and $\overline{\text{DSACK1}}$) pins are used for two purposes. One is to indicate the completion of data transfer, i.e., the same function as the $\overline{\text{DTACK}}$ signal of the MC68000. The other function is to inform the host processor of the port size. In this example, both pins are connected to their respective pins of the MC68020, indicating a 32-bit device. If the host is an MC68000, only the $\overline{\text{DSACK1}}$ pin is connected to the $\overline{\text{DTACK}}$ pin of the MC68000. Since communication between the host processor and the FPCP uses asynchronous bus cycles, the FPCP can be operated with an independent clock at a speed different from that of the host processor clock.

Coprocessor interaction

Since a floating-point instruction is to be executed by the FPCP, the host processor does not decode the op code of the instruction after being fetched from memory. In order for the MC68020 or MC68030 to forward a floating-point instruction to the FPCP in configurations that might include other coprocessors, such as the MC68851 paged memory management unit (PMMU), each floating-point instruction has a coprocessor identification (CP-ID), as shown in Fig. 11-11. For Motorola assemblers, the default identification number assigned to the MC68881/MC68882 is 001. This number can be changed to any other 3-bit value by using appropriate assembler directives. However, since the identification number 000 is reserved for the MC68851 PMMU, this number cannot be assigned to the FPCP in systems that have a PMMU. Note that since the MC68030 includes a PMMU on the chip, an FPCP must also be assigned a nonzero identification number when configured with an MC68030. Since coprocessor identification is used as part of the address

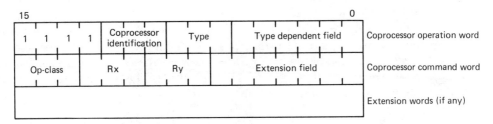

(a) General format of coprocessor instruction

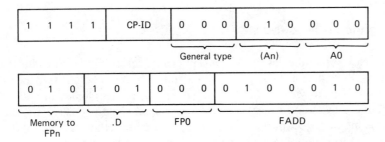

(b) Machine code for FADD.D (A0),FP0

Figure 11-11 Machine code format of FPCP instructions.

Sec. 11-3   Interface of the FPCP

383

in accessing a coprocessor interface register, it must match the address decoding logic that enables the FPCP.

In addition to a coprocessor identification, the first word of a floating-point instruction, referred to as the operation word, has a type and a type-dependent field. The type field indicates the type of coprocessor instruction such as general or branch. The usage of the type-dependent field varies according to the type field. Typically, this field specifies the effective address for a memory operand or the condition selected in a branch instruction. The most significant 4 bits of the operation words are always 1111, indicating to the host processor that this is a coprocessor instruction.

The second word in a floating-point instruction is the coprocessor command word. For a general-type instruction, the host processor writes this word to the coprocessor interface command register of the MC68881/MC68882. The coprocessor command word consists of four fields: op-class, Rx, Ry, and extension. The op-class specifies the class of the instruction and general types of operands—for example, memory to FP data register, or FP data register to memory. The values Rx, Ry, and the extension field depend on the specific op-class. For example, in a memory-to-FP data register instruction, Rx specifies the source data format, Ry specifies the destination register, and the extension field indicates the operation to be performed, such as add, log, or move. Following the coprocessor command word, there may be one to six extension words to specify an offset or immediate operand if needed.

Once the MC68020/MC68030 detects a coprocessor instruction, it initiates coprocessor interaction by writing the coprocessor command word to the command register of the coprocessor. The host processor then reads the response register of the coprocessor for any request for service—for example, to evaluate effective address and to transfer the operand to the coprocessor. If a service request is detected, the host processor performs the service and checks the response register again. If no further service is needed, the host processor is free to begin execution of the next instruction while the coprocessor is still executing the current instruction. Figure 11-12 illustrates this communication dialogues using the floating-point instruction

```
FADD.D      (A0),FP0
```

as an example.

Interfacing the FPCP to the MC68000

Because an earlier member of the M68000 microprocessor family does not contain coprocessor interface hardware, the FPCP must be connected as a peripheral processor when used with an MC68000, MC68010, or MC68008. In such a configuration, the FPCP coprocessor interface registers are accessed by the host processor as memory locations, just as in programming other peripheral devices. The 32-byte address block assigned to the coprocessor interface registers is determined by the chip-enable logic. Figure 11-13 shows the connection between the FPCP and MC68000. The chip-enable logic needs to decode all address bits

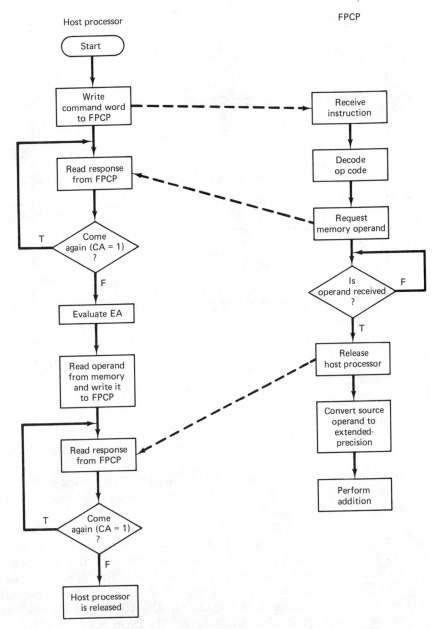

Host processor   FPCP

Start

Write
command word ----------------------------→ Receive
to FPCP   instruction

Read response   Decode
from FPCP   op code

Come   Request
again (CA = 1) ◄-------------   memory operand
?
T   Is
F   operand received F
                                             ?
Evaluate EA   T

Read operand   Release
from memory   host processor
and write it
to FPCP   Convert source
                                              operand to
Read response ◄------------   extended-
from FPCP   precision

Come   Perform
again (CA = 1)   addition
?
T
F

Host processor
is released

Figure 11-12 Interaction between the host processor and the FPCP.

except A4–A0. The A4–A1 pins are for selecting the register to be accessed, and the A0 pin together with the $\overline{\text{SIZE}}$ pin specifies the data bus width.

The FPCP has 32 data pins, capable of transferring data up to 4 bytes per bus cycle. When connected to an MC68020, which is also a 32-bit processor, the data bus width of the FPCP can be specified as 32 bits. However, the MC68000 or MC68010 has only 16 data pins. Therefore, as shown in the figure, the A0 pin

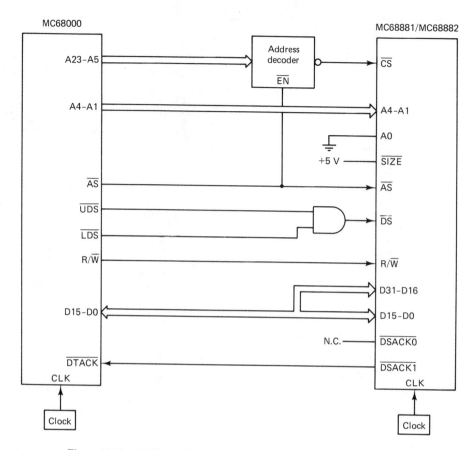

Figure 11-13 FPCP to MC68000 connection. (Courtesy of Motorola, Inc.)

is connected to ground and the $\overline{\text{SIZE}}$ pin to V_{cc}, indicating a 16-bit data bus. In addition, both the upper 16 data pins (D31–D16) and the lower 16 data pins (D15–D0) of the FPCP are connected to the 16 data bus lines.

If the host processor is an MC68008, which has only 8 data pins, the $\overline{\text{SIZE}}$ pin is grounded to indicate an 8-bit data bus, whereas the A0 pins of both devices are directly connected. The 8 lower data pins (D7–D0) and the 24 upper data pins (D31–D8) must be connected to the 8 data pins of the MC68008. This means that pins D0, D8, D16, and D24 are all connected to data bus line 0, pins D1, D9, D17, and D25 to data bus line 1, and so on. The $\overline{\text{DSACK0}}$ pin of the FPCP is connected to the $\overline{\text{DTACK}}$ pin of the MC68008, and the $\overline{\text{DSACK1}}$ pin is not used.

Programming the FPCP as a peripheral

When the FPCP is configured as a peripheral processor, communication between the host processor and the FPCP must be handled by host processor instructions. In other words, the coprocessor interface discussed earlier must be emulated by software. Therefore, in a configuration where the host processor is an MC68000, MC68010, or MC68008, each floating-point instruction needs to be replaced with several MC68000 instructions that pass the floating-point instruction to the FPCP for execution.

Let us use the floating-point instruction

```
FADD.D      (A0),FP1
```

as an example to illustrate how to instruct the FPCP as a peripheral processor to perform a floating-point operation. In an application program, instead of using this floating-point instruction, it should be replaced with the following MC68000 instruction sequence:

```
           MOVE.W    #$54A2,COMMAND      ;WRITE COMMAND
CHECK0     CMPI.W    #$8900,RESPONSE     ;READ RESPONSE
           BEQ       CHECK0
           MOVE.L    (A0),OPERAND        ;EVALUATE EA AND PASS OPERAND
           MOVE.L    4(A0),OPERAND
CHECK1     TST.B     RESPONSE            ;READ RESPONSE
           BMI       CHECK1
```

In the example, symbols COMMAND, RESPONSE, and OPERAND, respectively, represent the addresses assigned to the command, response, and operand interface registers of the FPCP.

The first instruction, MOVE.W, is used for the MC68000 to assemble and write the command word to the FPCP command interface register. Referring to the general insruction format given in Fig. 11-11, the command word associated with the instruction

```
FADD.D      (A0),FP1
```

is formed as follows:

010	101	001	0100010
(Memory to FPn)	(D)	(FP1)	(FADD)

In the hex format, this command word becomes 54A2. The next two instructions read the response interface register and repeat this operation until the FPCP requests the transfer of the needed external operand. When the FPCP receives a new floating-point instruction while a previous one is still being executed, the FPCP returns a null come-again response. This 16-bit response has five indication bits with the following format:

1	0	00100	1	000000	0	0	(i.e., $8900)
(CA)	(PC)		(IA)		(PF)	(T/F)	

The CA (come-again) bit indicates that the processor should process the service indicated in the response and read the response register again to seek further service request. If the CA bit is not set, the host processor is released from further services and may execute its own instructions. The IA (interrupt accept) bit is used to specify that the main processor may process pending interrupts if necessary. To simplify the implementation, in our example we assume no pending exceptions and errors. Therefore, if the response is not $8900, the MC68000 fetches the 64-bit memory operand specified by the addressing mode (A0) and loads it to the operand interface register. For the MC68000, transferring a 64-bit number requires two MOVE.L instructions. The last two instructions repeatedly check the CA bit in the response register until it is cleared. Once the CA bit is cleared, the MC68000 is released by the FPCP and may start to execute the next instruction in sequence while the FPCP is finishing the current instruction.

The preceding example illustrates the sequence required to execute a typical instruction FADD.D (A0), FP1. For an MC68000 system using the FPCP, each floating-point instruction in the program must be replaced with a similar but different emulation sequence. There are three methods to implement the necessary emulation software: macros, subroutines, and emulation traps.

The first approach is to generate emulation sequences by macro calls. Of course, a different macro, perhaps using the instruction mnemonic as the macro name, can be defined for each FPCP instruction with addressing mode and operand type included as parameters. Actually, the number of required macros can be substantially reduced by defining one macro for all instructions in a particular instruction group and by using the FPCP instruction mnemonic as a macro parameter. This is possible because two FPCP instructions in the same group have identical emulation sequence, except the operand word to be sent to the FPCP is different. For example, FADD, FSUB, FMUL, and so on are all in the same group, and therefore their emulation sequences can be generated by calling the same macro.

The second approach is to implement a library of subroutines that can be called to execute emulation sequences. Compared to macros, the advantage of using subroutines is saving memory space. However, this method is slower because the overhead associated with subroutine call and return is incurred each time a subroutine is called. In addition, parameter passing to a subroutine occurs during execution time, thus requiring code to detect the addressing mode and operand type being used in the FPCP instruction. On the other hand, for a macro, parameter substitution is performed by the assembler. This eliminates the need for parsing the actual arguments during execution time.

The third aproach is to execute emulation sequences in a trap service routine. Note that in the machine code of each FPCP instruction, the most significant 4 bits are always 1111. When an MC68000, MC68010, or MC68008 attempts to execute such an instruction, a line 1111 emulator exception with vector number = 11 is initiated. Therefore, a service routine can be designed to handle FPCP instructions; it is initiated whenever an FPCP instruction is encountered. This approach is even slower than the one using a subroutine because of the stacking overhead associated with an exception. In addition, the service routine must decode the FPCP instruction, which causes the exception in order to generate the correct emulation sequence. However, this approach has a desirable feature. It makes a user program containing FPCP instructions in the MC68000 system to be upward compatible to an MC680020 or MC68030 system without reassembling.

EXERCISES

1. Convert the following decimal numbers to single-precision real numbers (give the answers in hexadecimal):
   (a) -12.34×10^6
   (b) 3.625×10^{-4}
   (c) -25.3125

2. Convert the following decimal numbers to packed decimal real numbers (give the answers in hexadecimal)
   (a) 5432100
   (b) -12×10^{37}
   (c) 25×10^{-41}

3. Does 0.1 have an exact representation in a binary real data format? Justify your answer.

4. Assume that FP0 has -12.625 before the instruction

   ```
   FMOVE.L      FP0,D1
   ```

   being executed. Determine the result in D1 produced by this instruction for each of the following rounding options:
   (a) Toward the nearest integer
   (b) Toward 0
   (c) Toward $+\infty$
   (d) Toward $-\infty$

5. Repeat Exercise 4 with the initial condition that FP0 has 12.625.

6. In loading constant 10 into register FP0, what is the difference between the following two instructions?

   ```
   FMOVE.W      #10,FP0       and
   FMOVECR.X    #$33,FP0
   ```

7. Assume that array RLDATA stores 50 real numbers in the double-precision real format. Write an instruction sequence to calculate the root mean square value of those 50 numbers and store the result into RMS as an extended-precision real number.

8. Write a subroutine that performs inner product of two given real vectors. This subroutine should have four parameters: the two vectors to be multiplied, the vector size, and the variable to store the product. Assume that vector components and product are in the single-precision format and the vector size is given as a 16-bit integer.

9. Assume that the FPCP is configured as a peripheral processor. Show the necessary instruction sequence to replace each of the following floating-point instructions:
   (a) FADD.S   (A0)+,FP2
   (b) FADD.P   VAR,FP2
   (c) FADD.X   FP0,FP1

10. Show a typical application where the FSAVE and FRESTORE instructions are needed.

11. Show how to program the control register of the FPCP to have a specific bit pattern.

12. Draw a logic diagram to show the connection between the FPCP and the MC68008.

12

Memory Management

12-1 Memory Hierarchy

The memory hierarchy of a microcomputer system has at least three levels. The register set inside a microprocessor can be considered as the highest level memory. It is used for keeping small amounts of data temporarily between operations. The next level is the main memory, also called external memory, which is implemented with LSI MOS memory devices. The main memory is required for storing the program(s) currently being executed. The lowest level in the memory hierarchy is the mass storage, commonly provided by hard disks or diskettes as permanent storage media. As the memory capacity increases from one level to the next lower level, the speed and the cost per bit decrease.

Although both internal registers and external memory devices are implemented in MOS circuits, accessing registers is much faster. In accessing external memory, the access time must include the delay incurred in address decoding, the response time of the memory device, and the delay caused by the data bus interface. As a result, transferring data to or from external memory requires bus cycles rather than clock cycles, as for the registers. For high-performance microprocessors, the speed of the external memory cannot sustain the high processor clock rate, and so, wait states must be inserted in each memory cycle. In such cases, the main memory becomes the bottleneck of the system, thus substantially underutilizing the processing power of the processor.

A solution for resolving the speed mismatch between processor and main memory is to add another level of memory called a *cache*, as illustrated in Fig. 12-1. A cache is a fast memory of small size serving as a buffer between the processor and main memory. By keeping frequently used data and prefetched

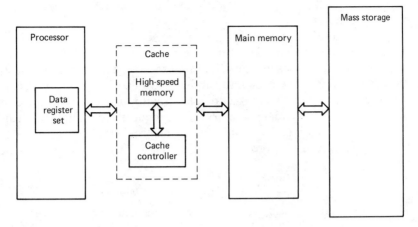

Figure 12-1 Memory hierarchy with cache.

instructions, a cache significantly reduces the need for the processor to access main memory; much of the time, the instruction to be executed next and the memory operand needed for the operation are already in the cache. Since the cache is accessed with no wait states, the average memory access time is minimized. Cache memory also improves the system performance by increasing the availability of the system bus and main memory which are shared by DMA controllers and other microprocessors in a multiprocessor configuration. A cache can be implemented with high-speed SRAM devices, as part of a microprocessor, or using a combination of the two approaches (i.e., two-level caching).

The main reason behind the concept of caching is that programs usually access memory in the neighborhood of locations that are accessed recently rather than in a completely random fashion. This phenomenon is known as *program locality* and is illustrated in Fig. 12-2. One major factor contributing to program locality is that in a typical program, instruction execution usually proceeds sequentially or in small loops. References of data operands also exhibit such locality. In many cases, elements in arrays are processed sequentially and variables are often accessed several times in succession. Another example of reference locality is the stack usage. Since operands are always pushed onto or retrieved from the

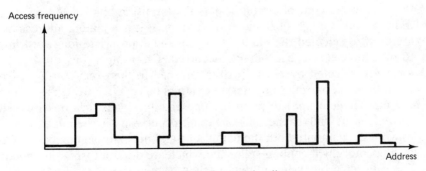

Figure 12-2 Program locality.

top of the stack, the next few accesses to the stack are all near the currently pointed location.

A cache can reduce average memory access time by duplicating portions of recently used code and data from the main memory into the fast cache. When the processor accesses memory, it checks the cache first. If the requested operand or instruction is in the cache, the access is called a *cache hit*. When a hit occurs, the processor's access can be completed with little delay because the cache is much faster than the main memory. If the requested operand or instruction is not in the cache, a case called a *cache miss*, the processor accesses the main memory in the usual way. Therefore, the average memory access time t_{ave} can be estimated as

$$t_{ave} = t_{cache} + (1 - h)t_{memory}$$

where t_{cache} and t_{memory} represent the cache and main memory access times, respectively, and h is the hit rate. Since t_{cache} is much smaller than t_{memory}, the average memory access time is reduced, and it becomes smaller as the hit ratio increases.

12-2 On-chip Caches

On-chip cache memory becomes a typical feature for later members in the M68000 microprocessor family. The MC68020 has a 256-byte instruction cache to keep instructions recently being executed. The MC68030 has added a 256-byte data cache in addition to the instruction cache. The MC68040 has further extended the two cache memories to 4K bytes each. To illustrate the on-chip cache facilities, let us consider the MC68030.

Figure 12-3 shows the organization of the MC68030s data cache. It consists of 16 blocks, with each block having 4 entries. Each entry contains 4 consecutive bytes. Since an entry has a valid bit associated with it, each entry is independently replaceable. Each block has a tag containing 27 bits to identify the function code FC2–FC0 and the upper 24 address bits A31–A8 of the 16-byte block. During a data fetch, upon receiving the operand address.

FC2–FC0, A31–A8, A7–A4, A3–A2, A1–A0

the data cache control circuit selects the tag using bits A7–A4 and compares it to the received FC2–FC0 and A31–A8 bits. If it is a match, address bits A3–A2 are used to selected the valid bit (V) for the appropriate longword in the block to determine if a cache hit has occurred. On a cache hit, the byte, word, or longword selected by A1 and A0 is returned to the execution unit. On a cache miss, the bus controller initiates an external bus cycle (through the on-chip memory management unit) to fetch the operand and loads it into the execution unit as well as the data cache. If a cache hit occurs on a write cycle, it is necessary to write the data into both the data cache and the external device. Otherwise, the main memory will contain stale data which are different from the modified cache line (i.e., data block in the data cache). Should this data block be loaded from

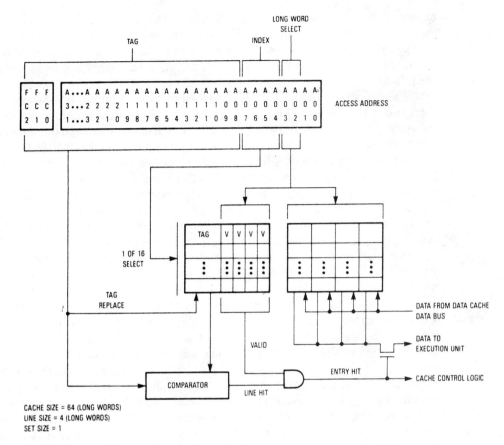

TAG

INDEX

LONG WORD
SELECT

F F F	A...A A A A A A A A A A A A A A A A A A A A A A A A-	ACCESS ADDRESS
C C C	3...2 2 2 2 1 1 1 1 1 1 1 1 1 1 0 0 0 0 0 0 0 0 0 0	
2 1 0	1...3 2 1 0 9 8 7 6 5 4 3 2 1 0 9 8 7 6 5 4 3 2 1 0	

1 OF 16
SELECT

TAG V V V V

TAG
REPLACE

DATA FROM DATA CACHE
DATA BUS

DATA TO
EXECUTION UNIT

VALID

ENTRY HIT

COMPARATOR

LINE HIT

CACHE CONTROL LOGIC

CACHE SIZE = 64 (LONG WORDS)
LINE SIZE = 4 (LONG WORDS)
SET SIZE = 1

Figure 12-3 MC68030 on-chip data cache organization. (Courtesy of Motorola, Inc.)

main memory into cache again at a later time, a read from this previously modified variable would no longer deliver its most recent value. If a write cycle generates a miss in the data cache, only the external device is updated, and no cache entry is replaced or allocated for that address. This is commonly known as the *write-through policy*.

Operation of the instruction cache is similar to that of the data cache except that the instruction cache does not have write operation and uses a different tag field. A tag in the instruction cache consists of the FC2 function bit and A31–A8 address bits, in contrast to 27 bits used in a data cache tag.

Both the instruction and data caches are automatically filled by the MC68030. By using burst transfer bus cycles, up to four longwords can be filled, with one longword being fetched from memory in every clock cycle. Neither cache can be manipulated directly by the programmer except through the CACR (cache control register), which provides cache clearing and cache entry clearing facilities. In addition, by programming the MMU, a page of addresses can be marked as noncacheable. An access within a noncacheable page causes the cache to be inhibited, thus forcing an external reference. This feature is necessary in programming I/O registers because the MC68030 uses memory mapped I/O. For example, if an input data register was cached as a memory location, a read would obtain the register content from the data cache, which might not be the current input data.

The MC68040's data cache is enhanced to support multiprocessor systems. There are two methods to keep memory and cache data consistent: write-through and copyback. For the write-through method, whenever a write to the data cache occurs the same data is also written to the main memory. The MC68030's data cache implements this write-through memory update method. Clearly, the write-through method increases main memory access, making it less available to other bus masters in the system. To better utilize the external bus, the copyback method does not update the main memory immediately each time a write to the data cache occurs. Instead it sets the dirty bit associated with the affected cache line. When a cache line needs to be replaced, its dirty bit is checked. If set, the modified line will be copied back to main memory before being replaced by a new line. The data cache of the MC68040 provides both write-through and copyback memory update options.

For a multiprocessor system, the problem of keeping cache data consistent with main memory becomes more complicated. Since there are other bus masters capable of accessing the main memory, it is possible that when shared data are cached by the MC68040, the copy in main memory may be modified by other bus masters. One simple solution to avoid this cache coherence problem is to make a writable shared data noncacheable. This guarantees that only one copy of the shared data exits in the system and forces the MC68040 to access the main memory for shared data. But, any reference to the shared data, either a read or a write, requires external memory access. As a result, usage of the external bus will increase accordingly.

A more sophisticated scheme is to allow shared data to be cached and meanwhile the MC68040 monitors memory accesses from other bus masters. If an external bus master accesses the shared data in main memory, the MC68040 can perform a bus-snooping operation to maintain cache coherence. To facilitate bus snooping in multiprocessor configuration, the MC68040 provides two snoop control signals, SC0 and SC1. The snoop control signals, which are inputs to the MC68040, allows an external bus master to specify the snoop operation to be performed by the MC68040 for the external bus master.

Two possible snoop operations may be required while an external master is accessing shared data which are also in the MC68040's data cache. One case is that an external bus master writes to shared data in the main memory. This causes the cached data in the MC68040 to be different from the copy in the main memory. To ensure that subsequent reads by the MC68040 access valid data, the MC68040 must either update its data cache with the new data from main memory or invalidate the affected cache line. If a cahe line is marked invalid, the next read from this cache line will force the MC68040 to bring in the modified data from main memory.

The other case requiring a snoop operation is that an external bus master reads data from main memory while the MC68040 modifies the same data in its data cache. In this case, the MC68040 must intervene the external bus master's access and supply it with valid data.

12-3 Memory Management and Virtual Memory

Another important subject related to memory is virtual memory. Under a virtual memory system, a program currently being executed is not stored as a whole in a single contiguous area in main memory. Instead, a program is divided into many pages, with each page being stored in a memory block not necessarily adjacent to each other. Furthermore, only portions of the program need to reside in memory at a time. Whenever needed, the next portion is brought in from the mass storage. This operation is transparent to the user and is handled by the memory management system. Virtual memory enables the system to execute a program whose size exceeds the capacity of the physical memory. Another advantage of virtual memory is that the main memory can be utilized efficiently, a feature particularly desirable for multiprogramming systems.

With the conventional approach, the processor sends the instruction or operand address directly to memory during a memory reference. This is satisfactory if there is only one program in memory at a time. But in a multiprogramming environment there may be several programs in memory simultaneously. For a multiprogramming system it is important to utilize the memory efficiently so that the system can execute as many programs as possible at the same time to reduce the processor idle time to the minimum.

Memory can be better utilized by having memory management logic that performs dynamic address translation. As illustrated in Fig. 12-4, for each memory reference the logical address output by the processor is translated into a physical address, which is then forwarded to the memory. A logical address is an address used in the user program, which is the effective address calculated according to the addressing mode. A physical address is the actual memory location to be accessed, and it may be different from its corresponding logical address.

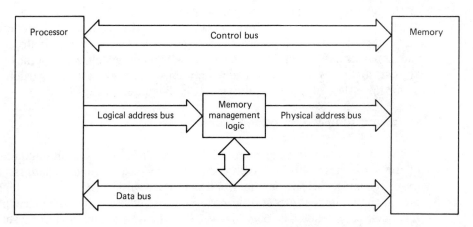

Figure 12-4 Dynamic address translation.

Page memory management

A typical memory management scheme is called *paging*. In a paged memory system, a program in the logical space is divided into several pages of fixed size. During execution, each page is stored in a memory block, and the memory management logic performs the necessary mapping between a page and a memory block. There are two significant advantages provided by this memory management: reducing memory fragmentation and offering memory protection.

In the conventional approach, several programs can be stored in memory at the same time, with each program occupying a single contiguous area. However, as current programs are completed and new programs are loaded, more and more small free areas begin to appear and scatter in memory. The system may not be able to load a program, even though the total amount of available memory is large enough. Because of this memory fragmentation problem, a significant portion of memory may be wasted. In a paged memory system, a program can be stored in several memory blocks, which are not necessarily adjacent to each other, as illustrated in Fig. 12-5. This significantly reduces memory fragmentation and therefore better utilizes the available real memory.

The MC68000 provides only limited protection for the supervisor from a user program with the supervisor and user operating modes. In a multiprogramming system, it is desirable to be able to protect user programs from each other. In a paged memory system, before a logical address is translated, the memory management logic can check whether the address is outside the boundary assigned to the current program. If a violation is detected, the access will be denied and control will be returned to the operating system. In addition, each page can be individually protected to prevent write accesses. This feature is useful in allowing a shared memory area to be accessed by several programs while still protecting the shared area from unauthorized modifications.

Paged memory management can be extended to provide virtual memory capability. In a paged virtual memory system, the user is given extended memory by treating mass storage as part of the real memory. Therefore, the size of a user program is limited only by the logical (virtual) space, not by the actual amount of real memory. While a program is being executed, only part of the program resides in memory. During a memory reference, if the needed page is not presently in memory, the memory management logic suspends the current instruction and causes a page fault exception. The page fault handler, which is part of the operating system, loads in the required page and then resumes the failing instruction. The major logic flow of a page fault handler is illustrated in Fig. 12-6.

Hardware required for paged memory

With paged memory management hardware, the program is partitioned into pages of the same size. This is accomplished by having each logical address divided into two fields, the page number and the offset within the page. The high-order bits in the address represent the page number, whereas the low-order bits correspond to the offset. The page size is determined by the number of bits allocated to the offset field. As an illustration, suppose that the logical address has 24 bits

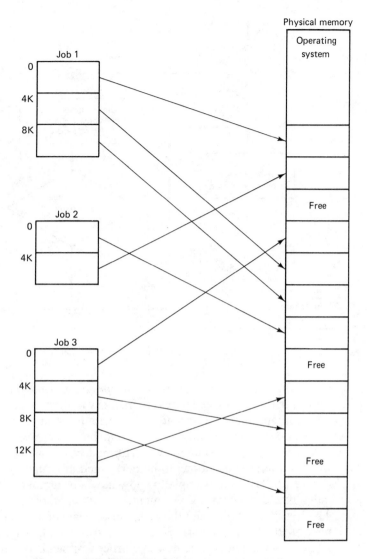

Figure 12-5 Paged memory management.

and the low-order n bits are allocated to the offset. Then, the page size is 2^n bytes and a program may have up to 2^{24-n} pages.

Figure 12-7 illustrates the mechanism of logical-to-physical address translation. The page number P in a logical address is used as the key to search the page table. If a match to the incoming page number is found, the corresponding physical base address is concatenated with the offset to form the physical address. In order to support multiple users, the page table may include a user number field and use a page table register to store the identification number of the currently executing job. When the system switches from one job to another, the page table register is updated, so that a new section of the page table is used for address translations.

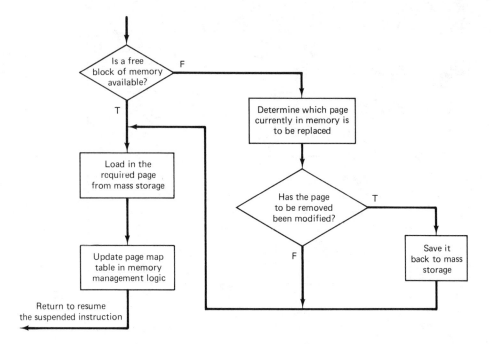

Figure 12-6 Logic flow of a page fault handler.

Each entry in the page table is called a *page descriptor*. Because the address translation must be performed for every memory reference, portions of the table—that is, recently used page descriptors—are kept in a content addressable memory (CAM) as part of the memory management hardware. Searching the CAM to match the received page number is performed by parallel combinational logic. This allows address translations to be performed at a high speed.

Figure 12-8 uses an example to show how a program can be executed properly under paged memory management. In this example the offset field of the logical address has 12 bits, and the program consists of 3 pages stored in memory beginning at locations $085000, $0A1000, and $150000, respectively. When the JMP NEXT instruction is executed, the processor sends out $000100 as the next instruction address. This address is then translated to $0A1100, the correct physical address where the target instruction is stored. Similarly, the instruction

        MOVE.W   OPER,D1

loads the word at location $150080, which corresponds to OPER, into register D1 rather than fetching the operand from logical address $000080. As illustrated by this example, a program becomes position-independent with no restrictions on addressing modes. Therefore, even if the program execution is suspended and the current page is replaced, execution can resume properly after this page has been reloaded into memory, most likely into a different area.

In addition to the page number and the physical base address, a page de-

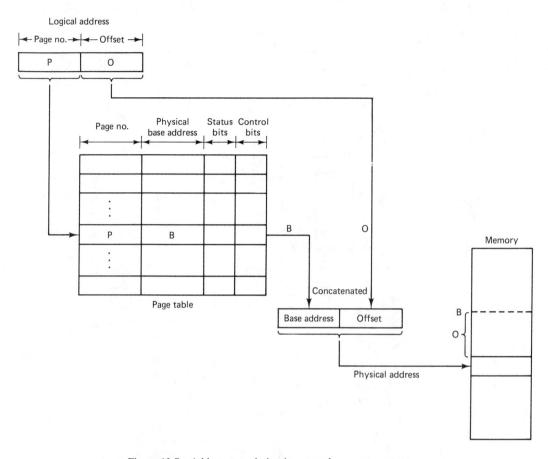

Figure 12-7 Address translation in a paged memory system.

scriptor includes certain status bits and control bits to provide useful information regarding the page. Among the commonly seen status and control bits are these:

Used bit: Set whenever the page is accessed. This bit is useful in determining which page is to be replaced when it becomes necessary to remove a page currently in memory to make more space available. Having a used bit associated with each page, the operating system can examine all used bits and choose one that has not been accessed recently. After all the used bits are set to 1, the operating system can reset them to 0.

Modified bit: Set whenever the page has been written to. This status bit indicates whether or not the page has been modified since being brought into memory. When the page is replaced, if it has been modified, it must be stored back into mass storage before loading the incoming page. If the page has not been modified, the incoming page is simply loaded from mass storage, thus saving a write operation.

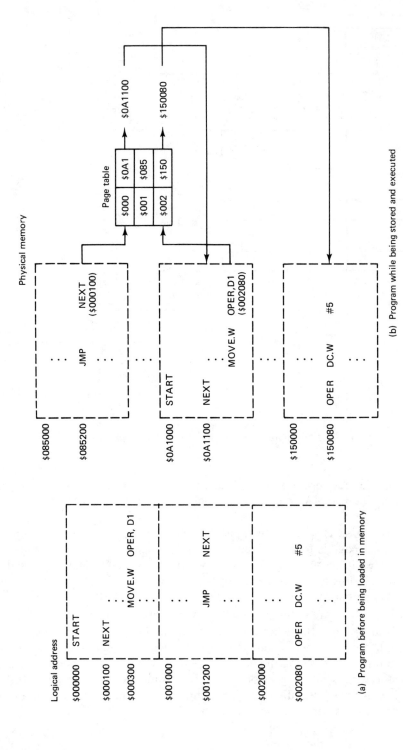

Logical address

(a) Program before being loaded in memory

Physical memory

Page table

(b) Program while being stored and executed

Figure 12-8 Program execution under the paged memory scheme.

400

Write protect bit: Provides protection against unauthorized writing. When the W control bit is set, a write to the page will cause a write violation, and control will be passed to the operating system.

Present bit: Indicates whether or not the referenced page is in the memory. Attempting to access a page whose P status bit is cleared generates a page fault, thus causing a trap to the operating system. The operating system then loads the required page into memory, updates the page table, and continues with the suspended instruction. When sufficient space is not currently available, one or more existing pages are swapped out to the mass storage.

As can be seen from the preceding discussion, implementing paged memory management logic requires complex hardware. Motorola made available two LSI memory management devices, the MC68451 and the MC68851, to simplify the hardware implementation in supporting paged memory capability for the M68000 family.

MC68451 MMU

The MC68451 MMU (memory management unit) is designed to be used with microprocessors MC68000 and MC68010 to provide memory management capability. This device implements a segmentation memory management scheme, which permits a program to be divided into segments of variable lengths rather than fixed-sized pages.

Connections between the MC68000 and MC68451 are shown in Fig. 12-9. During an address translation, the MMU translates logical address bits A8–A23 to physical address bits PA8–PA23. The low-order seven address bits A1–A7 are directly routed to memory, becoming physical address bits PA1–PA7. Therefore, the minimum size for a segment is 256 bytes. Along with the logical address the

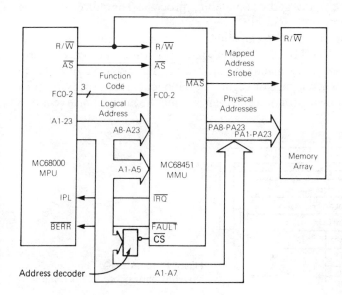

Figure 12-9 Connections of the MC68451. (Courtesy of Motorola, Inc.)

MMU also receives the 3-bit function code from the processor. This allows the protection mechanism of the MMU to distinguish five types of segments: user data, user program, supervisor data, supervisor program, and interrupt acknowledge. If the incoming segment number is not found in the translation table or a write protection is violated, the MMU activates its $\overline{\text{FAULT}}$ (fault detect) output. By connecting the $\overline{\text{FAULT}}$ pin to the processor's $\overline{\text{BERR}}$ pin, a translation error will cause a bus error exception. In setting up the descriptors in the translation table and programming the internal registers for the control of the MMU, the device is accessed as a peripheral to the processor with five register select pins.

As shown in Fig. 12-10, an MMU can hold 32 descriptors. Other descriptors of the translation table can be stored in memory. Through software, they can be loaded into the MMU, as needed. Additional MMUs can also be added to increase the number of descriptors that participate in the address translation.

Each descriptor has 72 bits divided into six registers. The logical base address register stores a 16-bit segment number. The logical address mask register specifies which bits in the logical base address register are to be ignored in searching for a match to the incoming segment number. This allows a segment to have any length, as long as it is a multiple of 256 bytes. The physical base address register together with the logical address mask and the incoming logical address are used to form the high-order 16 physical address bits. The address space number register and the space mask register are for the MMU to check for a match to the current bus cycle number, which is a function of the incoming function code and the current user number specified in the address space table.

The segment status register stores six status and control bits: U (used), I (interrupt), IP (interrupt pending), M (modified), W (write protect), and E (enable). Since U, M, and W bits have been discussed before, they are not discussed again here. The I control bit, when set to 1, causes an interrupt request upon access of the corresponding segment. The IP status bit merely indicates whether an interrupt request has been generated. The E control bit, when set to 1, enables the segment to participate in the address-matching process. Therefore, it can be used as the earlier-mentioned present bit.

Even though the MMU has the capability to perform address translations and detect segment faults, the MC68000/MC68451 configuration in Fig. 12-9 provides only segmentation memory management, not virtual memory. In order to support virtual memory, when a page or segment fault occurs, the processor must be able to suspend the failing instruction and then resume the instruction execution

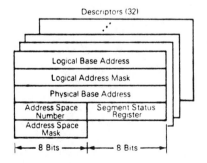

Figure 12-10 MC68451 programmer's model. (Courtesy of Motorola, Inc.)

after the fault is fixed. This process must be transparent to the user, as if the fault never occurred, a feature that the MC68000 lacks.

The system in Fig. 12-9 enables the MC68000 to recognize a segment fault through a bus error exception. But after the fault is corrected, we cannot simply reexecute the instruction that caused the fault. To explain this, let us consider a simple example. The instruction

    MOVEM.L   D0 – D7, – (A0)

moves registers D7 through D0 to memory using the predecrement addressing mode. If a fault occurs after registers D7 through D4 have been stored, address register A0 would have already been decremented by 16. When this instruction is reexecuted upon return from the fault-handling routine, register D7 through D0 would be stored into a wrong area starting from the supposed destination minus 16. To support virtual memory, the processor must save enough internal information during a fault exception so that it can restore its internal state to permit the instruction to be continued.

In principle, the bus rerun feature of the MC68000 could be used in handling a fault. When MMU's FAULT pin is connected to both HALT and BERR pins of the MC68000, a fault will force the MC68000 into the single bus cycle mode. Later, the execution of the suspended instruction can be resumed properly by rerunning the previous bus cycle. However, since the MC68000 must be in the halt state prior to a rerun cycle, the fault cannot be corrected unless there is another processor in the system to run the fault handler.

The major improvement of the MC68010 over its predecessor, the MC68000, is that it provides virtual memory support. In doing so, the MC68010 saves internal data latches and control registers in addition to the instruction and the status registers during a bus or address error exception. This feature allows the MC68010 to reconstruct the internal machine state, thus permitting the faulted instruction to be completed. Therefore, the MC68451 when used with the MC68010 can implement a virtual memory system.

MC68851 PMMU

The MC68851 PMMU (paged memory management unit) is designed primarily to provide a paged virtual memory capability for the MC68020 microprocessor. This device, which is based on the paged memory management scheme, has many enhanced features over the MC68451. First, the logical bus of the PMMU has 32 bits instead of 24 bits. This bus extension enables the PMMU to provide a virtual memory up to 4×10^9 bytes when configured with the MC68020 processor, which also uses a 32-bit address bus. Second, the PMMU is designed to operate as a coprocessor, which is capable of executing its own instruction set of 12 instructions. These instructions are specially designed for setting control functions, loading and storing internal registers, and testing various conditions. Because the PMMU instruction set simplifies the implementation of the software associated with memory management and releases the processor from actually programming the PMMU, the software overhead in providing a virtual memory is substantially reduced. Third, the PMMU keeps part of the page table resident, but unlike the MMU, if the needed page descriptor is not found within the PMMU, then the device automatically searches the remaining part of the table stored in memory. After being located, the page descriptor is loaded into the PMMU for performing address translation. All this is done by hardware, with no software intervention from the processor. Finally, the PMMU extends memory protection by providing a hierarchial protection. In addition to the protection mechanism based on the function code, a user program may be divided into regions of up to eight distinct privilege levels. A routine at a given privilege level has access to all areas that require the same or lower privilege level but cannot access areas of higher privilege levels. This hierarchical protection mechanism requires the MC68020 module call and return instruction pair (CALLM and RTM) to pass program control between two routines operating at different levels.

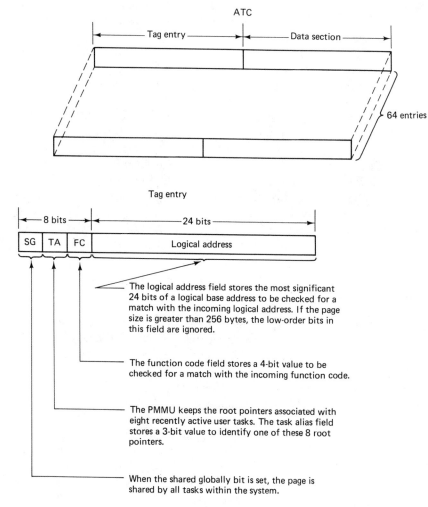

Figure 12-11   Organization of the address translation cache in the PMMU.

Data section

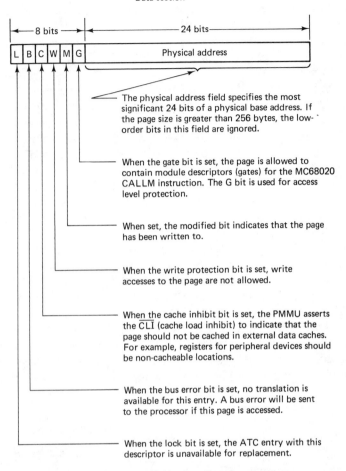

The physical address field specifies the most significant 24 bits of a physical base address. If the page size is greater than 256 bytes, the low-order bits in this field are ignored.

When the gate bit is set, the page is allowed to contain module descriptors (gates) for the MC68020 CALLM instruction. The G bit is used for access level protection.

When set, the modified bit indicates that the page has been written to.

When the write protection bit is set, write accesses to the page are not allowed.

When the cache inhibit bit is set, the PMMU asserts the $\overline{CLI}$ (cache load inhibit) to indicate that the page should not be cached in external data caches. For example, registers for peripheral devices should be non-cacheable locations.

When the bus error bit is set, no translation is available for this entry. A bus error will be sent to the processor if this page is accessed.

When the lock bit is set, the ATC entry with this descriptor is unavailable for replacement.

Figure 12-11 (*continued*)

The PMMU supports a logical space of 4G bytes. Even with a page size of 32K bytes, a page table may have up to 125,000 descriptors. To provide the needed flexibility in storing a page table of that size, each one is organized as a tree rather than a linear array. The PMMU has an address translation cache (ATC) to store up to 64 recently used page descriptors. Figure 12-11 shows the organization of the ATC and summarizes the meaning of each field in the descriptor.

Upon receiving a logical address along with a function code from the processor, the PMMU first searches the ATC for a match. If a match is found, the logical address is translated to the corresponding physical address, thus allowing the current bus cycle to complete. If no match is found, the PMMU asserts both $\overline{BERR}$ and $\overline{HALT}$ pins to abort the current bus cycle. Then, it becomes the bus master and searches the page table in memory. If the needed descriptor is found, the PMMU loads it into the ATC and lets the processor rerun the aborted bus cycle to complete the memory access. This is done entirely by the hardware of the PMMU, with no software intervention. If the needed descriptor cannot be found in memory, a page fault is detected, and the processor is forced into a bus error exception by the $\overline{BERR}$ signal. In the exception, the MC68020 saves its internal state on the supervisor stack, executes the page fault handler to fix the fault, and then restores the saved internal state to continue the suspended instruction.

As shown in Fig. 12-12, the connection between the MC68020 and the PMMU is straightforward. Because the communication between the MC68020 and the PMMU is handled by coprocessor interface implemented in hardware, no address decoder nor interface programming is required. Extensions to this simple configuration are possible; they include an external cache and additional bus masters such as a floating-point coprocessor and a DMA controller.

As a coprocessor, the PMMU is capable of executing its instructions. However, the PMMU relies on the host processor to fetch the instruction and to load or store the memory operand when needed during the instruction execution. If the fetched instruction is a PMMU instruction, the MC68020 writes the instruction, including a coprocessor identification, to the PMMU. The MC68020 then reads the PMMU's response, which might be a request for the MC68020 to evaluate the effective address and to transfer the operand to or from the PMMU. This interaction between the MC68020 and the PMMU is handled entirely by hardware and is transparent to the user.

The PMMU may also be used with the MC68010 to provide a virtual memory capability. Since the MC68010 does not support coprocessor interface, in such a configuration the PMMU is accessed as a peripheral. A software routine is required to emulate the coprocessor interface by explicitly accessing the interface registers of the PMMU. More on coprocessor interface was discussed in Chap. 11.

MC68030 memory management logic

The memory management unit of the MC68030 provides many of the features of the MC68851 PMMU. However, there are some differences between the two, and the major ones are discussed next.

1. The MC68030 has a smaller address translation cache (ATC) for keeping recently used page descriptors, 22 entries in contrast to 64 entires of the MC68851.

2. The MC68030 does not support the hierarchical protection mechanism used in the MC68851, which allows up to eight levels of protection. Instead, the MC68030 provides supervisor protection and write protection by means of the function code signals. These signals identify accesses to the user program space, the user data space, the supervisor program space, and the supervisor data space. By using the function code signals, the MC68030 is able to protect supervisor program and data spaces from access by user programs and user program and data spaces from access by other users. In addition, the MC68030 can prevent unauthorized write accesses to supervisor and user program spaces and to individual pages of memory.

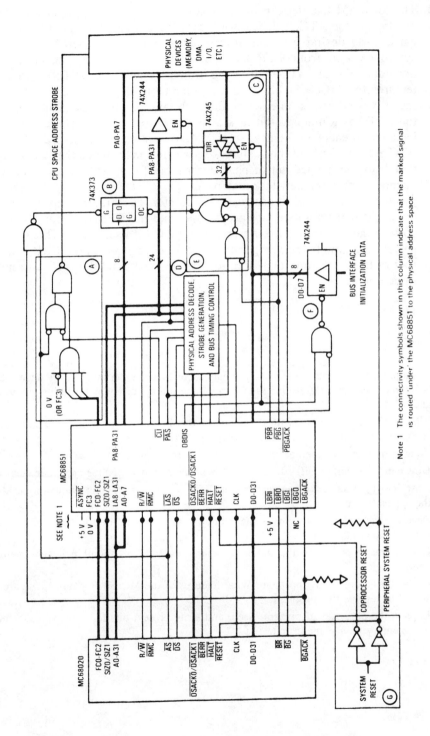

Note 1 The connectivity symbols shown in this column indicate that the marked signal
is routed 'under' the MC68851 to the physical address space

Figure 12-12 Example of a simple MC68020/MC68851 hardware configuration. (Courtesy of Motorola, Inc.)

3. The MC68851 has the capability of keeping page descriptors of more than one task in the ATC. This feature, which the MC68030 does not provide, is particularly desirable in a multiprogramming system. When the operating system switches from one task to another, the new task may begin execution immediately if the ATC holds some of its page descriptors. To provide this feature, the MC68851 has a root pointer table (RPT), which keeps eight recently used root pointers, one for each task. Each of the eight entries in the RPT has a unique 3-bit task alias associated with it. These 3 bits are included in each ATC entry, so eight tasks can be distinguished among all ATC entries. Without this feature, to perform a task switch the system must first load the needed set of page descriptors from the descriptor table in memory before the new task may begin. The MC68030 does not have a root pointer table. Instead, it uses two root pointer registers; the supervisor root pointer (SRP) for supervisor access only and the CPU root pointer (CRP) corresponding to the current translation table for user space. Therefore, to switch to a new task, the operating system needs to load the CRP with the root of the translation table tree for the new task, and the ATC also needs to be updated.

EXERCISES

1. Assume that cache access time is 100 nanoseconds and external memory access time is 300 nanoseconds. Determine the average access time for cache hit ratios of 0.9, 0.5, and 0.3.

2. What problem associated with data caching can be caused by memory-mapped I/O? How does the MC68030 data cache solve this problem?

3. What is memory fragmentation? How can it be reduced?

4. How can the modified bit reduce the overhead caused by paged memory management?

5. How does the number of page descriptors kept in the memory management logic affect the system performance?

6. Describe the two reasons why a cache improves the overall performance of a system with multiple bus masters.

7. Explain the purposes of valid and dirty bits that are typically found in a cache memory control logic.

8. Define cache coherence problem. What features of the MC68040's data cache are designed to resolve this problem?

9. Explain the purposes of present, used, and write protect bits that are typically found in a memory management unit.

Bibliography

1. Wilcox, Alan D., *68000 Microcomputer Designing and Troubleshooting* (Englewood Cliffs, N.J.: Prentice-Hall, Inc., 1987).
2. Clements, Alan, *Microprocessor System Design: 68000 Hardware, Software, and Interfacing* (Boston: PWS Computer Science, 1987).
3. Harman, Thomas L., and Barbara Lawson, *The Motorola MC68000 Microprocessor Family: Assembly Language, Interface Design, and System Design* (Englewood Cliffs, N.J: Prentice-Hall, Inc., 1985).
4. Triebel, Walter A., and Avtar Singh, *The 68000 Microprocessor Architecture, Software, and Interfacing Techniques* (Englewood Cliffs, N.J.: Prentice-Hall, Inc., 1986).
5. *MC68000 8-/16-/32-Bit Microprocessors Programmer's Reference Manual*, 5th ed. (Englewood Cliffs, N.J.: Prentice-Hall, Inc., 1986).
6. *MC68020 32-Bit Microprocessor User's Manual*, 2nd ed. (Englewood Cliffs, N.J.: Prentice-Hall, Inc., 1986).
7. *MC68030 Enhanced 32-Bit Microprocessor Users's Manual*, 2nd ed. (Englewood Cliffs, N.J.: Prentice-Hall, Inc., 1989).
8. *MC68040 32-bit Microprocessor User's Manual* (Tempe, Ariz.: Motorola, Inc., 1989).
9. *MC68851 Paged Memory Management Unit User's Manual* (Englewood Cliffs, N.J.: Prentice-Hall, Inc., 1986).
10. *MC68881/MC68882 Floating-Point Coprocessor User's Manual* (Englewood Cliffs, N.J.: Prentice-Hall, Inc., 1987).
11. *M68000 Family Reference* (Tempe, Ariz.: Motorola, Inc., 1988).
12. *M68000 Family Programmer's Reference Manual* (Tempe, Ariz.: Motorola, Inc., 1989).
13. *MC68000 Educational Computer Board User's Manual* (Tempe, Ariz.: Motorola, Inc., 1982).
14. *Motorola Microprocessors Data Manual* (Tempe, Ariz.: Motorola, Inc., 1981).

Appendix A

MC68000 Instruction Format Summary*

This appendix provides a summary of the primary words in each instruction of the instruction set. The complete instruction definition consists of the primary words followed by the addressing mode operands such as immediate data fields, displacements, and index operands. Table 1 is an operation code (op code) map that illustrates how bits 15 through 12 are used to specify the operations.

TABLE 1

Bits 15 through 12	Operation
0000	Bit Manipulation/MOVEP/Immediate
0001	Move Byte
0010	Move Long
0011	Move Word
0100	Miscellaneous
0101	ADDQ/SUBQ/Scc/DBcc
0110	Bcc/BSR
0111	MOVEQ
1000	OR/DIV/SBCD
1001	SUB/SUBX
1010	(Unassigned, Reserved)
1011	CMP/EOR
1100	AND/MUL/ABCD/EXG
1101	ADD/ADDX
1110	Shift/Rotate
1111	Coprocessor Interface (MC68020)

* Courtesy of Motorola, Inc.

TABLE 2

Address Modes	Mode	Register	Data	Memory	Control	Alterable	Assembler Syntax
Data Register Direct	000	reg. no.	X	–	–	X	Dn
Address Register Direct	001	reg. no.	–	–	–	X	An
Address Register Indirect	010	reg. no.	X	X	X	X	(An)
Address Register Indirect with Postincrement	011	reg. no.	X	X	–	X	(An) +
Address Register Indirect with Predecrement	100	reg. no.	X	X	–	X	– (An)
Address Register Indirect with Displacement	101	reg. no	X	X	X	X	(d_{16},An) or $d_{16}(An)$
Address Register Indirect with Index	110	reg. no.	X	X	X	X	(d_8,An,Xn) or $d_8(An,Xn)$
Absolute Short	111	000	X	X	X	X	(xxx).W
Absolute Long	111	001	X	X	X	X	(xxx).L
Program Counter Indirect with Displacement	111	101	X	X	X	–	(d_{16},PC) or $d_{16}(PC)$
Program Counter Indirect with Index	111	011	X	X	X	–	(d_8,PC,Xn) or $d_8(PC,Xn)$
Immediate	111	100	X	X	–	–	# < data >

Table 3. Conditional Tests

Mnemonic	Condition	Encoding	Test
T *	True	0000	1
F *	False	0001	0
HI	High	0010	$\overline{C} \cdot \overline{Z}$
LS	Low or Same	0011	C + Z
CC(HS)	Carry Clear	0100	$\overline{C}$
CS(LO)	Carry Set	0101	C
NE	Not Equal	0110	$\overline{Z}$
EQ	Equal	0111	Z
VC	Overflow Clear	1000	$\overline{V}$
VS	Overflow Set	1001	V
PL	Plus	1010	$\overline{N}$
MI	Minus	1011	N
GE	Greater or Equal	1100	$N \cdot V + \overline{N} \cdot \overline{V}$
LT	Less Than	1101	$N \cdot \overline{V} + \overline{N} \cdot V$
GT	Greater Than	1110	$N \cdot V \cdot \overline{Z} + \overline{N} \cdot \overline{V} \cdot \overline{Z}$
LE	Less or Equal	1111	$Z + N \cdot \overline{V} + \overline{N} \cdot V$

• = Boolean AND
+ = Boolean OR
$\overline{N}$ = Boolean NOT N

* Not available for the Bcc instruction

App. A   MC68000 Instruction Format Summary

STANDARD INSTRUCTIONS

OR Immediate

15	14	13	12	11	10	9	8	7	6	5	4	3	2	1	0
0	0	0	0	0	0	0	0	Size		Effective Address					
										Mode			Register		

Size field: 00 = byte 01 = word 10 = long

OR Immediate to CCR

15	14	13	12	11	10	9	8	7	6	5	4	3	2	1	0
0	0	0	0	0	0	0	0	0	0	1	1	1	1	0	0
0	0	0	0	0	0	0	0	Byte Data							

OR Immediate to SR

15	14	13	12	11	10	9	8	7	6	5	4	3	2	1	0
0	0	0	0	0	0	0	0	0	1	1	1	1	1	0	0
Word Data															

Dynamic Bit

15	14	13	12	11	10	9	8	7	6	5	4	3	2	1	0
0	0	0	0	Data Register			1	Type		Effective Address					
										Mode			Register		

Type field: 00 = TST 10 = CLR
            01 = CHG 11 = SET

MOVEP

15	14	13	12	11	10	9	8	7	6	5	4	3	2	1	0
0	0	0	0	Data Register			Op-Mode			0	0	1	Address Register		

Op-Mode field: 100 = transfer word from memory to register
               101 = transfer long from memory to register
               110 = transfer word from register to memory
               111 = transfer long from register to memory

AND Immediate

15	14	13	12	11	10	9	8	7	6	5	4	3	2	1	0
0	0	0	0	0	0	1	0	Size		Effective Address					
										Mode			Register		

Size field: 00 = byte 01 = word 10 = long

MC68000 Instruction Format Summary   App. A

AND Immediate to CCR

15	14	13	12	11	10	9	8	7	6	5	4	3	2	1	0
0	0	0	0	0	0	1	0	0	0	1	1	1	1	0	0
0	0	0	0	0	0	0	0	Byte Data							

AND Immediate to SR

15	14	13	12	11	10	9	8	7	6	5	4	3	2	1	0
0	0	0	0	0	0	1	0	0	1	1	1	1	1	0	0
Word Data															

SUB Immediate

15	14	13	12	11	10	9	8	7	6	5	4	3	2	1	0
0	0	0	0	0	1	0	0	Size		Effective Address					
										Mode			Register		

Size field: 00 = byte   01 = word   10 = long

ADD Immediate

15	14	13	12	11	10	9	8	7	6	5	4	3	2	1	0
0	0	0	0	0	1	1	0	Size		Effective Address					
										Mode			Register		

Size field: 00 = byte   01 = word   10 = long

Static Bit

15	14	13	12	11	10	9	8	7	6	5	4	3	2	1	0
0	0	0	0	1	0	0	0	Type		Effective Address					
										Mode			Register		
0	0	0	0	0	0	0	Bit Number								

Type field: 00 = TST   10 = CLR
            01 = CHG   11 = SET

EOR Immediate

15	14	13	12	11	10	9	8	7	6	5	4	3	2	1	0
0	0	0	0	1	0	1	0	Size		Effective Address					
										Mode			Register		

Size field: 00 = byte   01 = word   10 = long

EOR Immediate to CCR

15	14	13	12	11	10	9	8	7	6	5	4	3	2	1	0
0	0	0	0	1	0	1	0	0	0	1	1	1	1	0	0
0	0	0	0	0	0	0	0	Byte Data							

EOR Immediate to SR

15	14	13	12	11	10	9	8	7	6	5	4	3	2	1	0
0	0	0	0	1	0	1	0	0	1	1	1	1	1	0	0
Word Data															

CMP Immediate

15	14	13	12	11	10	9	8	7	6	5	4	3	2	1	0
0	0	0	0	1	1	0	0	Size		Effective Address					
										Mode			Register		

Size field: 00 = byte 01 = word 10 = long

MOVES (MC68010/MC68012)

15	14	13	12	11	10	9	8	7	6	5	4	3	2	1	0
0	0	0	0	1	1	1	0	Size		Effective Address					
										Mode			Register		
A/D	Register			dr	0	0	0	0	0	0	0	0	0	0	0

dr field: 0 = EA to register
          1 = register to EA

MOVE Byte

15	14	13	12	11	10	9	8	7	6	5	4	3	2	1	0
0	0	0	1	Destination						Source					
				Register			Mode			Mode			Register		

Note register and mode locations

MOVEA Long

15	14	13	12	11	10	9	8	7	6	5	4	3	2	1	0
0	0	1	0	Destination			0	0	1	Source					
				Register						Mode			Register		

MOVE Long

15	14	13	12	11	10	9	8	7	6	5	4	3	2	1	0
				Destination						Source					
0	0	1	0	Register			Mode			Mode			Register		

Note register and mode locations

MOVEA Word

15	14	13	12	11	10	9	8	7	6	5	4	3	2	1	0
				Destination								Source			
0	0	1	1	Register			0	0	1	Mode			Register		

MOVE Word

15	14	13	12	11	10	9	8	7	6	5	4	3	2	1	0
				Destination						Source					
0	0	1	1	Register			Mode			Mode			Register		

Note register and mode locations

NEGX

15	14	13	12	11	10	9	8	7	6	5	4	3	2	1	0
										Effective Address					
0	1	0	0	0	0	0	0	Size		Mode			Register		

Size field: 00 = byte 01 = word 10 = long

MOVE from SR

15	14	13	12	11	10	9	8	7	6	5	4	3	2	1	0
										Effective Address					
0	1	0	0	0	0	0	0	1	1	Mode			Register		

CHK

15	14	13	12	11	10	9	8	7	6	5	4	3	2	1	0
				Data			Size		0	Effective Address					
0	1	0	0	Register			Size		0	Mode			Register		

Size field: 10 = Longword (MC68020)
11 = Word

LEA

15	14	13	12	11	10	9	8	7	6	5	4	3	2	1	0
0	1	0	0	Address Register			1	1	1	Effective Address					
										Mode			Register		

CLR

15	14	13	12	11	10	9	8	7	6	5	4	3	2	1	0
0	1	0	0	0	0	1	0	Size		Effective Address					
										Mode			Register		

Size field: 00 = byte   01 = word   10 = long

MOVE from CCR (MC68010/MC68012)

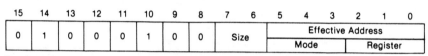

15	14	13	12	11	10	9	8	7	6	5	4	3	2	1	0
0	1	0	0	0	0	1	0	1	1	Effective Address					
										Mode			Register		

NEG

15	14	13	12	11	10	9	8	7	6	5	4	3	2	1	0
0	1	0	0	0	1	0	0	Size		Effective Address					
										Mode			Register		

Size field: 00 = byte   01 = word   10 = long

MOVE to CCR

15	14	13	12	11	10	9	8	7	6	5	4	3	2	1	0
0	1	0	0	0	1	0	0	1	1	Effective Address					
										Mode			Register		

NOT

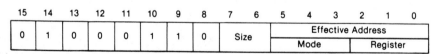

15	14	13	12	11	10	9	8	7	6	5	4	3	2	1	0
0	1	0	0	0	1	1	0	Size		Effective Address					
										Mode			Register		

Size field: 00 = byte   01 = word   10 = long

MOVE to SR

15	14	13	12	11	10	9	8	7	6	5	4	3	2	1	0
0	1	0	0	0	1	1	0	1	1	Effective Address					
										Mode			Register		

NBCD

15	14	13	12	11	10	9	8	7	6	5	4	3	2	1	0
										Effective Address					
0	1	0	0	1	0	0	0	0	0	Mode			Register		

SWAP

15	14	13	12	11	10	9	8	7	6	5	4	3	2	1	0
0	1	0	0	1	0	0	0	0	1	0	0	0	Data Register		

BKPT (MC68010/MC68012)

15	14	13	12	11	10	9	8	7	6	5	4	3	2	1	0
0	1	0	0	1	0	0	0	0	1	0	0	1	BKPT #		

PEA

15	14	13	12	11	10	9	8	7	6	5	4	3	2	1	0
										Effective Address					
0	1	0	0	1	0	0	0	0	1	Mode			Register		

EXT Word

15	14	13	12	11	10	9	8	7	6	5	4	3	2	1	0
0	1	0	0	1	0	0	Type			0	0	0	Data Register		

Type Field: 010 = Extend Word   011 = Extend Long

MOVEM Registers to EA

15	14	13	12	11	10	9	8	7	6	5	4	3	2	1	0
											Effective Address				
0	1	0	0	1	0	0	0	1	Sz	Mode			Register		

Sz field: 0 = word transfer   1 = long transfer

TST

15	14	13	12	11	10	9	8	7	6	5	4	3	2	1	0
										Effective Address					
0	1	0	0	1	0	1	0	Size		Mode			Register		

Size field: 00 = byte   01 = word   10 = long

TAS

15	14	13	12	11	10	9	8	7	6	5	4	3	2	1	0
										Effective Address					
0	1	0	0	1	0	1	0	1	1	Mode			Register		

ILLEGAL

15	14	13	12	11	10	9	8	7	6	5	4	3	2	1	0
0	1	0	0	1	0	1	0	1	1	1	1	1	1	0	0

MOVEM EA to Registers

15	14	13	12	11	10	9	8	7	6	5	4	3	2	1	0
										Effective Address					
0	1	0	0	1	1	0	0	1	Sz	Mode			Register		

Sz field: 0 = word transfer   1 = long transfer

TRAP

15	14	13	12	11	10	9	8	7	6	5	4	3	2	1	0
0	1	0	0	1	1	1	0	0	1	0	0	Vector			

LINK Word

15	14	13	12	11	10	9	8	7	6	5	4	3	2	1	0
0	1	0	0	1	1	1	0	0	1	0	1	0	Address Register		

UNLK

15	14	13	12	11	10	9	8	7	6	5	4	3	2	1	0
0	1	0	0	1	1	1	0	0	1	0	1	1	Address Register		

MOVE to USP

15	14	13	12	11	10	9	8	7	6	5	4	3	2	1	0
0	1	0	0	1	1	1	0	0	1	1	0	0	Address Register		

MOVE from USP

15	14	13	12	11	10	9	8	7	6	5	4	3	2	1	0
0	1	0	0	1	1	1	0	0	1	1	0	1	Address Register		

RESET

15	14	13	12	11	10	9	8	7	6	5	4	3	2	1	0
0	1	0	0	1	1	1	0	0	1	1	1	0	0	0	0

NOP

15	14	13	12	11	10	9	8	7	6	5	4	3	2	1	0
0	1	0	0	1	1	1	0	0	1	1	1	0	0	0	1

STOP

15	14	13	12	11	10	9	8	7	6	5	4	3	2	1	0
0	1	0	0	1	1	1	0	0	1	1	1	0	0	1	0

RTE

15	14	13	12	11	10	9	8	7	6	5	4	3	2	1	0
0	1	0	0	1	1	1	0	0	1	1	1	0	0	1	1

RTD (MC68010/MC68012)

15	14	13	12	11	10	9	8	7	6	5	4	3	2	1	0
0	1	0	0	1	1	1	0	0	1	1	1	0	1	0	0

RTS

15	14	13	12	11	10	9	8	7	6	5	4	3	2	1	0
0	1	0	0	1	1	1	0	0	1	1	1	0	1	0	1

TRAPV

15	14	13	12	11	10	9	8	7	6	5	4	3	2	1	0
0	1	0	0	1	1	1	0	0	1	1	1	0	1	1	0

RTR

15	14	13	12	11	10	9	8	7	6	5	4	3	2	1	0
0	1	0	0	1	1	1	0	0	1	1	1	0	1	1	1

MOVEC (MC68010/MC68012)

15	14	13	12	11	10	9	8	7	6	5	4	3	2	1	0
0	1	0	0	1	1	1	0	0	1	1	1	1	0	1	dr
A/D	Register			Control Register											

dr field: 0 = control register to general register
          1 = general register to control register

Control Register field: $000 = SFC $801 = VBR
                         $001 = DFC $802 = CAAR   (MC68020)
                         $002 = CACR (MC68020) $803 = MSP   (MC68020)
                         $800 = USP $804 = ISP   (MC68020)

JSR

15	14	13	12	11	10	9	8	7	6	5	4	3	2	1	0
0	1	0	0	1	1	1	0	1	0	Effective Address					
										Mode			Register		

JMP

15	14	13	12	11	10	9	8	7	6	5	4	3	2	1	0
0	1	0	0	1	1	1	0	1	1	Effective Address					
										Mode			Register		

ADDQ

15	14	13	12	11	10	9	8	7	6	5	4	3	2	1	0
0	1	0	1	Data			0	Size		Effective Address					
										Mode			Register		

Data field: Three bits of immediate data, 0, 1-7 representing a range of 8,
            1 to 7 respectively.
Size field: 00 = byte   01 = word   10 = long

Scc

15	14	13	12	11	10	9	8	7	6	5	4	3	2	1	0
0	1	0	1	Condition				1	1	Effective Address					
										Mode			Register		

DBcc

15	14	13	12	11	10	9	8	7	6	5	4	3	2	1	0
0	1	0	1		Condition			1	1	0	0	1		Data Register	

SUBQ

15	14	13	12	11	10	9	8	7	6	5	4	3	2	1	0
0	1	0	1		Data		1		Size		Effective Address				
											Mode			Register	

Data field: Three bits of immediate data, 0, 1-7 representing a range of 8,
1 to 7 respectively.
Size field: 00 = byte   01 = word   10 = long

Bcc

15	14	13	12	11	10	9	8	7	6	5	4	3	2	1	0
0	1	1	0		Condition					8-Bit Displacement					
16-Bit Displacement if 8-Bit Displacement = $00															

BRA

15	14	13	12	11	10	9	8	7	6	5	4	3	2	1	0
0	1	1	0	0	0	0	0			8-Bit Displacement					
16-Bit Displacement if 8-Bit Displacement = $00															

BSR

15	14	13	12	11	10	9	8	7	6	5	4	3	2	1	0
0	1	1	0	0	0	0	1			8-Bit Displacement					
16-Bit Displacement if 8-Bit Displacement = $00															

MOVEQ

15	14	13	12	11	10	9	8	7	6	5	4	3	2	1	0
0	1	1	1		Data Register		0			Data					

Data field: Data is sign extended to a long operand and all 32 bits are
transferred to the data register.

OR

15	14	13	12	11	10	9	8	7	6	5	4	3	2	1	0
1	0	0	0	Data Register			Op-Mode			Effective Address					
										Mode			Register		

Op-Mode field:
Byte	Word	Long	Operation
000	001	010	(<ea>)v(<Dn>) → <Dn>
100	101	110	(<Dn>)v(<ea>) → <ea>

DIVU/DIVS Word

15	14	13	12	11	10	9	8	7	6	5	4	3	2	1	0
1	0	0	0	Data Register			Type	1	1	Effective Address					
										Mode			Register		

Type field: 0 = DIVU   1 = DIVS

SBCD

15	14	13	12	11	10	9	8	7	6	5	4	3	2	1	0
1	0	0	0	Destination Register*			1	0	0	0	0	R/M	Source Register*		

R/M field: 0 = data register to data register
            1 = memory to memory
*If R/M = 0, specifies a data register
 If R/M = 1, specifies an address register for the predecrement addressing mode.

SUB

15	14	13	12	11	10	9	8	7	6	5	4	3	2	1	0
1	0	0	1	Data Register			Op-Mode			Effective Address					
										Mode			Register		

Op-Mode field:
Byte	Word	Long	Operation
000	001	010	(<Dn>) – (<ea>) → <Dn>
100	101	110	(<ea>) – (<Dn>) → <ea>

SUBA

15	14	13	12	11	10	9	8	7	6	5	4	3	2	1	0
1	0	0	1	Data Register			Op-Mode			Effective Address					
										Mode			Register		

Op-Mode field:
Word	Long	Operation
011	111	(<An>) – (<ea>) → <An>

SUBX

15	14	13	12	11	10	9	8	7	6	5	4	3	2	1	0
1	0	0	1	Destination Register*			1	Size		0	0	R/M	Source Register*		

Size field: 00 = byte   01 = word   10 = long
R/M field: 0 = data register to data register   1 = memory to memory
*If R/M = 0, specifies a data register
 If R/M = 1, specifies an address register for the predecrement addressing mode.

MC68000 Instruction Format Summary   App. A

CMP

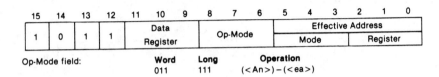

15	14	13	12	11	10	9	8	7	6	5	4	3	2	1	0
				Data						Effective Address					
1	0	1	1	Register			Op-Mode			Mode			Register		

Op-Mode field:

	Byte	Word	Long	Operation
	000	001	010	(<Dn>)−(<ea>)

CMPA

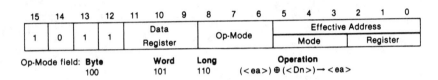

15	14	13	12	11	10	9	8	7	6	5	4	3	2	1	0
				Data						Effective Address					
1	0	1	1	Register			Op-Mode			Mode			Register		

Op-Mode field:

	Word	Long	Operation
	011	111	(<An>)−(<ea>)

EOR

15	14	13	12	11	10	9	8	7	6	5	4	3	2	1	0
				Data						Effective Address					
1	0	1	1	Register			Op-Mode			Mode			Register		

Op-Mode field:

	Byte	Word	Long	Operation
	100	101	110	(<ea>) ⊕ (<Dn>) → <ea>

CMPM

15	14	13	12	11	10	9	8	7	6	5	4	3	2	1	0
				Destination										Source	
1	0	1	1	Register			1	Size		0	0	1		Register	

Size field: 00 = byte 01 = word 10 = long

AND

15	14	13	12	11	10	9	8	7	6	5	4	3	2	1	0
				Data						Effective Address					
1	1	0	0	Register			Op-Mode			Mode			Register		

Op-Mode field:

	Byte	Word	Long	Operation
	000	001	010	(<ea>)Λ(<Dn>) → <Dn>
	100	101	110	(<Dn>)Λ(<ea>) → <ea>

MULU Word
MULS Word

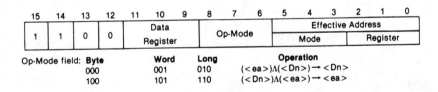

15	14	13	12	11	10	9	8	7	6	5	4	3	2	1	0
				Data						Effective Address					
1	1	0	0	Register			Type	1	1	Mode			Register		

Type field: 0 = MULU 1 = MULS

ABCD

15	14	13	12	11	10	9	8	7	6	5	4	3	2	1	0
1	1	0	0	Destination Register*			1	0	0	0	0	R/M	Source Register*		

R/M field: 0 = data register to data register   1 = memory to memory
* If R/M = 0, specifies a data register
   If R/M = 1, specifies an address register for the predecrement addressing mode.

EXG Data Registers

15	14	13	12	11	10	9	8	7	6	5	4	3	2	1	0
1	1	0	0	Data Register			1	0	1	0	0	0	Data Register		

EXG Address Registers

15	14	13	12	11	10	9	8	7	6	5	4	3	2	1	0
1	1	0	0	Address Register			1	0	1	0	0	1	Address Register		

EXG Data Register and Address Register

15	14	13	12	11	10	9	8	7	6	5	4	3	2	1	0
1	1	0	0	Data Register			1	1	0	0	0	1	Address Register		

ADD

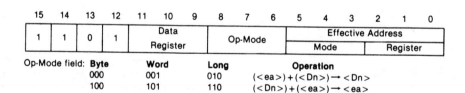

15	14	13	12	11	10	9	8	7	6	5	4	3	2	1	0
1	1	0	1	Data Register			Op-Mode			Effective Address					
										Mode			Register		

Op-Mode field:

Byte	Word	Long	Operation
000	001	010	$(<ea>) + (<Dn>) \rightarrow <Dn>$
100	101	110	$(<Dn>) + (<ea>) \rightarrow <ea>$

ADDA

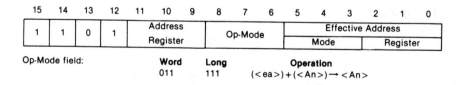

15	14	13	12	11	10	9	8	7	6	5	4	3	2	1	0
1	1	0	1	Address Register			Op-Mode			Effective Address					
										Mode			Register		

Op-Mode field:

	Word	Long	Operation
	011	111	$(<ea>) + (<An>) \rightarrow <An>$

ADDX

15	14	13	12	11	10	9	8	7	6	5	4	3	2	1	0
1	1	0	1	Destination Register*			1	Size		0	0	R/M	Source Register*		

Size field: 00 = byte   01 = word   10 = long
R/M field: 0 = data register to data register   1 = memory to memory
* If R/M = 0, specifies a data register
  If R/M = 1, specifies an address register for the predecrement addressing mode.

SHIFT/ROTATE — Register

15	14	13	12	11	10	9	8	7	6	5	4	3	2	1	0
1	1	1	0	Count/ Register			dr	Size		i/r	Type		Data Register		

Count/Register field: If i/r field = 0, specifies shift count
                      If i/r field = 1, specifies a data register that con-
                      tains the shift count

dr field: 0 = right   1 = left
Size field: 00 = byte   01 = word   10 = long
i/r field: 0 = immediate shift count   1 = register shift count
Type field: 00 = arithmetic shift   10 = rotate with extend
            01 = logical shift   11 = rotate

SHIFT/ROTATE — Memory

15	14	13	12	11	10	9	8	7	6	5	4	3	2	1	0
1	1	1	0	0	Type		dr	1	1	Effective Address Mode			Register		

Type field: 00 = arithmetic shift   01 = logical shift   10 = rotate with extend   11 = rotate
dr field: 0 = right   1 = left

Appendix B

The MC68000 Instruction Set in Alphabetical Order

Name	Mnemonic	Size or Postfix	Operand Format	Allowable EA Modes	Operation	N	Z	V	C	X	Section Referenced
Add decimal with X flag	ABCD	Byte	Dx,Dy −(Ax),−(Ay)		$Dx_{10} + Dy_{10} + X \to Dy$ $(SRC)_{10} + (DST)_{10} + X \to DST$	u	*	u	*	*	3-8
Add binary	ADD	.B,.W,.L	EA,Dn Dn,EA	All Memory alterable	$(EA) + Dn \to Dn$ $Dn + (EA) \to EA$	*	*	*	*	*	3-7
Add address	ADDA	.W,.L	EA,An	All	$(EA) + An \to An$	—	—	—	—	—	3-7
Add immediate	ADDI	.B,.W,.L	#I,EA	Data alterable	$I + (EA) \to EA$	*	*	*	*	*	3-7
Add quick	ADDQ	.B,.W,.L	#I3,EA	Alterable	$I3 + (EA) \to EA$	*	*	*	*	*	3-7
Add with X flag	ADDX	.B,.W,.L	Dx,Dy −(Ax),−(Ay)		$Dx + Dy + X \to Dy$ $(SRC) + (DST) + X \to DST$	*	*	*	*	*	3-7
AND logical	AND	.B,.W,.L	EA,Dn Dn,EA	Data Memory alterable	$(EA) \land Dn \to Dn$ $Dn \land (EA) \to EA$	*	*	0	0	—	3-9
AND immediate	ANDI	.B,.W,.L Byte Word	#I,EA #I,CCR #I,SR	Data alterable	$I \land (EA) \to EA$ $I \land CCR \to CCR$ $I \land SR \to SR$	*	*	0	0	—	3-9
Arithmetic shift left	ASL	.B,.W,.L Word	Dx,Dy #I3,Dy EA	Memory alterable	$\boxed{C\,X} \leftarrow \boxed{DST} \leftarrow 0$	*	*	*	*	*	3-10
Arithmetic shift right	ASR	.B,.W,.L Word	Dx,Dy #I3,Dy EA	Memory alterable	$\boxed{DST} \to \boxed{C\,X}$	*	*	*	*	*	3-10
Branch conditionally	Bcc	.S or none	DST		If cc then $DST \to PC$	—	—	—	—	—	3-6

Where cc designates the condition to be tested as given below.

Flag Setting for Causing a Branch in Bcc or a Termination in DBcc, or FF to Be Moved to EA in Scc

Syntax	Test Condition	
BEQ, DBEQ, SEQ	Equal	$Z = 1$
BNE, DBNE, SNE	Not equal	$Z = 0$
BGT, DBGT, SGT	Greater	$Z + (N \oplus V) = 0$
BLT, DBLT, SLT	Less	$N \oplus V = 1$
BGE, DBGE, SGE	Greater or equal	$N \oplus V = 0$
BLE, DBLE, SLE	Less or equal	$Z + (N \oplus V) = 1$

Name	Mnemonic	Size or Postfix	Operand Format	Allowable EA Modes	Operation	N	Z	V	C	X	Section Referenced
	BVS, DBVS, SVS		Overflow		V = 1						
	BVC, DBVC, SVC		No overflow		V = 0						
	BPL, DBPL, SPL		Plus		N = 0						
	BMI, DBMI, SMI		Minus		N = 1						
	BHI, DBHI, SHI		Higher		C + Z = 0						
	BLS, DBLS, SLS		Lower or same		C + Z = 1						
	BCS, DBCS, SCS		Carry set (Lower)		C = 1						
	BCC, DBCC, SCC		Carry clear (Higher or same)		C = 0						
	DBF, SF		False (Never)		None						
	DBT, ST		True (Always)		None						
Test bit and change	BCHG	Byte or longword	Dn,EA / #I,EA	Data alterable	$\overline{\text{DST[bit no.]}} \rightarrow$ Z, DST[bit no.]	—	*	—	—	—	3-11
Test bit and clear	BCLR	Byte or longword	Dn,EA / #I,EA	Data alterable	$\overline{\text{DST[bit no.]}} \rightarrow$ Z; 0 → DST[bit no.]	—	*	—	—	—	3-11
Branch	BRA	.S or none	DST		DST → PC	—	—	—	—	—	3-6
Test bit and set	BSET	Byte or longword	Dn,EA / #I,EA	Data alterable	$\overline{\text{DST[bit no.]}} \rightarrow$ Z; 1 → DST[bit no.]	—	*	—	—	—	3-11
Branch to subroutine	BSR	.S or none	DST		PC → −(SP); DST → PC	—	—	—	—	—	5-2
Test bit	BTST	Byte or longword	Dn,EA / #I,EA	Data	$\overline{\text{DST[bit no.]}} \rightarrow$ Z	—	*	—	—	—	3-11
Check register against bounds	CHK	Word	EA,Dn	Data	If Dn.W < 0 or Dn.W > (EA) then PC → −(SSP); SR → −(SSP); (24) → PC	*	u	u	u	—	6-5
Clear	CLR	.B, .W, .L	EA	Data alterable	0 → EA	0	1	0	0	—	3-7
Compare	CMP	.B, .W, .L	EA,Dn	All	Dn − (EA)	*	*	*	*	—	3-5
Compare address	CMPA	.W, .L	EA,An	All	An − (EA)	*	*	*	*	—	3-5
Compare immediate	CMPI	.B, .W, .L	#I,EA	Data alterable	(EA) − I	*	*	*	*	—	3-5
Compare memory	CMPM	.B, .W, .L	(Ax)+,(Ay)+		ROPR − LOPR	*	*	*	*	—	3-5
Decrement and branch conditionally	DBcc	Unsized	Dn,DST		If cc then Dn.W − 1 → Dn.W If Dn.W ≠ −1 then DST → PC	—	—	—	—	—	3-6

Where cc designates one of the condition tests as described in Bcc.

Operation	Mnemonic	Size	Operand	Addressing	Operation	X	N	Z	V	C	Page
Sign divide	DIVS	Word	EA,Dn	Data	Dn / (EA) Quotient (signed) → Dn[15:0] Remainder (same sign as dividend) → Dn[31:16]	*	*	*	0	—	3-7
Unsigned divide	DIVU	Word	EA,Dn	Data	Dn / (EA) Quotient (unsigned) → Dn[15:0] Remainder (unsigned) → Dn[31:16]	*	*	*	0	—	3-7
Exclusive OR logical	EOR	.B, .W, .L	Dn,EA	Data alterable	Dn ⊕ (EA) → EA	*	*	0	0	—	3-9
Exclusive OR immediate	EORI	.B, .W, .L / Byte / Word	#I,EA / #I,CCR / #I,SR	Data alterable	#I ⊕ (EA) → EA / #I ⊕ CCR → CCR / #I ⊕ SR → SR	* / * / *	* / * / *	0 / * / *	0 / * / *	— / * / *	3-9
Exchange registers	EXG	Longword	Rx,Ry		Rx ↔ Ry	—	—	—	—	—	3-4
Sign extend	EXT	.W, .L	Dn		Dn.B sign-extended → Dn.W or Dn.W sign-extended → Dn.L	*	*	0	0	—	3-7
Jump	JMP	Unsized	EA	Control	EA → PC	—	—	—	—	—	3-6
Jump to subroutine	JSR	Unsized	EA	Control	PC → −(SP); EA → PC	—	—	—	—	—	5-2
Load effective address	LEA	Longword	EA,An	Control	EA → An	—	—	—	—	—	3-4
Link and allocate	LINK	Unsized	An,#I16		An → −(SP); SP → An; SP + I16 → SP	—	—	—	—	—	5-5
Logical shift left	LSL	.B, .W, .L / Word	Dx,Dy / #I3,Dy / EA	Memory alterable	C/X ← [DST] ← 0	*	*	0	*	*	3-9
Logical shift right	LSR	.B, .W, .L / Word	Dx,Dy / #I3,Dy / EA	Memory alterable	0 → [DST] → C/X	*	*	0	*	*	3-9
Move data	MOVE	.B, .W, .L	EA,EA	SRC: All DST: Data alterable	(SRC EA) → DST EA	*	*	0	0	—	3-4
Move condition codes or status register	MOVE	Word	EA,CCR or SR / SR,EA	Data / Data alterable	(EA) → CCR or SR / SR → EA	* / —	* / —	* / —	* / —	* / —	3-4

Name	Mnemonic	Size or Postfix	Operand Format	Allowable EA Modes	Operation	N	Z	V	C	X	Section Referenced
Move user stack pointer	MOVE	Longword	USP,An / An,USP		USP → An / An → USP	—	—	—	—	—	3-4
Move address	MOVEA	.W, .L	EA,An	All	(EA) → An	—	—	—	—	—	3-4
Move multiple registers	MOVEM	.W, .L	Reg List,EA / EA,Reg List	Control alterable or predecrement / Control or postincrement	Registers → EA / (EA) → Registers	—	—	—	—	—	3-4
Move peripheral data	MOVEP	.W, .L	Dx,D16(Ay) / D16(Ay),Dx		Dx → DST / (SRC) → Dx	—	—	—	—	—	3-4
Move quick	MOVEQ	Longword	#I8,Dn		I8 (sign-extended) → Dn	*	*	0	0	—	3-4
Signed multiply	MULS	Word	EA,Dn	Data	(EA) * Dn[15:0] → Dn / Product is signed	*	*	0	0	—	3-7
Unsigned multiply	MULU	Word	EA,Dn	Data	(EA) * Dn[15:0] → Dn / Product is unsigned	*	*	0	0	—	3-7
Negate decimal with X flag	NBCD	Byte	EA	Data alterable	$0 - (EA)_{10} - X \to EA$	u	*	u	*	*	3-8
Negate	NEG	.B, .W, .L	EA	Data alterable	$0 - (EA) \to EA$	*	*	*	*	*	3-7
Negate with extend	NEGX	.B, .W, .L	EA	Data alterable	$0 - (EA) - X \to EA$	*	*	*	*	*	3-7
No operation	NOP	Unsized	None		No operation	—	—	—	—	—	3-6
Logical complement	NOT	.B, .W, .L	EA	Data alterable	$\overline{(EA)} \to EA$	*	*	0	0	—	3-9
OR logical	OR	.B, .W, .L	EA,Dn / Dn,EA	Data / Memory alterable	(EA) ∨ Dn → Dn / Dn ∨ (EA) → EA	*	*	0	0	—	3-9
OR immediate	ORI	.B, .W, .L / Byte / Word	#I, EA / #I,CCR / #I,SR	Data alterable	I ∨ (EA) → EA / I ∨ CCR → CCR / I ∨ SR → SR	*	*	*	*	—	3-9
Push effective address	PEA	Longword	EA	Control	EA → −(SP)	—	—	—	—	—	3-4
Reset	RESET	Unsized	None		Low → $\overline{\text{RESET}}$ pin	—	—	—	—	—	6-2
Rotate left	ROL	.B, .W, .L / Word	Dx,Dy / #I3,Dy / EA	Memory alterable	(rotate diagram: C → DST → C)	*	*	0	*	—	3-10
Rotate right	ROR	.B, .W, .L / Word	Dx,Dy / #I3,Dy / EA	Memory alterable	(rotate diagram: DST → C)	*	*	0	*	—	3-10

430

Description	Mnemonic	Size	Operands	Operation	X	N	Z	V	C	Page
Rotate left through X flag	ROXL	.B, .W, .L	Dx,Dy / #I3,Dy / EA (Memory alterable — Word)		*	*	0	*	*	3-10
Rotate right through X flag	ROXR	.B, .W, .L / Word (Memory alterable)	Dx,Dy / #I3,Dy / EA		*	*	0	*	*	3-10
Return from exception	RTE	Unsized	None	(SP)+ → SR; (SP)+ → PC	*	*	*	*	*	6-1
Return and restore condition codes	RTR	Unsized	None	(SP)+ → CCR; (SP)+ → PC	*	*	*	*	*	5-2
Return from subroutine	RTS	Unsized	None	(SP)+ → PC	—	—	—	—	—	5-2
Subtract decimal with X flag	SBCD	Byte	Dx,Dy / -(Ax),-(Ay)	$Dy_{10} - Dx_{10} - X \to Dy$ $(DST)_{10} - (SRC)_{10} - X \to DST$	u	*	u	*	*	3-8
Set conditionally	Scc	Byte	EA (Data alterable)	If cc then FF → EA else 00 → EA	—	—	—	—	—	3-6
		Where cc designates one of the condition tests as described in Bcc.								
Stop	STOP	Unsized	#I	I → SR; Stop	*	*	*	*	*	3-6
Subtract binary	SUB	.B, .W, .L	EA,Dn (All) / Dn,EA (Memory alterable)	Dn - (EA) → Dn / (EA) - Dn → EA	*	*	*	*	*	3-7
Subtract address	SUBA	.W, .L	EA,An (All)	An - (EA) → An	—	—	—	—	—	3-7
Subtract immediate	SUBI	.B, .W, .L	#I,EA (Data alterable)	(EA) - I → EA	*	*	*	*	*	3-7
Subtract quick	SUBQ	.B, .W, .L	#I3,EA (Alterable)	(EA) - I3 → EA	*	*	*	*	*	3-7
Subtract with X flag	SUBX	.B, .W, .L	Dx,Dy / -(Ax),-(Ay)	Dy - Dx - X → Dy / (DST) - (SRC) - X → DST	*	*	*	*	*	3-7
Swap register halves	SWAP	Word	Dn	Dn[31:16] ↔ Dn[15:0]	*	*	0	0	—	3-4
Test and set	TAS	Byte	EA (Data alterable)	(EA) - 0; 1 → EA[7]	*	*	0	0	—	5-6
Trap	TRAP	Unsized	#I4	PC → -(SSP); SR → -(SSP); ((32 + I4) × 4) → PC	—	—	—	—	—	6-5
Trap on overflow	TRAPV	Unsized	None	If V = 1 then PC → -(SSP); SR → -(SSP); (28) → PC	—	—	—	—	—	6-5
Test	TST	.B, .W, .L	EA (Data alterable)	(EA) - 0	*	*	0	0	—	3-5
Unlink	UNLK	Unsized	An	An → SP; (SP)+ → An	—	—	—	—	—	5-5

Appendix C

The MC68881/MC68882 Instruction Set in Alphabetical Order

Name	Mnemonic	Size or Postfix	Operand Format	Allowable EA Modes	Operation	Section Referenced
Absolute value	FABS	.B, .W, .L, .S, .D, .X, .P .X .X	EA,FPn FPm,FPn FPn	Data	$|(SRC)| \rightarrow$ FPn	11-2
Arc cosine	FACOS	.B, .W, .L, .S, .D, .X, .P .X .X	EA, FPn FPm,FPn FPn	Data	Cos^{-1} (SRC) $\rightarrow$ FPn	11-2
Add	FADD	.B, .W, .L, .S, .D, .X, .P .X	EA,FPn FPm,FPn	Data	(SRC) + FPn $\rightarrow$ FPn	11-2
Arc sine	FASIN	.B, .W, .L, .S, .D, .X, .P .X .X	EA,FPn FPm,FPn FPn	Data	Sin^{-1} (SRC) $\rightarrow$ FPn	11-2
Arc tangent	FATAN	.B, .W, .L, .S, .D, .X, .P .X .X	EA,FPn FPm,FPn FPn	Data	Tan^{-1} (SRC) $\rightarrow$ FPn	11-2
Hyperbolic arc tangent	FATANH	.B, .W, .L, .S, .D, .X, .P .X .X	EA,FPn FPm,FPn FPn	Data	Tanh^{-1} (SRC) $\rightarrow$ FPn	11-2
Branch conditionally	FBcc	.W, .L	DST		If cc then DST $\rightarrow$ PC	11-2
Compare	FCMP	.B, .W, .L, .S, .D, .X, .P .X	EA,FPn FPm,FPn	Data	FPn $-$ (SRC)	11-2
Cosine	FCOS	.B, .W, .L, .S, .D, .X, .P .X .X	EA,FPn FPm,FPn FPn	Data	Cos (SRC) $\rightarrow$ FPn	11-2
Hyperbolic cosine	FCOSH	.B, .W, .L, .S, .D, .X, .P .X .X	EA,FPn FPm,FPn FPn	Data	Cosh (SRC) $\rightarrow$ FPn	11-2
Decrement and branch conditionally	FDBcc	Unsized	Dn,DST		If $\overline{cc}$ then Dn.W $- 1 \rightarrow$ Dn.W If Dn.W $\neq -1$ then DST $\rightarrow$ PC	11-2
Divide	FDIV	.B, .W, .L, .S, .D, .X, .P .X	EA,FPn FPm,FPn	Data	FPn / (SRC) $\rightarrow$ FPn	11-2
e to the x power	FETOX	.B, .W, .L, .S, .D, .X, .P .X .X	EA,FPn FPm,FPn FPn	Data	$e^{(SRC)} \rightarrow$ FPn	11-2

Name	Mnemonic	Size or Postfix	Operand Format	Allowable EA Modes	Operation	Section Referenced
e to the x power $-$ 1	FETOXM1	.B, .W, .L, .S, .D, .X, .P .X .X	EA,FPn FPm,FPn FPn	Data	$e^{(SRC)} - 1 \rightarrow$ FPn	11-2
Get exponent	FGETEXP	.B, .W, .L, .S, .D, .X, .P .X .X	EA,FPn FPm,FPn FPn	Data	Exponent of (SRC) $\rightarrow$ FPn	11-2
Get mantissa	FGETMAN	.B, .W, .L, .S, .D, .X, .P .X .X	EA,FPn FPm,FPn FPn	Data	Mantissa of (SRC) $\rightarrow$ FPn	11-2
Integer part	FINT	.B, .W, .L, .S, .D, .X, .P .X .X	EA,FPn FPm,FPn FPn	Data	Integer of (SRC) $\rightarrow$ FPn	11-2
Integer part, round to 0	FINTRZ	.B, .W, .L, .S, .D, .X, .P .X .X	EA,FPn FPm,FPn FPn	Data	Integer of (SRC) $\rightarrow$ FPn (Round to 0)	11-2
Log base 10	FLOG10	.B, .W, .L, .S, .D, .X, .P .X .X	EA,FPn FPm,FPn FPn	Data	$Log_{10}(SRC) \rightarrow$ FPn	11-2
Log base 2	FLOG2	.B, .W, .L, .S, .D, .X, .P .X .X	EA,FPn FPm,FPn FPn	Data	$Log_{2}(SRC) \rightarrow$ FPn	11-2
Log base e	FLOGN	.B, .W, .L, .S, .D, .X, .P .X .X	EA,FPn FPm,FPn FPn	Data	$Log_{e}(SRC) \rightarrow$ FPn	11-2
Log base e of X + 1	FLOGNP1	.B, .W, .L, .S, .D, .X, .P .X .X	EA,FPn FPm,FPn FPn	Data	$Log_{e}[(SRC) + 1] \rightarrow$ FPn	11-2
Modulo remainder	FMOD	.B, .W, .L, .S, .D, .X, .P .X	EA,FPn FPm,FPn	Data	FPn mod (SRC) $\rightarrow$ FPn	11-2
Move data register	FMOVE	.B, .W, .L, .S, .D, .X, .P .X .B, .W, .L, .S, .D, .X .P .P	EA,FPn FPm,FPn FPm,EA FPm,EA{Dn} FPm,EA{#k}	Data Data alterable Data alterable Data alterable	(SRC) $\rightarrow$ FPn FPm $\rightarrow$ EA	11-2
Move control register	FMOVE	.L .L	EA,FPcr FPcr,EA	All Alterable	(EA) $\rightarrow$ control register Control register $\rightarrow$ EA	11-2

Description	Mnemonic	Size	Operand	Addressing Category	Operation	Page
Move constant ROM	FMOVECR	.X	#ccc,FPn		ROM constant → FPn	11-2
Move multiple data registers	FMOVEM	.X .X .X .X	Reg List,EA Dn,EA EA,Reg List EA,Dn	Control alterable or −(An) Control or (An)+	Data registers → EA (EA) → Data registers	11-2 11-2
Move multiple control registers	FMOVEM	.L .L	Reg List,EA EA,Reg List	Alterable All	Control registers → EA (EA) → Control registers	11-2
Multiply	FMUL	.B, .W, .L, .S, .D, .X, .P	EA,FPn FPm,FPn	Data	(SRC) * FPn → FPn	11-2
Negate	FNEG	.B, .W, .L, .S, .D, .X, .P .X .X	EA,FPn FPm,FPn FPn	Data	−(SRC) → FPn	11-2
No operation	FNOP	Unsized			None	11-2
Remainder	FREM	.B, .W, .L, .S, .D, .X, .P .X	EA,FPn FPm,FPn	Data	Remainder of FPn / (SRC) → FPn	11-2
Restore internal state	FRESTORE	Unsized	EA	Control or (An)+	(EA) → Internal state (Privileged)	11-2
Save internal state	FSAVE	Unsized	EA	Control alterable or −(An)	Internal state → EA (Privileged)	11-2
Scale exponent	FSCALE	.B, .W, .L, .S, .D, .X, .P .X	EA,FPn FPm,FPn	Data	FPn * $2^{(\text{integer of } (SRC))}$ → FPn	11-2
Set Conditionally	FScc	Byte	EA	Data alterable	If cc then FF → EA else 00 → EA	11-2
Single-precision divide	FSGLDIV	.B, .W, .L, .S, .D, .X, .P .X	EA,FPn FPm,FPn	Data	FPn / (SRC) → FPn (Single precision)	11-2
Single-precision multiply	FSGLMUL	.B, .W, .L, .S, .D, .X, .P .X	EA,FPn FPm,FPn	Data	FPn * (SRC) → FPn (Single precision)	11-2
Sine	FSIN	.B, .W, .L, .S, .D, .X, .P .X .X	EA,FPn FPm,FPn FPn	Data	Sin (SRC) → FPn	11-2
Sine and cosine	FSINCOS	.B, .W, .L, .S, .D, .X, .P .X	EA,FPc:FPs FPm,FPc:FPs	Data	Sin (SRC) → FPs Cos (SRC) → FPc	11-2
Hyperbolic sine	FSINH	.B, .W, .L, .S, .D, .X, .P .X .X	EA,FPn FPm,FPn FPn	Data	Sinh (SRC) → FPn	11-2
Square root	FSQRT	.B, .W, .L, .S, .D, .X, .P .X .X	EA,FPn FPm,FPn FPn	Data	$\sqrt{(SRC)}$ → FPn	11-2

Name	Mnemonic	Size or Postfix	Operand Format	Allowable EA Modes	Operation	Section Referenced
Subtract	FSUB	.B, .W, .L, .S, .D, .X, .P .X	EA,FPn FPm,FPn	Data	FPn − (SRC) → FPn	11-2
Tangent	FTAN	.B, .W, .L, .S, .D, .X, .P .X .X	EA,FPn FPm,FPn FPn	Data	Tan (SRC) → FPn	11-2
Hyperbolic tangent	FTANH	.B, .W, .L, .S, .D, .X, .P .X .X	EA,FPn FPm,FPn FPn	Data	Tanh (SRC) → FPn	11-2
10 to the x power	FTENTOX	.B, .W, .L, .S, .D, .X, .P .X .X	EA,FPn FPm,FPn FPn	Data	$10^{(SRC)} \to FPn$	11-2
Trap conditionally	FTRAPcc	None .W, .L	None #Data		If cc then TRAP	11-2
Test	FTST	.B, .W, .L, .S, .D, .X, .P .X	EA FPn	Data	(SRC) − 0	11-2
2 to the x power	FTWOTOX	.B, .W, .L, .S, .D, .X, .P .X .X	EA,FPn FPm,FPn FPn	Data	$2^{(SRC)} \to FPn$	11-2

Appendix D

M68000 Family Summary*

   * This Appendix summarizes the characteristics of the microprocessors in the M68000 Family. The M68000PM/AD, *M68000 Programmer's Reference Manual* includes more detailed information on the M68000 Family differences. (Courtesy of Motorola, Inc.)

MC68020, MC68030, and MC68040 Instruction Set Extensions		Applies To		
Instruction	Notes	MC68020	MC68030	MC68040
FNEG	New Instruction			✔
FRESTORE	New Instruction			✔
FSAVE	New Instruction			✔
FScc	New Instruction			✔
FSQRT	New Instruction			✔
FSUB	New Instruction			✔
FTRAPcc	New Instruction			✔
FTST	New Instruction			✔
LINK	Supports 32-Bit Displacement	✔	✔	✔
MOVE16	New Instruction			✔
MOVEC	Supports New Control Registers	✔	✔	✔
MULS/MULU	Supports 32-Bit Operands	✔	✔	✔
PACK	New Instruction	✔	✔	✔
PFLUSH	MMU Instruction		✔	✔
PLOAD	MMU Instruction		✔	
PMOVE	MMU Instruction		✔	
PTEST	MMU Instruction		✔	✔
RTM	New Instruction	✔		
TST	Supports Program Counter Relative Addressing Modes	✔	✔	✔
TRAPcc	New Instruction	✔	✔	✔
UNPK	New Instruction	✔	✔	✔

Addressing Modes

MC68020, MC68030, and MC68040 Extensions	Memory indirect addressing modes, scaled index, and larger displacements. Refer to specific data sheets for details.

MC68020, MC68030, and MC68040 Instruction Set Extensions		Applies To		
Instruction	**Notes**	**MC68020**	**MC68030**	**MC68040**
Bcc	Supports 32-Bit Displacements	✔	✔	✔
BFxxxx	Bit Field Instructions (BCHG, BFCLR, BFEXTS, BFEXTU, BFFFO, BFINS, BFSET, BFTST)	✔	✔	✔
BKPT	New Instruction Functionally	✔	✔	
BRA	Supports 32-Bit Displacements	✔	✔	✔
BSR	Supports 32-Bit Displacement	✔	✔	✔
CALLM	New Instruction	✔		
CAS, CAS2	New Instructions	✔	✔	✔
CHK	Supports 32-Bit Operands	✔	✔	✔
CHK2	New Instruction	✔	✔	✔
CINV	Cache Maintenance Instruction			✔
CMPI	Supports Program Counter Relative Addressing Modes	✔	✔	✔
CMP2	New Instruction	✔	✔	✔
CPUSH	Cache Maintenance Instruction			✔
cp	Coprocessor Instructions	✔	✔	
DIVS/DIVU	Supports 32-Bit and 64-Bit Operands	✔	✔	✔
EXTB	Supports 8-Bit Extend to 32-Bits	✔	✔	✔
FABS	New Instruction			✔
FADD	New Instruction			✔
FBcc	New Instruction			✔
FCMP	New Instruction			✔
FDBcc	New Instruction			✔
FDIV	New Instruction			✔
FMOVE	New Instruction			✔
FMOVEM	New Instruction			✔
FMUL	New Instruction			✔

Control Registers

MC68000, MC68008	None
MC68010	SFC, DFC, VBR
MC68020	SFC, DFC, VBR, CACR, CAAR
MC68030	SFC, DFC, VBR, CACR, CAAR, CRP, SRP, TC, TT0, TT1, MMUSR
MC68040	SFC, DFC, VBR, CACR, URP, SRP, TC, DTT0, DTT1, ITT0, ITT1, MMUSR

Stack Pointer

MC68000, MC68008, MC68010	USP, SSP
MC68020, MC68030, MC68040	USP, SSP (MSP, ISP)

Status Register Bits

MC68000, MC68008, MC68010	T, S, I0/I1/I2, X/N/Z/V/C
MC68020, MC68030, MC68040	T0, T1, S, M, I0/I1/I2, X/N/Z/V/C

Function Code/Address Space

MC68000, MC68008	FC2–FC0 = 7 is Interrupt Acknowledge Only
MC68010, MC68020, MC68030, MC68040	FC2–FC0 = 7 is CPU Space
MC68040	User, Supervisor, and Acknowledge

Indivisible Bus Cycles

MC68000, MC68008, MC68010	Use $\overline{AS}$ Signal
MC68020, MC68030	Use $\overline{RMC}$ Signal
MC68040	Use $\overline{LOCK}$ and $\overline{LOCKE}$ Signal

Stack Frames

MC68000, MC68008	Supports Original set
MC68010	Supports Formats $0, $8
MC68020/MC68030	Supports Formats $0, $1, $2, $9, $A, $B
MC68040	Supports Formats $0, $1, $2, $3, $7

Attribute	MC68000	MC68008	MC68010	MC68020	MC68030	MC68040
Data Bus Size (Bits)	16	8	16	8, 16, 32	8, 16, 32	32
Address Bus Size (Bits)	24	20	24	32	32	32
Instruction Cache (In Bytes)	—	—	3[1] (Words)	256	256	4096
Data Cache (In Bytes)	—	—	—	—	256	4096

NOTE 1: The MC68010 supports a 3-word cache for the loop mode.

Virtual Interfaces

MC68010, MC68020, MC68030	Virtual Memory/Machine
M68040	Virtual Memory
MC68010, MC68020, MC68030, MC68040	Provide Bus Error Detection, Fault Recovery
MC68030, MC68040	On-Chip MMU

Coprocessor Interface

MC68000, MC68008, MC68010	Emulated in Software
MC68020, MC68030	In Microcode
MC68040	Emulated in Software (On-Chip Floating-Point Unit)

Word/Long Word Data Alignment

MC68000, MC68008, MC68010	Word/Long Data, Instructions, and Stack Must be Word Aligned
MC68020, MC68030, MC68040	Only Instructions Must be Word Aligned (Data Alignment Improves Performance)

Index